Alaska
Science
Nuggets

Neil Davis

University of Alaska Press

ISBN 0-912006-38-2
(previously ISBN 0-915360-02-0)
Library of Congress Catalog Card Number: 82-80679
Printed in the United States of America

Geophysical Institute
        First Printing, 1982
        Second Printing, 1984
University of Alaska Press
        Third Printing, 1989, 2500 copies
        Fourth Printing, 1992, 2500 copies

This material is based in part upon work supported by the National Science Foundation under
Grant No. OSS-7917901 and by a grant from the Alaska Humanities Forum. Any opinions,
findings, conclusions or recommendations expressed in this publication are those of the authors
and do no necessarily reflect the views of the National Science Foundation or the Alaska Humanities Forum.

The University of Alaska is an EO/AA employer and educational institution.

Foreword

This volume contains 400 of the approximately 520 articles written for the Alaska Science Forum, a weekly series of short columns discussing facts about the north and questions interesting to northerners. The series commenced in the *Fairbanks Daily News-Miner* in March 1976 and later appeared in other newspapers in Alaska and northwestern Canada under various headings: The *Fairbanks Daily News-Miner* used the title Community Science Forum and the articles have appeared in the *Anchorage Times* under the column name Diggings. Other papers carrying the articles regularly or sporadically are the *Cheechacko News* (Kenai), *Cordova Times*, *Copper Valley Views* (Copper Center), *The Frontiersman* (Palmer), *Homer News*, *Ketchikan News*, *Kodiak Daily Mirror*, *Lynn Canal News* (Haines), *The Nome Nugget*, *Peninsula Clarion* (Kenai), *Southeast Alaska Empire* (Juneau), *Tundra Times* (statewide), *Valdez Vanguard*, and *Yukon News* (Whitehorse, Yukon Territory, Canada).

The primary motivation for making this compilation has been the many requests for such a volume from teachers in Alaskan schools and others who have found the articles useful for reference. Previously published articles not included here are those deemed of passing interest or those which largely duplicate information contained in others, though some duplication remains. Except for a few minor wording changes and correction of errors, the articles are presented here as originally written.

Articles written by other contributors are followed by the authors' names. The month and year of initial publication appears at the end of each article together with a keying number that ties to a filing system wherein reference materials are retained.

I am most grateful to the 36 others whose contributions have broadened the scope of the series. Also, I gratefully acknowledge the many members of the faculty of the University of Alaska and other professionals whom I have consulted to obtain accurate information during the preparation of articles. It would indeed be difficult to prepare the articles without the availability of the immense talent pool that exists on the Fairbanks campus of the University of Alaska and elsewhere in the Fairbanks area — in no field did I lack for expert advice.

Despite the fact that the text of all articles was preserved on magnetic cards and, consequently, little typing was required to prepare this volume, the effort was still considerable. It was performed by the staff of *The Northern Engineer* under the direction of that journal's editor Carla Helfferich. Teri Lucara typeset the text and Deborah Jo Davis did the layout. It was an education for me and a pleasure to work with these three. Patricia Ann Davis not only did the cartoons scattered throughout the volume but also the cover art. The cover is based upon an original drawing by David Stone of the Geophysical Institute. Photographs and drawings presented without acknowledgment are mine or from collections held by the Geophysical Institute.

I am pleased to acknowledge University of Alaska historian Dr. Claus-M. Naske whose urging started the writing of the articles appearing here. The Alaska Humanities Forum provided initial funding. Later, both the National Science Foundation and the Geophysical Institute supported the work.

The many people who wrote letters and orally communicated suggestions and questions have made substantial contribution to what appears in this volume. Finally, I wish to thank the Director of the Geophysical Institute, Dr. Juan G. Roederer, and the Institute's Assistant Director, Professor Albert E. Belon, for their encouragement and support.

— *Neil Davis*

CONTENTS

CHAPTER THREE
NORTHERN SKY AND WEATHER

CHAPTER FOUR
WATER AND ICE

CONTENTS

CHAPTER FIVE
THE SEA

CHAPTER SIX
VOLCANOES, EARTHQUAKES, TECTONICS

CHAPTER SEVEN
NORTHERN PLANTS

CHAPTER EIGHT
NORTHERN ANIMALS

CHAPTER NINE
OUR HERITAGE

CHAPTER TEN
LIVING IN THE NORTH

CONTENTS

CHAPTER ONE
AURORAS AND RELATED THINGS

Names and Definition of the Aurora

The Northern Lights and the aurora borealis are two names for the same thing. The term aurora borealis was first used by Galileo in 1619 to suggest the likeness of the Northern Lights to an early dawn in the northern sky, an appearance it sometimes has to those who live at low or intermediate latitudes in the Northern Hemisphere.

Once the term aurora borealis was introduced, Galileo and others used it as the name for the Northern Lights. The early history of auroral terminology is somewhat clouded because, at the time, Galileo was already under duress from the Roman Inquisition and was not supposed to be writing on astronomical matters. Therefore, his writings on the subject were appearing under the name of his student, Mario Guiducci. Galileo referenced the aurora as part of his arguments against the established idea that the earth was the center of the Universe. He wrongly thought that the aurora is caused by sunlight reflecting from the high atmosphere.

Galileo's original error has propagated through nearly four centuries to the present time. Misinformed by geography books written as late as fifty years ago, a surprising number of people still labor under the misconception that the aurora is sunlight glinting off the high atmosphere, off the polar icecap or off falling snow or ice crystals.

Instead, the aurora is an actual light source created in the high atmosphere. It is a glow given off by the atoms and molecules of which the atmosphere is composed. That glow is caused by the atoms and molecules being struck by charged particles, mostly electrons and protons, that originated on the sun. These particles stream out from the sun and normally are guided by the earth's magnetic field into the polar regions where they enter the atmosphere and make it glow.

The proper name for the aurora of the Southern Hemisphere is the aurora australis. Together the aurora australis and the aurora borealis are known as the aurora polaris.

Nowadays the simple name aurora is mostly used, as is the name Northern Lights.

Jan 80:A1

The Solar Wind

Over the course of the year, northerners receive less sunlight than those farther south, but, in one sense, they make up for it by getting more of the direct effects of the solar wind. Like sunlight, the solar wind derives from the sun, but it has quite different characteristics. Sunlight is composed of electromagnetic waves whereas the solar wind is made up of tiny particles, mostly electrons and protons.

Sunlight travels to the earth in only about eight minutes, but it takes a day or two for the particles in the solar wind to make the trip. Even so, the solar wind moves right along, traveling at 300 to more than 500 kilometers per second, fast enough to make the trip to earth in a day or two. Despite the high wind speed, a person exposed to it would be incapable of sensing the solar wind directly because of the low density in the wind. However, the particles in the solar wind travel so fast that they would mortally damage a person's exposed body in a short time.

The bulk of the particles in the solar wind are the basic building blocks of matter, electrons and protons. They continuously boil off the sun's surface and speed outward in all directions, to distances well beyond the earth. Compared to the number of air molecules at the earth's surface, the number of particles in a unit volume of the solar wind is tiny, in fact, more than a billion billion times less. The density of particles in the wind is only about one per cubic centimeter, a density considered on earth to be an excellent vacuum.

Even though the solar wind has so few particles per unit volume, the wind has a profound effect upon the earth, especially at high latitudes. The earth's magnetic field interacts with the particles in the solar wind to deflect them away from the equatorial region. But at higher latitudes, they do move down into the high atmosphere. When they impact the atmospheric gases there they heat up the gases and also create the visible aurora and electrical currents in the high atmosphere. These currents, in turn, induce other currents in the earth and in long pipelines and power transmission systems. Current in the pipelines increases their rate of corrosion, and the current in the transmission lines trips breakers to cause power outages.

Extra strong blasts of solar wind emanate from sunspots. When these more intense blasts arrive at earth, auroras tend to be bright and widespread, and there are disturbances to radio communications and to the direction a compass needle points.

It is conjectured, but not proven, that variations in the solar wind may affect the earth's global weather. Evidence is mounting that past solar wind variations have influenced the climate, so it seems likely that an effect on weather will someday be found.

Jul 81:A5

The Earth's Magnetosphere

Only three planets in the solar system have magnetospheres and this is because only Earth, Jupiter and Saturn generate their own magnetic fields. Since the existence of auroras on a planet requires a magnetic field, only Earth, Jupiter and Saturn can have this beautiful phenomenon.

The people of Earth did not know they had a magnetic field until they discovered lodestones and began to use them for navigation. The magnetic field is generated within the earth by electrical currents flowing deep inside it. (Every electric current generates its own magnetic field; a current in a straight wire generates a magnetic field pointed at right angles to the wire; the magnetic field becomes weaker the greater is the distance from the wire.)

As far as is known, people do not directly sense the earth's magnetic field, although there is now strong evidence that the birds do it, bees do, and even sewage bacteria move in directions dictated by the local magnetic field. People have been able to map out the strength and direction of the magnetic field everywhere on the earth's surface. This mapping can be done simply by hanging a needle-shaped magnet by its center on a fine string. A human hair, a glass fiber or a gold thread makes an excellent suspension string.

Using the suspended magnet technique, both the strength and direction of the magnetic field can be measured at any point. At the equator the needle hangs horizontally and points north-south. Over Alaska and western Canada, the needle hangs nearly vertically; there it is found that the strength of the field is nearly twice that at the equator.

Using more sophisticated magnetometers that can be flown in aircraft, rockets and satellites, the earth's magnetic field also can be measured at all altitudes above the surface. The higher one goes the weaker becomes the magnetic field, but it maintains an orderly pattern of direction at all altitudes.

However, at very high altitude a boundary is reached where it is evident that the magnetic field being measured is no longer that of the earth, but is instead that of the interplanetary medium which really is a weak extension of the sun's magnetic field. In this distant region the magnetic field is very weak and of an irregular nature that depends upon the sun's level of sunspot activity. Here there also is a continuous flow of charged particles, mostly electrons and protons, moving at high speed in a direction away from the sun, the so-called solar wind.

The boundary between the earth's magnetic field and the solar wind is called the magnetopause and the region inside the magnetopause — everywhere down to the earth's surface — is named the magnetosphere. Actually, the magnetosphere is bounded below by the ionosphere, lying roughly 100 km above the earth's surface. This is the same altitude where most auroras occur.

The solar wind blowing against the magnetosphere compresses it on the side of the earth toward the sun. There the boundary is about 10 earth radii from the center of the earth. Away from the direction of the sun, the magnetosphere stretches far out behind the earth, even farther than the distance to the moon.

Most of the electrons and protons in the solar wind sweep past the magnetosphere and journey on out to the fringes of the solar system but some find their ways across the magnetopause and on down to the polar atmospheres where they hit the atmosphere. Their impact is what produces the auroras.

Jul 81:A6

Energy Source for the Aurora

Rather large amounts of power are required to produce the aurora seen in the two polar regions. During a moderate to large auroral display lasting one to three hours the energy dissipated by the auroral processes is about the same as released in a Richter magnitude 6 earthquake, in a cyclone, or in a small nuclear bomb.

It is almost certain that the energy required to power the aurora comes from the sun. From the sun there is a continual outflow of matter in the form of electrons and nuclei of atoms, mostly hydrogen nuclei (protons). This flow, called the solar wind, streams at speeds near 400 km/sec (900,000 mph) and therefore takes several days to reach the earth, whereas light takes only eight minutes.

Near the earth, the energy of motion within the solar wind is converted to electromagnetic energy — by the same process that an electrical generator converts energy of motion to electrical energy. That energy is again converted to energy of motion of those electrons and protons which stream down into the atmosphere to collide with the air to cause the aurora we see.

The details of energy conversion and energy transfer processes are very complex and not yet entirely understood. If we can understand the details, the knowledge should give valuable insight into cosmological processes, since we suspect that the processes in the aurora are those which also occur in stellar bodies and perhaps elsewhere in the Universe.

— *Daniel Swift*
Oct 77:54

Decline of the Aurora

Auroras tend to be most extensive in the maximum years of the 11-year solar sunspot cycle. Similarly, those solar cycles of highest sunspot activity yield more auroras than the cycles of low activity.

The most active solar cycle in many decades began in April 1954 and peaked in 1958 (cycle 19 on diagram). It produced numerous beautiful auroras worldwide. The next cycle beginning in October 1964 (cycle 20) was much less active with only about half as many sunspots in peak years as the previous cycle 19. The current cycle 21, starting about now, probably will be even weaker, since there seems to be a trend toward several low-activity cycles immediately after an especially active one. Hence those of

us who were adults during the spectacular years of 1957 and 1958 are unlikely to see in our lifetimes such numerous, brilliant displays again.

Nov 76:127

A False Solar Alarm

On April 12, 1978, the national news media distributed the prediction that extensive auroras and radio blackout would cover much of the world. The reason for the prediction was the occurrence of a giant flare on the sun the day before, the largest flare to be observed in several years.

Solar flares jet out high-speed clouds of electrons and protons that reach to the earth's orbit in a day or two. If these clouds are aimed to hit the earth, a portion of them penetrates through the earth's magnetic field to strike the polar atmospheres. There, auroras and disturbances to the radio wave-reflecting ionosphere are caused.

On the night of April 13, big auroras were supposed to be seen far equatorward of their normal high-latitude habitats. But these auroras were not seen.

The problem was that the solar flare did not occur at the right place on the sun for its ejected cloud to strike the earth. If a large flare develops in the center of the sun, as seen from the earth, or a bit to the left of center, then the earth is likely to be struck by the ejected cloud. However, the solar flare of April 11

Decline of the Aurora: *Predicted and observed sunspot numbers.*

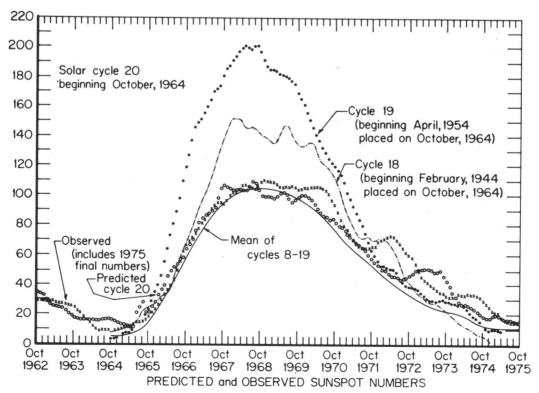

PREDICTED and OBSERVED SUNSPOT NUMBERS

4

occurred about 40 degrees of solar longitude to the west (to the right of center as we view the sun). The material it ejected mainly shot out past the earth.

The earth intercepted the fringe of the blast and did experience rather nice auroras over Alaska and at other high-latitude locations. But the contiguous states were, as usual, not so lucky.

Apr 78:93

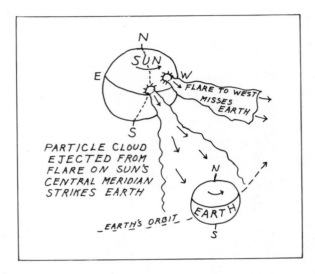

A False Solar Alarm.

Jupiter's Red Spot — The Auroral Connection

Since it was discovered in 1665, Jupiter's Giant Red Spot has come and gone — for reasons not known. At times, it merely may have been that no one with adequate telescopes was paying attention. The Red Spot was weak or not observed at all during the rest of the 17th century.

However, this period was the time of the Maunder Minimum — an epoch when there were very few sunspots. For reasons such as this, the suggestion has been made that Jupiter's Red Spot, like the Earth's aurora, is strongly affected by solar activity.

When the 11-year solar cycle is at its peak, sunspots are most numerous and conspicuous. From these regions on the sun's surface copious quantities of particles, mostly protons and electrons, are cast out. The ever-present outward flowing solar wind is enhanced by these additional particles; the result on Earth is more auroras, magnetic disturbances and disruption to radio communications.

Jupiter, too, has its auroras, and likewise these undoubtedly are affected by the flow of particles reaching that planet from the sun. However, associated with the changes in particle emission from the sun are related changes in ultraviolet radiation. It is this ultraviolet light rather than the solar wind

particles which causes changes in Jupiter's Red Spot, according to a recent suggestion by Dr. Kenneth Schatten of Boston University.

If the ultraviolet hypothesis is true, and Dr. Schatten is not entirely convinced that it is, 1979 and 1980, being years of sunspot maximum, will continue to be good years for seeing Jupiter's Red Spot just as they will for seeing the Northern Lights.

Sep 79:341

Predicting Auroras

Despite all that is known about the aurora, predicting when the Northern Lights will appear still is a dicey business.

One well-known trend is the 11-year solar cycle; auroras are more numerous in years of maximum numbers of sunspots. Right now we are on the decline from a maximum that occurred a year or so ago.

Another cyclic trend relates to the 27-day period of the sun's rotation on its own axis. Sometimes sunspots last for months. Hence one that sprays the earth with aurora-generating solar wind particles on one solar rotation may well do so 27 days later.

There also seems to be a slight tendency for more auroras to occur in spring and fall rather than in summer and winter, owing to the changing annual relationship of Earth to the plane of the sun's equator.

When it comes to predicting whether or not spectacular auroras will be seen on any given night, the best bet is to notice what happened the night before. If there was little aurora last night, the chances are that the aurora will be no better tonight. That scheme sometimes fails miserably because a period of relatively quiet must sometime get interrupted by new activity. That new activity can only be predicted by recalling the 27-day solar cycle and, better yet, being able to observe the new appearance of sunspots or to make direct instrumental observations of the solar wind with a satellite flying high above the earth and off in the direction of the sun.

When new activity does commence, it usually lasts several days. The first night is usually the best, with a decline in activity each night thereafter — unless a new sequence of activity shows up.

Within any one night there are cycles lasting an hour or two. On a particularly active night the cycles follow one right after the other, but sometimes only one or two will appear.

Sound hopeless? Almost, but a little regular experience watching the night sky gives anyone some predictive ability.

Oct 81:508

Hints for Aurora Watching

Sometimes one is surprised by the appearance of bright active auroras directly overhead as soon as it gets dark in the evening. When this happens, it is a good bet that the sky will be worth watching the rest of the night. Very likely the aurora will weaken from time to time through the night, but it usually will brighten up and become active again several times.

More usually one notices arcs and bands building up in the northern sky and slowly spreading southward. Especially when several close-spaced arcs appear without showing much motion, one should expect spectacular activity to follow within the next few minutes to an hour.

Once the arcs begin to break up into swirling bands, it is common to see fast-moving rays with reddish lower tips racing back and forth along the auroral forms. Then after a few minutes of splendor, the whole scene grows disappointing, and everyone goes back inside the house to warm up.

However, if one will just go back outside a few minutes to an hour later, the aurora usually will present a special treat relatively few people are aware of. This will be a display of pulsating aurora. It occurs mostly in the hours near and past midnight, after the bright, spectacular part of the display. To see the pulsating aurora well, one must have dark-adapted eyes. This means one must stay outside without looking at any bright lights for five or ten minutes; twenty is best.

Then if one looks overhead, one will see large, weak patches of light blinking on and off every few seconds. It is not bright but it is awe-inspiring. The pulsating aurora may persist for many minutes or even several hours. Thus even when you get cold or tired and go in, it will continue to play on in your absence.

Oct 81:509

Photographing the Aurora

The aurora is one of nature's most beautiful dramas. Played against a cosmic backdrop, the colors and motions are often subtle and quick, but such a show is not difficult to photograph if strict attention is paid to certain procedures which are peculiar to auroral photography. First, find someplace where you have a clear view of the sky and horizon, away from streetlights. You will need a sturdy tripod, a camera with an f/2.8 lens or faster, a high-speed black and white or color film, and a cable release. The wider angle lenses are easier to work with if they are fast enough. Between 10:30 p.m. and midnight, you'll have the best chance of seeing the bright arcs and forms which are most photogenic. Pay attention to the foreground; it provides a stable means of

composition and orientation, as well as an attractive setting. Use a "night light" in the foreground, such as a cabin window. Regular outside lights are too bright and may overexpose the film during the 3 to 30 seconds it takes to catch ordinary auroral arcs. These arcs follow a daily pattern, so if you notice a composition you missed, chances are it will occur again some other night. Open the camera's shutter while the arcs are more or less stationary or "painted' across the sky. Too much motion during exposure results in blurry non-descript forms. Don't let the film and camera "cold soak" by standing out for hours. Put it in an airtight plastic bag before going inside so moisture from the warm air will not condense on the cold metal and rust some delicate part inside.

When the skies are clear, it's usually cold. If you can't dress warmly enough for an hour's watch, plan on taking a walk, stopping now and then to watch the biggest show on earth.

— Charles Deehr
Nov 76:129

Divining the Aurora

All it takes to find the aurora, day or night, is a pair of sticks. Willow wands will not work because the sticks must be conducting. And, instead of walking across the ground with them, one must drive the metal rods into the ground, at locations several hundred feet apart. A wire is attached to each rod and also attached to one post of a sensitive ammeter or voltmeter.

When the aurora appears overhead, a voltage will be induced in the earth between the rods and electricity will flow in the wire attached between the rods and the meter. If the meter has the ability to record the voltages or currents passing through it, a record similar to the one shown here will be produced.

During quiet times, when there is no aurora, the recording meter will draw a straight line down the center of the graph. When really bright aurora is overhead, the pen of the meter will sweep back and forth across the paper in response to the auroral activity. The meter can be converted into an auroral alarm by rigging it to ring a bell when major voltage changes appear. Dr. Victor P. Hessler used such an alarm to help him acquire his excellent set of black and white auroral photographs, taken over a period of years.

The reason the earth current meter works is that huge electrical currents flow in the high atmosphere when the aurora appears. These currents induce secondary currents in the earth's surface where they can be easily measured. Despite the simplicity of the earth current recorder, it remains, down through

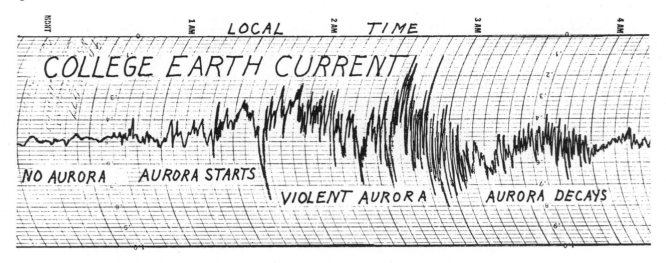

Divining the Aurora: *Earth currents indicate overhead auroral activity.*

the years, as about the best method to tell when there is aurora overhead. It works day or night, whether the sky is cloudy or clear.

Anyone interested in building an auroral alarm system using the earth current technique should contact us for a few additional hints on how to make the system work best.

Jul 77:41

Magnetic Storms

The magnetic storm is among the first of several aspects of the earth's environment to be recognized as caused by variations on the sun. During the last century, people noticed that there were occasional periods of a day or longer when the magnetic field of the earth changed in strength and direction. They called these periods magnetic storms.

Later, scientists realized that the times of magnetic storm were the times of most extensive auroral displays, and they realized that magnetic storms typically followed, by a day or two, large flares on the sun. When radio came into use about 60 years ago, people soon found that long-distance radio propagation was erratic or impossible during magnetic storms.

Erupting solar flares, typically associated with major sunspots, spew out large numbers of charged particles, mostly electrons and protons, which stream outward to the earth to create the magnetic storms and related phenomena.

During storms, intense electrical currents flow in the earth's ionosphere, especially in the auroral zones. These currents — as do all currents — generate magnetic fields. Just as the aurora is quite variable, the auroral zone ionospheric currents are variable and it is their created magnetic fields that are most responsible for the jumpiness of a compass needle placed at high latitude. Variations of a large fraction of a degree commonly occur, and variations by several degrees in a few minutes' time have been observed.

Magnetic storms often last for several days, but the first day usually is the most severe. The bright, extensive auroras often seen near the onset of the storm typically will be followed the next night by a somewhat lesser display, and the night after that usually will have fewer still. It is hard to predict major auroral displays, but the knowledge that they are related to magnetic storms helps.

Dec 80:449

Magnetic Substorms

Many years ago people gave the name "magnetic storms" to those intervals lasting a few days wherein there appear the most extensive auroral displays and during which marked variations in the earth's magnetic field occur. A more recent discovery, made some years ago by Dr. Syun-Ichi Akasofu of the Geophysical Institute, is that magnetic storms contain shorter periods of increased activity, called magnetic substorms or auroral substorms.

Substorms typically last about an hour or so. When a substorm begins, the number of auroras seen in the sky may increase, and those that exist will brighten perceptibly. Rapid motions within the auroral forms and violent motions of the forms themselves occur. In a few minutes the aurora can change from barely noticeable to a brilliant display extending across the visible sky.

Observations from satellites and from widely spaced observing points on the earth's surface show that substorms typically originate at the auroral zone on that part of the earth opposite the sun. In other words, the substorm usually begins near local midnight at the auroral zone. The enhanced activity expands to the west and to the east away from the midnight meridian. For that reason an observer often sees enhanced activity move his direction from the eastern horizon in the hours before local midnight. If the observer's local time is post-midnight, he often sees enhanced activity moving toward him across the western horizon. Also, an observer located north of the auroral zone, for example on the northern coast of Alaska or Canada, often observes the region of enhanced activity expanding toward him from the south.

Thus, while a substorm usually starts in one region, the midnight region of the auroral zone, it quickly expands east and west, and also somewhat poleward, to spread around the earth. Consequently, it is a global, not a local phenomenon. When a substorm is in progress, all of the earth's auroras are affected.

During the substorm there are rapid variations in the earth's magnetic field. Then, the magnetic compass needle fluctuates in direction, sometimes by several degrees.

After several tens of minutes the substorm decays, and the aurora grows weaker. Some hours may pass before a new substorm starts, but during particularly large magnetic storms the substorms may follow one after the other.

The substorm behavior explains why auroras come and go on any particular night. On some nights there may be only one substorm, and on others several may occur. If one happens to walk outside to look at the sky between substorms he might not see much aurora, even on a night that is generally active. But an hour or two later, after a new substorm has started, the sky might be full of aurora.

Nov 81:447

Auroral Electrojets

During a major auroral display, intense electrical currents exist in the ionosphere over western Canada and Alaska. Flowing mostly east-west at altitudes near 100 km (60 miles), the currents can be as large as a half million amperes.

Called the auroral electrojets, because the currents flow in relatively confined regions in and near the aurora, the currents nevertheless are diffuse, compared to currents in wires. At times, the electrojets spread over a zone several hundred miles wide.

So far, no one has any concept of how the auroral currents could be harnessed for useful purpose. In fact, as far as the works of man are concerned, the intense currents are more harmful than helpful.

Though the auroral electrojets are high above our heads, they do induce similar currents in the conducting earth beneath our feet, and in other conductors such as electrical transmission lines and metal

pipelines. Like the aurora, the auroral electrojets change rapidly with time. The strongest currents may last only a few minutes, and much of the time they are quite weak.

Currents induced in the Trans-Alaska Pipeline and other pipelines can promote corrosion which limits the lifetime of the pipe. Also, the auroral electrojet currents induce so much current in long electrical transmission lines that power outages can result when protective breakers are tripped. This is a consideration to be taken into account in the design of transmission lines, such as the intertie between Anchorage and Fairbanks, now being contemplated.

Dec 80:446

The Continuous Aurora

Only during the last decade, when highly sophisticated satellites began to circle the polar regions, have we become aware that the aurora is a truly continuous part of the earth's environment. A person on the ground can see only a comparatively small part of the polar atmosphere wherein the Northern Lights reside, but the properly instrumented satellite can skim across the polar region to look downward and detect whatever aurora exists, wherever it may be. These satellites find that the aurora is always there.

Twin auroral halos crown the two polar regions. Each sits atop the denser part of the atmosphere, rarely penetrating down to altitudes below 70 km (40 miles); more usually the base of the aurora is near altitude 100 km. Called the auroral ovals, the two halos often consist of weak, parallel arcs embedded in a diffuse auroral glow a few hundred kilometers in width. At such times, the auroral ovals typically have a diameter of only four or five thousand kilometers. Then, of course, only persons living at very high latitude can see the aurora, and then only if they look closely on a dark, clear night. One living on the north coast of Alaska or western Canada would see aurora only by looking northward.

During times of high auroral activity, the ovals widen and expand toward the equator. Then the aurora might be seen overhead in central Alaska or Canada. On the average, auroras extend this far equatorward perhaps one night in three, or four. Once in a great while, perhaps once in ten years or so, the twin ovals expand so much they cloak practically all of the earth's sky except for that of the tropical region.

Oct 80:436

The Transient Aurora

Just as bright auroras come and go in the night sky, major auroral displays flit in and out among the years according to the prevalence of spots on the sun. Those persons living at moderate latitudes in the time from about 1640 to 1720 had little chance to see Northern Lights simply because very few of significance occurred.

The whole of the eighteenth century was a good time for auroras. Even then, because of the 11-year cycle of solar activity, some years were better than others. Auroral observing was not quite so rewarding for most at the outset of the 1800s, but it improved during the last half of that century, peaking in about 1870.

Surprisingly enough, records of sunspot activity show that the Klondike gold rush era, 1896 to 1902, was a low time for the aurora. Nevertheless, the people who wintered over in Dawson, the Fortymile or other northern gold camps saw plenty of aurora. Robert Service certainly saw enough to cause him to spice up many of his poems with allusions to the aurora.

Except for the ups and downs of the 11-year sunspot cycle, aurora watching got steadily better up until the fantastic winter of 1957-58, the time known as the International Geophysical Year because of intensive studies established worldwide during those years. That was a great year; night after night bright auroras flashed across the Alaskan-Yukon sky and sometimes spread as far south as Cuba. If the trends continue as they have for the past four centuries the world will not be treated to the equal of the 1957-58 auroral grandeur before about the middle of the 21st century. Even so, one of the happinesses of living in the north is that the major variations in auroral activity — the 11-year cycle and longer cycles — are not so obvious to us. Those living at more lowly latitudes see few if any auroras during the off parts of the cycles, but we still can observe auroras in central and northern Alaska and Yukon on essentially every clear, dark night.

Aug 80:423

The Auroral Oval

Though most of us see the aurora only occasionally, the aurora is, in fact, a permanent feature of the earth. It is always there to see if one is in the right place, and darkness conditions permit.

Twin halos called the auroral ovals encircle the two polar regions of the earth. Each oval consists of a band of hard-to-see auroral glow within which are embedded visible auroral arcs, bands and other shapes. The oval in the Southern Hemisphere is nearly a carbon copy of the one in the north, so when one sees an aurora, he or she can be certain that a similar aurora is occurring in the other hemisphere at the same time. This statement is not quite correct because observations have shown that when a particularly extensive and bright aurora is in one hemisphere the exact counterpart to it in the other might not be found, or at least not at the expected location.

The two auroral ovals pivot around the earth's geomagnetic poles, located near Thule, Greenland and Vostok, Antarctica. They are displaced somewhat toward the nightside of the earth with the consequence being that the ovals extend to lower latitude at night than they do in daytime. Usually the dayside of the northern auroral oval lies about 500 km north of the Alaska-Canada coast of the Beaufort Sea, but at night the oval extends down over the land in this region.

When conditions in the solar wind blowing out from the sun to the earth are quiet, the auroral ovals contract poleward and become quite narrow. During active conditions the ovals enlarge in diameter and widen. Under highly active conditions the northern oval might extend from Barrow to Ketchikan, Alaska. On rare occasions the northern oval may expand to reach southern California; likewise, the southern oval will expand toward the equator, simultaneously.

Mar 81:450

The Auroral Arc

A remaining mystery of the aurora is the reason why the thin auroral arc is the most common shape seen. Arcs stand in the sky like giant ribbons set on edge. In length they often extend from horizon to horizon, a distance of a thousand kilometers or more; sometimes arcs are several thousand kilometers long. Arcs reach upward from their lower borders in the direction of the magnetic field, which at auroral zone latitudes is nearly vertical. The height extent of the arc is usually a few tens of kilometers and sometimes far in excess of a hundred kilometers.

Considering the great length and height extent of arcs, it is truly amazing that they sometimes are less than a hundred meters thick. Furthermore, the brighter an arc becomes the thinner the structure is. As yet, there is no universally accepted theory that explains this extreme thinness.

Seeing an arc low in the northern or southern sky, one is unable to discern the arc's thickness. Only when the arc sweeps up into the zenith region can this aspect of the arc's shape be recognized. A precise measurement of arc thickness can be made only when the arc appears exactly in the observer's magnetic zenith. Every observer has his or her own private magnetic zenith.

If one holds a compass needle suspended by a string tied to its center of mass, the needle will turn to point upward to the magnetic zenith. The north-seeking end of the compass needle will point downward and northward. Thus the south-seeking end is upward and is pointing somewhat southward of the true zenith, the true zenith being that point in the sky vertically above the observer's head. In Alaska and western Canada the magnetic zenith appears 10 to 20 degrees to the south of the true zenith; the exact angle depends upon where the observer is located.

One has no trouble locating the magnetic zenith if there is aurora overhead since it is the point toward which ray structures within auroral arcs appear to converge, and if an arc sweeps through the zenith the arc will appear thinnest there. Part of the fun of watching the aurora is picking out the location of the magnetic zenith and seeing how auroras appear to change shape — and exhibit their thinness — as they sweep through the zenith.

Dec 80:445

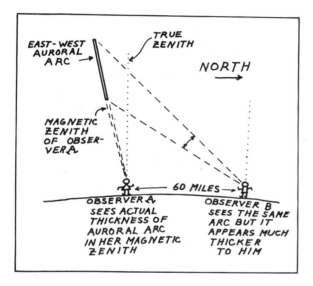

The Auroral Arc: *The apparent thickness of an aurora depends upon the location of the observer.*

Auroral Rays

One of the aurora's mysteries that took a long time to solve was the nature of the ray structure often seen in auroral arcs and bands.

Standing in the aurora like pickets in a fence, the rays sometimes move sideways across the arcs and bands at high speeds. Sometimes one even sees them appear to move past each other both to the left and the right.

Rays line up along the direction of the earth's magnetic field, which points nearly vertically and somewhat to the northeast over Alaska and western Canada. To recognize the cross-sectional shapes of the rays, one needs to see them directly overhead in the sky. When they are in that position, they don't look like rays anymore, one reason why it took so long to discover their true shapes.

Not until very sensitive, high-speed television cameras were aimed at the bottoms of rays overhead was the mystery resolved. This solution to the enigma yielded a masters degree for now-a-Ph.D. Tom Hallinan of the Geophysical Institute. He found that the rays were tightly wound up spirals only a kilometer or two across. Their form is difficult to recognize with the naked eye because the curled up shapes develop so quickly — sometimes in a second or so — and they often move very rapidly.

With a television camera capable of taking 30 pictures each second, it was possible to record the development of the spiral-shaped rays and measure their motion. Sometimes they move across the sky at speeds one hundred times that of a jet aircraft. To the observer on the ground, they do not appear to move quite that fast because the rays are so far away.

Mar 81:451

(See photos next page.)

Auroral Arcs and Bands

The sky provides no guides to give the visual observer depth perception. Consequently an observer of the aurora cannot tell how high the aurora is above him nor can he determine the true shape of the configurations being seen.

However if one knows ahead of time the normal shapes and orientations of auroral forms, an observer can more readily follow and understand the changes that occur in a display, and also better appreciate the true size of auroral phenomena.

Those long arches that extend roughly east-west (actually magnetic east-west) from horizon to horizon are called arcs. If of non-uniform curvature, these forms are called bands. No really meaningful difference exists between arcs and bands, except that the more convoluted form, the band, is often brighter than the arc, and the appearance of bands usually signifies that the overall display is becoming more active.

Arcs and bands are thin ribbons set on edge parallel to the ground. The thickness of an arc or band may be as little as 100 meters (100 yds). The lower edge is typically 80 to 120 km (50 to 75 miles) above the earth and the upper edge is usually 10 to 100 km above that. Off out to the east or west, arcs and bands appear to meet the horizon. Still roughly 100 km above the surface, the aurora there is more than 600 miles distant. Hence, the aurora seen to meet the eastern horizon at Fairbanks is actually nearly directly overhead at Whitehorse, and visa versa. Similarly, an arc or band seen from Fairbanks to be 20 degrees above the north horizon is directly overhead Fort Yukon.

The ray structure often seen in arcs and bands marks out the orientation of the magnetic field, nearly vertical at high latitude. The vertical extent of

Auroral Rays: *When seen from the side the rays resemble a picket fence. (Photo by V.P. Hessler.)*

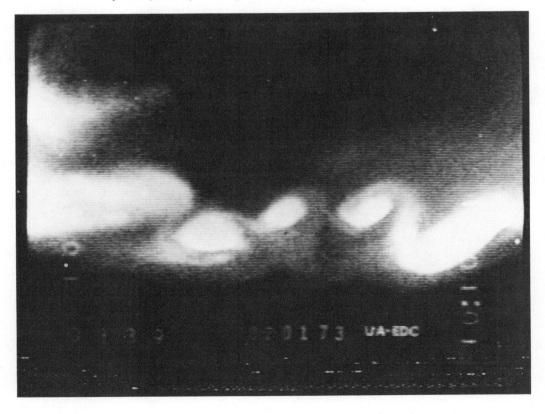

Auroral Rays: *Auroral rays as seen from directly below. This high-speed television photograph shows the rays to be tightly wound spirals interconnected by a thin arc.*

arcs and bands is also along this direction. Though the rays appear to converge upward, they are, in reality, essentially parallel shafts of light.

If rayed aurora is directly overhead, the point to which the rays appear to converge is the magnetic zenith. A line from that point to the observer marks out the local direction of the earth's magnetic field.

Dec 79:362

Spirals: *Spirals in low clouds downwind from the pass west of Umnak.*

Aurora Arcs and Bands: *An array of sub-parallel auroral arcs. (Photo by Takeshi Ohtake.)*

Spirals

Swirling one's hand through the soapy waters of the bathtub sets up a visible turbulent spiralling pattern of flow. That spiral pattern is observed frequently in nature, in many different ways. Wherever seen, the spiral pattern signals the existence of shear motion in the medium. By shear, one means motion of a part of the medium past another part.

Beautiful spiral patterns in the clouds are sometimes seen to leeward of mountains obstructing the general flow of air. The accompanying photograph shows a row of spirals in the clouds carried by winds rushing through a pass west of Umnak Island in the Aleutian Islands.

Clear air turbulence encountered when an aircraft passes near a high-speed stream of air is another example of the spiralling flow in a region of shear in air. Spirals are seen in the eddies of rivers, and they are what makes a whistle work. If one holds the mouth just right, the turbulent spiral pattern can be formed in the air blowing past the teeth thereby creating a high-pitched sound. The cloud photograph portrays what happens in a whistler's mouth if one imagines that the Aleutian volcanoes are the whistler's teeth.

Within the last few years, spirals have been discovered in the aurora. A graduate student at the University of Alaska, Thomas J. Hallinan, discovered that auroral rays seen from below were another form of the common spiral pattern. This discovery began an intensive study into the shear motions in auroras and what the spiral patterns might imply about the cause of the aurora. Through Hallinan's work, for which he received the Ph.D. in 1976, it is now known that the spiral patterns in the aurora are signs of very large electric fields and currents in the aurora. That knowledge, in turn, helped lead to the development of a new theory that seems to explain most of the auroras we see.

Jan 78:215

Spirals: *Fisheye photo of spiral in aurora over Fort Yukon.*

More on Spirals

Several readers have called in with essentially the same question: Is the funnel one sometimes sees as water goes down the bathtub drain caused by the same processes that cause spirals in clouds and in the aurora? And is it true that the direction of the swirling water is opposite in the Southern Hemisphere?

Usually, when one pulls the plug in the bathroom sink the water tends to be moving either clockwise or counterclockwise. As the water moves toward the drain, the pre-existing clockwise or counterclockwise motion is enhanced because of a law of physics that requires the circular motion to be maintained. It is maintained only if the speed of the rotating water increases as it nears the drain. The truth is that one can create in the draining water a spiralling funnel that is either clockwise or counterclockwise, depending upon how you stir the water just before opening the drain.

However, if the water is perfectly still and there is no disturbance as the drain is opened, the water should tend to develop a counterclockwise flow pattern as it drains away in the Northern Hemisphere, and a clockwise pattern if it drains in the Southern Hemisphere. This preference is caused by the earth's rotation, the so-called Coriolis force. The Coriolis force in the Northern Hemisphere is stronger the closer one is to the North Pole.

This fact allows Alaskans to claim bigger and better Coriolis forces than exist elsewhere in the Union, and especially in Texas. Within our state, Ketchikan sits at the bottom of the Coriolis totem pole and Barrow at the top.

There is shear flow in the water spiralling down the drain; however, the shear itself is not the cause of the rotating pattern. Therefore, the pattern in the water is not caused by the same mechanism that creates spirals in the aurora or that can sometimes be seen in clouds when one air mass moves past another.

Jan 78:221

Flickering Aurora

One of the stranger kinds of aurora is one rarely recognized by eye. Called flickering aurora by the University of Alaska researchers who first described it, this aurora undergoes rapid change somewhat akin to that seen when a candle's flame is struck by a sudden draft of air.

After more than a year of recording flickering auroras on sensitive television systems used to observe the night sky, the flickering aurora was finally recognized as being something other than a problem with the TV sets. The crucial observation came one night in 1966 when such an intense display of flickering aurora occurred that it was easily seen by the unaided eye as well as the sensitive TV systems.

Flickering occurs only near the time of the auroral breakup, the time when quiet auroral arcs rapidly grow brighter and twist into contorted shapes that sweep across the sky. Why flickering occurs only at this time and why it occurs at all are unknown.

Curiously, in each display flickering aurora oscillates at a rather fixed frequency between 7 and 13 cycles per second. This is just the frequency range of alpha waves in the human brain.

Alpha waves become dominant when a person changes from an active thinking state to a passive, blank state. Apparently persons prone to epilepsy can sometimes be caused to undergo petit and grand mal seizures when exposed to light flashing near 10 cycles per sec., the frequency of flickering aurora. It has also been suggested that some auto and aircraft accidents have been caused by persons being lulled into a blank alpha-dominant state by rapidly flashing lights. So far, the flickering aurora has not been blamed for accidents or epileptic seizures, but who knows?

Oct 79:349

Pulsating Aurora

It is no surprise that comparatively few people have ever seen pulsating aurora, even though it is one of the more common, if not the most common, type of Northern Lights. One reason is that the pulsating aurora normally occurs late in the night, usually from about midnight to dawn, when most everyone is, or should be, tucked into bed. Another reason is that pulsating aurora is relatively weak. Even during a strong display of pulsating aurora, a person looking up at the sky immediately after leaving a lighted room will usually fail to see this weak aurora.

Pulsating aurora does not swish across the sky like the bright, active auroras typically seen earlier in the night. It just blinks on and off, for reasons that auroral scientists do not yet understand.

Both pulsating arcs and patches are seen; the most obvious to the human observer are large pulsating patches, usually bigger than the Big Dipper from handle to cup. These patches blink on and off every few seconds; the most common periodicity is 6 to 10 seconds. Many pulsating auroral patches may be seen in the sky at one time. Each seems to have its own temporal behavior pattern, quite independent of its neighbors.

Excellent displays of pulsating aurora can be seen on many winter nights throughout central Alaska and northern British Columbia. During particularly active nights, equally beautiful displays of pulsating aurora can be seen at least as far south as Seattle.

Dec 78:267

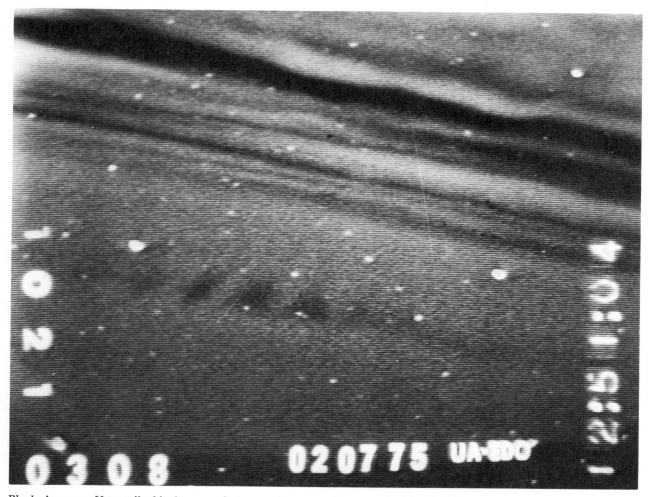

Black Aurora: *Unusually black spaces between close-spaced auroras in this television photograph of the sky give rise to the name "black aurora." The white spots are stars, and the numbers around the edge tell the camera pointing direction and the date and time of the photograph.*

Black Aurora

The name "black aurora" was coined mostly in fun by graduate students and others at the Geophysical Institute, somewhat more than 20 years ago.

When making visual observations of the Northern Lights, these observers noticed that there sometimes occurred overhead in the sky what appeared to be close-spaced auroral forms with unusually black dark spaces between them. This situation did not occur often, but when it did, the auroral display seemed distinctive enough that people recognized it as special and commented about the apparent blackness of the sky between the auroras.

Being aware that the human eye and brain combination has a remarkable ability to distinguish between different shades of grey, the young observers thought that the apparent blackness between the auroras was not real, instead that it was an optical illusion. So as a joke aimed at themselves and their own limitations, and because the whole concept was obviously ridiculous, the students applied the name black aurora to this type of display. The word black, of course, referred to dark spaces between the real auroras.

It turned out, however, that these visual observers were seeing a real effect. In later years, new types of observations using various instruments revealed that the black auroras were more than an optical illusion. Most bright auroras are embedded in regions of less bright, perhaps barely visible aurora. Between these auroral forms the sky is brighter than the sky some distance away from the aurora, a fact that the careful observer can verify the next time he or she sees aurora overhead.

But, for reasons not yet known, there sometimes appear truly black voids between close-spaced auroras. In these voids there is an abnormal absence of auroral light, so the sky there looks and truly is abnormally black. So what started out as a joke has become an unexplained mystery.

14

When the mystery is explained, the new knowledge acquired by solving it may be comparatively trivial, or it might be quite important. That uncertainty adds spice to every unsolved problem, be it one in science or in everyday life.

Aug 80:422

Aurora in Eskimo Legend

Cultural Eskimo views on a person's destination after life vary widely from Alaska to Greenland. Eskimo parents of the Mackenzie region must always remember that the soul of the departed may enter the body of a new-born child where it will remain until death — unless that child be punished too often, in which case the spirit will leave. In other regions, the departed spirit goes to various levels of afterlife, the hereafter depending upon behavior in life and the manner of death.

A person who dies of sickness or other routine cause and who has not been a good person in life generally will end up in a bad place. That place may be beneath the sea or perhaps down in the bowels of the earth. The bad place is not necessarily a site for punishment (the views differ from Alaska to Greenland) but it may be very dark there, much snow and ice cover the land, and it is always stormy.

In general, it is believed that there is no assurance that life in the final land will be better or worse than here on earth. There can be a sort of intermediate form of the hereafter which may be rather monotonous to live in but which will be free of cold and hardship.

The better places to go are one of the levels of heaven, the highest of which is in the aurora borealis. This is a happy place where there is no snow or storm. It is always bright, and there are many easily caught animals. A common belief is that the aurora is caused by the spirits playing ball. They are playing football with a walrus head, and the contra-streaming movements of the lights across the sky are the evidence of struggles among the spirits.

The person who goes to the highest heaven in the aurora is the man who dies in the hunt, the person who is murdered or who has committed the noble act of suicide or the woman who has died in childbirth. It helps if one has always been generous to the poor and starving.

Among some Greenlander Eskimos, the aurora is thought to be caused by the spirit of stillborn or murdered children playing ball with their afterbirths. The Copper Eskimos view the aurora as the manifestations of the spirits that bring fine weather. In Alaska it is known that the aurora will come closer if one whistles at it. It also has been said that the aurora will cut your head off if you whistle at it. Prior to 1900 it was written that the Eskimos of Point Barrow were afraid of the Northern Lights and carried knives in self-protection. Further protection could be gained by throwing dog excrement or urine at the aurora. Others believe that one must be careful not to offend the auroras because these ghostly spirits somehow control the supply of game and weather.

Nov 77:197

Conjugate Aurora

We are often asked whether the aurora is seen only in the Northern Hemisphere. The answer is "no, there is aurora in the Southern Hemisphere also". Until recently, very little was known about the Southern Hemisphere aurora; it was known to exist and it was known that, during times of high auroral activity in the north, aurora was also observed in the south. But do they occur at exactly the same time and do they look exactly the same?

The first opportunity to answer this question came in 1957-1958 during the International Geophysical

26 March 1968, 10:48:05 UT

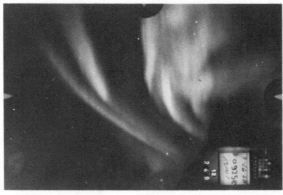

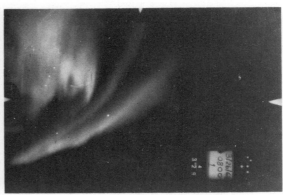

Northern Hemisphere   Southern Hemisphere

Conjugate Aurora: *Simultaneous photographs taken from cockpits of aircraft flying conjugate paths in the Northern and Southern Hemispheres.*

Year. Auroral cameras were operated routinely from many locations in the Northern and Southern Hemispheres. On the basis of this data, researchers at the Geophysical Institute demonstrated that auroras are conjugate, i.e., they occur simultaneously and they look alike.

Since then many programs have been devoted to worldwide investigation of the conjugacy of auroral phenomena. One of these programs originated at the Geophysical Institute and was made possible by cooperation with the Los Alamos Scientific Laboratory. Observations were made from jet aircraft flying simultaneously on a precalculated flight path over Alaska and south of New Zealand. A total of 18 such flights have been made so far with more than 60 hours of conjugate auroral observations.

The conjugate flight data have demonstrated that when an aurora is seen over Alaska, a similar aurora is seen south of New Zealand and that they behave alike. A beautiful example is shown here.

On the basis of our present understanding of the physics of the aurora, we would expect that if an aurora is seen over Alaska, a similar aurora should be seen at the opposite end of the magnetic field line which is south of New Zealand. The data, however, show some fairly systematic differences which indicate that the aurora over Alaska is brighter than almost anywhere else, a phenomenon not yet fully understood.
                                                         — *Hans Nielsen*
                                                         Apr 76:34

Alaska's Auroras the Best?

Flights of instrumented aircraft over Alaska and south of New Zealand have shown that the southern aurora can duplicate the boreal aurora. Also, the flights have shown that the auroras over Alaska are typically 20-30% brighter.

Putting this observation and others together, scientists at the Geophysical Institute have concluded that the aurora over Alaska and eastern Siberia is probably brighter than over eastern Canada, Iceland and northern Scandinavia.

An explanation for the difference in brightness with longitude comes from the knowledge that the earth's magnetic field strength varies with longitude. The magnetic field strength helps determine how many electrons and protons can enter the earth's atmosphere to cause the aurora. The more charged particles entering, the brighter the aurora.
                                                         May 76:38

Auroral Flights

The aurora is another reason, besides cheaper fares and good ongoing connections, to take those late night flights between Anchorage or Fairbanks and

Alaska's Aurora Best? *Alaska aurora wins the contest. (Drawing by Pat Davis.)*

Seattle. A person sitting in a window seat on the proper side of the airplane can have a grandstand seat on one of nature's finer spectacles.

At altitude 30,000 feet (10 km), most of the earth's atmosphere is below the airplane where it cannot shield out the auroral light. Consequently, any auroras seen will be roughly twice as bright as they would be observed at ground level.

On a night of average auroral activity, the aurora will be to the east-northeast or north of an aircraft flying between Seattle and Alaska's major cities. Therefore, the best auroral watching is from a left-hand seat flying south to Seattle or a right-hand seat when flying north. Cabin lights reflecting off the aircraft windows can prevent one from seeing the Northern Lights well, but a blanket held up as a shield eliminates this problem.

Do not be misled by the sight of aurora below the wing. This aurora is probably 60 miles (100 km or more) above the earth's surface, but far distant from the aircraft — as Columbus proved in 1492, the world is round. Earth curvature allows one flying at 30,000 feet to see auroras more than 1000 miles away. Sometimes on the Seattle-Alaska flights, one can see with one sweep of the eye approximately one-fourth of all the aurora occurring in the Northern Hemisphere.

                                                         Nov 78:266

Auroral Sounds

One of the elusive mysteries of the aurora is the question of auroral sound. So far, no person has made a truly comprehensive investigation of this problem or managed to record sounds in the audio range that could be associated with the Northern Lights. Yet many northerners have received the sensation of sound while observing bright, fast-moving auroras overhead. When something moves rapidly, one is inclined to think it should make a noise. That idea might explain some observations. But there are reported instances of people hearing the sounds before becoming aware of the aurora overhead.

People who are used to listening to the sounds of the wilderness away from the noisy background of urban living are most likely to have heard aurorally associated sound usually described as a rustling or crackling noise. Also, women and young people tend to report the sounds more often than older people or men. This tendency suggests that the auroral noise may be at the high-frequency end of the human hearing range. Men and older people tend to have comparatively poor hearing at high frequencies.

Winter's darkness is the time for viewing and listening to auroras. At the Geophysical Institute, we are interested in collecting reports of auroral sounds. It is important to note the time of the observation, the appearance of the aurora, the weather conditions and any other factors that might help unravel the mystery of what auroral sounds are. It is fairly certain that the sound cannot be generated within the aurora itself and propagated to the hearer. A more likely explanation is that the sound is generated at or near the ground by electrical phenomena associated with the aurora. Also, it is possible that there are no sound waves as such, but that the sensation of sound is produced inside the hearer's head by physical or psychological processes.

Whatever the answer, we need to find out. We might learn more both about the aurora and how our minds and bodies work.

Nov 78:265

Insight into Auroral Sounds?

There can be no doubt that some people hear swishing or crackling sounds accompanying bright auroral displays. Usually the reports indicate that the aurora is directly overhead and fast-moving when the sounds are heard.

Since the aurora is at high altitude where the air is too thin to effectively transmit sound waves to the ground, it is certain that no audible sound is produced by the aurora itself. One possiblity is that electric fields produced on or near the ground surface by the aurora are somehow causing audible sound.

Another suggestion is that the sounds are a form of self-delusion. The idea here is that one is so used to fast-moving objects also making sound that he or she assumes the fast-moving aurora makes a sound and thereby 'hears' a sound. Yet another idea is that there is perhaps no real sound but that electromagnetic fields produced by the aurora might create the sensation of sound within a person's nervous system.

Recently, Dr. Juan G. Roederer, Director of the Geophysical Institute, has made another suggestion of how people might hear aurora. Dr. Roederer's suggestion comes out of his broad background that includes study of the physics of the brain and the nervous system.

He points out that in the brain there is provision for mixing of signals from the different senses prior to conscious perception of those signals. Thus it may be possible for a signal coming from the eyes to be interpreted as having originated in the ears. (Recall that a sharp blow on the head sometimes causes an apparent bitter taste in the mouth.)

One test of the signal mixing hypothesis suggested by Roederer is for observers of auroral sound to close their eyes to see if the sounds go away, a requirement of this hypothesis.

Nov 79:357

Auroras and Migrating Birds

Do great auroral displays affect migrating birds? It now seems that there is some connection, though how it comes about is obscure. The most spectacular auroras occur during intervals known as magnetic storms; during these times it appears that migrating birds shift from their normal tracks.

There is a hint that migrating birds have a tendency to fly left of normal track during magnetic (and auroral) disturbances. More obvious is an observed variation in migrating track direction as much as twenty or thirty degrees to either side of normal during disturbances.

According to an article by Frank R. Moore of Clemson University that appeared in the May 6, 1977 issue of *Science*, these effects have been seen in migrating robins, warblers and other passerine (perching) birds. Tests with homing pigeons also show that birds may sense change in the earth's magnetic field. So far, there is evidently no proof that birds actually use the magnetic field for navigation.

If, as suggested, migrating birds move in more variable directions when experiencing magnetic field changes, one wonders what happens to them when they reach the auroral zone. It is here that the magnetic field varies the most and most rapidly. Could it be that the magnetic disturbance accompanying the aurora tends to disperse birds east and west along the auroral zone and thus affect where they do their summer nesting?

Jun 77:170

More on Auroras and Birds

Commenting on the question of whether migrating birds are affected by the magnetic disturbances accompanying auroras, geologist Florence Weber cites an incident that suggests that birds are at least aware of auroras.

Last fall she and others were boating down the Yukon and had camped near the mouth of Stewart River. That evening, at sunset, several thousand sandhill cranes paused in their southward migration to land on nearby sandbars. Later in the night an intense aurora appeared overhead. When it abruptly ceased, the cranes set up an intense gabbling noise and then quieted down.

Still later, a bright meteor flashed across the sky and the cranes again gabbled loudly. Sunrise again set off the chattering.

Florence Weber described the incident to ornithologist Brina Kessel, who, as it turned out, that same night was waiting at Big Delta hoping to observe the sandhill crane migration along the normal route. But the cranes never appeared there. Whether the cranes departed from their normal migration route because of auroral disturbance is, of course, unknown. Another possibility, suggested by Dr. Kessel, is that strong winds from the west carried the birds far to the east of their normal path.

Jul 77:173

Abnormal Radio Propagation

Like many others, J. Raymond of Fairbanks has noted the vagaries of AM radio reception in Alaska and has asked if reception is better in Alaska than elsewhere. He rightly notes that the peculiarities of broadcast band radio in Alaska are related to the aurora.

Those same incoming charged particles (mainly electrons) that stream down along the direction of the earth's magnetic field over central and northern Alaska to create the visible aurora also modify the ionosphere. Irregularly shaped regions of enhanced electron density associated with aurora in the ionosphere, altitude 100 km (60 mi) and above, both absorb and reflect radio waves.

For the most part, the auroral particles interfere with ionospheric radio propagation, making it less reliable in Alaska and other polar regions than at lower latitudes. But sometimes the auroral effects lead to weird and wondrous propagation paths. This is why listeners in Chalkyitsik sometimes receive AM radio from Hungary, China, or South America. It explains why Fairbanks cab drivers sometimes receive instructions from dispatchers in Miami or New Jersey. Such radio waves may bounce several times between the ionosphere and the earth's surface before reaching the destination where heard. The radio waves used to send television and telephone messages via satellite are of much higher frequency. These travel only line-of-sight paths from antenna to antenna and are little deviated by the ionosphere.

Nov 77:195

Radio Waves and Aurora

Listeners of "shortwave" radio bands, ham radio operators and "CB'ers" all have one thing in common — their activities are interfered with by the aurora. The same energetic particles that come in from outside the atmosphere to create the visible aurora alter the ionospheric layers that affect radio propagation. These particles have a variety of effects. One is to cause absorption of radio waves that normally would be reflected by the mirror-like ionospheric layers. Then long-distance communication that depends upon ionospheric reflection may cease simply because of the absorption. The incoming particles can also create peculiar reflecting regions. In such instances it may be possible for a ham operator in Anchorage to talk with one in Fairbanks even though both their antennas are pointed northward — in such a case they are actually bouncing their signals off the auroral region. This also is the reason why a "CB'er" can sometimes receive signals from distant Alaskan locations or even from the lower 48. A Fairbanks cab driver once received instructions from a dispatcher in New Jersey.

Equally frustrating is the rapid fading (called fluttering) that garbles communications as a result of changing or multiple paths that radio waves traverse during auroral disturbance conditions.

For the most part, satellite communications avoid these problems because of the propagation paths and the very high frequencies employed.

— Robert D. Hunsucker
Oct 76:117

The Aurora Versus CB'ers

Why have CB communications been particularly difficult in Alaska the past few months? The answer to this question posed by Mr. C. A. Boyd of the Delta Junction area involves the ways of both Man and Nature.

Citizens Band is intended for local, essentially line-of-sight communications. The frequency range for the most popular CB band, near 27 megahertz, is particularly suited to portable short-distance communication. This band is high enough in frequency to permit short antennas and light-weight transmitters and receivers — the higher one goes in frequency, the smaller become the equipment and the power requirements. It is also more costly to build CB equipment designed for high frequency, and the higher in frequency the less able are the radio waves to be refracted or reflected around objects. Thus, if substantially higher frequency is used, for instance the 462 megahertz CB band, it is more costly and more necessary to be truly line-of-sight between radios. The 27 megahertz Citizens Band is low enough in frequency that, at least to a limited extent,

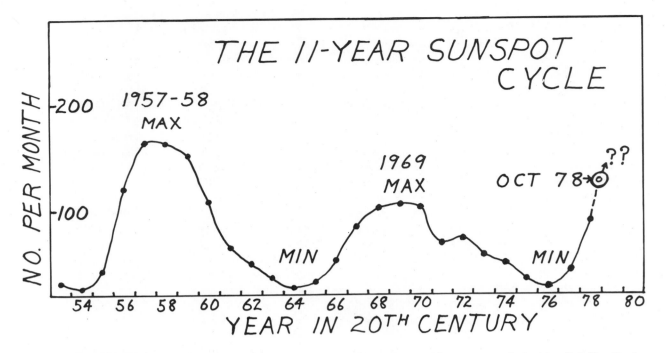

THE 11-YEAR SUNSPOT CYCLE

NO. PER MONTH

200
100

1957-58 MAX

1969 MAX

OCT 78

??

MIN

MIN

54 56 58 60 62 64 66 68 70 72 74 76 78 80

YEAR IN 20TH CENTURY

The Aurora Versus CB'ers: *The ups and downs of the 11-year sunspot cycle are somewhat unpredictable. During 1978, the number of sunspots per month rose dramatically and contributed to more auroras and more radio interference in the polar regions. The maximum of the current cycle is predicted for winter 1979-80.*

the signals can be reflected or bent around hills and valleys to permit non-line-of-sight reception.

Still, the frequency of CB is too high to permit it to bounce off the normal ionosphere located 50 to 400 miles (80 to 600 km) above the earth. Thus, normally, CB transmissions cannot be "skipped" off the ionosphere to be received at distant locations up to several thousands of miles away.

The recent problem with CB in Alaska arises now because the ionosphere is no longer the "normal" one we have been used to the past few years. We are rapidly approaching the maximum of an 11-year solar cycle, a maximum that has all the signs of being higher than the last maximum. In fact, already during October 1978 there were more sunspots than during any month of the last maximum. During sunspot maximum years, there is more aurora at high latitudes, and the ionosphere is made more reflective of radio waves through the action of the same incoming particles that cause aurora.

The last few months it has been usual for the daytime ionosphere over Alaska to be dense enough to reflect radio waves in the 27 megahertz Citizens Band. Consequently, distant signals, typically those from a few hundred to a few thousand miles away, are being skipped in to compete with locally originated signals. The result is often an incomprehensible babble of noise that destroys the usefulness of CB.

This problem has become particularly severe for the first time because this is the first time we are

approaching a sunspot maximum period since CB came into heavy use near the auroral zone. Furthermore, the rapid onset of the new solar maximum period during 1978 makes the radiowave pollution problem especially apparent this year.

The interference problem noticed in recent months by CB'ers near the auroral zone is mostly restricted to the daytime signals being skipped off the high (F-region) ionosphere from locations to the south. A similar problem would exist at night if there were more CB'ers scattered along the auroral zone in western Canada or eastern Siberia. At night, CB signals are most likely to be reflected off the lower ionosphere (E-region) in a direction parallel to the auroral zone, that is, mostly east-west.

So far, the CB interference problem is mostly restricted to the auroral regions. As we more closely approach the maximum of this solar cycle, the problem likely will spread farther south, just as does the aurora.

How long will the interference problem last? The maximum of this solar cycle is predicted to occur during the 1979-1980 winter. So Alaskan and northern Canadian CB'ers using the 27 megahertz band can expect serious interference problems well beyond the time of sunspot maximum, at least another two years. The best permanent solution is to assign much higher frequencies to Citizens Band use.

Jan 79:283

Aurora Versus Power Lines

The Northern Lights are pretty to look at, but we all know that every silver cloud has a dark lining. At least it does for the electrical engineer.

One problem is that intense electrical currents in the ionosphere accompany large auroral displays. Sometimes currents as large as a few hundred thousand amperes flow along the aurora, 60 miles above the earth's surface. As these currents wax and wane from minute to minute, they induce voltages in the conducting surface of the earth. The induced voltage can be as large as one volt per kilometer, about six-tenths of a volt per mile.

This voltage also appears in wires such as telegraph or electrical transmission lines which are grounded to earth at each end. The voltage appearing is proportional to the length of the line, hence a long line can acquire a large voltage. A thousand volts will sometimes appear in a line a thousand kilometers long if there are strong auroras overhead.

In the olden days of overland telegraph lines, the key operators sometimes were in for nasty surprises during auroral displays. Unwanted sparks erupted around their telegraph terminals, and the telegraph systems became unusable. Had the Alaska-Siberia Telegraph not been abandoned in 1867 before being completed, the system surely would have had much trouble with the aurora.

More important now is the current induced in long electrical transmission lines. The aurorally induced current is small compared to the 60 hertz current intentionally placed in a power transmission line, but even so, the auroral current surges have characteristics that do cause problems. The current finds its way into protective relays in the line and can cause them to trip off, stopping the power transmission. Power grids in eastern Canada and northeastern United States have undergone blackouts for this reason. Similarly, extensive auroral storms tripped off the power line between Winnepeg and Minneapolis during October 1980 and again in April 1981.

Still another problem with the auroral currents in power lines is that they create undesirable noise in the lines. The noise bothers people living near the power transmission lines and it may indicate undesirable mechanical and thermal stresses which reduce the useful lifetime of transformers; the damaging effects are thought to be cumulative.

Also, the induced currents can cause catastrophic failure of transformers during an auroral storm. An expensive 735,000-volt transformer at St. James Bay, Canada, had to be replaced after the December 19, 1980 great red aurora, but it blew again during another display in April 1981.

The great red aurora seen by many Alaskans and Canadians on the early morning of December 19, 1980 fed current into the protective relays at the Gold Hill substation on the power line between Healy and Fairbanks, Alaska, but did not trip the relays. This line is comparatively short, so the induced current was not large.

Because of concern over problems they expect to occur as more long intertie power lines are built in the North, Drs. John Aspnes and Syun Akasofu and other scientists at the University of Alaska's School of Engineering and Geophysical Institute have begun investigating auroral induction in power lines in cooperation with the Golden Valley Electric Association in Fairbanks. Curiously enough, lack of funding now threatens to curtail this work, work which may save operators of power lines much money in the long run and which may help avoid power outages on such projects as the proposed intertie between Anchorage and Fairbanks.

Oct 81:506

Aurora and Climate

Only a few years ago almost every meteorologist and auroral physicist scoffed at the suggestion that the earth's weather might be influenced by variations in sunspots. True, statistical relationships between the 11-year cycle in sunspot occurrence and weather or climatic phenomena were being claimed. But it was common knowledge that one could find 11-year cycles in the stock market, the quality of wines, the length of women's dresses and almost anyplace one chose to look.

The problem has been that scientists could find no mechanism by which the particles streaming from the sun in association with sunspot variability could have an influence on weather or climate, even though these particles were known to create auroras and other so-called solar-terrestrial effects.

It seems to be characteristic of scientists that they are sceptical of apparent associations between different phenomena if it is not obvious why the two phenomena should be related. But give a scientist a good reason why two phenomena should be related, and he is prone to accept the flimsiest of evidence as undeniable proof.

A number of scientists are seriously searching for an understanding of how solar-terrestrial influences might cause climatic change or variations in weather patterns. Mechanisms are needed because the evidence is growing that there is a relation between solar activity and climate. Examination of climate over the past 7000 years has shown that those centuries of low solar activity, and hence least aurora, were colder than the centuries of high solar activity.

Out of the searches for mechanisms are starting to appear some plausible ideas. The best so far, I think, is the idea that the small amounts of energy carried by particles into the auroral zones do influence the configuration of the sub-polar jet stream. It was the persistent distortion to the jet stream that caused the record winter of 1975-1976.

Nov 77:194

Red Aurora

Early on the morning of December 19, 1980, a blood-red auroral arc suddenly appeared in the skies over British Columbia, Yukon Territory and Alaska. Because of the hour — the event started about 6:20 a.m., Pacific time, 4:20 a.m. Alaska time — not many people were up to see it, even though it lasted for some time and was seen in central Alaska as late as 7:00 a.m.

Totally red auroras occur infrequently; not more than a few have been seen in this part of the world during the last twenty years. The most widely-seen in North America in recent times was the spectacular red aurora of February 11, 1958. That night the sky over almost all of the continent was clear, so millions of Americans and Canadians, even those as far south as Florida and southern California, saw this beautiful display. All night long, the Alaskan sky was filled with red aurora so bright it made the snow on the ground look red.

All-red auroras are seen near the beginnings of large magnetic storms, and only during some of these. At such times, large numbers of electrons originating on the sun stream into the high atmosphere. There they strike oxygen atoms resident at altitudes of 200 to 500 km and cause them to emit quanta of pure red light.

Normal green auroras and green auroras tinged with reddish lower borders occur at much lower altitudes, typically near 100 km. The electrons that produce these auroras are more energetic than those creating blood-red auroras so they penetrate more deeply into the atmosphere. During their passage through the upper reaches, these electrons also cause red emissions from oxygen atoms but the red color usually is so much weaker than the green that it is detected only with special instruments.

Eye-witness reports of the December 19, 1980, aurora are needed because moonlight prevented most instrumental observations of this unusual aurora. They can be sent to me at the Geophysical Institute, Fairbanks, Alaska, 99701.

Dec 80:456

December 19, 1980 Red Aurora

Although all data from far-flung stations are not yet available, it is possible to piece together a description of the unusual auroral display of December 19, 1980 using reports from those who saw the display and instrumental data acquired at Fairbanks and Fort

Yukon, Alaska. Aside from the rarity of the blood-red auroras, this display is of special interest because it induced very large currents in the electrical transmission line between Nenana and Fairbanks between 5:00 a.m. and 7:00 a.m. on the morning of December 19 (Alaska Standard Time).

Black and white pictures taken each minute by an all-sky camera at Fort Yukon showed that a normally-appearing auroral arc — probably a green one — developed directly overhead that location just after 7:00 p.m. on the evening of December 18, 1980. Several arcs and bands swirled overhead Fort Yukon during the next hour, not an unusual occurrence at that auroral zone location. The aurora then quieted down.

The first hint that this might be an unusual night was visual sighting of aurora directly overhead Anchorage shortly after midnight. This in itself was not really unusual, since auroras do often appear over Anchorage; when they do, it means a larger-than-average display is underway.

At 1:43 a.m., the aurora over Fort Yukon started anew, and by 2:30 a.m. the arcs were showing unusually tall ray structures; perhaps they were more reddish than usual. Things started to get exciting about 3:45 a.m., and the aurora came on like gangbusters over the whole of the southern half of Alaska. However, the best of the action appears to have been seen in the Anchorage area and the areas easterly of it over into British Columbia. The aurora was seen overhead Seward between 5:15 a.m. and 6:30 a.m. and overhead Ketchikan near 6:20 a.m.

A red glow was seen on the north horizon in the Anchorage area near 4:00 a.m. There was deep red aurora to the west of Clear, Alaska at 6:45 a.m., and then truly red aurora mixed in with auroras of green and yellowish hues spread over Anchorage-area skies in the hour or two after 6:30 a.m. The last aurora seen was being entirely obscured by sunlight by 9:00 a.m.

A number of people living within a hundred miles of Anchorage saw long ray structures, of mixed colors, stretching up toward the center of the sky and converging to a point called the magnetic zenith. In the Anchorage area this point is somewhat to the southeast of the true zenith which is directly overhead the observer. Called the corona, this rayed auroral structuring signifies that the aurora is overhead, since the coronal appearance cannot happen otherwise.

Several persons rightly noted that the red portions of this aurora were of unusual purity of color and quite different from the reddish hues that sometimes tinge the bottoms of normal, active green auroras. The deep blood-red color of the unusual all-red auroras is truly pure, as is light from a lazer, since it is not a mixture of colors. Instead it is, in this case, composed of light of only two red wavelengths, at 6300 and 6364 Angstroms.

Most of the aurora we see are a mixture of many colors. There usually is much bluish light near 3900 Angstroms, but our eyes are poor in the blue, so we detect it poorly. Our eyes see best in the green, and there usually is strong auroral light at 5577 Angstroms (a yellowish-green color), hence we see green aurora frequently.

The rare all-red auroras and the tall ray structures or tall featureless masses in which the red auroras appear are caused by a preponderance of incoming particles (electrons and protons) having lower speeds than those that cause the common garden-variety green auroras usually seen. Moving too slowly to penetrate down to an altitude near 100 km (60 miles) where green auroras are created, the slow-moving particles lose most of their energy to oxygen atoms in the high atmosphere, at altitudes in the range 200 to 400 km. The interaction of the incoming particles with the oxygen atoms gives the pure red light at 6300 and 6364 Angstroms.

By contrast, the red tinge sometimes seen at the bottoms of green auroras is a mixture of many different shades of red caused by the incoming particles striking oxygen and nitrogen molecules lying comparatively low in the atmosphere, at altitudes 60 to 90 km.

Jan 81:461

Historical Auroras

Written records telling of the observation of great auroral displays extend back to Roman times in the western world and to well beyond that in the Orient. Even as far back as the seventh century, there are written accounts of aurora being seen at middle latitudes in both the eastern and western worlds.

All this is of more than casual interest because the written record of great auroral displays over the past 1500 years indicates changing levels of auroral activity. The change can be the result of long-term variations in sunspot activity and can also be due to long-term variations in the earth's magnetic field. Very likely, solar variability is the main cause. Since solar variability also affects weather, any insight into that variability acquired through study of auroral history can have consequence beyond just learning more about the aurora.

Another line of evidence on variation in solar activity appears in the content of radioactive carbon (carbon-14) contained in trees. The solar activity at any time determines how much carbon-14 is available in the atmosphere for plants to take up. Hence, using tree-ring dating and carbon-14 measurement, one has another means to observe solar variability over past

centuries. Fair agreement pertains between the carbon-14 content and auroral history methods.

Written auroral records show that the present is an era of auroral maximum that began about the middle of the nineteenth century. A definite low, known as the Maunder Minimum, began in the mid-1600s and ended in 1716. During that minimum few if any auroras were seen at middle and low latitudes. Other minimum auroral periods existed in the seventh and fifteenth centuries.

A particularly good time for seeing auroras was the twelfth century, a period called the Medieval Maximum. The century preceding the birth of Christ also was good; it is called the Roman Maximum. Prior to that time, the studied record of observed auroral displays becomes too sparse to indicate the level of activity which existed at any particular era.

Those who are studying records of historical auroras are of the opinion that further systematic investigation will reveal even more information, enough to obtain a rather detailed picture of the auroral history of the past 2000 years. To the non-historian that idea is somewhat surprising because it would seem that all the past records might have been examined by now. That this may not be so reminds one of how recent in human history is the practice of systematically examining those records of the past obtained around the globe, many of which are still being uncovered after centuries of storage.

One interesting result of the studies of past auroras is the indication that our familiar 11-year sunspot cycle may have been somewhat different about a thousand years ago. At that time it seems that this cycle had a period closer to 10 years than 11 years. Though the 11-year cycle has much influence over the numbers of auroras seen at middle and low latitudes, it is not as noticeable at high latitudes where auroras are common regardless of time within the cycle. Similarly, during those prolonged periods of auroral quiet of past centuries, there probably was plenty of aurora for northerners to see.

Nov 81:448

Man-Made Aurora

Proof that scientists really do understand the direct cause of the Northern Lights comes from a series of rocket experiments performed in Alaska, Hawaii, Virginia and elsewhere in the world.

The first experiment was at the NASA rocket base at Wallops Island, Virginia, in 1969. An electron gun, a device capable of shooting out beams of high-speed electrons, was placed in the nose cone of a rocket and lofted high above most of the atmosphere. Using gas jets, the rocket payload was rotated until it pointed downward along the direction of the earth's magnetic field, which, even as far south as Virginia, points more downward than northward.

When all was ready, bursts of electrons were shot from the gun. Traveling at speeds near twenty thousand miles per hour, the electrons followed the direction of the magnetic field and penetrated the atmosphere. There they struck the atoms and molecules of the atmosphere and made them glow, producing the first controlled man-made aurora. The thin, pencil streaks of aurora that resulted were too weak to be seen by eye. Still they were recorded by sensitive ground-based television systems developed by the University of Alaska and placed around the launch site.

Having proved that auroras can be generated by man, the experimental team next moved to Hawaii for an even more difficult experiment. Another electron gun was flown up from a launch site on Maui. This time, the gun was aimed upward instead of down.

Shooting from the gun, the electron beams sped away from the earth, following the magnetic field direction upward. Reaching high above the equator, the electrons then curved to follow the magnetic field back downward into the Southern Hemisphere. They produced an aurora recorded by the University of Alaska television cameras carried aboard jet aircraft flying above the South Pacific Ocean, east of American Samoa.

Having shot electrons from the Northern Hemisphere to the Southern, the experimenters had proved that beams of electrons would follow along the direction of the earth's magnetic field for great distances. And, of course, they verified again that when the electrons hit the atmosphere, they generated an observable aurora.

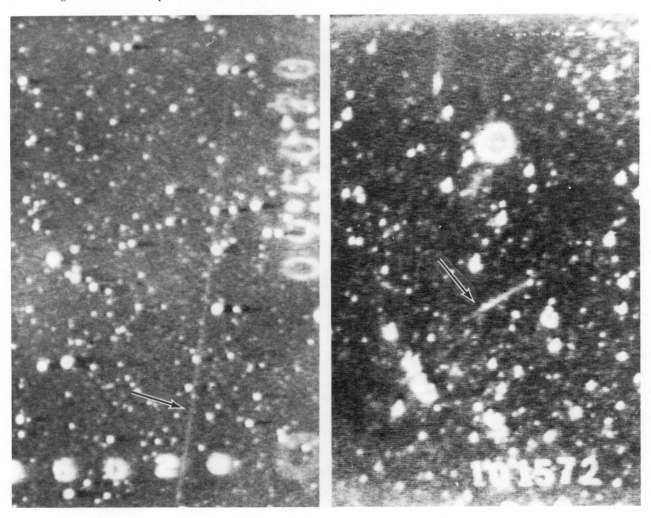

Man-Made Aurora: *Man-made auroras created over Virginia in 1969 (left) and over the South Pacific in 1972 (right). The thin auroral streaks indicated by the arrows were too weak to be seen by the human eye. These pictures were taken by the Geophysical Institute's television cameras used to observe the natural aurora. The round white spots are stars magnified in size by the extreme sensitivity of the special cameras.*

Several similar experiments have been performed from the Poker Flat rocket range near Fairbanks. Soviet and French-Soviet teams also have generated artificial auroras over Russia, using similar rocket devices. When NASA's space shuttle flies, it too will perform more artificial aurora experiments.

Aside from giving straightforward proof of how auroras are caused, such experiments help to solve some of the mysteries that still remain about the aurora and about other complex phenomena occurring in our universe. What goes on in producing an aurora is similar to the processes taking place in the stars and in the vast reaches of space between them.

Mar 81:462

Barium Releases

Again this year rockets are being flown from Poker Flat Research Range, near Chatanika, to create high-altitude barium releases. Five rockets, each carrying four to twelve releases, are being flown on clear nights sometime in late March and early April.

Each release ejects a small quantity of barium vapor that is visible from the ground and which permits measurement of the wind and the electric field in the upper atmosphere. The release first appears in the form of a rapidly expanding yellow-green ball. Part of the barium vapor remains neutral and drifts with the wind forming a green cloud. From this cloud a reddish-purple cloud of ionized barium vapor emerges. This cloud drifts away under the influence of the electric field. Since the releases are at very high altitude, 150-300 km, they can be seen everywhere in central and northern Alaska. When feasible, there is an attempt to notify area radio stations of impending launches so that Alaskans can observe the releases if they choose.

Apr 76:19

International Barium Releases

Strange lights seen in Alaskan skies on late February and early March 1978 evenings have a reasonable explanation. These were chemical releases performed at high altitude aboard rockets flown from the University's Poker Flat rocket range near Fairbanks.

The two most beautiful sequences, on February 27 and March 1, were conducted by a group of Danish scientists, the first truly international users of Alaska's scientific rocket range.

Each Danish rocket released a chemical called trimethylaluminate (TMA, for short) as it sped upward through altitude 80 km (50 miles). At this altitude the rocket was still in darkness and the TMA formed a yellowish trail. Then as the rocket entered sunlight, the TMA being released glowed a beautiful blue color.

By photographing the deformation of the TMA

Barium Releases: *A barium jet painting the configuration of a magnetic field line against the stars. The wing of the aircraft from which this montage television photograph is made shows at lower left. Just over the wing are auroras. The barium jet was ejected from a rocket near the point marked 480 km. It took 110 seconds to rise to 2000 km altitude. Such experiments helped in the discovery of the auroral acceleration mechanism.*

trail with cameras at Arctic Village, Fort Yukon and Fairbanks, the Danish scientists measured the wind in the region through which the rocket was flying.

A minute or so later, the rocket released a puff of barium gas. The barium release soon formed two clouds that drifted apart. One part, composed of ionized barium, drifted away westward under the influence of the electric field in the high atmosphere. Thus by tracking it, the Danes could measure the electric field. Two more barium releases and then a second TMA release, performed as the rocket fell back toward the earth, allowed additional measurements of the wind and electric field over an extended region above Alaska.

The highest barium releases were at altitude 270 km, high enough to be easily seen all over Alaska and western Canada wherever the sky was clear.

People have wondered if there was a connection between the barium releases and the extensive auroras that occurred throughout each night following the chemical release. The answer is yes, but the releases did not cause the aurora. It was the other way around. By observing with various instruments, it was known that extensive auroras were already occurring over Alaska when the releases were made in evening twilight. Since the objective was to measure the effects of the aurora on the high-altitude winds, the rockets were purposely flown during times of extensive naturally occurring aurora.

Mar 78:28

Barium Releases from Orbit

Those Alaskans and Canadians ambitious enough to stay up and watch the sky Saturday night, October 28, 1978, had the opportunity to see a new type of scientific experiment likely to be the forerunner of many to come. It was the first time that an earth-orbiting vehicle was used to inject visible chemicals into the high atmosphere.

At 2:07 a.m. Sunday morning (Daylight Saving Time), a command was sent up from the NASA Gilmore satellite tracking station north of Fairbanks to a Delta rocket flying over the polar cap southward towards Alaska. This rocket had launched a Nimbus G weather satellite from Cape Vandenberg five days earlier and was following the satellite along in its orbit 600 miles above the earth. Upon receipt of the command, the Delta vehicle ejected four puffs of barium vapor, spaced 40 seconds apart.

Though it was dark at the ground, sunlight impinging upon the released barium atoms plucked off electrons and thereby left the barium atoms in the charged (ionized) state. In that condition, the barium atoms could move freely along the direction of the earth's magnetic field but not transverse to it.

Then the fact that the barium had been released from a fast-moving vehicle came into play. Carrying the orbiting release vehicle's forward speed of 8 km per sec (18,000 mph), the barium ions slammed against the steeply inclined geomagnetic field and scooted upward along the direction of the field. The ions moved so high up over Alaska that they could be seen well up in the northern sky of California and Hawaii. The clouds also were photographed by camera crews at Fairbanks, Fort Yukon, Barrow, Barter Island and Cape Parry, N.W.T.

The primary objective of the experiment was to measure electric fields in the polar cap, but the rapid upward motions of the barium ions proved equally interesting, especially since early results indicate that the barium moved upwards faster than anyone expected.

Nov 78:269

Lithium Red Sky

Red sky at night: scientist's delight. Natural blood-red sky at night is comparatively rare. Perhaps once a decade, huge flares on the sun generate red auroras that spread over much of the earth's surface and sometimes cause the sky to appear red.

In recent years, artificially red nighttime skies have been created over limited parts of the earth. Rocket-borne releases of a few pounds of the element lithium make markers in the sky that can be easily photographed to measure winds in the high atmosphere.

Many Alaskans and Yukoners are familiar with the barium releases made aboard rockets launched from the Poker Flat rocket range near Fairbanks. These releases create two types of cloud. One is a neutral green cloud that moves with the wind. The other is a bluish purple cloud that striates like a rayed aurora and moves under the influence of the electric field in the high atmosphere.

In somewhat similar fashion it is possible to slowly spew out lithium metal from a rocket to produce a long, visible red trail. Sunlight shining on the lithium atoms causes them to be excited so that they glow with a red light. Unlike the barium, lithium released in the high atmosphere yields only a neutral gas tracer. The neutral tracer is useful only for measuring the direction and speed of the wind in the high atmosphere at altitudes well above 100 km.

This week scientists from NASA's Goddard Space Flight Center are at Poker Flat attempting to fly two rockets that will release both lithium and barium. These releases are high enough to be visible to all persons with clear sky in Alaska, eastern Siberia and northwestern Canada.

The red lithium trails are easy to see and do persist for a long time. Lithium is such a light element that it remains aloft for hours drifting with the wind. Eventually the lithium becomes invisible as it disperses and combines with other elements in the air.

The overall objective of the research using chemical releases at high altitude is to understand how energy is transferred from one level to another in the atmosphere and the near-earth regions of space above. That energy transfer may have some influence upon climate.

Apr 79:312

Flying Rockets

Over the past ten years, more than 170 major rockets have been flown from the Geophysical Institute's Poker Flat rocket range, north of Fairbanks. Each of these was an "unguided" rocket, meaning that once it left the ground no further guidance control was possible.

Despite the lack of in-flight guidance, it is possible to fly the rockets several hundred miles into the atmosphere and still have them hit a target only a few miles across, some distance downrange. Downrange from Poker Flat is to the north or east.

Most of the rockets have two stages. The first-stage motor lifts the rocket from the ground and gets it well underway. Its fuel being spent after a few seconds, this first motor falls away and lands within a few miles of the launch site. The second-stage rocket with its attached payload coasts upward for about twenty seconds, and then it fires for a few more seconds to give the velocity needed to lift the payload up into the high atmosphere.

The launch crews use a steerable launcher to aim the rockets, one that can be aimed with a precision of one-tenth of a degree. Once the first-stage rocket motor is fired, the rocket moves a few inches or feet before flying freely on its own.

Before launching a rocket, the crew carefully measures the winds by means of anemometers spaced along a 200-foot tower at the site and radar-tracked balloons flown to altitudes above 20,000 feet. The winds are critical because a rocket drifts with the wind when its motors are coasting and it cocks over into the wind when they are firing. Thus, the crew must know the wind at all altitudes and must set the launcher according to complex formulas based upon the wind direction and speed.

Adjustment for the wind sometimes requires setting the launcher direction up or down by one or two degrees, or right or left up to twenty degrees, from the direction it would be aimed were there no wind. When the winds are strong or highly variable, the launch team waits for a better day.

Mar 81:474

Old Reliable

The old-reliable Model A Ford of transportation to the high atmosphere is the Nike (Nī′kē) rocket

Old Reliable: *A Nike rocket lifts a second-stage rocket and a payload from Poker Flat at night.*

motor. Like the old Fords, some of the Nike rockets flown at the Poker Flat Research Range near Fairbanks are vintage-class vehicles. As they emerge from packing crates, they display markings showing manufacture dates as far back as the early 1950s.

Nike rockets originally were mass-produced for military purposes, the prime use being for ground-to-air flights against aircraft. They are no longer manufactured. Some years ago NASA and other civilian agencies acquired the remaining several hundred Nikes for scientific rocket flights.

A Nike rocket is used mostly as the first stage of a two-stage vehicle intended to carry 80- to 300-pound payloads to altitudes ranging from 60 to 200 miles. If the system fails to work properly, the fault usually is in the performance of the newer second stage and almost never with the old military surplus Nike.

At launch a Nike weighs in at about 1300 pounds, is 16 inches in diameter and is 12 feet long. Hotter than any dragster, the Nike goes from 0 to 1600 mph in less than 4 seconds flat. Then, it has risen a mile high and is nothing more than a hollow tube with fins, all its fuel being spent. A few seconds later the Nike ends its first flight — also its last — by crumpling into the ground a few kilometers downrange from the launch site. By then the burning of its separated second-stage motor has increased the vehicle speed to about 4500 mph. That speed enables the second stage and its attached payload to coast to an altitude of 150 miles.

The fuel of a Nike is a rubbery black solid formed from a liquid poured into the steel rocket shell and cast into place leaving a star-shaped central hole extending the full length of the motor. An ignitor at the front end initiates burning that almost immediately extends to the confining nozzle at the rocket's rear. Burning proceeds from the central hole outward toward the rocket case; at any instant the remaining unburnt fuel helps shield the case from the hot gases inside.

Feb 79:287

Whistlers

Lacking radio receivers built into them, human beings are unable to hear radio waves without special electronic devices. However, these devices need not always be the radio receivers we normally think of.

For example, some people who have two or more different kinds of fillings in their teeth are able to hear high-power A.M. broadcast stations when located within a few hundred feet of the stations. In such cases, the strong radio waves act upon the teeth fillings in such a way that the electromagnetic oscillations get transformed to mechanical vibrations in the person's head, and these are heard as sound.

A quite different but equally curious phenomenon was discovered before the end of the last century. People listening to telephones sometimes have heard strange whistling noises in addition to whatever other sounds were coming over the wires. The whistling noise starts out with a high-frequency tone and steadily decreases to lower tone, over a period of a second or two. It sounds very much like the second of the two-syllable whistle that appreciative boys sometimes emit when seeing attractive girls, or vice versa.

It is now known that these sounds, called whistlers, are created by lightning strokes traveling over a surprising path. A lightning stroke emits a wide range of radio waves, the most powerful being at about 5000 Hertz. Some of the radio waves pass through the ionosphere and travel along geomagnetic field lines. Guided by the magnetic field, the waves pass high above the earth's equator and then follow along the field lines back down to the opposite hemisphere. The higher-frequency signals travel fastest and consequently get back to earth sooner than the lower frequencies, hence the decreasing tone of the whistler when it is heard.

Any long wire, such as a fence or a long telephone line, makes a good antenna for receiving these space-traveling signals. An audio amplifier such as is contained in a home music system, a radio or a tape deck hooked to a long wire makes a satisfactory receiving system for whistlers.

With such a system, a person in Alaska or western Canada can hear lightning strokes in the South Pacific Ocean. Each stroke sounds not like a crash, but rather is a whistle with tone decreasing with time. One can also hear a whistler that starts out from a local lightning stroke. When this happens, one first hears the crash of the lightning stroke in the receiving system, followed a few seconds later by the whistler. In this case, the radio waves creating the whistler travel along the magnetic field lines to the other hemisphere where they bounce off the ionosphere and speed back along the same path to the point of origin. Such a two-hop whistler is more drawn out in time than one caused by the radio waves making a single passage.

When auroras are active, other sounds, often semi-musical, also are heard on the receiving equipment. Sometimes both ascending- and descending-tone whistlers are heard, at other times the sound is a jumble of murmurs and rustling. Because of their musical nature, the name 'dawn chorus' is given to some of these sounds. Since all these sounds come in as radio waves, they apparently have no direct relation to the auroral sounds many people report when observing active auroral displays.

Apr 81:473

CHAPTER TWO
ASTRONOMY AND KEEPING TIME

The Stars at Night

Is it really true that the stars seen in a northerner's sky do not seem as numerous and as bright as those in more southerly skies? Since almost everything is better in the Yukon and Alaska, it hurts to admit that our view of the stars is, in fact, inferior.

The reason has nothing to do with the stars themselves. Although the stars are not uniformly distributed in the heavens, the spinning of the earth on its axis exposes to all stargazers similar stellar concentrations through the night. The greatest concentration is seen by viewing regions of our own galaxy, the Milky Way. It appears essentially overhead in Alaskan skies, though only about 30 degrees above the horizon at the North Pole.

At high latitudes, the stars do not stand out against the blackness of the sky because the sky there is not black. Even at middle and low latitude the sky is not truly black because of weak luminosity of the high atmosphere. Called airglow, this light emission arises largely from chemical reactions and is about as strong as the integrated, i.e., the total, light from all the stars. Thus at lower latitudes, starlight and the night airglow equally illuminate the earth.

Night airglow typically is brighter at high latitudes than at low. Also diffuse auroral glow adds to the light of the night sky. Together the airglow and diffuse auroral emissions provide a rather bright background to view the stars against. In photographic terms, the northern sky scene has reduced contrast compared to the sky farther south. The weakest of the usually visible stars cannot be seen, and the brightest stars do not stand out as well.

So even if our stars do not appear as bright and numerous, at least our night skies are brighter than those to the south.

Mar 79:292

The Night Airglow

Far from being truly black, the night sky casts down upon the earth's surface a soft, weak illumina-tion. Half or less of this light comes from the stars; the rest is produced in the air itself by a number of different processes. Called the night airglow, this dim, relatively uniform light is so weak that only the aware observer can detect its existence with the naked eye.

The night airglow has its daylight counterpart, too. Sunlight shining upon the high atmosphere during daytime and twilight gives energy to the atoms and molecules of the air, causing them to directly re-emit some of this energy in the form of light. The resulting dayglow and twilight airglow emissions can be quite bright. Still, they pale into near-insignificance compared to the brightness of direct sunlight, so we are generally unaware of them in our daily living.

The night airglow also derives its energy from the sun, but various delayed-action processes permit storage of the energy and its later emission of light after the sun is gone. These processes act only in the upper atmosphere, at altitudes of 60 km (40 mi) and above.

Like its brighter and fast-moving relative the aurora, night airglow has strong emissions at specific wavelengths. At a wavelength of 5577 Angstrom units there is a strong green emission from oxygen. There is a deep red emission at 6300 Angstroms, also from oxygen, and a yellow emission at 5893 Angstroms from sodium atoms in the atmosphere.

In addition to these single-wavelength emissions, it seems that the night airglow may have a continuum of weak emission at all wavelengths, much as the sun itself has. Students of the airglow are not certain about this, though, because the appearance of a continuum can arise from the overlapping of many emissions at specific wavelengths.

The night airglow sometimes produces more light than the stars, and consequently can be the major nighttime source of natural light, especially at high latitude where the airglow emissions are brightest. If there is snow on the ground, the combined starlight and night airglow can provide light for people to see reasonably well by. Despite the fact that the night airglow is a major source of nocturnal illumination, there has not been enough scientific investigation to give a really satisfactory explanation of the phenomenon.

Mar 79:293

"The Jupiter Effect"

Forum's first correspondent, Mrs. Claude Swaim, requests comment on *The Jupiter Effect*, a recent book by two scientists suggesting unusual occurrences of geophysical events in 1982. This book suggests a major increase in auroras with attendant disruption to radio communications, changes in weather patterns and major storms that could devastate coastal cities. It also predicts potentially devastating earthquakes.

The authors of *The Jupiter Effect*, John Gribben and Stephen Plagemann, suggest a major change in sunspot activity in 1982 due to magnetic and gravitational effects of the planets which, in 1982, will be aligned on one side of the sun. Much evidence exists that such effects will be minor and that 1982 will not be a markedly unusual sunspot year.

The authors then further speculate that the supposed change in sunspot activity will produce major effects on the earth's weather, air circulation and rotation. Though changing sunspot activity may affect the earth's rotation, climate and weather, the evidence available so far indicates that the effects are too subtle to create sudden cataclysmic geophysical disasters of the type suggested in *The Jupiter Effect*.

In summary, *The Jupiter Effect* is far too speculative to cause major concern.

Mar 76:22

"The Jupiter Effect": *A sceptic better be sure of his ground. (Drawing by Pat Davis.)*

Venus

Human beings and other higher life forms are patterned to be aware of the unusual and to ignore the usual. Were it otherwise, an individual could not cope with the huge amount of information the eyes and other sensors can present to the mind.

It bothers no one that the sun comes up each morning and that it goes down each night — except for those fortunates who live at high latitude. Nor do the monthly comings and goings of the moon and its apparent changes in shape bother people. In fact, the moon's 28-day cycle has served as a familiar and useful calendar through the ages.

But let there be a total eclipse of the sun. The sudden unexpected disappearance of the sun often causes terror and concern that the world's end has finally come.

More regular and less spectacular, but still sometimes leading to concern and confusion, is the highly variable appearance of the planet Venus — the brightest and most conspicuous planet.

Venus spends most of its time far from the earth, up to 160 million miles away. When distant, Venus is comparatively dim and mostly forgotten. But every 584 days — a year and seven months — Venus approaches the earth, and its apparent brightness increases. Confusingly, Venus appears first as a bright "evening star." Then 72 days after being brightest in the evening, it becomes brightest as a "morning star." This duality led the Greeks to give Venus two names, Phosphorus in evening and Hesperus in morning. When brightest, Venus is 30° from the sun and is crescent-shaped like the moon near the time of new moon. The light seen is, of course, like that from the moon, reflected sunlight.

Almost every time Venus approaches the earth and shows its brightest face, there are new UFO reports. A person looks up in the evening or morning sky and is startled to see an extremely bright object that was not there the last time he looked, a few days or weeks earlier, and he has forgotten that the object was there many months ago. Furthermore, a bright light in the sky such as Venus, stared at long enough, often gives the impression of motion, sometimes making it difficult to believe that one is seeing our closest planetary neighbor, still several tens of millions of miles distant.

Feb 79:286

Reporting Unusual Events

The University of Alaska's Geophysical Institute keeps a valuable file of reports of sightings of unusual events. Sometimes a report of apparently only passing interest at the time is found, years later, to be of real significance.

Many of the reports are by staff members, but

most are telephoned or written in from residents around Alaska. The reports concern earthquakes, unusual animal behavior, atypical water motions or waves, meteor sightings, peculiar cloud formations, satellite sightings, unusual auroras, reports of hearing the aurora, unidentified flying objects, etc. — a whole host of curious or unexplained events.

The most valuable reports are usually those that contain detailed information of a factual nature. The timing and duration of an event are always important, as is the location of the observer. Especially if an observer does not understand the event, it is worth reporting as many features of it and the general environment as possible. The temperature, wind, cloud cover, moisture in the air and proximity to man-made or natural objects can be important as can the color, shape or apparent size of an unknown object. Especially if the sighted object or phenomenon is in the sky, it may be difficult to tell how far away it is. Reports of angles from known directions or objects often are more useful than an observer's estimate of distance.

The clenched fist with extended thumb at arm's length is a useful device for measuring vertical angles. If the base of the fist is placed on the observer's horizon, the tip of the thumb will be 20 degrees above the horizon. By "walking" the clenched fist up the sky 20 degrees at a time, a fairly accurate measure of elevation can be made. Above all, note the time and write down what has been observed as quickly as possible.

One of the most interesting reports we have ever received was from a woman at Huslia. She said, "I was cleaning fish at the river, and an unusual wave came across the water; I think there has been an earthquake somewhere." The details she gave, plus a similar independent report from a man several miles away, made it possible to verify that she had observed the effects of an earthquake near Yakutat, 800 miles distant.
— *Neil Davis and John Miller*
Jan 77:145

Unusual Events in the Sky

Careful observations of unusual lights or of other unidentified objects in the sky can be of significant value. Fireball meteors, auroras, noctilucent clouds, mirage phenomena, atmospheric dust, city lights reflected from clouds, earthquake lights, lightning, forest fires, ice crystals and raindrops in the air, plus a host of other phenomena can create strange effects. Whether or not a person can identify the cause of the phenomenon seen, visual observations can be useful. In those cases where the object is not recognized, after-the-fact review of the observations usually will permit identification, especially if several different persons report their observations.

What should one look for and report?

TIME OF OBSERVATION — Knowing when is probably more important than anything else. Note down the date and the time as closely as you know it. After the observation, you can compare your watch to a time standard such as the radio or telephone to find any error in timing. Given only the time of your observation, we can easily determine if certain phenomena such as the aurora, noctilucent clouds or sunrise-sunset effects could have been responsible for the sightings.

DURATION OF THE EVENT — Did it last just a few seconds, a few minutes or an hour?

LOCATION IN THE SKY — North, south, east or west? How high above the horizon in angular measure? Remember that if you extend your arm and place the bottom of your fist on the horizon so that your thumb is stretched upward, the tip of your thumb will be 20 degrees above the horizon. You can "walk" your fist up the sky to measure angles everywhere; 4½ fist plus thumb lengths brings you to the zenith (straight overhead). The "pointer stars" of the Big Dipper are about 5 degrees apart, and the moon and the sun are about ½ degree across. Do not bother to try to estimate the distance from yourself to an object in the sky; such estimates are usually so unreliable as to be meaningless.

SIZE OF THE OBJECT — As with location, a report of the angular size is important. Either give the size in degrees or compare it to familiar objects such as trees or buildings near you or the moon, sun or stellar constellations. If the object is large, you might indicate the fraction of the sky filled.

Reporting Unusual Events. *(Drawing by Pat Davis.)*

CONDITION OF THE SKY — How bright was the sky? Was it perfectly clear, haze covered, totally cloudy, broken clouds, scattered clouds? Was it raining or snowing? What was the wind? Were the sun and moon up or down? Where were they relative to the object seen? Were stars visible?

BRIGHTNESS OF THE OBJECT — If the object gave off light, was it bright enough to cast shadows or was it much weaker? Try to compare its brightness to familiar objects such as moonlit clouds or the moon itself. Another measure is how much light the object creates on the ground. (Whether or not the ground is snow covered will be important here.)

INTERNAL STRUCTURE — Did the object appear uniform everywhere or did it exhibit structure? If the structure was ray-like, did the rays appear to be parallel or did they appear to converge to some point, either within or outside the object?

MOTION — If the object moved, try to indicate the direction of motion and the angular speed. Since it is so difficult to estimate actual size and distance, estimation of actual speed, say in miles per hour, is equally difficult. Hence, the rate of movement given in degrees per second or per minute is much more valuable. Comparisons are useful: as fast as a satellite, or a small aircraft near the ground or a jet aircraft at cruising altitude.

Almost no one will be able to note and record all of the eight characteristics listed above, especially if the object is observed for a short time. Still, an awareness of what kinds of observations are most valuable results in the making of better observations.

At the Geophysical Institute we maintain a valuable file of sightings of all sorts. Your contributions will be welcomed and preserved.

Feb 79:286

An Unidentified Flying Object

On a cold winter afternoon just as the sun was setting in the southwest, a strange flying object was seen from the Geophysical Institute in Fairbanks. It hung apparently motionless in the southern sky about 20 degrees above the horizon.

Viewed through binoculars, the object appeared to consist of two reddish-white flat-sided flying saucers lying back-to-back, as shown in Sketch 1. After viewing for several minutes, we announced over our loudspeaker system that the object was there and asked other people to look at it. When you don't know what you are seeing, it is good to have as many observers as possible join in the viewing.

Several minutes later the object changed its orientation and appeared as in Sketch 2. By then it was lower in the sky and weaker. Some minutes later

yet, it appeared as in Sketch 3. Only then we knew that we had been watching a contrail from a jet flying from Fairbanks to Anchorage.

At first, we had seen the contrail end-on as the jet climbed away from us and, from our vantage, hung motionless in the sky. Later the jet achieved altitude and was perhaps moving slightly left to right as we saw it. Finally when the aircraft headed down toward Anchorage, the contrail could be seen stretching out behind and being distorted by air turbulence.

Long ago, I gave up being embarrassed at not being able to immediately recognize familiar objects in the sky. They take on strange shapes that easily fool one. The best one can do is observe carefully and try to note and write down all the conditions. If the object is not a flying saucer from another world, careful unbiased observing will probably eventually bring out the truth. And if it really is a flying saucer, one wants to get all the facts possible.

Jan 78:208

An Unidentified Flying Object: *The Geophysical Institute's UFO as seen at three different times.*

Seeing Satellites

Orbiting satellites are visible from the ground only because they reflect sunlight. Sometimes it is not the satellite we see, but the much larger rocket used to put it in orbit and which also orbits.

The requirements for seeing an orbiting object are that it be in sunlight and that there be no sunshine on the lower atmosphere near the observer. We can, of course, see the moon in the daytime, but it subtends a large angle to our eyes. Satellites normally can be seen only during the times of nautical or astronomical twilight. Civil twilight is the time when the sun is 0 to 6 degrees below the horizon; nautical twilight is when it is 6 to 12, and astronomical twilight is when it is 12 to 18 degrees. When the sun is below 18 degrees, it no longer shines on the high atmosphere (below about 400 km). A very high satellite, one above 400 km, could perhaps be seen during the night.

The best times for viewing satellites are those marked AT (astronomical twilight) or NT (nautical twilight) in the diagram. This diagram was prepared twenty years ago by C. T. Elvey, then director of the Geophysical Institute. That was when satellites were first being seen.

Feb 78:206

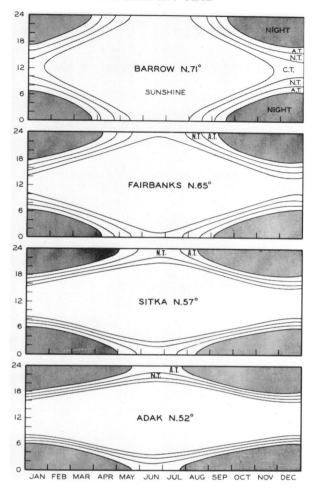

24
18
12
6
0

NIGHT

A.T.
N.T.
C.T.
N.T.
A.T.

BARROW N.71°

SUNSHINE

NIGHT

24
18
12
6
0

N.T. A.T.

FAIRBANKS N.65°

24
18
12
6
0

N.T. A.T.

SITKA N.57°

24
18
12
6
0

A.T.
N.T.

ADAK N.52°

JAN FEB MAR APR MAY JUN JUL AUG SEP OCT NOV DEC

Seeing Satellites: *Sunset, twilight and sunrise hours. A.T. indicates astronomical twilight, N.T. indicates nautical twilight, and C.T. indicates civil twilight.*

The Truth About Sputnik

For twenty years it has been said that the first persons in the Western Hemisphere to see a satellite, Sputnik I, were scientists of the Geophysical Institute at Fairbanks. All these years I have remained silent, but now I reveal the truth — they were not the first.

Early on the morning of October 6, 1957, the Geophysical Institute's scientists picked up the radio signal from Sputnik. One of them stepped outside to view the sky and immediately saw, high overhead, the Sputnik. This was the first reported sighting on this continent.

Several days later I was discussing the sighting of the Sputnik with my neighbor, Dexter Stegemeyer, and he casually said, "Oh yes, I saw it, too." At first he was reluctant to give details but finally came out with the full story.

That morning, well before dawn, he was sitting in his outhouse. The door of the outhouse was open and faced to the west. Mr. Stegemeyer said he was just sitting there enjoying the beauty of the stars twinkling in the sky when he saw a strange moving

star come up out of the west. Though not a scientist by training, Stege, as we called him, was a good observer and a thinker. He said that he did not know that the Russian satellite had been launched some hours before. Yet he reasoned that the object he saw was a strange new thing. From its speed and uniform passage across the sky, he knew it could not be an airplane, a meteor or any other familiar phenomenon.

Stege and his family left Alaska some years after the launch of Sputnik, but the outhouse from whence he made the sighting still stands. His was the first sighting since he did see Sputnik lower in the western sky than did those at the Geophysical Institute.

Sometimes it takes a long time for the truth to come out. Even our artist was reluctant to illustrate the full truth in his rendition of Stege making that first sighting. Instead he only shows Stege walking to the outhouse on a brisk winter morn, typically Alaskan in his parka and with warm toilet seat in hand.

Oct 77:186

The Truth About Sputnik. *(Drawing by Charles Deehr.)*

Skylab Predictions

A striking, and somewhat confusing, aspect of Skylab's fall onto the Indian Ocean and Australia on July 11, 1979 was the multiplicity of reentry predictions we heard. Differences in the predictions eminating from different organizations gave one cause to wonder which, if any, of the predictions to believe and why different predictions should exist at all.

The reason for differences in the predictions being given out by NASA and NORAD (North American Air Defense Command) was that calculations of reentry times being performed by the two organizations were based upon different assumptions about the atmospheric drag on Skylab. One organization's calculations were made by assuming that the drag during future orbits would be the same as the drag experienced by Skylab during the past 24 hours. The other organization's calculation apparently was identical in every respect except for incorporating the assumption that the drag would increase with time in a particular fashion.

The atmosphere at lower altitudes is denser and gives greater resistance to an object moving through it. So in principle, the latter time-dependent calculation should give the most accurate prediction — at least it should if one could know exactly how the drag would increase as Skylab slipped lower into the atmosphere.

Regardless of which type of calculation one preferred, it was expected that the two would give results more exactly alike as the time of reentry was neared. Further, it was hoped that the conver-gence of the two predictions would occur early enough to permit with confidence a decision on whether or not to tumble the Skylab in order to adjust the reentry time.

In retrospect, it all worked out reasonably well. About six hours before reentry, the convergence in the predictions was sufficient to allow NASA to tumble Skylab somewhat earlier than first planned. The result was reentry on about the safest of Skylab's orbital tracks and in a portion of the orbit having minimal population, although NASA preferred to have Skylab fall just a little earlier than it did, so as to avoid Australia altogether.

Jul 79:332

Alaskan Eclipses

Within a few weeks during late 1977 both solar and lunar eclipses will be visible from Alaska. The lunar eclipse on Monday, September 26, will be followed by a solar eclipse on October 12.

During the lunar eclipse, the moon will be full and therefore directly opposite the sun from the earth. Note that lunar eclipses can only occur when the moon is full. The moon will enter the earth's lightest shadow region (the penumbra) at 9:30 p.m. Alaskan Daylight Saving Time on September 26, 1977. The

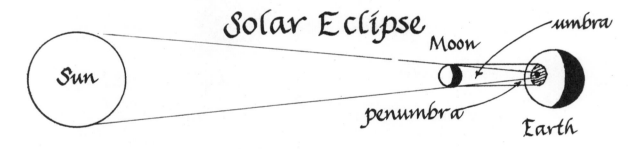

Alaskan Eclipses: *The relative geometry of the sun, moon and Earth during an eclipse. (Drawing by Charles Deehr.)*

moon will pass nearest the earth's dark shadow (the umbra) at mid-eclipse near 11:30 p.m. The eclipse will be over by 1:40 a.m. Tuesday.

Photographers will find the penumbral eclipse a good subject, using the same methods one applies to photographing the midnight sun except for allowing about ten times the exposure. The lunar eclipse can be viewed with the naked eye or through binoculars or telescopes.

The solar eclipse of October 12, 1977, will start about 9:50 a.m. At mid-eclipse, near 10:30 a.m., the moon will cover approximately 16% of the sun visible from Alaska. Total eclipse will occur in the eastern Pacific; Alaskans will see only a bite out of the edge of the sun. Note that a solar eclipse can only occur during the dark of the moon.

Never look directly at the sun during a solar eclipse, even through photographic negatives. The eye can be damaged from a very short exposure, so be extra careful. An image of the sun can be projected onto a surface using a telescope or binoculars. Also one can use a "pinhole camera" made by punching a small hole through one side of a cardboard box. Let the sun shine through the hole so that the image appears on the interior of the opposite side of the box.   — *Charles Deehr*
                                                       Sep 77:185

February 1979 Eclipse

Each year the earth experiences at least two eclipses of the sun. At most, there can be seven eclipses, five solar and two lunar, or alternately, four solar and three lunar eclipses.

Despite the high frequency of solar eclipses, the last total solar eclipse visible in the United States this century will occur on the morning of February 26, 1979. The next such eclipse will occur in the year 2017.

The path of totality of the eclipse will begin about 1000 km (600 miles) west of Seattle at about 8:10 a.m. Pacific Standard Time. It races eastward to pass over Portland at 8:13 a.m. and arcs gently over Helena, Montana, northward into Canada to pass over Hudson Bay to its termination two hours later in central Greenland.

Although a partial or total eclipse will be visible everywhere in Canada and in the lesser forty-eight, Alaskans will be mostly left out in the sunshine. No eclipse effects will be seen west of a line running from Prudhoe, through Bettles, Tanana, Farewell and Kodiak. On this line, the eclipse ends just at sunrise.

To the east, at locations such as Anchorage and Fairbanks, minor eclipsing may be visible. Residents of the Whitehorse area and of southeastern Alaska will see a larger portion of the sun occluded by the moon.

In the Anchorage area, whatever effects to be seen will occur at and just after sunrise, about 7:15 a.m. Alaska Standard Time. The same is true of the Fairbanks area, where sunrise will be about 7:28 a.m. Residents of British Columbia and southeastern Alaska should begin observing at sunrise. At Ketchikan the maximum coverage of the sun will be at 6:30 a.m. Pacific Standard Time, and about ten minutes later at Whitehorse.

                                                       Jan 79:277

Streakers in the Night

Social streakers come and go, but Hecate, the dreaded green Goddess of Night, has been at it for a long time, and she is more predictable. Her meteors can be seen on any dark, clear night and are most numerous during meteor showers. These showers occur when clouds of debris in orbit around the sun intersect the earth's atmosphere. Among the predictable showers are Lyrids, occurring April 20-22; Aquarids, May 4-6; and Perseids, August 10-13. For serious sky watchers, the radiant points (points from which the meteors appear to radiate) of the three showers are most easily specified relative to the constellations. Lyrids appear between Vega and Hercules, Aquarids southwest of the square of Pegasus and Perseids in Perseus.

Most meteors are tiny bits of dust that burn up high in the atmosphere. Not infrequently, very bright meteors flash across the sky creating daylight brilliance. Only rarely does a meteoric particle survive the fiery passage through the air long enough to strike the ground and become known as a meteorite. Such an incident is reported to have occurred in China on March 8. A large meteor broke up and many tiny meteorites were found. Among them was one fragment weighing over 3400 pounds. This is the largest meteorite ever found.   — *Judy Holland*
                                                       May 76:59

Alaskan Meteorites

The number of meteorite finds and observed falls in any region seems to depend mainly upon how many people live there and whether the ground is such that old meteorites or meteorite craters are easily found. With its low population and its tree and moss cover, Alaska loses on both counts, so it is no surprise that few meteorite finds have been made.

In fact, Alaska can boast only one confirmed meteorite. A nickel-iron meteorite, it was raised by a gold dredge at Aggie Creek near Council on the Seward Peninsula. Found in 1942, the main part of the meteorite now resides at the University of Alaska Museum in Fairbanks.

A meteorite shower may have been observed many years ago by an Eskimo of Kwigillingok. He said that one day while out hunting on the sea he heard stones rattle down on the ice nearby. The man picked one up and later gave it to his son, telling him that the stone would someday be worth a great deal of money. The son did bring the stone to a geologist at the University of Alaska who said the stone appeared to be a small chronditic meteorite. Though the geologist offered the man several times the going rate for meteoritic material, the amount was far less than the Eskimo expected. He refused to give the stone up for analysis, so confirmation of its being a meteorite was not possible.

With the recent discovery that Sithylemenkat Lake near Bettles sits in a depression perhaps caused by a giant meteorite perhaps 100,000 years ago, there are now three suspected impact craters in Alaska. The other two are the Savonoski Crater, roughly 500 meters across, in Katmai, and a small one only 63 meters across on Amak Island north of the Alaska Peninsula. Dr. Juergen Kienle of the Geophysical Institute notes that the Amak crater might be a maar rather than a meteorite crater.

Nov 77:191

The Aggie Creek Meteorite

About the size and shape of a small ham, Alaska's Aggie Creek meteorite weighs a hefty 58 pounds. Its metallic nature is obvious from the appearance of the two faces from which samples have been cut away, otherwise it looks like a rusty orange rock.

The Aggie Creek meteorite was lifted by a gold dredge in 1942. From its original location, 15 miles east of Council on the Seward Peninsula, it was taken to Nome by Eskil Anderson and sent on to the University of Alaska Museum. The listed donor is F. K. Dent.

The meteorite is about 90% iron and 8.5% nickel, a composition typical of iron meteorites. Six other meteorites found elsewhere in the world share the exact same composition. That identity has led to the suggestion that the seven objects may be fragments of one original cosmic mass, parts of which have fallen at different places and times.

Proof that the Aggie Creek object truly is a meteorite comes from the pattern exhibited by its cut faces. This is called the Widmanstätten pattern after the man who discovered its existence in iron meteorites. The pattern appears when the polished cut face is treated with acid. The acid etches away most easily one of two minerals the meteorite is composed of (kamacite and taenite) and reveals that the meteorite is a particular laminated structure called an octahedrite.

This octahedral structure is thought to have developed when the meteoritic material first solidified deep within a parent body, now broken up and

scattered through the reaches of the solar system. Within our earthbound laboratories, it has not been possible, so far, to exactly duplicate the Widmanstätten pattern — another among many indicators that there is much we have yet to learn.

Dec 77:200

The Aggie Creek Meteorite: *A cut section shows the tell-tale Widmanstätten pattern.*

The 1929 Kuskokwim Meteor

Sometime near the end of January 1929, Clark M. Garber and a group of Lower Kuskokwim Eskimos were completing a roundup that netted thirty-three thousand reindeer. Mr. Garber, then the Superintendent of Eskimo Education, Medical Relief and Reindeer Herds in the Yukon-Kuskokwim Rivers District, said it was the largest such roundup ever held in the area. The roundup was located three days' travel via reindeer sled from the Bethel-Akiak area — possibly at Kasiglook to the northwest in the Kuskokwim-Yukon delta.

Working inside his tent, Mr. Garber heard a distant high-pitched noise that grew louder as though it were approaching rapidly. At first he thought it was an airplane in trouble; then a herder burst into the tent asking him to quickly come and see the big ball of fire approaching from the southeast. The fiery meteor appeared to be heading directly toward them, but slowly enough that most of the workers were able to hide behind trees before it arrived overhead.

Writing in an unpublished manuscript held in the University of Alaska Archives at Fairbanks, Mr. Garber estimated that the meteor passed over not a thousand feet above them and stated that it had a short incandescent tail. Wind accompanying the meteor blew one man against a stump, knocking him unconscious. It also more or less devastated the camp. Mr. Garber's tent was blown unharmed into a nearby ravine, while others were never found; it took all day to find the cookstove. The wind also blew down much of the nearby reindeer corral which, fortunately for the workers, was empty of animals at the time.

The next day, Eskimos traveling from the northwest reported that the meteor had fallen into a small lake and exploded, blowing a five-foot-thick ice covering away.

Jun 78:231

The Savonoski Problem

So far, Savonoski Crater is one of life's deep dark mysteries.

From the air, Savonoski Crater in Katmai National Monument has every appearance of having been caused by a meteorite impact. It occurs high on a sandstone ridge between two valleys, it is nearly circular and it is deep. Savonoski Crater is about 500 meters (1600 feet) across, the lake inside is 50 meters deep and the rim rises up to 60 meters above the water.

Despite the superficial appearance of being a meteorite crater, extensive investigation by geophysicists failed to find evidence linking Savonoski to a meteoritic origin. Proof, if it could be found, would consist of locating meteoritic material or some evidence in the crater's rock of it having been shocked by a meteoritic impact. Microscopic examination of rock can identify such evidence.

Much of the problem is that Savonoski Crater was formed during or before the last time glaciers covered the area. Any evidence of the crater's origin left above the crater's rim has been swept away by glacial action.

If Savonoski Crater was not formed by a meteorite, the best bet is that it is a volcanic maar. In a sense a maar is a volcano that tried but failed. A maar is formed when a magma pipe reaches to near the earth's surface and strikes the water table. Steam generated by the hot magma explosively blows away the overlying rock to form a circular pit. Smoke, ash and some rocks usually are ejected from the maar for several days. Then, evidently because there is not enough pressure to continue the eruption — the maar becomes inactive. Often water runs in to form a lake just as there is within Savonoski Crater.

Sep 78:250

Cold Meteorites

My mind's eye has always viewed a meteorite impact as involving a fiery object striking the earth, so I was much surprised recently to learn that this view is not necessarily correct.

Meteors enter the atmosphere at such high speed that they create a glow of light in the upper atmosphere. The light is partly from the burning of the meteor and partly emission from the surrounding air, which is heated by the passage of the meteor. Most of the meteors we see are tiny specks which quickly burn up before the meteor reaches to within several tens of miles of the earth's surface. But what about those that do reach the surface and hence become called meteorites?

A meteor weighing from several pounds to several hundred pounds will, indeed, partially burn up before striking the ground. Entry to the atmosphere may be at speeds as great as 90,000 miles per hour (40 km/sec). Roughly half of the meteor will be burned away due to heating as the meteor is slowed down by the air. Depending upon the meteor's initial speed and initial weight, it will reach a terminal speed of about 500 miles per hour. It will reach that low speed roughly ten miles above the ground.

As the meteor falls the last ten or so miles it cools off. Meteorites picked up immediately after they fell were usually no more than lukewarm. Never has a meteorite of intermediate size been known to start a fire, even when landing in a haystack or in other combustible material.

The slow final fall rate explains also why intermediate-size meteorites penetrate so shallowly when

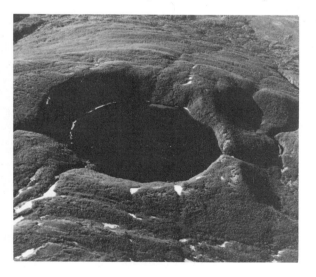

The Savonoski Problem: *Geologists Bevan French of NASA, Ernest Muller of Syracuse University, and Peter Ward of USGS have carefully investigated Savonoski Crater in Katmai National Monument without being able to determine its cause.*

they hit. Most go no deeper than a few feet. A meteorite weighing 2200 pounds (1000 kg) that fell in Norton County, Kansas, in 1930 made a hole only nine feet deep.

Huge meteorites, those weighing thousands of tons, do not reach terminal velocity before striking the earth's surface. Therefore, these can remain fiery until impact.

Oct 77:190

Meteor Sounds

If a person hears sounds while observing a meteor's descent, these can be used to help pinpoint the location of the fall.

Single or multiple loud reports, like cannon fire, are sometimes heard a minute or two after the meteor is seen. Identical to sonic booms, these are caused by shock waves (zones of high air pressure) arriving at the observer's location. They are created high up along the meteor's path while it is still moving faster than the speed of sound in air. Unless the observer is almost exactly at the impact point, the shock wave detonations are the last thing to be heard. At that location, the observer will not see a streak as the meteor approaches, only a light that grows brighter and larger.

If an observer is near the projected impact point — the point where the meteor falls or would fall if it has not entirely burned up or broken up into tiny pieces that might scatter widely — sounds like thunder, a train rumbling over a viaduct or the tearing of cloth may be heard before the shock waves are heard. The tearing sounds arise near the end of the visible path of the meteor, usually only a few miles above the ground. These sounds are thought to be associated with the breaking up of the meteor, perhaps from thermal expansion due to rapid heating as the meteor plows through the dense air of the lower atmosphere.

People sometimes report a slight whistling, crackling or sizzling sound before hearing anything else, and usually while the meteor fireball is in sight. The cause of these noises is not known. Some authorities think the sounds are illusory even though the sensation of hearing them is genuine, the idea being that the sound may be a trick of the brain since human experience suggests that anything bright and fast-moving should whistle or sizzle.

Such sounds, first the sizzling, then the tearing and finally the cannon-like detonations, are heard if the observer is within 50 km (30 miles) or so of the impact point, except that the detonations are heard first if the observer is essentially at the impact point. There is a zone of quiet roughly 50 km to 100 km away; outside that region the shock waves may be heard. The zone of quiet is caused by refraction of sound waves in the lower atmosphere.

Nov 78:273

Halloween Fireball Meteor

The bright fireball meteor that plunged down through the atmosphere over Alaska on Halloween night 1978 appears to be typical of others sighted elsewhere around the world. Trick-or-treaters and other night travelers reported that the event occurred near 6:15 p.m. Alaska Standard Time.

The meteor was probably first seen near altitude 100 miles (150 km). Reports from Black Rapids, Big Delta, Healy, Tok and Fairbanks suggest that the meteor was traveling nearly straight down. If it struck the earth, the point of impact appears to be south of Delta, north of Black Rapids, well west of Tok and well east of the Fairbanks area. Many persons reported that the fireball appeared to land nearby. Such reports occur because the human eyes are unable to distinguish distance to an object seen in the sky, but it seems that the human brain assumes that a moving bright light must be nearby. This is why reports of angle are so valuable, and why estimates of distance to objects in the sky are essentially useless.

As is typical of fireball meteors observed at night, this one was variable in color, mostly white, but blue, green, yellow and orange were reported. The change in color is caused partly by the slowing down of the meteor as it plows through the air and partly by the variable burning of the different elements of which the meteor is composed. By the time the meteor reaches terminal velocity — typically not faster than 300 meters per sec or 1000 feet per sec — the meteor no longer glows. This apparent burnout usually occurs several miles to several tens of miles above the ground. Repeated flaring up and breaking up into fragments are common occurrences. Apparently, only a small fraction of observed fireball meteors yield findable meteorites at the ground.

Booming and hissing noises associated with the Halloween night fireball were heard in the vicinity of Big Delta and Black Rapids. Similar noises are frequently reported within 40 or 50 miles of a fireball meteor's trajectory. The booming noises are analogous to the sonic boom of a high-speed aircraft; the hissing noises are unexplained. The Geophysical Institute's seismograph station at Black Rapids recorded the sonic boom at 6:23 p.m., several minutes after the meteor was seen.

Nov 78:272

The Missing Night

On the evening of June 30, 1908, there was no night at all in central Siberia. Early that morning there had been a huge explosion in the air above the basin of the Stony Tunguska River, about 1000 kilometers north of Lake Baikal. Trees beneath the blast were flattened in an area more than 50 km across, and the heat of the explosion started forest fires that raged for several days.

Even yet it is not certain what happened that morning. Most of the evidence points toward the explosion of a giant meteoritic mass high above the tiaga swamplands. Or it might have been a comet. Two almost science fiction ideas are that Siberia was struck by a "black hole" or a piece of "anti-matter." A recent book suggests the explosion was that of a malfunctioning nuclear-powered spacecraft from another world.

Whatever the cause, the sky was lit up each night for more than a month afterwards. Massive glowing silvery clouds and brilliant, colorful sunsets were seen in Europe and Asia. The "white night" of June 30 was the brightest, but strange twilights were observed until the end of August that year.

Evidently the cause of the bright summer nights of 1908 was extensive dust debris from the explosion circulating in the high atmosphere. During summer nights at the higher latitudes the sun still shines on the upper air, even if there is darkness at the ground.

If this is the correct explanation, the dust should have circulated so as to cover Alaska and perhaps Canada. Yet no reports of strange nights in 1908 came from North America.

There are still people in Alaska who were here in 1908 and might remember seeing strange nights or twilights that year. Entries in diaries also could be a source of information. We would appreciate hearing from anyone with information on Alaskan sightings. Since northern Alaska is light in late June, any early sightings of the phenomenon probably were in southern Alaska. In late July or August strange twilights could have been seen in northern Alaska also.

Dec 77:201

Snowball in Siberia

One of the major mysteries of the century is the violent explosion occurring June 30, 1908 over the Stony Tunguska River, north of Lake Baikal in central Siberia. This explosion was about the same size as the Mt. St. Helens eruption on May 18, 1980; i.e., about the same as a ten-megaton atomic blast.

Much more so than the Mt. St. Helens eruption, the Tunguska blast felled forests in the vicinity. Trees within 30 miles (45 km) were blown down in a radial pattern pointing back to the site of the explosion. The local destruction plus the seismic and sound waves that spread around the world from the

Tunguska explosion pointed to the impact of a giant meteorite.

However, extensive searches made over a period of many years failed to reveal an impact crater or any significant lasting evidence much other than the felled and burned trees. Russian investigators concluded that no object had actually struck the earth but that something had exploded a mile or two above the earth.

Whereas certain characteristics of the Tunguska explosion fit with the idea of a meteorite or comet exploding upon impact with the earth's dense lower atmosphere, more than a few investigators have thought there has to be another explanation. The result has been a collection of exotic suggestions involving earthly impacts with such heavenly bodies as antimatter, black holes and damaged spaceships from another world.

The latest suggestion comes from scientists Thomas Ahrens and John O'Keefe whose work at Caltech gives added credence to a cometary explanation. They suggest that an ice-rich comet — in essence, a giant snowball — impacting at Tunguska would cause a giant explosive flash of steam. The explosion would create the requisite combination of immediate and lasting effects, according to Ahrens and O'Keefe. Of course, the cometary snowball itself would not be found since it would last no longer than its proverbial brother placed elsewhere.

Jul 80:400

Shortest Day — Shortest Night

Why, asks Mr. Jim Schneider of KUAC, is the shortest day longer than the shortest night? Looking over sunrise-sunset times, he noticed that the shortest night (June 21) at Fairbanks is only 2 hours, 11 minutes long, but the shortest day (December 21) is 3 hours, 42 minutes. Were it not for refraction of the sun's rays in the atmosphere, the shortest day would equal the shortest night at a particular latitude. Atmospheric refraction bends the rays so that they can pass over the horizon. Hence the sun appears to rise before it actually reaches the horizon and it is still visible at night after it is below the horizon. Consequently every day is longer than it should be if there were no refraction.

Jun 76:66

Twilight Zone

Partly compensating for the miseries of winter in interior Alaska are the long twilights year-round. Soft light casting long patterns through the trees and beautiful sunrises and sunsets are the result of the low sun in its slanting path across the horizon.

Near the equator, the sun rises and sets rapidly because its path is near perpendicular to the horizon.

There, the setting sun moves from the horizon, at equinox, to 6° below the horizon in only 24 minutes. By definition, civil twilight ends when the sun is 6° below the horizon, though the sky is still light for some minutes afterward.

But at Fairbanks, the end of civil twilight is nearly an hour after sunset on equinoctial dates. From May 15 until July 23, civil twilight never ends because the sun never falls as low as 6° below the horizon. Even in December civil twilight lasts about an hour. The reason for the long twilights at high latitude is the slanting path taken there by the sun as it passes the horizon. A greater rotation of the earth on its axis is required to bring the sun 6° below the horizon at the higher latitudes.

Jun 76:61

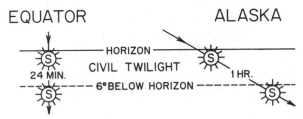

Twilight Zone: *Why twilights at high latitude last a long time.*

Photograph the Midnight Sun

Contrary to your first impression of June nights in Fairbanks, the sun actually sets every evening for at least two hours. The "midnight sun" can be seen from Eagle Summit which is about 100 miles north on the Steese Highway. Eagle Summit is not north of the Arctic Circle but the midnight sun can be seen from there between June 17 and 24. Two effects combine to make this possible. First, the altitude at the summit is roughly 3600 feet above sea level. This gives enough height so that an observer can see over the sea-level horizon. Another effect is atmospheric refraction. This is the bending of light rays by the atmosphere in such a way that the sun can be as much as three degrees below the horizon of an observer and still be seen.

The orientation of the earth's axis with respect to the sun at midnight during the winter and summer is shown in the accompanying figure. You can see that twilight (shaded area) occurs at noon in the winter and midnight in the summer. We offer the following tips to those who would photograph the midnight sun from Eagle Summit.

If you want to take photographs you will need to do some planning. First, make sure you have the necessary equipment. The most critical item is mosquito repellent — several gallons. You also will need a camera that takes multiple exposures and a steady tripod.

At Eagle Summit, the sun is at its lowest point at 12:48 a.m. Put the camera on the steady tripod, and place the sun in the left side of the viewfinder, then take the first photo at 11:48. Taking care not to move the camera, take photographs every ten minutes over a period of two hours. That's 13 clicks of the shutter. The last photo will be at 1:48: at this time the sun should be near the right edge of the viewfinder. The photo will show 13 images of the sun arranged in an arc with the lowest point in the center.

A light reading into the sun taken at the beginning of the sequence will provide an estimate of the exposure to use. Close the camera aperture down

MIDNIGHT at EAGLE SUMMIT

Summer

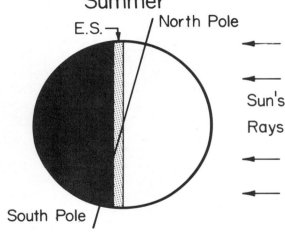

Winter

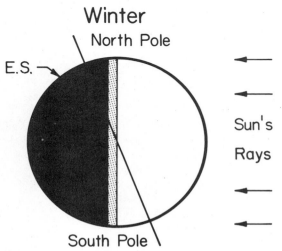

Photograph the Midnight Sun: *Even though it is south of the Arctic Circle, Eagle Summit (E.S.) is high enough to be in sunlight at midnight in summer.*

two steps from the indicated reading. Do not vary the exposure in subsequent shots.

Be careful the mosquitoes don't fly away with your camera.

The Bureau of Land Management (BLM) has built and maintained parking areas and hiking trails in the Eagle Summit area. They have a brochure describing the area and in particular the 23 mile Pinnell Mountain Trail going from Eagle Summit to 12 Mile Summit along the mountain ridges. A new brochure is being prepared by BLM for release later this year which describes the phenomena of the midnight sun from Eagle Summit.

— Glenn Shaw and Charles Deehr
Jun 77:171

Moon and Sun Chart for Fairbanks

Diagrams and charts are often used to display a great deal of information in a small space. Consequently, they sometimes are hard to understand without study. This complex diagram has been compiled in response to a question from Mrs. Louise Hollister of Fairbanks; it goes far beyond her question about whether or not the moon rises every month. With the diagram one can pick any local time (left margin) on any date (bottom margin) in 1977 and determine for that time whether the sun is up or down and whether the moon is up or down. Diagrams such as this are rare because they require so much work to prepare. Since the calendar year is not composed of an integral number of lunar months, a new diagram must be made each year. Furthermore, a different diagram is required for each location on the earth's surface.

The curved lines running across the pages, approximately horizontally, show the times of sunrise and sunset and the times each day when civil, nautical and astronomical twilights end. These twilight times correspond to the times when the sun is 6°, 12° and 18° below the Fairbanks horizon, respectively. This part of the diagram is unchanged year after year. It tells us that we have only sunlight or civil twilight between May 15 and July 25 each year. The overhead sky is only fully dark after the end of astronomical twilight. Thus we have no truly dark sky between April 7 and September 4.

The curved lines running nearly vertically on the diagram show the periods of moon up and moon down at Fairbanks. Follow a date line up the chart to find the moonrise and moonset times. Doing so, one finds that the moon rises and sets every day at Fairbanks. But, each lunar month, the moon goes through its phases from new (dark) moon to full moon, as shown by the circles at the bottom of the chart. On dates of new moon, the moon is not visible in the sky, either in daylight or at night. If it rises once every day of the year, why do we not see the moon block out the stars behind it? The chart shows the answer to be that the new moon is never up during the night hours.

Since the times shown at left on this diagram are standard Alaska time, remember, in summer, to

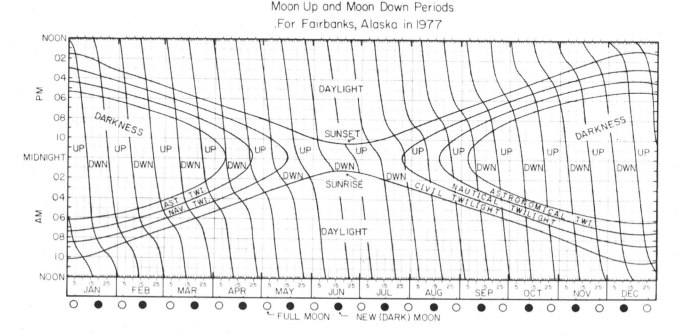

Moon and Sun Chart for Fairbanks: *The near-vertical lines indicating moon-up and moon-down times are good only for the year 1977.*

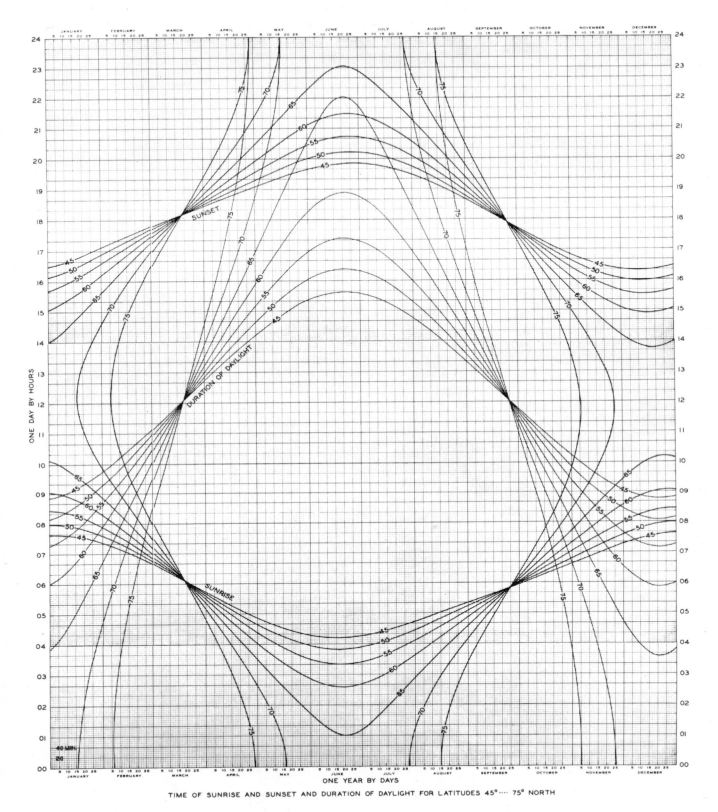

TIME OF SUNRISE AND SUNSET AND DURATION OF DAYLIGHT FOR LATITUDES 45°····75° NORTH

Sunrise and Sunset Times: *This chart is independent of the year; it is useful for all time.*

convert from Daylight Saving Time by subtracting one hour from the time shown on the clock.

Jan 77:198

Sunrise and Sunset Times

Exactly at the North Pole, the day is six months long and so is the night. The equator, too, receives exactly one-half year of daylight, as does every other place on earth. (We ignore topographic effects and atmospheric refraction.)

But as Alaskans are well aware, equality of daylight pertains not on a daily basis. In winter, northern Alaska ends up on the short end of the proverbial day. To see just how much variation there is across the span of Alaska, one can examine the accompanying diagram.

Both the duration of daylight and the sunrise-sunset times (in standard local time) are given at latitudes 45° to 75° in 5-degree increments. The hour of the day and total hours of daylight appear at left and right; the day in the year is shown at top and bottom.

This rather pretty diagram with its attractive symmetry was designed and drawn by Dan Wilder, longtime draftsman at the Geophysical Institute until his death in 1967. While the supply lasts, we will send copies to readers upon request.

Dec 77:198

Changing Time

Fiddling around with time has been a pastime of governments for thousands of years. Today's often hotly debated decisions on shifting a time zone by an hour or so seem penny ante compared to some past machinations.

Roman politicians were known to shift days around to reduce or extend the terms of office of certain officials. Fed up with this, Julius Caesar, in 45 B.C., established a new calendar, the Julian, named for himself. He gave the year 365¼ days; made the year start in January instead of March; stole one day from February to add to the month of July, also named for himself; and he invented the leap year. Open complaints likely were few.

The Julian calendar created much-needed order for the conduct of civil and astronomical affairs, but it fouled up the reckoning of church festival dates. Previously these had been dated by means of the Jewish lunar calendar which used years ranging from 352 to 386 days long. Between various segments of the Christian church, battles raged for the next thousand years in attempts to reconcile the religious and civil calendars.

Most of the Western world shifted over to the Gregorian calendar during the two hundred years starting in 1582. This calendar is similar to the Julian but, unlike it, the Gregorian has provision for fine-tuning to keep the months from slowly shifting through the seasons as the centuries go by.

When Great Britain finally shifted in 1752, the changeover to the Gregorian calendar required advancing the date by eleven days. This caused great opposition, and a few people were killed as opponents rioted in the streets shouting, "Give us back our fortnight."

Russia was among the last to change to the Gregorian calendar. Hence, when Alaska was purchased, the United States and Russia were eleven days out of whack. But since the annexation shifted Alaska across the International Date Line, the date in Alaska only had to be changed by ten days.

Jul 80:409

Solstices, Equinoxes and Leap Years

Ready or not, summer solstice comes early this year — eighteen hours ahead of last year. In 1980 it occurs at Universal (Greenwich meridian) Time 5:47 a.m. on June 21. Since it takes almost half a day for the sun to get from the Greenwich meridian around to our sky, solstice comes at 8:47 p.m. on June 20, Alaska Daylight Saving Time (10:47 p.m. Yukon Time).

Summer solstice occurs at that instant when the sun attains its maximum excursion above the earth's equator. Winter solstice is when the sun is farthest south on or about December 21. The instant when the sun moves back north across the equator, on or about March 21, is the vernal (spring) equinox. On this day the shadow of the top of a pole or other object will march eastward in a straight line across the ground, just as it will on the autumnal equinox, about September 22.

Each year the time of a solstice or an equinox comes about five hours and forty-nine minutes later than the one the year before, except on leap years when it comes about eighteen hours and twelve minutes earlier. The main reason for the jerky annual pattern is the use of the leap year to partially correct for the year being about 365¼ instead of a whole number of days long.

Since the year is not exactly 365¼ days long, yet another adjustment is required once in a while. The method adopted in the Gregorian calendar, which we use today, is to not always have leap years every four years. Years divisible by 100 are not leap years unless they are also divisible by 400. Hence the years 1800, 1900 and 2100 have no February 29, but the years 2000 and 2400 do. (Thanks to Edee Rohde of Fairbanks for suggesting this article.)

Jun 80:406

(See drawing next page.)

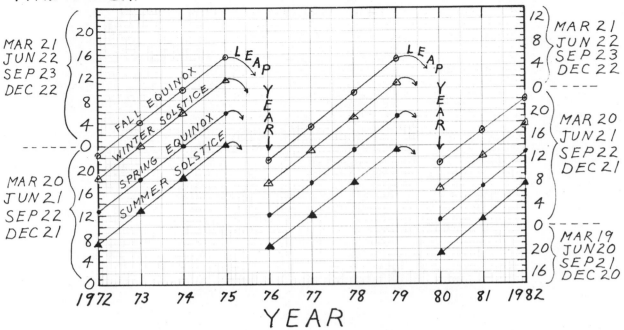

UNIVERSAL TIME AND DATE

ALASKA STANDARD TIME AND DATE

YEAR

Solstices, Equinoxes and Leap Years: *To use this diagram remember that summer solstice is in June, winter solstice in December, and that the equinoxes are in March and September. Pick a year and then read from the equinox or solstice point to the left to find the Universal (Greenwich) hour and date. Read to the right-hand scale to get the hour and date in Alaska Standard Time.*

Tanana Moon Calendar

Unable to see stars in summer, the Indians of the Upper Tanana Valley, in olden times, utilized a self-adjusting calendar based on the moon. The year began in October and involved 13 months, each equal to the period of the revolution of the moon about the earth — 29 days, 12 hours, 44 minutes. As the lunar months were described in terms of familiar natural phenomena, the discrepancy between 13 lunar months (384 days) and one solar year (365 days) was of little consequence, nor was the exact day of the month. The calendar was as follows:

October — Moon when the bull moose ruts

November — Moon when the sheep ruts

December — Hook-game moon (month of social activities and game playing)

January — Moon when the sun appears again after long sleep

February — Moon when days grow longer

March — Moon of the cold winds, or the Eagle Moon

April — Hawk Moon

May — Moon when the snow is soft in day and freezes at night

June — Moon when young animals are born

July — Moon when new hair appears on animals, or moon when the moose comes down off the hill

August — Moon when the moose fat is ready

September — Moon when the animals take on winter coats

13th Month — Moon when the leaves turn red

(Reference: R.A. McKennan, The Upper Tanana Indians, Yale University, 1969.)

Aug 76:110

A Sundial for Fairbanks

Sundials were on their way out a thousand years ago when fledgling inventions led to the development of modern clocks. In those early times the hour had no fixed length; it depended upon season and latitude.

Simplest of all sundials is one with a vertical pointer (a gnomon) which casts its shadow on a flat surface marked to show the passage of the hours. We show here such a sundial designed specifically for Fairbanks. In one sense it is a rather fancy sundial because it tells both the hour of the day and the day of the year. This ability comes from the use of the University's high-speed computer, which gives us a leg up on the old-time sundial designers. The design is based upon calculations by Professor Hans Nielsen showing the length of a vertical stick's shadow each hour of the day and the direction to the shadow tip.

Dashed lines show the paths of the end of the pointer's shadow across the sundial on the days indicated. We drew in only the twenty-first day of each month to illustrate the extreme positions occurring on the solstices (June 21 and December 21) and at equinox (March 21 and September 21).

Moving along the line marked June 21, one sees that the Fairbanks sundial works from before 3 a.m. until after 9 p.m. But on the shortest day of the year, December 21, it only works from about 11 a.m. until 1 p.m., the time when the sun is above the horizon.

Notice that the sundial is 25 pointer lengths in radius. On December 21 the shadow doesn't even fall on the sundial; we indicate that by using a dotted line and the special distance scale marked by asterisks.

The radial hour lines of the sundial are curved to account for the changes in the sun's apparent motion across the sky with season. If the lines were not curved, the sundial "clock" would run faster than a normal clock at some times of the year and at other times, slower.

This sundial illustrates that Alaska truly is the land of long shadows, with remarkable variations through the course of the year. One curiosity — notice that the shadow of the tip of an object marches across the ground in a perfectly straight line on two days of the year, the equinox days.

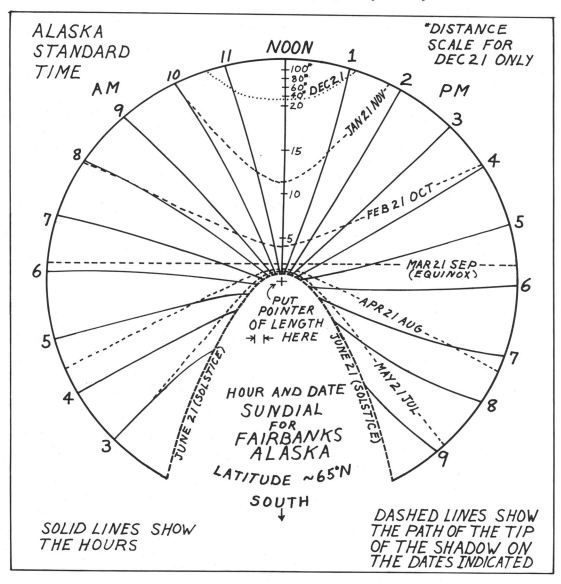

A Sundial for Fairbanks: *This sundial will work at any location with the same latitude as Fairbanks (64½°N).*

Though called a sundial for Fairbanks, this one will work reasonably well at any location of similar latitude, locations such as Dawson, Eagle, Tanana, Nulato and Nome.

Nov 77:196

Compass Accuracy

Why are magnetic compasses so notoriously inaccurate at high latitude? The reason is not the weakness of the magnetic field near the pole. In fact, the earth's magnetic field near the north or south pole is about twice as strong as near the equator. The trouble is that, near the poles, the magnetic field points the wrong direction — it is nearly vertical. At the equator the magnetic field is horizontal, and there it points roughly north-south.

In navigation one wants to know the direction in the horizontal plane, that is, the direction of north, south, east and west. But in the polar regions, a compass needle suspended from its center will align itself almost vertically — not too useful when one is seeking the direction of north.

At Ketchikan the free compass needle points 17 degrees from the vertical: in the Nome and Anchorage areas, about 15 degrees; at Whitehorse, 14 degrees; at Fairbanks, 13 degrees; and at Barrow, only 11 degrees from vertical. Hence in Alaska and northern Canada, the magnetic field exerts little horizontal force on a compass needle. The force that is exerted causes the compass to point horizontally well east of north, by amounts ranging from less than ten degrees in the Aleutians to as much as 40 degrees near Barter Island.

Jun 78:230

CHAPTER THREE
NORTHERN SKY AND WEATHER

Sun and Weather

The ultimate source of energy on earth is the sun. Life itself would not exist without its steady radiation, nor coal, nor oil, nor plants, nor wind and rain. Whether the air is hot or cold, windy or calm, wet or dry, clear or cloudy is directly dependent on the sun. Any changes in weather patterns, then, should be due to changes in the sun and its relationship to earth. Thus, the constancy of the weather with the days and seasons is a result of the sun's unchanging brightness and its steady trek across the sky.

As weather records improve, however, it is tempting to compare them with the small changes in solar output connected with sunspots or disturbances on the sun which were first recorded by Chinese astrologers a thousand years ago. The yearly growth rings of our oldest trees like ancient, wizard chieftains tell of droughts that seem to vary with the numbers of these sunspots. In recent times the spots have appeared and disappeared in an eleven-year cycle. Associated with these cycles are disturbances in the high atmosphere of the earth such as aurora and radio blackouts.

The direct effect of these small variations of solar radiation on the earth's *lower* atmosphere must be small. If the weather system were a ten-ton truck, then the effect of changes due to sunspots would be the same as hooking it up to a little red wagon. The truck would not notice the wagon until perhaps the wagon bounced high enough due to road corrugations to cut an electric wire or brake line and trigger a change in the action of the truck. Thus, if the aurora changes the amount of heat or light reaching the earth in a critical place like the Gulf of Alaska, the storms forming there could, on the average, be more severe or move more northward, producing noticeable effects which could vary roughly with the eleven-year cycle.

Historic records indicate that the eleven-year sunspot cycle disappeared for as long as one hundred years at least twice. Historical references to the aurora, weather and sunspots are now being studied to determine if these longer absences of sunspots will emphasize effects on earth which are not evident in the eleven-year cycle. Thus, the "Little Ice Age", an extended cold period which occurred in Europe during one of the extended absences of sunspots, may provide a model to allow prediction of future changes in solar activity and its effects on earth.

— Chuck Deehr and Henry Cole
Sep 78:260

The Moon and Weather

Every weather forecaster wishes he could do as well as did Lieutenant S. M. Saxby of the British Navy one day in November 1868. He predicted, nearly a year in advance, that on October 5, 1869, the northeastern United States would experience an exceptionally violent hurricane with abnormal tides. A friend predicted the landfall of this storm to be Halifax, Nova Scotia. Sure enough, within 12 hours of the designated time a hurricane of great violence did strike, and it landed within 100 miles of Halifax.

Lt. Saxby stated that his prediction was based upon the moon's position. He knew that on October 5, 1869, the moon would be at its closest approach to earth, and it also would be very nearly on the line joining the center of the earth to the sun — conditions that cause the moon and the sun to pull best in unison to create the highest tides. Thus, Saxby's prediction of abnormal tides on October 5 was firmly based on known facts.

About the basis for his prediction of a hurricane on that date, one cannot be so sure. But certainly if a strong hurricane did occur on that date of abnormal tide, it was bound to create unusual flooding damage.

Though scientists have generally been unable to find physical reasons to explain a lunar influence, weather prophets, down through the years, have relied heavily on the moon. In New England it was said that "the number of days old the moon is at the first snow tells how many snows there will be that winter." Ben Franklin in *Poor Richard's Almanac* based his weather predictions upon the lunar phase. He hedged his bets slightly by stating: "I should ask the indulgence of the reader for a day of grace on either side of the date for a specific weather prediction."

The ability to predict the weather is a definite asset for many reasons, social, scientific and economic. Consequently, searches are underway to detect relationships between weather and other phenomena, and eventually to learn the mechanisms that create such relationships.

One recent study by the National Weather Service indicates that, in the country as a whole, about 10% more rain and occasions of heaviest rain occur in the days following new or full moon — that is, in the days following the greatest tidal variation each lunar month. Another study indicates the greater tendency for tropical storms to attain hurricane status at these same times.

Why these tendencies should exist is not known. The nature of the reported tendencies suggests the influence of tidal forces, but no one seems to know how they might act to affect the development of storms. If Lieutenant Saxby knew, the secret seems to have died with him.

— *Henry Cole*
Oct 78:259

High-Altitude Winds

Although noted for its harsh winters, Interior Alaska enjoys a climate notably free of severe wind. However gale-force winds are present on most evenings high overhead, at altitudes above 100 miles. Winds exceeding 100 mph occur sometime during nearly every day; sometimes they are in excess of 200 mph. The high-altitude wind is usually westward in late afternoon and eastward in early morning.

While not entirely understood, these winds near the fringe of space are known to be caused by the interaction between the earth's magnetic field and the solar wind, a never-ending stream of matter flowing out from the sun. The interaction causes charged particles in the atmosphere to move rapidly. These collide with the air and cause it to move as well. Even though of very high speed, these winds have little effect because the air at this high altitude is only about one billionth as dense as that at the surface.

— *Howard Bates*
Apr 77:156

Noctilucent Clouds

Like blue-white spiderwebs laced across the twilight sky, noctilucent clouds form a wispy filigree in the heavens. Truly a polar phenomenon, noctilucent clouds are never seen at latitudes below 45°. Thus, in North America, noctilucent clouds are pretty much the property of Alaska and Canada.

Nor are noctilucent clouds an everyday occurrence. In 1885, they were first recognized as something strange in the sky. Since then more than a thousand sightings have been recorded in the world. Several displays occurred over central Alaska in the summer of 1979.

The characteristic that distinguishes noctilucent clouds from all others is their remarkably high altitude, 82 (plus or minus a few) kilometers (about 50 miles). Rarely do normal clouds extend as high as 15 kilometers. Noctilucent clouds are seen only in deep twilight, when the sun is 6° to 16° below the horizon. Then the sky is dark enough for the thin noctilucent clouds to be seen and yet the sun is still in position to reflect enough light from the clouds to make them visible to an observer.

In the Northern Hemisphere, noctilucent clouds are seen from early March to late October and are most frequently observed in mid-summer. Similarly, austral summer is the time the clouds are seen in the Southern Hemisphere.

Though noctilucent clouds have been recognized for nearly a century, no one quite knows why they occur. Almost certainly, the clouds consist of ice-coated dust particles, the dust presumably coming from meteors striking the atmosphere. Beyond that, not much is known.

Oct 79:346

On Climatic Cycles

Weather and climate link closely together since climate is nothing more than the long-time average of the weather. By weather, we mean the air temperature, air humidity, wind, cloudiness, storminess and any other condition of the atmosphere.

If the weather is unusual a few years in a row, one wonders if a long-term climatic change is being signaled. Usually that seems not to be the case because there are cyclic or quasi-cyclic variations of atmospheric conditions. Short cycles — measured in tens or hundreds of days — might be thought of as weather cycles. Cycles lasting years obviously can be thought of as climatic.

Searches through old ships' logs and other historical documents dating back to 1700 have allowed identification of a climatic cycle near 30 to 40 years long. Changes of patterns of wind strength over the Pacific Ocean and ocean temperature show this cycle, according to Dr. Joseph Fletcher, discoverer of Fletcher's Ice Island (Ice Island T-3). He received an honorary doctoral degree from the University of Alaska in 1979 in recognition of his contributions to arctic science.

The 30- to 40-year cycle also shows up in the amount of water discharged from the Nile River over the years and perhaps in the extent of the arctic ice pack. It may be the chief cause of the 1930s dust bowl in the United States. Perhaps it is the reason why northern lakes, such as Harding Lake near Fairbanks, show changing levels.

Dr. Fletcher suggests that the 30- to 40-year climatic cycle is created by interaction between the atmosphere and the ocean. The coupled ocean-atmosphere system transports energy from the hot equatorial regions towards the poles in a not-quite steady fashion. The ability of the ocean water to store heat for a long time may be the chief cause of the 30- to 40-year cycle.

May 79:314

1816, Year Without Summer

Famous in the annals of weather is the year 1816, during which the temperature dipped to freezing every month in Madison County, New York. It was a bitter year for farmers in both America and Europe as their crops froze, were replanted and froze again. On the Fourth of July, men of Plymouth, Connecticut wore heavy overcoats as they played quoits in the bright sunshine. Snow fell in Montreal on June 6 and 8 and Quebec City had a 12-inch accumulation on June 10.

In fact, 1816 was just the worst of a series of cold years from 1812 to 1817, years that were cold worldwide. The accepted explanation is that several major volcanic eruptions in those years loaded the atmosphere with dust which girded the globe. The dust does a better job of keeping the sun's radiation out than keeping the earth's in and so causes the average temperature to lower by a degree or so. Local effects can be much more severe, as unfortunate farmers have found out. Extensive volcanic dust perhaps has played a major role in past climatic changes; it may again have profound effect, even so great as to cause a new ice age. *(Reference: Patrick Hughes writing in the May 1976 issue of EDIS, a publication of the Environmental Data Service of NOAA.)*

Jul 76:98

Predicting Local Weather

A reader, Mrs. L. Hollister, reports that a neighbor lady claims to be fairly successful in predicting local wind conditions by observing the nature of the clouds in certain directions from her house. The question is whether such claims make sense and why is it that one sometimes can do better than the experts in predicting weather.

To some extent everyone learns to be an expert on the weather that affects them directly. A person interested in gardening worries about frost and learns within a few years whether his garden location is likely or not to suffer frost if a frost warning is given. Those who launch rockets from the Poker Flat Research Range have learned to pay attention to weather forecasts, but they have found that nighttime

skies are usually clearer than the Weather Service predicts.

It does seem true that an observant, self-taught weather watcher can do rather well in many instances, especially if he or she remains in one location for a long time. Official weather forecasts are usually for a general area. Since conditions vary even within a few miles, one can use one's own observations to improve the official forecasts for a specific location.

Sep 76:114

Serious Weather Predictions

Weather prediction is probably nearly as old as mankind. Which has advanced farthest over the years is perhaps a matter of conjecture. In *EDIS*, a publication of the National Oceanographic and Atmospheric Administration, Patrick Hughes notes that as early as Babylonian time, circa 2100 B.C., weather phenomena were being associated with the positions of heavenly bodies. At that time, weather prediction was done by priests who developed schemes of astrological-meteorological prediction, and weather prediction was based mostly upon myth. By 750 B.C. the Greeks were beginning to codify sound predictive techniques based upon observational experience. Later, the Romans included weather "signs" in handbooks and almanacs prepared for farmers.

No doubt the most serious weather forecasters were those feudal astrologers who, after the fall of the Roman Empire, were responsible for forecasting weather for military campaigns. If the forecaster made the correct forecast and the campaign was a success, the astrologer was allowed to live to forecast again, but if his forecast was wrong, the penalty was sometimes death. Think how many of those unfortunates wished they had been clever enough to have thought up the modern practice of saying "Tomorrow there will be a fifty percent chance of rain."

Feb 79:290

Climatic Variations

When one lacks knowledge about the climate of the past, the safest guess as to what the climate might have been is to assume it is the same as now. But knowledge is accumulating to suggest that things were not always as they are at present.

Tree ring growth over the past 2000 years indicates several serious droughts between 500 A.D. and 1700 A.D. In North America particularly severe droughts began near the years 510, 610, 830, 860, 1165, 1276, 1390, 1495, 1570 and about 1625 A.D.

During the droughtless eleventh century northern Alaska was several degrees warmer in summer than it is now, but during the more drought-ridden sixteenth century, tree ring growth rates show the Mackenzie

Valley and northern Alaska had colder summers than exist currently.

Evidently, since about 1670, North America has not experienced any truly great droughts such as occurred in the centuries before. Most of those early severe droughts lasted ten to twenty years, so they surely had serious consequences for agriculture and perhaps for other activities of mankind.

Dealing with a somewhat longer time scale, a recent book written in Danish suggests the possibility of radically different climatic conditions in northern Europe prior to about the year 1200. It also is suggested that global wind patterns may have been quite different prior to 1200 and that these patterns may have profoundly affected Viking exploration and settlement.

Instead of bucking westerly winds to cross the Atlantic, the Vikings may have been able to sail comfortably before steady easterlies on the way to Greenland and North America. A pattern of steady easterly rather than westerly winds might also explain why the Vikings settled the nowadays relatively godforsaken western coast of Scotland. Perhaps then the western coast was more like today's eastern Scottish coast.

Evidence for a change in wind pattern also comes from the configuration of the homeland Viking coastline itself. Today's smooth western Danish coastline is created by ocean currents largely driven by the westerly winds. In earlier years the coastline was somewhat inland from its present location and more jagged, affording harbors from which the Vikings could sally forth.

One wonders to what extent the rise and fall of ancient cultures may have been dictated by major climatic changes. Certainly the time around 1200 A.D. was one of profound change in Europe. Could a change in weather patterns have been at least a partial cause? Even the lesser fluctuations that caused droughts for a few years or a few tens of years might have toppled dukes and an occasional king or queen.

— *Hans Stenbaek-Nielsen*
Nov 79:353

Fairbanks' Changing Climate

In March of 1973, *Nature* published a short report of research on global climate changes during the past 20 years or so stating that climatologists generally accept the fact that the earth's climate is tending toward an ice age of some sort, and that a new North American ice sheet may be forming. Since we are talking about the relatively near future, what is the implication for Alaska? Probably not much. Although one tends to think of ice sheets occurring when the weather is very cold everywhere, this is not necessarily true. Even at the maximum of the last ice

age, temperatures around Fairbanks were probably much as they are now. Of course, then as now, one could say that an ice age descends upon Fairbanks every winter.

But a changing climate affects weather patterns also and here Fairbanks shows some effect. Precipitation records for the last 20 years show a steady decrease in rainfall. (1967 was a spectacular exception.) The average annual rainfall in Fairbanks 20 years ago was 11.9 inches; since that time it has dropped to 10.7 inches. Local weather reports now show that the summer of 1976 was the sixth driest on record. Records for Anchorage also show a decrease. It is not as noticeable in that area because the climate tends to be damper to begin with. Other records for the rest of Alaska have not as yet been examined.

— *W. Murcray*
Jan 77:116

Glaciers Advancing or Retreating?

When Vancouver explored the southeastern Alaska coast in 1794 he found Glacier Bay filled with ice. Today it is mostly ice-free, but glaciologist William O. Field predicts that it may fill with ice again over a period of hundreds of years. Though many Alaskan glaciers are retreating, quite a few others are advancing. Dr. Field, still active after fifty years of glacial observation, cites examples of glaciers nearly side by side some of which are retreating and others advancing. He concludes that factors other than climate change must be responsible. Especially when glaciers spill into the sea, it appears that an unstable equilibrium exists. While the glacier ice always flows forward, the glacial snout advances and retreats, its position being determined by a complex interplay of snowfall, temperature through the year, deposition of rock debris and effects of ocean tides on iceberg calving rates. Studies lasting many tens of years are necessary to unravel these effects, effects that can have serious consequences to coastal shipping and land transportation facilities in glaciated areas.

Aug 76:102

Increasing Glaciation

As we all know, things are going to get worse before they get better: The Northern Hemisphere is in for a period of increasing glaciation during the next few thousand years. That is the conclusion of three researchers reporting in the December 10, 1976, issue of *Science* magazine. The three, J. D. Hays, John Imbrie and N. J. Shackleton, have examined the geologic record over the past 450,000 years by analyzing drill cores of sediments on the floor of the South Atlantic Ocean. By measuring the relative abundance and composition of life species in the sediments and being able to date when the sediments were laid down, they were able to obtain an index of the global climate over the 450,000-year period.

The scientists found cyclic variations in the climate that they could relate both to periods of glaciation and to cyclic variations in the earth's orbit. Wobbling of the earth's rotation axis (period 41,000 years), shift of the date of the equinoxes (period 21,000 years) and change in the degree of circularity of the earth's motion about the sun (period 100,000 years) all are found to be important. By extending the past behavior into the near future, Hays, Imbrie and Shackleton predict a long-term trend over the next 20,000 years toward extensive glaciation and cooler climate.

Assuming the correctness of the prediction, the effect on Alaska will be profound. Many mountain valleys will again become ice-filled. Ground transportation corridors through the Alaska Range and the Brooks Range will be closed. As more sea water is tied up in ice, the coastlines will expand outward and the Bering Land Bridge will reappear. Someday it will be possible to drive a car past Nome to Moscow.

Jan 77:141

Carbon Dioxide Increase

The world's air now is increasing its carbon dioxide content by about 1% per year. If the trend continues another decade or so, we may be headed rapidly into climatic change that will increase the world's deserts and reduce the areas suitable for agriculture.

Carbon dioxide, unlike its deadly sound-alike carbon monoxide, is a harmless minor constituent of air (0.03%). Most of the world's carbon is locked up either in carbon dioxide (CO_2) molecules or in rock and mineral compounds.

In sunlight, green plants photosynthesize water and CO_2 from the air into starches and sugars required for plant growth. Sooner or later the CO_2 is returned to the air by the plants themselves or by the bacteria, yeasts and animals that consume the plants as foods. Another way for the so-called biological "carbon cycle" to be completed is through combustion, either slow (rot) or fast (fire).

Just in the last few years, scientists have come to realize that living plants and humus matter are a major reserve of CO_2, in addition to the huge store in fossil fuels. Fear is being expressed that the clearing of forested land, especially in the tropical rain forests, may be releasing huge amounts of carbon dioxide to the air each year. As man both burns fossil fuels and clears the forests, the air receives a double-barreled insult that it may not be able to cast off. Increased CO_2 in air leads to increasing absorption of infrared light to cause a greater greenhouse effect and consequent climatic changes.

Even the ice pack on the polar seas may be a source of carbon dioxide to the atmosphere. New measurements of carbon dioxide at Point Barrow and offshore have been reported by the University of Alaska's Tom Gosink. These results lead him to think that the sea ice helps transfer CO_2 in sea water to the air more rapidly than it would if the ice were absent. Maybe his idea will provide the world with a safety valve. If the world gets too hot because of increasing CO_2 in the air, perhaps the polar ice will melt and reduce the upward flow of CO_2 to the air and thereby allow a return to normal.

Feb 78:223

Warmer Years Ahead?

Predictions of doom are so common that most of us treat them like cries of wolf. Contributing to our disbelief at times is the long-term nature of some predictions, especially those of geophysical nature, such as the warning about the effects of spray cans on the ozone layer. Though scientists consider valid the warning that the world must cut down on its release of fluorocarbons to the atmosphere, it's hard for us to maintain for years a high level of excitement about such issues.

Unfortunately, here is another issue of special concern to northerners. It is the steady rise of carbon dioxide in the atmosphere, a change that is most likely to affect the high latitudes more than other regions of the world. Just prior to the age of industrialization, the earth's atmosphere contained 288 to 295 parts per million (ppm) carbon dioxide. By 1958, the carbon dioxide content had risen to about 314 ppm, and by 1978 it was near 330 ppm.

The increase in atmospheric carbon dioxide is attributed to man's burning of fossil fuels, mainly coal and petroleum, and also to burning associated with deforestation for agricultural or logging purposes. The atmospheric content of carbon dioxide is expected to increase by at least several ppm each year, well into the next century. Sometime in the next hundred years or so the fossil fuels will be fairly well used up and the injection of excessive carbon dioxide into the air will decline.

Still, at the rate we are burning fuel we can expect to create worldwide warming of near-surface air by 1.5° to $3.5^\circ C$ (3° to $6^\circ F$) and even more warming at high latitude. Offhand, this sounds like a good deal for the north country. The winters might get warmer and some of the permafrost should disappear.

That's such a happy note to end on, perhaps its best not to mention possible bad effects of the carbon dioxide increase.

Jun 80:404

Is The World Warming Up?

Some years in the future, Alaska and northwestern Canada may face some interesting policy questions created by what appears to be a warming up of the world's climate. The effects of the predicted change are likely to be greatest in this part of the world, and, being suppliers of fossil energy to the world, we northerners may be contributing to the change.

The overall global temperature is determined by the requirement that, in the long run, the earth must radiate to space as much energy as it receives from the sun. If the amount of energy coming in increases, the global temperature will increase so that the outward radiation increases — the outward radiation is proportional to the earth's temperature. Alternately, changes in the earth's radiation characteristics can create temperature changes without there being any change in the solar energy coming in.

Carbon dioxide in the earth's atmosphere traps outgoing radiation. This is the so-called greenhouse effect which keeps the earth warmer than it would be were there no carbon dioxide in the atmosphere.

Right now, there is certainty about two things. Firstly, the amount of carbon dioxide in the air has increased from about 280 to 300 parts per million in 1880 to 340 parts per million in 1980. Secondly, the global temperature has risen by about $0.4^{\circ}C$ during the same period. The increase in carbon dioxide this past century is caused by the great increase in human use of fossil fuels, a use that puts carbon dioxide into the air. Also, the observed increase in global temperature is consistent with what scientists calculate it should be from the increase in carbon dioxide.

The question of what future world temperatures will be is muddied by the knowledge that a variety of natural fluctuations in temperatures do occur. There may be upward or downward fluctuations in solar luminosity. Large volcanic eruptions spill aerosols into the air and cause temporary global cooling. Running means (8-year averages) of the composite Alaska average annual temperature show oscillations of one Centigrade degree and a period of roughly 13 years, for unknown reasons. Other cyclic or quasi-cyclic variations occur with much longer periods. All together, these natural fluctuations create a lot of noise that makes it difficult to recognize a particular change such as that thought to be associated with the carbon dioxide increase.

However, it is now predicted that there will be substantial warming during the 1980s and that the carbon dioxide warming trend will clearly emerge from the noise by the end of this century.

During the 21st century the global warming could amount to $2^{\circ}C$ or even more. The kicker is that the warming at high latitudes will be much more, perhaps about $5^{\circ}C$. That is close to $10^{\circ}F$, and that is a lot.

One of the more serious consequences is melting of the arctic ice pack and melting of Antarctic glacier ice. Sea level could rise by ten or twenty feet in less than a hundred years. Think what that means for every coastal village and city in the world. Louisiana and Florida would grow smaller by 25% and the Northwest Passage could open to shipping. Large portions of North America and Asia would become drought-prone because of accompanying meteorological changes.

A major effect in Alaska and northwestern Canada would be melting of permafrost over large areas. Foundations and roads in discontinuous permafrost areas will be greatly affected, so there would be high repair costs.

All this might be avoided if the world curtails its consumption of oil, natural gas and coal. If it comes to a decision on that issue, how will the energy-producing areas such as Alaska and northwestern Canada react? Will they be willing to reduce their income from fuel sales to alleviate the situation? Or will they have any say in the matter?

Sep 81:504

Unusual Weather

Why such a mild early winter in Fairbanks? Why more than 100 inches of rain in Cordova since August? Why the driest fall in 90 years near Seattle? Why unusual cold and storm in the northcentral states?

All these unusual weather patterns are related, and they have a single cause — they are the predictable result of an unusually persistent pattern that has developed these past few months in the air circulation of the Northern Hemisphere.

Normally the upper average jet stream air flow over the Gulf of Alaska is west to east. Having moved across the Pacific Ocean, this air is warm and moist. Its normal flow across the Panhandle and the Pacific Northwest gives the rainfall usually experienced there. Central Alaska in winter normally receives cold air from the north and west, dry air that has swept across Siberia or the ice-covered Arctic Ocean.

The normal west to east flow pattern around the earth at middle latitudes sometimes develops a wavy pattern, as shown in the top of the diagram. Sometimes the wavy structure is influenced and reenforced by the presence of mountain masses. This winter that seems to have happened — a northward undulation of the flow pattern has developed over the mountains of the northwest coast and it has remained fixed there for many weeks.

In consequence, warm, moist air has been forced northward from the Gulf of Alaska. Rising over the

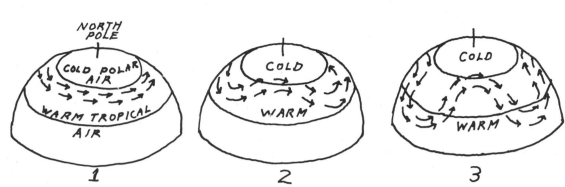

STEP 1 – UNIFORM WESTERLY (EAST-FLOWING) SUBPOLAR JET STREAM.
STEP 2 – JET STREAM GROWS UNSTABLE AND DEVELOPS WAVY STRUCTURE.
STEP 3 – WAVY STRUCTURE GROWS AND SOMETIMES THE DISTORTED
           STRUCTURE PERSISTS – AS IN WINTER 1976.

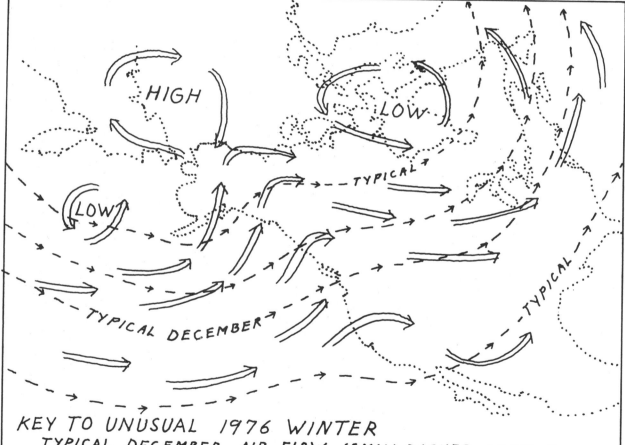

KEY TO UNUSUAL 1976 WINTER
   TYPICAL DECEMBER AIR FLOW (SMALL DASHED ARROWS)
HAS BEEN PUSHED NORTHWARD BY A PERSISTENT PRESSURE
PATTERN FIXED OVER THE WEST COAST OF NORTH
AMERICA. HEAVY ARROWS SHOW THE AVERAGE DEC. 1976 FLOW.

Unusual Weather: *This pattern has persisted during several years after 1976, giving unusually warm winters during those years.*

Coast Range it has dumped heavy rain on Cordova and nearby areas. Loss of water precipitated on the flanks of the Coast Range and the Alaska Range has actually made the air warmer yet; by the time this air has settled in the Tanana Valley the air is quite warm and dry — hence, our pleasant winter here.

Our gain is to the loss of those living south and east of us. The unusual flow pattern has brought cold arctic air southward down over central Canada and the northern tier of states. Those living in the Pacific Northwest have not received their normal rainfall because the persistent northward air flow in the Gulf of Alaska has diverted the rain-giving moist air northwards and presented it to Cordova and Yakutat. Residents there normally receive enough rainfall to be less than enthused, but they are experiencing warmer than normal temperatures.

— *Neil Davis and Sue Ann Bowling*
Jan 77:140

Asian Dust Invades Alaska

Working with researchers from the University of Rhode Island, the Geophysical Institute's Dr. Glenn Shaw has discovered that the air over Alaska may regularly receive large injections of dust originating with sandstorms in the Takla Makan and Gobi deserts of Asia. As much as a half-million tons of desert dust may pass over Alaska during a five-day event.

The dust is carried in horizontal bands of "arctic haze" blowing over the Pacific Ocean and into northern Alaska. Dr. Shaw and his co-workers are now beginning to take ground-level air samples at Fairbanks and Barrow to learn how much of the dust falls on Alaska and what effects the airborne dust might have on Arctic climate.

Nov 76:121

Arctic Haze

Distinct reddish-brown layers have been observed many times by jet pilots flying across the Arctic on the trans-polar air route. Especially pronounced in winter, these haze layers were first reported more than twenty years ago. When an aircraft is within a layer of arctic haze, pilots report that horizontal visibility can drop to one tenth that of normally clear sky.

Much of the haze seen in the air is of natural origin, but arctic haze evidently is man-made. Measurements made by sampling air at Point Barrow, Alaska and other arctic locations show that the haze contains small amounts of vanadium. The vanadium, being a natural component of crude oil, is injected into the atmosphere in areas of heavy industrial activity.

The Geophysical Institute's Glenn Shaw and his co-workers at other research institutions around the country who are making the measurements are fairly certain that their results imply that the arctic haze originates in the industrialized portions of Europe. The researchers think that the injected pollution is carried northeasterly toward the Arctic Ocean where some of it is transported directly across the polar region to the Alaskan and Canadian coasts.

Arctic haze is mostly composed of particles of sulfuric acid and organic compounds formed in the air from the combination of naturally occurring chemicals and pollutant sulfur dioxide or hydrocarbon gases. Called aerosols, these resultant particles are small enough to float in the air but are large enough to reflect sunlight, and hence cause haze.

Acid rains created when the pollutant-caused aerosols are washed from the air have destroyed fish in the lakes of Scandinavia and New York. Slightly acidic rains have been detected at Barrow but no damaging ecological effects have been noted there so far.

Jan 80:363

Arctic Haze Confirmed

Large jet aircraft are not the only sign of civilization penetrating the high arctic on a daily basis. Distinct reddish-brown layers of man-made pollution haze now add color to the Arctic's whiteness.

Suspected for some years, it is now confirmed that industrial pollution from Europe, North America and Asia finds its way into the arctic atmosphere via normal air circulation patterns. Measurements made at Barrow, Alaska, and at Mould Bay and Igloolik in Northwest Territories, Canada, show that the arctic pollution is not as bad as near most cities. Peak values are about one-third the average air pollution measured in Berkeley, California. This arctic pollution is bad enough to concern scientists because it might alter the polar climate if the current rate of pollution input to the Arctic persists.

The pollution tends to accumulate in the arctic air because there is little rain or snowfall to strip out the pollutant particles during much of the year. The pollutants, mostly black soot, sulfuric acid and industrially-produced organic compounds, are light enough to float in the air unless washed out by precipitation. Then, of course, the pollutants contribute to the production of acid rain which makes some people vitriolic when they think about it, especially Canadians, whose forests and lakes are suffering most from acid rain's effects.

In early winter, most of the arctic pollution appears to emanate from industrial areas in the Soviet Union. Later in winter, the pollution comes mostly from western Europe. By spring, the circulation into the Arctic may shift to bring up pollution from eastern North America. So it looks like many of the industrialized regions of the Northern Hemisphere are contributing to the problem.

Jun 81:490

Acid Rain

Acid rain was thought to be a European problem ten years ago. Next the loss of fish populations in eastern portions of Canada and the United States showed that damaging acid rain was more widespread. So far, there is not much acid rain in Alaska and northwestern Canada, but the Rocky Mountain states and even the West Coast from Washington state southward are beginning to see some signs.

The worst American locality seems to be the Ohio Valley. Rain more acidic than vinegar, actually nearly as acidic as stomach acid, has fallen there. Besides killing fish, acid rain can cause soil to lose quickly the valuable plant nutrients that have built up over the ages. Thus its effects can be very serious and long-lasting.

The Geophysical Institute's Dr. Glenn Shaw voices concern that as industrialization spreads northward through Canada, Alaska and Siberia, the accompanying increased ejection of sulfur dioxide and nitrogen oxide will cause more acidic rain and snowfall in the north. This is something to think about as we develop greater usage of the huge coal deposits available in Alaska. As we use this coal, large investments in air pollution control devices may be necessary to preserve our water, fish, soil and clear sky.

Jun 80:408

Aleutian Lightning

Tropical islands often are the locations of lightning storms, but lightning is rarely seen in the Aleutian Islands. Residents of Adak have asked for an explanation of why this is through a teacher who has spent some time there, Virginia Van den Noort.

Lightning is an electrical discharge of the air that can occur only when the atmospheric electric field is strong enough to break down the air. Such strong electric fields develop only when there is considerable vertical mixing of the air.

A condition that leads to thunderstorms and lightning is one where the ground surface is warmer than the air just above it. The ground warms the near-surface air, which then rises causing an overturn of the air mass. Upward-moving air together with downward-falling water droplets are thought to create the high electric fields required for production of lightning.

Such conditions occur over tropical islands and over warm land masses. But in the North Pacific, in the region of the Aleutians, the ground and water surface often is colder than the air above, at least in

summer. Consequently the air near the land and sea surface is kept cool. That coolness stabilizes the air rather than causing it to convect vertically.

Thus, the reason why the Aleutians have so little lightning is the same one that creates so much low cloud and fog there — stable moist air in contact with a comparatively cold sea and land surface.

Jun 79:311

Thunderstorms in Alaska

As we move into summer weather, clouds change from widespread layered (or stratus) to a discrete cauliflower-type of cumulus cloud. These cumulus clouds, due primarily to ground heating by the sun, often develop into thunderstorms. Many Alaskan forest fires are caused by lightning from these thunderstorms. Because these fires often remain undetected for a long time, they account for most of the forest acreage burned (about one million acres per year). A single thunderstorm lasts almost 20 minutes. Thunderstorms are associated with updrafts inside and downdrafts below it. These drafts can be as fast as 50 knots. The sudden wind shifts associated with downdrafts under a storm are most dangerous to aircraft.

Thunderstorms do not occur uniformly over the state. Very few, if any, are recorded north of the Brooks Range. Of the few preferred areas, the most extensive thunderstorm formation occurs in the mountainous region between the Yukon and Tanana rivers, extending into Lake Minchumina. Fairbanks is in the middle of this active region. Lightning from thunderstorms can occur between two clouds or from cloud to ground. The thunder associated with the former is heard as a rumbling noise while the latter is heard as a crack. Cloud to ground lightning is what causes damage to trees and can kill animals.

If you are caught in a treeless plain during a thunderstorm, lie flat until the storm passes, as lightning prefers to strike elevated objects which act as antennas. One person or animal in a group can act as an antenna causing all to be struck by lightning. (Herds of caribou sometimes found dead on the plains are so killed.) Another simple precaution is to avoid standing under trees or touching their trunks. Tall trees around your house, especially if you are living in the hills, will help deflect lightning; also make sure your television antenna is well grounded.

— K.O.L.F. Jayaweera
Apr 77:155

Northern Thunderstorms

Even during fair weather, small puffy clouds are common in northern skies. A warm area on the ground surface creates an updraft carrying moisture

54

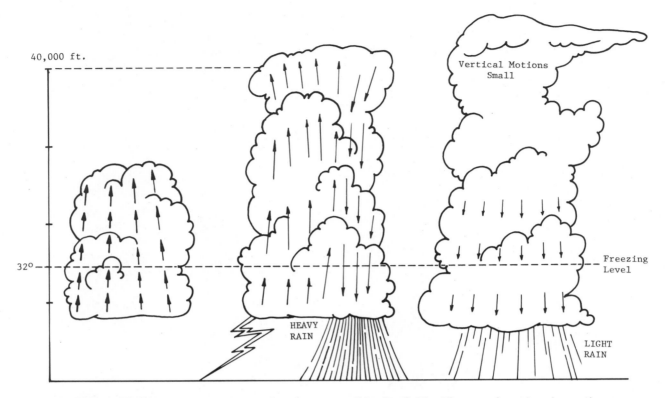

40,000 ft.

32°

Vertical Motions
Small

Freezing
Level

HEAVY
RAIN

LIGHT
RAIN

Northern Thunderstorms: *The life cycle of a thunderstorm cell begins (left) with upward-moving air creating a cumulus cloud. Then in the mature stage (center) rain, cold air, and perhaps hail fall down in a part of the thundercloud, and lightning is common. Finally, the updrafts and the lightning cease and the tall cloud dissipates. (This diagram is redrawn from one given by H.R. Byers and R.R. Braham, Jr.)*

up which condenses to form clouds. Each cloud might last only a few minutes, especially if the nearby air is dry.

But when the moisture content of the middle atmosphere is high, and if the temperature decreases rapidly with altitude, minor updrafts can develop into major upward convective flows. Tall thunderclouds appear, reaching to altitudes above 20,000 feet (6000 meters) as air rushes upward carrying moisture high above the freezing level.

In the upper part of the cloud the moisture particles condense into water droplets and ice particles. For a time these may be carried upward on the rising air. As the droplets and particles grow in size they become so heavy that the pull of gravity becomes stronger than the force of the upward-rushing air. Then as the particles fall, they drag against the surrounding air and pull it down too. The descending air is also cooled by the cold ice and water particles and thereby becomes much heavier than the air outside the cloud, accelerating the downdraft. This, the mature stage in a thunderstorm's life cycle, is characterized by maximum rain, electrical effects, and wind gusts at the earth's surface.

As downdrafts begin to dominate the cloud — typ-

ically an hour or so after the cloud forms — the energy provided by the updraft is diminished. When the entire cloud consists of descending air, the thunderstorm exhausts itself and dissipates.

Huge thunderstorms, like the ones of middle and southwestern North America that can produce hailstones as large as baseballs, do not occur here in the north because of the lack of strong surface heating which helps to build the taller cells of overturning air within thunderclouds. Even so, thunderstorms are common enough in summer to be the cause of most fires in northern forests and tundra regions.

Jul 79:324

Arctic Thunderstorms

The history of thunderstorms observed in the high arctic reads like that of great auroras at low latitude — it dates back many years, but the number of events is not large.

Part of the historical sparseness of observed thunderstorms in the Arctic Ocean and on surrounding shores is due simply to the lack of people to observe the thunderstorms. But mainly, thunderstorms are rare in arctic regions because the conditions necessary for formation of the tall clouds are lacking. A warm earth surface, irregular terrain and plenty of moisture in the middle atmosphere contribute to the formation of strong updrafts and the associated condensation of moisture at high altitudes involved in the development of thunderstorms.

Looking into thunderstorm history, Mr. Arne Hanson of the Naval Arctic Research Laboratory at Barrow, Alaska, has uncovered an observation of an arctic thunderstorm made in 1580. A manuscript Hanson has prepared contains a quotation written aboard a ship sailing the Kara Sea, north of Siberia: ". . . the winde with a showre and thunder came to the Southwest and then wee ranne East Northeast."

Several thunderstorms on the north Siberia coast were recorded in the late 1700s, and at least nine were observed on the northern coasts of Canada, Alaska or Siberia by explorers in the period 1815-1826.

During the last 30 years, Hanson reports that three thunderstorms have been observed far offshore and well out over the icepack. These observations proved the error of a prediction made in 1933 by the famous oceanographer H. U. Sverdrup. He suggested that thunderstorms would never be observed out in the icepack area more than 100 km from shore.

Since arctic-region thunderstorms are comparatively rare, it is worthwhile to write down the details of any observations of them that might be made. At the Geophysical Institute we happily collect and archive descriptions of unusual events of this type.

Aug 79:325

Hail Formation

A raining down of hailstones as large as golfballs — or even baseballs — will quickly destroy crops, maim or kill animals and damage roofs. How do such large hailstones materialize out of thin air?

A clue to the formation of hailstones is seen when a hailstone is cut in half. Most show an onion-like layering of alternating clear and opaque ice. This layering demonstrates that the stone is built up by coatings of ice successively frozen onto the surface of the hailstone. Each coating evidences a buildup in an environment different from that in which the coat below formed. Clear ice forms in the part of the cloud where water is copious; ice with many trapped air bubbles, hence opaque, forms in drier portions.

Important to the buildup of hailstones is the existence in thunderhead clouds of supercooled water: water that remains in liquid form well below normal freezing temperature. Supercooled water droplets colliding with a foreign object — a piece of dirt, an embryonic hailstone — will freeze to it and thereby increase its size.

Much of the water in the upper part of a tall thunderhead cloud is supercooled. Once a hailstone starts to form in this part of the cloud, it can rapidly grow as it moves either upward or downward through the supercooled water.

Violent updrafts and downdrafts in thunderheads can carry hailstones, water droplets, (and airplanes) upward and downward at speeds to 180 mph (300 kmph). A single trip through a tall thunderhead can cause a hailstone to grow about one-half inch, so several trips are necessary to build up a large hailstone.

In the north, large hailstones are rare because the lack of strong ground surface heating does not favor the buildup of the gigantic thunderstorms common in some temperate climates. It would be interesting to know how the largest hailstone found by an Alaskan or Yukoner would compare with those found by residents of Potter, Nebraska in 1928. Hailstones there were about the size of large grapefruit with an average diameter of 5½ inches. The biggest weighed a pound and a half.

— Dan O'Neill
Aug 79:328

Raindrop Size

"Why are raindrops sometimes large and sometimes small?" — Another one of those seemingly simple questions that can be difficult to answer, this particular one is asked by reader Jennifer Jolis of Fairbanks.

Drop size in rain seems to be directly related to the upward speed of the air from which the rain falls. Clouds tend to dissipate and no longer release rain when the cloud layer decreases in altitude. Clouds form and produce rain as they rise in altitude.

Horizontally stratified clouds — the kind that sometimes stretch for hundreds or thousands of kilometers — produce raindrops of small size when the air containing the clouds is caused to ascend slowly at speeds less than 20 centimeters per sec (one kilometer per hour [kmph]). Gentle, drizzle-like rains are common along the coast and in interior Alaska and Yukon Territory when air masses are being moved from lowland to upland areas. The drop size of such gentle, wind-less rain is near one-half millimeter (mm), roughly the diameter of a straight pin. Falling at a speed of about 6 kmph, those tiny drops are still far larger than the 0.02-mm sized particles in a non-precipitating cloud.

Large raindrops evidently grow mainly through collision of smaller drops when there is sufficient updraft and turbulence to keep the drops circulating in the cloud and in various directions so that they will collide. The very largest raindrops, those up to 4 mm in diameter, fall at a speed of about 30 kmph. However, updrafts in thunderclouds can be twice this fast, so even these very large raindrops can be supported within the cloud. The 4-mm maximum diameter of raindrops probably results because raindrops larger than this size tend to break up when colliding with other large raindrops.

The appearance of large raindrops always signals strong updrafts and turbulence. When one feels that sudden cool gusty wind that experience tells often comes just before the rain, one should expect to be pelted with big raindrops. The gusty wind is a downdraft wind positioned just outside the updraft containing the big raindrops.

Jul 78:236

Tornadoes

Extending from the tropics to the polar regions, the continental plains of North America and Asia are the favored locations of tornadoes. Most occur in summer during the daytime; each year they kill hundreds and cause many millions of dollars in damage.

A tornado is a violently revolving funnel cloud usually a few hundred meters in diameter. Intense upward flow of air at its center leads to very low pressure there. The funnel itself is visible because it contains small water droplets formed by cooling and condensation of air expanding into the low pressure region. Heat given up by the condensation evidently provides the energy to drive the rapidly rotating air of the outer funnel at speeds as high as 500 miles per hour.

Buildings explode from the force of the air within when the low pressure of the funnel center passes over them; then the high wind in the outer funnel completes the devastation. Strange things happen in tornadoes — straw drives through posts and cows, oil is sucked out of tractor engines, a house is destroyed and hand towels from inside are found a half-mile away, still neatly folded. Most tornadoes make a roaring noise and some are silent. They often occur in pairs. A man in Iowa watched a tornado pass by his farm, then turned around to find his chicken house, located only a few feet from where he stood, silently stolen away by a second tornado. Has anyone ever seen a tornado in Alaska?

Jul 76:89

Why is the Sky Blue?

If you could go to the moon and look at the sky from there, you would see black. So the sky is not blue at all — what we see is simply the air glowing blue. This is caused by reflected sunlight, and it is blue because tiny air molecules reflect blue light more efficiently than the other colors. If the reflecting molecules were larger, however, such as the large water drops in a cloud, then all colors would be scattered. That is why clouds appear white.

Strangely enough, the blue hue of the sky depends on the reflectivity of the underlying surface. Thus, the sky looks bluer over the oceans than it does over a reflecting ice- or snow-covered surface. This fact was used by early polar explorers to detect open water. Haze or pollution causes the sky to look washed out. The bluest skies are seen in pure mountain air at locations far from urban pollution. Sadly enough, as industrial haze continues to build up, it is rarer all the time to see a really blue sky in many parts of the world. Perhaps the bluest sky in the world can be seen from the summit of Mauna Loa, Hawaii (14,000 feet). From this location on a clear day, the sky looks almost violet, the surrounding oceans, the altitude and the clear air all contributing to the hue.

— Glenn Shaw
Apr 76:55

Why is the Sky Blue? *Children sometimes ask nasty questions. (Drawing by Pat Davis.)*

Blue Haze

As the summer traveler goes south from Alaska and northwestern Canada, one of the most noticeable changes is the deterioration in air quality and seeing ability. No longer do distant mountain ranges stand out clearly — one may be lucky to see them at all.

As the sky seems to close in around him, the northerner may sense a loss of freedom. Do Americans not realize how bad their summer skies are? Why don't they stop pouring pollutants into them?

Actually, most of the obscuring haze in the air is quite natural. It would be there whether or not people lived in the area. At least this is true of the blue haze.

Blue haze is densest in forested regions. The haze consists mainly of organic particles in the air. Called aerosols, these particles are bigger than simple molecules, but they are light enough to float in air for a long time. Organic aerosols are those built up of compounds containing hydrocarbons, that is, hydrogen and carbon.

It is thought that the hydrogen and carbon boils

off in vapor form from plants and trees. Shining of the sun's rays onto the emitted hydrocarbon vapors causes them to interact with each other and with other naturally occurring elements to build larger particles. As they grow in size, these aerosol particles become large enough to scatter light. Blue light is most easily scattered — hence one sees blue haze. Worldwide, it is estimated that the amount of natural organic haze is 5 to 500 times greater than man-made haze. Of course, near industrial areas, the man-made part can easily exceed the natural component.

The reason we have much less blue haze at high latitudes evidently is that our low summer temperatures do not yield a high rate of boiling off of organic vapors from vegetation. Also, the low sun angle helps to shield out the ultraviolet component of sunlight that causes the vapors to form into aerosols. In coastal regions where there is frequent rainfall, both natural and man-made organic aerosols are washed out of the air since the aerosols are water-soluble.

Attesting to the relative permanence of the blue haze in forested temperate regions are several geographic names: the Blue Ridge Mountains of West Virginia, the Great Smoky Mountains of North Carolina and Tennessee, and the Blue Mountains of Oregon and Washington. These names were given long before industrial pollutants existed.

Jul 79:326

Pre-Storm Green Sky

Changes in sky color have long been known to portend change in the local weather. There is good reason for this association since changes in sky color can be caused by the movement of heavy cloud decks, and heavy clouds often produce rain, snow and lightning.

Such an instance was reported by residents of Kodiak who saw a peculiar green sky for about a half-hour during late evening in July 1978. Immediately following the appearance of the green sky, a

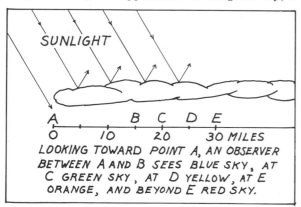

Pre-Storm Green: *Clouds overhead affect apparent sky color.*

rainstorm with much thunder and lightning struck the area.

Sky coloration is caused by the scattering of sunlight as it passes through the atmosphere. As we view the sky it is the scattered light that we are seeing. If there are no clouds in the sky, the sun illuminates all of the air near an observer and thereby causes his eye to receive scattered light from all parts of the atmosphere.

But the brightest light is that which has traveled the shortest distance through the atmosphere, the light that comes down to the observer from most nearly overhead. This light is bluish because blue and violet light is scattered much more than the other colors of the solar spectrum, green, yellow, orange and red.

Scattered light that comes to the eye from parcels of air located different distances away is richest in various colors. Whereas the scattered light coming to the eye from the overhead sky is richest in blue light, that which comes from 20 miles (30 kilometers) away is richest in green light. Light from 25 miles away is richest in yellow, that from 30 miles away is richest in orange, and that from a greater distance is richest in red. Consequently, the sky near the rising or setting sun is orange and red since the brightest scattered light is coming from air many miles from the observer.

Hence if a heavy cloud deck covers an observer's sky out to a distance of about 20 miles away, the light the observer will see will have green color because the clouds are shielding out the blue light scattered from nearby. If the cloud deck expands out to successively cover the sky to distances 25, 30 and more miles away, the observer will see the color of light below the clouds change to yellow, orange and then more reddish.

Green sky like the one seen at Kodiak is seen far less often than yellow, orange and red skies simply because the exact cloud cover extent required (to about 20 miles) does not occur all that often. But in high latitudes the sun is low to the horizon so much of the time that beautiful yellow, orange, and red skies are often seen.

Oct 79:262

The Green Flash

Clear, cold winter days in Alaska are conducive to seeing the green flash. Though a bit rare, the green flash happens often enough to pay to look for it just as the sun rises or sets. An observer in Fairbanks recently reported seeing the green flash at sunset when there was a strong temperature inversion (and much ice fog) in the Tanana Valley.

The green flash may last only a second or so near the time when the first edge of the sun comes up in

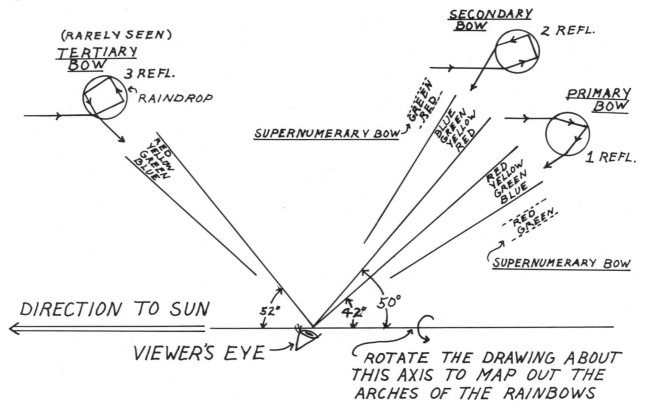

How Many Rainbows? *The geometry of rainbows.*

the morning, or the last edge goes down in the evening. The green flash is the result of the atmosphere acting like a weak prism to bend each color of the sun's light by different amounts. The separation of color is small, but sometimes enough to remove from view the red and yellow light coming from the edge of the sun above the horizon. This leaves only blue and green light, but the blue tends to be scattered most by the air. So, if conditions are just right, a portion of pure green sun, the green flash, will be seen briefly. It might flash several times because of air motion in the light path. Sometimes, for the same reason, the green edge of the sun seems to detach itself and then is suddenly gone.

The green flash was familiar to the ancient Egyptians who apparently saw it often in the clear desert air. Observation of the green color at sunrise and sunset evidently led to the idea that the sun was green at night. Night was the Egyptian emblem of death. Hence, Osiris, the god of the dead and who was identified with the nighttime sun, was always painted green.

Dec 77:209

How Many Rainbows?

Another advantage to living in the far north is the high frequency of seeing rainbows, a consequence of the low sun angle. Rainbows are caused by internal reflection and refraction of sunlight or moonlight inside raindrops.

Light entering a raindrop is bent by an amount that depends upon the wavelength (color) of the light. Each raindrop acts as a tiny spherical prism. A rainbow is seen whenever there are enough raindrops distributed properly with respect to the viewer and the sun and there is not too much absorption of the light in the rain. But rainbows are seen only in specific directions relative to the direction of the sun, directions that are determined by the number of reflections within individual raindrops.

A single reflection in the raindrop produces the brightest rainbow seen. This primary bow has a red outer boundary which is located at an angle of 42 degrees away from a line from the sun to the viewer. To see the primary bow the viewer must face away from the sun.

A secondary bow with colors reversed so that the red edge is toward the inner border is frequently seen about eight degrees outside the primary bow. It is weaker than the primary bow because the light undergoes two reflections, and consequently more absorption, inside the raindrops.

Three reflections inside the drops cast the light back toward the sun to create a tertiary rainbow only 52 degrees away from the sun. This bow is rarely seen because it is weaker than the primary and secondary bows, and the brightness of the sky this close to the sun overpowers the rainbow light. Furthermore, a person watching the primary and secondary bows would have the tertiary bow at his back.

An extra partial copy of the primary bow is sometimes seen parallel to and just inside the primary bow. Similarly, a partial copy of the secondary bow may be seen outside it. These usually narrow bands of red or red and green are called supernumerary rainbows. They are caused by light leaving the raindrops along different paths in such a way that the colored rays destructively and constructively interfere with each other so that colors are seen to be bright in certain places and absent in others. Hence, the supernumerary bows are "interference fringes" of the primary and secondary rainbows.

Jul 78:237

Rings Around the Moon

Have you ever seen a ring around the moon? Folklore has it that this means bad weather is coming — and this particular "old wives tale" happens to be true.

The ring that appears around the moon arises from light passing through six-sided ice crystals high in the atmosphere. These ice crystals refract, or bend, light in the same manner that a camera lens bends light. The ring has a diameter of approximately 22°, and sometimes, if one is lucky, it is also possible to detect a second, larger ring, twice the diameter of the first.

How can rings around the moon be used as a weather predictor? The ice crystals that cover the halo signify high-altitude, thin cirrus clouds that normally preceed a storm front by one or two days. Nowadays scientists are increasingly able to verify and understand the physical reasons behind many folklore tales as natural phenomena. — *Glenn Shaw*
Oct 76:24

Sun Dogs and Light Shafts

"Diamond Dust" or tiny ice crystals in the winter air over Fairbanks cause many curious optical phenomena in the sky. They sometimes cause a multicolored halo around the sun or moon. Within the solar halo ring, on either side of the sun, one often sees two bright spots called "sun dogs" or "mock suns". At night one frequently sees pillars of light extending vertically upward from street lights or other bright sources. These forests of glowing vertical shafts can be easily mistaken for displays of the rayed aurora.

These optical effects and others like them are caused by the reflection and refraction (bending) of light by the small ice crystals. The ice crystals are flat and they fall through the air with their flat sides horizontal. Light reflecting from the flat faces of the ice crystals causes vertical light shafts. Reflection alone does not alter the color of light, so the vertical pillars are the color of the light source, usually white.

On the other hand, sun dogs and related phenomena are multi-colored because they are caused by refraction of the light through the ice crystals. Refraction breaks sunlight up into the colors of the rainbow. Sun dogs and halos always are at an angle of 22° from the sun. That particular angle, curiously enough, occurs because the refracting ice crystals have hexagonal (six-sided) faces.

— *K.O.L.F. Jayaweera*
May 76:36

Vertical Light Shafts

Winter is the time of falling snow and ice crystals. Ice and snow crystals can take on many forms, ranging from six-sided cylinders to flat plates and complex flat forms having hexagonal symmetry.

If the air temperature is not far below freezing, in the range 15^OF to 25^OF (-9^OC to -4^OC), only needle-like cylinders form. In the range -5^OF to 15^OF (-20^OC to -9^OC), the flat plate-like crystals grow.

The flat crystal forms tend to orient with their flat sides in the horizontal plane as they fall through the air, though like a falling leaf, they oscillate about this orientation.

The majestic vertical light columns that one sees so often during the northern winter are caused by reflection of light sources from the flat undersides of the falling crystals. These columns can be seen above any bright light source — the sun, moon, street lights and auto lights. Sometimes one sees the columns extend down below the headlights of an automobile.

Whenever the vertical light shafts are seen, one knows that the temperature of the air in the vicinity where the responsible crystals formed must be well below zero.

If there is a brightening of the vertical light shaft 22° above the light source, it means that light is entering and refracting within the ice crystals instead of only reflecting from their undersides. That happens when ice crystals other than flat plates are present and so indicates somewhat warmer air temperature. The resulting sun dogs, moon dogs or light dogs tend to be multicolored because the prismatic refraction in the ice crystals breaks up the light into its component colors.

Dec 78:232

(See photo next page.)

The Parry Arc

Among reports of peculiar mirages or other strange phenomena observed in the Arctic is one described by

60

Vertical Light Shafts: *Partial vertical light shafts photographed in April 1978 by Mary Ford of the* Peninsula Clarion. *A combination of needle- and plate-like ice crystals falling over the industrial area north of Kenai has created these images, which are akin to both vertical light shafts and sun dogs.*

P. Berwick of Fairbanks. In that instance several people at a DEW-Line site saw, on two different nights, what appeared to be the lights of a large city on the horizon. Was this a mirage, the Northern Lights or what?

A possible explanation is the Parry arc named after the explorer, W. E. Parry, who first reported seeing the phenomenon while searching for a northwest passage in 1819-1820. The Parry arc is actually moonlight or sunlight deflected by passing through elongated airborne ice crystals. As the crystals fall, they tend to align themselves with their long axes horizontal. In effect they make many prisms that deflect light by about 22° and spread it out into the colors of the rainbow.

The Parry arc will appear below or above the sun or moon and so can be seen when these celestial bodies are obscured by clouds or the horizon. Its configuration is such that it could, in some circumstances, be mistaken for the lights of a city just on or just over the horizon. The Parry arc is but one of several related phenomena caused by sunlight or moonlight being deflected by airborne water or ice particles.

Mar 77:151

Snow Crystals

Just as no two human fingers have identical prints, it is reported that no two snowflakes are the same. Perhaps no two snow crystals are identical, but like fingers, many show similar characteristics.

Falling snow particles are classified into ten categories, according to shape. To classify falling snow crystals may sound like a scientific make-work project, but there is some reason for this apparent folly just as there is reason why snow crystals come in different shapes.

The basic hexagonal (six-sided) shape of all snow crystals derives from the shape and bonding of water molecules. Beyond that fundamental constraint, it boils down to a matter of micro-climate, the climate the snow crystal finds itself in as it grows. The two key factors in the micro-climate are temperature and humidity.

If the air is extremely wet and just a few degrees below freezing, only needles and columnar snow crystals form. Six-sided plate crystals grow if the temperature is somewhat colder (plus 10°F, minus 15°C). At plus 5°F (-15°C) star-like crystals grow. The more saturated is the air the more lacy and dendritic they are.

Even for a snowflake, there is no peace and stability in this world of ours. As the crystal grows it moves through the air within an ever-changing micro-climate that dictates a changing growth pattern. A crystal that started out to be a column may fall into cooler air that creates plate-like growth, so then it becomes a capped column. In extremely wet air, lumpy masses called graupel, ice pellets or hail develop. Evidently, the growth is so fast that the molecular forces trying to create beauty in the form of plates, stellar crystals, and columns cannot control the growth pattern.

Mar 80:375

Graphic Symbol	Examples			Symbol	Type of Particle
				F1	Plate
				F2	Stellar crystal
				F3	Column
				F4	Needle
				F5	Spatial dendrite
				F6	Capped column
				F7	Irregular crystal
				F8	Graupel
				F9	Ice pellet
				F0	Hail

Snow Crystals: *The International Snow Classification for falling snow. After the snow falls it is sometimes altered to other forms.*

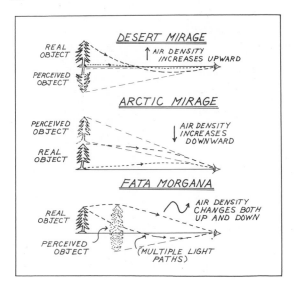

Mirages: *Light rays travelling from an object to the eye through the atmosphere are bent up or down depending upon whether the density of air increases upward or downward. The result can be a desert mirage, an arctic mirage or the fata morgana, which is a combination of both types.*

Arctic Mirage (Hillingar)

Just as cold snow differs from hot sand, arctic mirages differ from those of desert regions.

Desert mirages result from the heating of air overlying a warm surface, the hot sand. In a desert mirage objects appear to be lower than they actually are. Also, the image is inverted top for bottom.

Just the opposite happens in an arctic mirage because it results from the existence of relatively cold air next to the ground surface. That cold layer exists because the cold snow, ice or water surface extracts heat from the air just above. In the arctic mirage a distant object appears right way up but higher up than the actual location.

Though arctic and desert mirages seem to be quite different, they share a common fundamental cause. It is that light rays passing from an object through air to an observer always refract (bend) in the direction of increasing air density.

In a "normal" atmosphere, air is less dense the higher up above the earth's surface. Consequently, light rays travelling horizontally over the earth's surface actually bend downward as though trying to follow the curved surface. For this reason one sees distant mountains that actually are below the horizon, ones invisible if light truly travelled in straight lines in the atmosphere.

If the earth's surface is hot, it heats the air just above, making the air there less dense than air higher up. Consequently light rays traversing such a region bend upward causing false lakes and inverted moun-

tains to appear. These images tend to dance or otherwise change rapidly since dense air above lighter air is too unstable to remain static.

Contrasting with this instability is the steadiness of an air mass which is coldest at the bottom, the condition creating the arctic mirage. Especially over cold ocean areas, the air density can change with altitude so rapidly that the horizon appears to lift up like the edges of a saucer. Coastlines normally well below the horizon are raised up into view.

Early Norsemen called these mirages hillingars. The hillingar effect may well have contributed to the Norse discoveries of Iceland and Greenland, according to the suggestion of H.L. Sawatzky and W. H. Lehn, writing in the June 25, 1976 issue of *Science* magazine.

The hillingar even has an Alaskan connection in the form of a lodging house, the Captain Bartlett Inn in Fairbanks. The inn is named after Captain John Bartlett who seems to hold the distance record for seeing objects below the horizon with the aid of the hillingar effect. His ship, the *Effie N. Morrissey*, was located more than 500 km (300 miles) away from Iceland one day in 1939 when Captain Bartlett spotted one of the Icelandic mountains.

Sometimes, complex mirages called *fata morganas* are seen in conditions transitional between those favorable for desert mirages and arctic mirages. The fata morgana mirage may consist of a double image of an object, one image inverted, the other right side up. These appear frequently in broad valleys such as Alaska's Tanana Valley where temperature inversions and complex air layering are common.

Oct 79:347

Fata Morgana

Fata Morgana, also known as Morgan le Fay, was a fairy enchantress skilled in the art of changing shape. In one traditional story she was King Arthur's sister and learned many of her skills from Merlin the Magician.

A special type of complex mirage, one that sometimes gives the impression of a castle half in the air and half in the sea, is named after Fata Morgana. She was known to live in a marvelous castle under the sea. Sometimes the enchantress made this castle appear reflected up in the air, causing seamen who mistook it for a safe harbor to be lured to their deaths.

The fata morgana mirage is one that can occur only where there are alternating warm and cold layers of air near the ground or water surface. Instead of travelling straight through these layers, light is bent towards the colder, hence denser, air. The result can be a rather complicated light path and a strange image of a distant object. A fata morgana actually is a superposition of several images of one object. Typically one image is upright more or less above two inverted images that may be mingled together. The images may undergo rapid changes as the air layers move slightly up and down relative to the observer.

In Alaska the best chance of seeing the relatively rare fata morgana is in winter when temperature inversions develop in the larger valleys. When seeing a complex mountain image out across a valley or bay one can attempt to sort out in the mind the paths that the light rays must have taken. Perhaps it's best just to acknowledge that it is Morgan le Fay beckoning.

Sep 78:261

The Brocken Spectre

Most air travelers have observed glories in the vicinity of their aircraft's shadow on the clouds below. The glory is a part of a phenomenon familiar to mountaineers who know it as the Brocken Spectre.

According to legend, the name came from the unhappy circumstance of a climber on northern Germany's highest mountain, the Brocken. Working his way across a narrow precipice, the climber was startled by the sudden appearance in the nearby mists of a human figure with a ring of light around its head. Frightened, the climber fell to his death. If this event really took place, it was the climber's own shadow that he saw, and the ring of light was his own "glory" ring.

Two requirements must be met if one is to see her or his own glory. One must look exactly in the anti-solar direction and there must be many water droplets in the region where the glory is to appear. Since the shadow of one's own head appears only in the anti-solar direction, it makes sense that the glory ring will always be in the vicinity of the head's shadow.

Glories are common in high-latitude regions where the low sun angle allows a person to easily come between the sun and a fog or cloud bank. But glories are most easily seen when one is riding on the shadow side of an aircraft above the clouds. The clouds below provide the necessary water droplets.

The glory ring is caused by the phenomenon called diffraction. Sunlight penetrates individual water droplets, be they in rain, fog or clouds, and reflects off the back sides of the droplets. Some of the light emerges from the droplet to come back essentially toward the sun. But the sunlight coming back toward the sun from the different raindrops interferes with itself to create circular zones of darkness and brightness. The diameter of the zone for each color of light is different. Consequently, the glory an airplane passenger sees always is red on the outside, just as is a primary rainbow. If more than one glory

is seen, the color pattern repeats, red always being outermost.

Jan 79:282

The PCB Problem

When petroleum-based solvents like paint thinner and jet fuel are combined with chlorine a number of useful products result: dry cleaning fluid, pesticides, and electrical transformer oil, to name a few. Pure petroleum distillates flushed into our oceans are digested by bacteria as are all naturally occurring products of photosynthesis. But chlorination prevents digestion because the unusual compounds formed resist enzymatic attack. So compounds such as polychlorinated biphenyls (PCB's) eventually find their way into the ocean where they accumulate. PCB's are easy to find in water because they prefer not to get wet. They will penetrate plastics just to dry off. Scientists can easily obtain PCB samples from the ocean by letting pieces of styrofoam cup soak them up. The problem with PCB's is that they are collected in the fatty parts of microorganisms. This concentration factor between the organism and the water can be as much as a million. Concentrations may be further amplified as the microorganisms become food for animals farther up the food chain. Although detoxification mechanisms are common in higher organisms, some mammals and fish wind up with a large dose of PCB's and other recalcitrant (metabolism resistant) man-made molecules anyway. While an understanding of PCB toxicology mechanisms is just emerging, it is known that these substances do make animals sick. There are localized examples of other effects, such as thinning eggshells, that have led to declining populations of falcons and other birds at the top of the food chain.

Because of these problems industry is using biodegradable substitutes for PCB's. Researchers here in Alaska are seeking to find which PCB's can safely be used and the distribution of organisms that can manage to eat them. *— Don Button*

Jun 77:169

PCB's in the Alaskan Environment

According to recent media accounts PCB is the latest chemical insult to the Alaskan environment. PCB (shorthand for "polychlorinated biphenyls") is not a single chemical but a complex mixture of substances produced from petro-chemicals and chlorine gas. The PCB's are chemically stable, and this property enhances their utility as heat exchange fluids, fire retardants, and plasticizers.

Chemically and biologically, PCB's are similar to DDT. Both are inert chlorinated hydrocarbons which persist in the environment, concentrate in most organisms (including man), and exhibit toxicity. The biological effects of PCB's are sufficient to raise concern. They alledgedly contribute to reproductive failure, induce mutations, and cause chloracne (a severe skin disorder).

What will happen to the PCB's which have been introduced to the Alaskan environment? Recent research at the University of Alaska has shown that the waters of Port Valdez contain microorganisms which convert PCB's to harmless substances. However, they do so very slowly. The most reactive of the PCB components will reside unchanged in Port Valdez for five to ten years, and the more stable components are expected to remain intact up to ten times that long.

What can we learn from this unpleasant situation? Unlike DDT — which man has willfully distributed throughout the environment — the major uses of PCB's have been in localized, physically contained situations. They enter the environment primarily through man's carelessness. Undoubtedly a portion of Alaskan PCB's are "gifts" from our more industrialized neighbors. Airborne PCB's, primarily from refuse burning, are transported by wind to the Arctic. However, the high PCB levels found near Delta, Alaska, for example, must have come from a more highly concentrated source. The problem then resides with all of us and our "throw-away society." If we learn the proper handling of noxious substances from the Alaskan PCB episode, then perhaps the present problem will be beneficial. If, however, we ignore the question of how PCB's appeared at Delta, PCB's could well become a continuing serious problem.

— Paul Reichardt
Oct 79:348

Carbon Monoxide For Breakfast

A common question asked of scientists investigating carbon monoxide pollution in Fairbanks is: "How can a town as small as Fairbanks, with so few cars compared to the large metropolitan areas of the lower forty-eight, rank so high as a city severely affected by carbon monoxide pollution?" It doesn't seem right, does it? Even with an inversion, you would not expect Fairbanks CO levels to be as high as Los Angeles. The truth is that Fairbanks in the winter normally has CO levels higher than Los Angeles. Why? There are several reasons; one is that, as you know, Fairbanks is cold in the winter. When automobiles are started with cold engines they produce remarkably large quantities of CO until they reach normal operating temperature. In fact, a good estimate of how much CO is produced during a cold start when the temperature is 0^OF is one gram for every cubic inch of engine displacement. Since a typical car might have a 350 cubic inch engine, estimate ¾ pound of CO produced during a cold start.

It would take a warmed-up vehicle about 20 miles of driving to produce as much CO as a 5-minute warm-up.

One way to help is to plug your car in when it's cold. An all-night plug-in will usually eliminate the cold start effect, but then there goes the electric bill. At 0^OF, your car will probably start without a plug-in. But the next time you're sitting at the kitchen table having that last cup of coffee and watching your car warm up, think about this — there are about 50,000 cars in Fairbanks and most of them start up cold every morning. That is a lot of CO for breakfast.

— Lee Leonard
Oct 76:125

Daily Temperature Variations

A characteristic of life in the north is the small daily range in air temperature, at least compared to regions to the south.

The main reason for the relative constancy of air temperature is the comparatively small change in solar elevation each day at high latitude. In the extreme, above the Arctic Circle, the sun does not come up at all in midwinter and so provides no warming heat. In midsummer, the sun scoots around the sky without changing its elevation angle by more than a few tens of degrees.

When the sun is low in the sky a large fraction of the energy in sunlight is absorbed by the atmosphere. Also, the sunlight that does get through strikes a larger area of the ground. Consequently a unit area of ground surface receives far less solar energy when the sun is near the horizon than when the sun is high overhead.

Even when the sun is directly overhead (elevation angle 90°), only about 60% of the sun's energy impinging upon the earth's atmosphere reaches the ground. That percentage is nearly halved by the time the sun drops to 45° above the horizon.

When the sun is within 10° of the horizon, there is such minor heating at the base of the atmosphere that on northern midwinter days we see little noontime warming.

May 79:303

Temperature Inversion — What Causes It?

Fairbanks is surrounded on three sides by hills and has one of the lowest wind conditions in the world. The lack of wind allows the air over the city to remain relatively stagnant.

When the sky is clear, the ground and the air near it radiate heat energy to outer space. Clouds over the city prevent this radiation. That is the reason why, at the same temperature, it feels warmer outside under a cloudy sky than it does when the sky is clear. It is also the reason why you should shutter or curtain

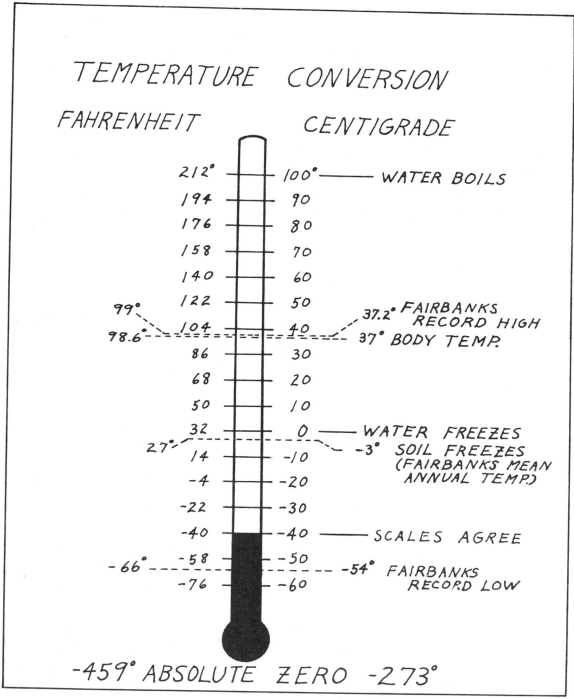

TEMPERATURE CONVERSION
FAHRENHEIT   CENTIGRADE

212° — 100° —— WATER BOILS
194 — 90
176 — 80
158 — 70
140 — 60
122 — 50
99°
98.6° ---- 104 — 40 ---- 37.2° FAIRBANKS RECORD HIGH
                        37° BODY TEMP.
86 — 30
68 — 20
50 — 10
32 — 0 —— WATER FREEZES
27° ---- 14 — -10 -3° SOIL FREEZES (FAIRBANKS MEAN ANNUAL TEMP.)
-4 — -20
-22 — -30
-40 — -40 —— SCALES AGREE
-66° ---- -58 — -50 --- -54° FAIRBANKS RECORD LOW
-76 — -60

-459° ABSOLUTE ZERO -273°

your windows on clear nights — to prevent radiation to the cold sky.

When the sky is clear, the ground cools and cools the air near it. Thus an inversion forms near the ground, an inversion being the condition of higher temperature at altitude than at ground level.

The strongest inversions occur in winter; weaker ones occur in summer when the air is still. During winter nights and days there is an inversion more than 70% of the time.

Mar 76:7

Ice Fog Effect on Temperature Inversions

The temperature inversion over Fairbanks forms because the ground radiates energy to the sky. When thick, dense ice fog forms, the ice fog partly replaces the ground surface as the radiating source. The temperature inversion then moves up toward the top of the ice fog dome. Within the ice fog, the temperature is colder and more nearly constant. The result is a thicker layer of cold air near the ground.

Because of the increasing density of the ice fog layer over the past few years, those area residents who built or bought homes on the lower hills are losing the temperature advantage they once had. A few years ago, a home 50 or 100 feet above the valley floor often enjoyed winter temperatures perhaps 10° or 20° warmer than homes in the city. Only those residents in the higher hills now avoid the deepest cold.

How much longer will they? If the city continues to expand and the ice fog to increase, there may be less reason to live in the hills. Could this affect future trends of residential living in the Fairbanks area?

— Charles Deehr
May 76:42

Differences in Air Temperature

In locations such as Fairbanks, where protecting hills still winter winds, dramatic differences in air temperature develop at various ground elevations. Furthermore, at a single location, in mid-winter, the passage of a few hours can result in a substantial temperature change even though there is little diurnal variation in solar heating.

The cause of these differences and temporal changes is the development and decay of inversions in air temperature. About half the time, there is no inversion in a locality such as Fairbanks. Then, if there is no wind or change in weather, the vertical profile of air temperature shows a fall with increasing altitude at a rate of approximately 0.6°C per 100 meters (0.3°F per 100 feet). This is the so-called adiabatic lapse rate. An air column with this temperature distribution is stable, that is, there will be no tendency for air in the column to move up or down. Consequently, this is the temperature distribution that would pertain if there never were disturbing influences such as solar heating or wind. Under such conditions a house on a hill 500 feet above the valley floor where Fairbanks sits will have an outside air temperature a few degrees cooler than exists in the city. Hillside residents around Fairbanks have, at certain times, seen such differences.

But when winter skies are clear and when there is no wind, a condition develops that upsets the 'normal' temperature profile. If there is no cloud cover to intervene, the ground surface is able to radiate heat energy directly to space, just as does a person's bare face when exposed to the sky. The ground cools, and the air in contact with it also cools, not by radiation but by conduction to the ground.

The consequence of this transfer of heat energy — from the air to the ground by conduction and thence from the ground to space by radiation — is a cold layer of air near the ground, air that is colder than the air above. Thus the 'normal' trend of decreasing temperature with increasing altitude is inverted, hence the name inversion.

As time goes on, the thickness of the inversion layer grows because the cold layer of air near the ground cools the air just above, again by conduction. Within the near-ground inversion layer, very steep gradients in temperature can develop, as much as 16°F per 100 feet (9°C per 100 m) although gradients near 10°F per 100 feet are more common.

Now, the person who built a house up on the hillside has the advantage. Instead of being colder as at those times when the inversion was lacking, the air temperature becomes noticeably warmer as the inversion develops. One person who lives on a hillside 1500 feet above Fairbanks reports that the air outside his house typically is about 30°F warmer than reported in the city, after the inversion has lasted several days. Those living at intermediate altitudes on hillsides surrounding northern cities which experience inversions observe lesser differences, depending upon how high they are above the valley floor and how long the inversion has lasted.

Minor air currents sometimes make the cold lower air slosh back and forth across the valley floor, much like water in a tipped basin. Then, hillside residents may notice rather rapid oscillations in air temperature, perhaps as much as 5 or 10°F in a few hours.

Jan 81:458

Air Pollution in Fairbanks

The influence of a particular geographic setting and of certain weather conditions can make dispersion of pollutants especially difficult. An excellent example is provided by Alaska's second largest metropolitan area, Fairbanks, situated within a three-sided basin (Birch Hill to Chena Ridge) within a still larger three-sided basin (the Salcha Bluffs behind Eielson Air Force Base to Chena Ridge). These hills protect Fairbanks from strong winds on three sides. On the fourth side, the south, the Alaska Range and the Coast Range beyond it are distant but effective blockades against wind and storms.

As a result, Fairbanks has, at ground level, one of the lowest wind conditions in the world. The lack of wind allows the air over the city to remain relatively stagnant. A further effect of this highly sheltered location is that Fairbanks is typically clear-skyed (except for summer thunderclouds which often form *within* the valley).

Without the insulating effect of a cloud cover, heat from the earth's surface radiates directly into space, cooling the ground. When the ground cools sufficiently (as in winter or on a summer night), it cools the nearby, lower layers of air. Then the usual trend toward cooler air at higher altitudes becomes inverted: the air closest to the ground becomes colder than the air at higher altitudes. This temperature inversion is very stable because the cold air is heavier and tends to just sit, inert on the ground. Fairbanks' inversions are considered among the most extreme in the world, with temperatures sometimes increasing 16°F (9°C) with each 100 feet of altitude.

Since an inversion resists vertical mixing of air, any pollution put into the air tends to stay in the layer it enters. Strong winds can break up inversions by mixing up the air, as occurs at Delta or Healy where wind funnels through nearby mountain passes. However, in the highly sheltered Fairbanks basin strong winds are infrequent. Therefore pollutants tend to move away from their sources horizontally and quite slowly — especially near the ground. As a result pollution levels in Fairbanks are comparable with those in Los Angeles even though that city has a population more than 200 times greater.

There is no known way to change the low wind or the inversion layers such as occur at Fairbanks. Consequently, the only ways to reduce pollution are to limit pollution sources. Decreasing auto traffic, for example, or use of care in selecting sites for power plants or other industrial developments will help. The mine-mouth power plant at Healy, Alaska is an example of a site well chosen to avoid buildup of air pollution. The Delta, Alaska area can probably also dilute pollution far better than sites closer to Fairbanks.

— Sue Ann Bowling
Oct 79:46

Ice Fog

An important characteristic of the arctic and subarctic environment, especially in winter, is the stillness of the air. Aircraft pilots in particular notice the change that winter brings as their craft speed steadily along, instead of bouncing around through summer's turbulent air.

As the sun retreats to near or below the horizon, less heating of the ground surface and the near-surface air occurs. If the sky is clear, the earth radiates its heat energy to the frigid reaches of space and then cools the air in contact with it. Cold, stagnant air near the ground results, often inverting the normal trend for decreasing air temperature with increasing altitude. Sometimes extreme inversions develop. At Fairbanks, where hills surround the city to further hamper air movement, the near-ground inversions are among the world's most extreme, as much as 16°F (9°C) each 100 feet (30 meters) of altitude.

The stagnation and horizontal layering of the air creates spectacular mirages and some effects that are less pleasing. Industrial pollution from urban areas of the Northern Hemisphere finds its way into the Arctic where it hangs suspended in multiple reddish-brown layers to signal the passersby that they haven't entirely escaped civilization.

Of immediate concern to residents of northern cities is the trapping of man-made pollutants by the steep inversions such as occur at Fairbanks. Most are concerned with one particular pollutant, ice fog, because they can see it, or more precisely, because of it they cannot see vehicles on the streets, or land at the local airport.

Ice fog forms from water vapor expelled into the air by people breathing, but mostly from water vapor ejected into the air from automobiles and smokestacks. Compared to warm air, cold air is able to hold very little water vapor. Air at room temperature, if saturated, can contain about 20 grams of water vapor per cubic meter, but air at -40°C can hold a maximum of only 0.1 grams, 200 times less. When air is cooled to the point of saturation, excess water condenses into either liquid or ice crystals, depending upon the temperature and also upon the presence of other particles which help supercooled water droplets to turn into ice crystals. (Supercooled water is that remaining liquid even though its temperature is below 32°F [0°C]). In clean air the resulting ice fog may not form until the temperature falls to -40°C, but if the air is dirty, the fog of tiny spherical, blocklike or platelet ice crystals can start to develop at temperatures as warm as -20°C.

In a way, ice fog is but a warning of conditions that also trap more lethal urban pollutants. The stagnant air within the near-ground inversion also traps carbon monoxide, nitrogen and sulfur oxides, lead and hydrocarbons. Even tiny amounts of carbon monoxide are bad, especially for young children, since prolonged exposure can permanently retard their mental processes. However, the ice fog particles perhaps combine, as do liquid water droplets, with other pollutants to create obnoxious or dangerous acid compounds.

The air in a place such as Fairbanks can be so stagnant and the inversions so severe (inversions of at least some degree occur here approximately 240 days each year) that the city's pollution becomes trapped in a comparatively tight box of small volume. It is for this reason that scientists say that this particular city is so susceptible to pollution and that control of pollution sources is essential. They point out that though Fairbanks has a population two hundred times less than Los Angeles, the levels of the pollution in the two cities are sometimes comparable.

Jul 81:497

CHAPTER FOUR
WATER AND ICE

The Recharge of Groundwater

A major concern of Borough planners is the adequacy of groundwater resources for domestic use. A standard estimate of personal use is from 75 to 100 gallons of water each day. Thus, a family of four requires from 110,000 to 150,000 gallons of water each year. For residences outside the city this water must come mainly from individual wells.

The wells draw water from aquifers that are mainly recharged each spring by the melting snow. The actual pathway of water to the well is not entirely known, but for those living above the valley, it must originate in the surrounding hills. The University's Institute of Water Resources estimates that from 1½ to 3 inches of the annual precipitation is effective in recharging the goundwater resources that are utilized by households. This amounts to about 0.9 to 1.9 gallons of recharge per square foot of land. Hence a family of four will use the amount of water collected by 1.4 to 3.8 acres of land.

This area can be compared to the one to five acre lot sizes required by Borough zoning codes. However, wells do not necessarily go dry if the recharge areas are covered with houses on one acre lots because the wastewater going into septic tanks and drainfields is effective in recharging aquifers. Without really meaning to, you may be practicing conservation through multiple use of a valuable resource. If so, be comforted as you slake your thirst — the neighbor is still alive who drank it first. — *Daniel W. Swift*
Apr 76:52

Recharge of Groundwater — Aquifers

Household wells draw water from aquifers that are recharged from precipitation which falls on the surrounding hills. The total annual average precipitation that falls on the Fairbanks area is only 12 inches, and of this amount only 10 to 25% ever reaches the aquifers where it becomes available for use. The rest is lost through evaporation and runoff. From the point of view of managing our groundwater resources, it is important to identify the areas and the characteristics of areas which have the highest efficiency for groundwater recharge.

The runoff of water is controlled by the slope of the land, the vegetative cover and the permeability of the soil. There is less runoff from ridge tops than from hillsides; from this point of view ridge tops are more efficient for groundwater recharge. Loess, which is wind-blown silt, is the common soil type in the surrounding hills and has a rather low permeability. Water-saturated frozen soils have zero permeability. On the other hand, broken rock covered only by a thin layer of topsoil has high permeability and this type of structure would be highly efficient in collecting groundwater. Buildings, roads and other types of human development may be considered poor collectors.

Plant covering tends to inhibit runoff, so from this point of view it greatly increases the efficiency of groundwater collection. On the other hand, plants during the summer months contribute to evaporation. For example, during the summer months much of the rainfall remains on the needles or leaves of trees where it is subsequently evaporated. Water that does reach the soil is taken up by the roots where it eventually goes back into the air by evaporation.

Only moisture that gets below the root level or that gets into the ground during inactive periods is effective in recharging the aquifers. As a result, groundwater is recharged only as a result of a heavy and prolonged rain or during the spring melt. However, penetration of moisture into the ground during inactive periods is inhibited by the frozen soil.

At present not enough is known to identify the prime recharge areas. However, studies being carried out by the University's Institute of Water Resources should help in identifying those areas.
— *Daniel W. Swift*
Jun 76:80

Freezing of Water

From the time we are in diapers until we are ferried across the River Styx, water is so much a part of life that we mostly take it for granted.

More than half of each living thing on Earth is water. In addition to being the all-pervading fluid of life, water is the custodian of most of the earth's available energy. More so than most substances, water is capable of storing much heat energy. As water moves within the global circulation of the atmosphere and the oceans it helps transport solar energy received in the tropics to the polar regions and thereby moderates the environment of the whole planet.

Water is said to be the universal solvent, able to dissolve most other substances. Also, it is the best wetting agent by virtue of its ability to bond onto and coat the surfaces of many materials, even hard, slick substances such as glass.

Water owes its array of strange properties to the unusual way oxygen and hydrogen atoms cling together to form water molecules. The atoms in most molecules are bonded together by only one of two kinds of forces, but a water molecule is held together by both kinds. This causes a tricky balancing act because the two forces each try to establish different spacings between the hydrogen and oxygen atoms. Furthermore, at least one of the forces is temperature-dependent and extends outside the molecule to affect nearby molecules.

This complex interplay of forces causes water to behave in a strange way when it is frozen into ice. Most substances become more dense as they are cooled, and are more dense in the frozen state than when liquid. But when water is cooled below $+4^{\circ}C$ it begins to expand. When the water freezes, the crucial bonding force that sets up the ice crystal array actually pushes the randomly milling crowds of liquid molecules apart into less-dense, uniform ranks. This is why ice floats on water and why frozen plumbing breaks.

In school we learned that a stirred beaker of ice and water remains exactly at $0^{\circ}C$ ($32^{\circ}F$), and therefore that this temperature is the freezing point. (The water tries to thaw the ice, and the ice tries to freeze the water, so the mixture must go to an equilibrium temperature which is the freezing point.) But water found in nature can undergo the establishment of fixed ordering of the molecules — the process we call freezing — over a wide range in temperature. In some circumstances, water will remain in liquid form down to $-40^{\circ}C$ (also $-40^{\circ}F$, the two scales being equal at this particular temperature).

Thin layers of water molecules around protein molecules or hydrocarbon molecules will freeze at temperatures as high as $+4^{\circ}C$ ($+39^{\circ}F$). Thus plants, being partly made up of protein, can receive frost damage at temperatures above "freezing" — something the northern gardener should keep in mind on cool spring or fall nights.

Aug 79:330

Permafrost

Permafrost forms when the mean annual temperature is approximately $27^{\circ}F$ ($-3^{\circ}C$).

The mean annual temperature in Fairbanks is near $27^{\circ}F$. Consequently, Fairbanks is a region of discontinuous permafrost. In areas of south slope, good drainage or little vegetation cover, the soil temperature will generally be above average and no permafrost will exist. On the other hand, north slopes or heavily vegetated areas often contain permafrost. The type of soil also is a factor; the wind-deposited silty soil on many of the hills around Fairbanks is prone to permafrost and lenses of nearly pure ice.

Serious problems have occurred when houses have been built on frozen soil containing a high percentage of ice. When the ice melts due to heat from the house, damaging collapses can occur. Unless special precautions are taken, it is unwise to build on permafrost.

Though it may not cause any special problems, permafrost is now forming on the north side of large buildings constructed on previously unfrozen ground. The buildings shield the soil from sunlight and thereby allow the average soil temperature to fall below $27^{\circ}F$.

Apr 76:21

Fox Permafrost Tunnel

Sloping gradually down into a frozen hillside near Fox, the CRREL (Cold Regions Research and Engineering Laboratory) permafrost tunnel provides a fascinating portal into the past. Originally dug by the U. S. Army to test methods of tunneling in frozen silts and gravels, the tunnel penetrates through a 40,000-year-old accumulation of soil, gravel, ice, wood and bones. Enough organic material is distributed in the material to enable radiocarbon dating of many of the objects seen in the tunnel wall.

Down at the bottom are the gold-bearing gravels, laid down perhaps as long as 100,000 years ago. Above the gravels are layers of debris-laden mucks composed mainly of fine-grained windblown soil (loess). Downslope creep over the years has mixed up this material. Pieces of trees and ancient bones show in the tunnel walls; some are tagged with signs showing their ages.

Spectacular ice wedges are cross sectioned by the tunnel as are lenticular lenses of pure ice, stacked one atop the other. How these lenses form is evidently a mystery, but it is known that water migrates through

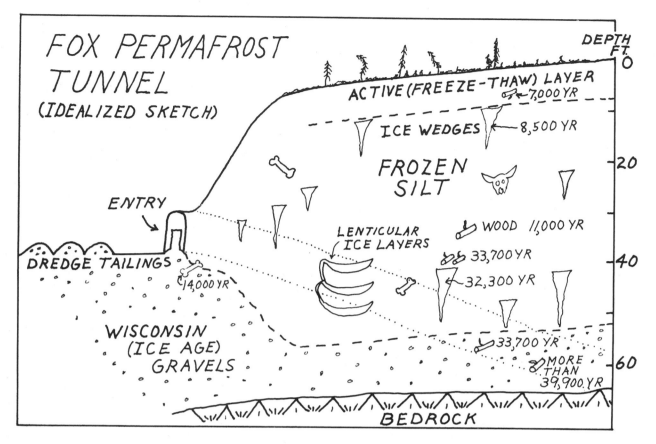

FOX PERMAFROST TUNNEL (IDEALIZED SKETCH)

the muck when it is near the freezing point and somehow accumulates to form the ice bodies.

Those lucky enough to have the University's Dr. Earl Beistline guide them on a tour through the Fox tunnel receive a valuable short course in the recent past. In the dim lamplight one can almost see the old miners of 70 years ago picking away in their hand-driven tunnels much like this one. And the -5°C temperature almost carries one back to the ice ages when the now-entombed bones jutting out of the wall were parts of living animals ranging over the Tanana Valley.

Jul 77:176

Permafrost and Water Runoff

In temperate climates, precipitation tends to percolate into the ground rather than to run off in open stream flow. Less than 20% of precipitation falling on the watershed of the Mississippi River actually flows down Ole Man River.

But in arctic and subarctic areas, rivers typically carry 55 to 65% of precipitation falling onto their watersheds. The reason is that permafrost prevents the downward percolation of water and forces it to run off at and very near the ground surface.

One of the consequences of the high runoff is that northern streams are much more prone to flooding

than temperate zone rivers. Another is that they have higher eroding and silt-carrying capabilities.

Critical to the control of water runoff in the north is the cover of moss and other vegetation of the tundra, bogs and forests. A thick layer of moss acts much like a sponge laid over the permafrost to slow down the movement of water across the ground surface.

The removal of moss and timber for mining apparently had severe effects on stream flow during gold rush days in Alaska and Canada. It is said that in the course of just a few years miners began to notice faster runoff and less evenness in stream flow. No doubt the removal of overburden also melted some of the permafrost and allowed greater downward percolation of water.

Fortunately, the mosses and forests do recover from the effects of mining, just as they do from the temporary destruction of forest fires. Many areas that old photographs show to be totally barren through the actions of early-day miners now have recovered so well that they show little obvious evidence of man's having been there.

May 79:316

Permafrost and Artesian Water

Most people are greatly pleased when they strike artesian water, but recent events on Farmers Loop

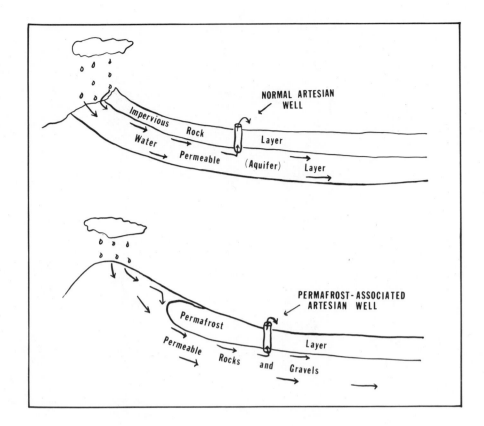

Road near Fairbanks show that an artesian well can constitute a geologic hazard instead of being beneficial. A well driven there yields an artesian flow that, so far, cannot be stopped. The result is unwanted flooding and icing of nearby property.

Artesian wells are common in some parts of the country, especially in the midwestern states. Artesian wells there result from drilling through an impervious capping layer into a water-bearing layer which is sloping. Water enters the aquifer layer at a higher elevation than the top of the well and thereby creates a pressure head to drive water up the well.

As shown in the diagram, the situation on Farmers Loop Road is much the same. Water enters the soil on the hills above the road and is trapped under the permafrost layer at the foot of the hills. Since the permafrost extends uphill above the wellhead, a pressure head is created, and so water flows up the well.

A normal artesian well can be stopped by simply capping the pipe. Apparently, water flowing upward through the well on Farmers Loop Road has thawed the surrounding permafrost and made the soil around the well permeable to water. To stop the flow it probably will be necessary either to refreeze the soil around the pipe or in some other way make it impervious to water pressure.

May 77:162

Ice at the Door

Last year some area residents had problems with wolves at the door. This year Bill Russell, near Fox, has a worse problem — ice has formed at his door and all around his house.

For the last three months, ground water has been rising up in a heated crawl space under Russell's new house. Now two to three feet of ice covers his yard and contributes to continued flooding of his attached garage.

A mile or so beyond Mr. Russell's house, Felix Pedro's monument is having a similar problem. Overflow ice forming from ground water has half-submerged the monument. Before spring, the monument may entirely disappear.

Trying to forestall further damage, Russell uses a large digging machine to cut trenches in the ice covering his yard. This way he hopes to drain away the water trapped beneath the overflow ice. For years, road maintenance crews have had the same problem, especially with the roads leading north from Fairbanks.

Mar 76:5

Cause of Overflow Ice

Two conditions are required for the formation of overflow ice.

Ice at the Door: *Overflow ice threatens the livability of a house near Fairbanks.*

Ice at the Door: *Debbie Davis (who did the layout of this volume) stands tall beside nearly ice-covered Pedro Monument.*

The first requirement is rather obvious — the air temperature must be low enough to cause freezing. Freezing of the ground surface and of the surface of a stream or lake forms an impervious layer that water cannot flow through. Once this happens, it can contribute to the second requirement for the formation of overflow ice.

That requirement is for the existence of water under enough pressure (i.e., with enough of a hydrostatic head) to rise to the surface. Even with a thick ice layer over stream or ground water, a strong enough hydrostatic head will cause the water to break through and overflow the surface.

If it is cold, the water breaking through will soon freeze before flowing far. Thus, peculiar glacier-like formations are built up, layer upon layer.

To see the effects, drive out to the vicinity of the monument to Felix Pedro on the Steese Highway beyond Fox.

Mar 76:20

Ice Lenses Versus Highways

Over much of their length, Alaska's highways have, like a wrinkled old man, special character. It's not the horizontal curves that make these roads interesting, it is the ones that go up and down.

It takes the neophyte Alaskan driver only one broken axle or battered head to realize that a DIP sign usually means business. If there is a SLOW sign and a DIP sign, be extra careful. And if, in addition, there is a yellow sawhorse beside the road, it may be wise to get out and walk ahead of the car before proceeding onward.

The culprit is usually the thawing of ground ice beneath the highway. In some permafrost areas crossed by roads, there are extensive near-surface sheets of ice that have been formed over hundreds or thousands of years. Several feet of settling can occur within the few years following the removal of tree and moss cover that previously protected the ice from the sun's heat.

Sometimes the roads cross over near-vertical ice lenses which are usually less than a meter (three feet) across but several meters tall. Thawing of these lenses allows extensive settling of the roadway overhead.

In the years before blacktop, the Alaska Road Commission personnel used to decorate the resulting ditches with red flags; sometimes they shoved more gravel into them. Nowadays the solution is to add more blacktop to these precipitous trenches across the roadway. In some places so much blacktop is poured in over the years that extended stalactite-like sheets of tar have been built up below the road surface.

May 78:94

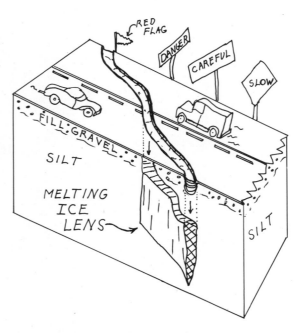

Ice Lenses Versus Highways: *A somewhat mislabeled diagram; the ice object below the roadway is actually an ice wedge.*

Ice Wedges

Probably the world's most well-known ice wedge (also called ice lens) is the one shown in the accompanying photograph by geologist Troy Péwé. Since Dr. Péwé took this picture near Livengood, Alaska in 1949, it has appeared in many widely-distributed publications. The picture is particularly useful because it clearly illustrates those characteristics of ice wedges that have been used to explain wedge formation.

A vertical ice wedge like the one shown is thought to start out as a crack created by contraction of fine-grained soil masses when the ground temperature falls below about 0°F (-17°C) for a long period. The cracking forms large polygon structures, in shape similar to that seen when mud dries. The cracking is reported to make loud popping noises, so it happens suddenly.

Afterwards, the crack is filled with new ice formed from summer thaw water or water molecules that migrate through the frozen soil and ice to deposit as ice in the crack. Then when the next prolonged cold spell comes along the crack opens again through contraction of the cold ground. This cycle repeats for many years, leading to the highly folliated (sheet-like) structure apparent in the wedge itself. Each growth cycle may increase the thickness of the wedge only by a millimeter or so, more at the top than at the bottom, as would be expected by a crack opening at the top.

The flat top of the wedge marks the line of annual freeze and thaw, and hence the top also of the

Ice Wedges: *The foliated structure of this classic example of an ice wedge indicates a layer-by-layer buildup of the wedge over hundreds of years. Annual thawing prevents the ice wedge from growing above the top of the permafrost line and thereby gives it a distinct, flat top. (Photo by Troy Péwé.)*

permafrost on either side of the wedge. Though the soil above the wedge probably also undergoes the cracking that could lead to wedge formation, each year's summer thaw would destroy the embryonic development and thereby prevent growth in the soil above the permafrost.

Dec 79:257

Summer Freezing of Wells

During the course of a year, the temperature of the air fluctuates more than the temperature of the soil just at the ground surface. In addition to having a lesser seasonal variation, the ground normally has a higher mean annual temperature than the air. The reason is that snow cover insulates the ground and thereby inhibits heat loss from the soil in winter. During summer, when the snow is gone, the flow of

energy from the air to the colder soil below is comparatively efficient, especially if there is not a moss layer.

During the year the soil temperature right at the ground surface typically varies by 35° to 90°F (20° to 50°C). The variation is least in wetter terrains. Below the ground surface, the seasonal variation in temperature diminishes rapidly with depth. Approximately every 20 feet the variation reduces by a factor of 10.

Consequently, at a depth of 20 feet the ground temperature fluctuates seasonally only a few degrees, and at 40 feet the fluctuation is only a few tenths of a degree. At 60 feet the variation is hard to measure.

Seasonal fluctuations in temperature propagate downward at a rate of about 5 feet per month. Thus, the coldest temperature at a depth of 10 feet may occur in March, two months after the month of coldest average air temperature. At 30-foot depth, the coldest temperature is reached in midsummer.

One result of the lag in ground temperature at depth can be the shock of having one's well freeze up any time during the year. This happens to wells driven through permafrost with temperature enough below freezing so that the presence of the warmer well, with its flowing water, is unable to maintain the soil around the well unfrozen. The wave of low temperature creeping down each year may be just enough to cause the soil around the pipe to freeze up.

Nov 78:271

Spring Freeze-up

Warmer springtime weather and lengthening daylight should signal to the northerner that winter's troubles are over. But just when you think you have it made, the sewer or the well freezes up. If not unfair, this quirk of fate seems a bit illogical.

One easy way to understand why the pipes freeze up so late in the season is to think about coming in from the cold wearing heavy rubber boots. One's feet stay cold for many minutes, even if the booted feet are propped up near a hot stove. It takes a long time for the heat to penetrate the boots. Then one may suddenly realize that the boots have become very hot, and will feel hot for many minutes after they are taken away from the stove. This example shows that energy is not transferred instantaneously.

So it is with freezing soil in winter except that the transfer of heat energy is much slower than in the rubber boot. As the top soil layer freezes, it gives up heat that is carried away by the air. Heat given up by the freezing of the soil below must be conducted away through the soil, a slower process. The level of freezing in soil can move downward as fast as three feet (one meter) per month in water-saturated gravel cleared of moss and snow. However, in ground that is snow covered or which has a high humus content, the freezing will proceed downward more slowly.

Hopefully, the buried water pipes and the sewer are below the level of deepest annual freezing. If not, they usually will freeze long after the coldest weather. In extreme cases, the freeze-up might even come in early summer.

Apr 80:394

Soft Springtime Roads

Why is it that northern roads which can be dry in fall are almost invariably wet in springtime?

One possible source of moisture is the melting of snow and ice on the road surface, and sometimes runoff water flows onto the roadway. But roads that have no runoff problem and which have been kept clear of snow and ice all winter still can be wet at breakup.

The real culprit is upward migration of soil moisture during and after freeze-up. The seriousness of the problem depends upon the composition of the roadbed and the availability of moisture in the roadbed material or the soil below. Normally, water exists in the soil in three forms — vapor, liquid water that is free to move through pore spaces in the soil, and liquid water that is relatively tightly adhered to the surfaces of soil particles.

In fine-grained soils (silts and clays) with high water content, the free liquid water in the pore spaces moves toward that part of the soil having the lowest temperature. Since in winter the ground surface is colder than the soil below, the free water moves upward. At the freezing line much of the free water is converted to ice.

Water in vapor form moves upward too. Vapor pressure is highest where the temperature is highest, and water vapor, like any gas, moves from a region of high pressure to low pressure. The resulting upward transport of water vapor is particularly important in sandy or gravelly soils. These soils have large pore spaces through which the water vapor can move easily. Where the pore spaces are large, the forces that move liquid water upward are less effective. Being something akin to capillary forces, they operate best when the pore spaces are small.

Even after the roadbed is frozen, there still is upward migration of moisture through the frozen soil toward the cold road surface. Frozen soil is funny stuff since it still contains liquid water. The liquid water is probably mostly that tightly adhered to soil particles; perhaps it takes part in the continuing upward migration of moisture.

As winter progresses, more and more water moves upward. The frozen water content can become so high after several months of freezing weather that the soil volume can, in extreme cases, nearly double — the phenomenon called soil heave.

Then comes spring, and anyone having lived through northern breakup knows the sort of quagmire that results from the melting of ice-rich, fine-grained soils.

Dec 78:268

Frost Heaving of Pilings

Freezing soil can create such great upward forces on telephone poles, bridge pilings and similar objects that they are literally lifted out of the ground. Several factors control the amount of frost heaving and the consequent lifting force on a piling.

Frost heaving is greatest in wet, fine-grained soils — clays and silts — since they undergo the greatest expansion of their volume as they freeze.

This Old Bridge: *Frost-heaved piling of a bridge spanning the outlet of Clearwater Lake, eight miles southeast of Big Delta, Alaska. (Photograph by Mark F. Meier, 8/15/51, provided by Troy Péwé.)*

The expansion is not caused only by the freezing of the water contained in the soil but also by the freezing of new water that migrates upward from below the frost line during and after the freezing of the soil.

The colder the ground surface, the greater is the transport of water upward. Freezing of this new water can create layers of pure ice within the top layers of the soil, even after the soil has become frozen. Consequently, frost heaving can continue right on through the winter if there is an adequate supply of water from below.

Russian experiments have shown that some clays, as they freeze, can nearly double in volume, especially if saturated with water rich in aluminum, iron or calcium. These elements help foster the upward migration of water as the soil freezes.

Upward frost heaving pressure on the bottom of a piling set in wet, fine-grained soil can easily be 60 pounds per square inch (4 kilograms per square centimeter). Similar forces act on the sides of the piling if the soil can form a bond to the piling as it freezes. If the temperature drops well below freezing, the upward forces become even larger.

Thus, a piling 20 inches (50 centimeters) in diameter set four feet (120 centimeters) into soil that freezes at least that deep will be lifted upward with a total force of approximately 200,000 pounds (90,000 kilograms). Ninety percent of this force is on the sides rather than the bottom of the piling. It is just about enough force to lift an engine of the Alaska Railroad. In one year, a piling may be lifted upward a foot (25 centimeters) or more, though in most instances the heaving is less. If conditions are favorable to continued heaving year after year — repeated freezing and thawing of the soil wherein the piling is set plus plenty of available ground water — the piling eventually will be lifted entirely out of the ground.

Jan 79:279

This Old Bridge

Bridges can fall both up and down, as is illustrated by this unusual photograph taken in 1951 by geolo-

78

gist Mark F. Meier and provided through the courtesy of another well-known geologist, Troy Péwé.

Built over the outlet to Clearwater Lake, near Delta, Alaska, the bridge has wooden pilings. Those set near the center of the river are in soil that remains unfrozen all year long. Near the edges of the stream, the pilings are in wet soil that undergoes annual freezing and thawing.

During the freezing process there is expansion of water-laden soil beneath each piling. In water-saturated, fine-grained soil, the expansion during freezing can nearly double the volume of the soil. The result is terrific upward force on the bottom of the piling — as much as 60 pounds per square inch (4 kilograms per square centimeter). Each year a piling can be pushed upward a foot (25 cm) or more, so the tenting up of the end of the Clearwater bridge is the result of repeated frost heaving over a period of several years.

Jan 80:368

Solifluction

Like loose folds of mossy skin hanging down the flanks of sleeping giants, solifluction flows can be seen on the sides of hills of interior Alaska. Travelers along the Steese and Taylor and other highways traversing the upland country can observe these flows, often lobe-shaped on their lower edges.

Solifluction is a slow downward flow of water-saturated soil. It is promoted by the existence of permafrost which traps snow and ice melt within the surface layer, making it more fluid. The whole surface layer tends to move together as a cohesive mass.

Another mechanism by which soil moves slowly downhill is creep. Each year as the soil freezes, it is pushed upward perpendicular to the sloping ground surface. When melting occurs in spring, the soil falls vertically downward, thereby ending up slightly farther downhill than where it was the previous fall. In contrast to unitary flow in solifluction, soil creep moves the soil particles individually and thereby tends to mix them up as the creep proceeds.

May 78:229

Roadcuts

A source of cheap, sometimes mind bending, entertainment is a new roadcut. From the car window a cut may not look especially exciting, but closer inspection often reveals the fresh cut to be a revealing window into the past — if one can understand what there is to see.

Recent roadway improvements on the University's Fairbanks campus opened up a 40,000-year record of windblown silt (loess) deposition, volcanic ash falls, soil formation and disturbances caused by frost action. Several knowledgeable geologists, including Robert M. Thorson and Richard D. Reger, were close at hand so it was possible to develop a fair interpretation of the sequence of events that caused the complex layering seen in the cut bank.

The picture is one of changing climate. Silt exposed near the bottom of the cut appears to be laid down by winds blowing off the glacial outwash plains to the south during a period of extensive glaciation that occurred more than 40,000 years ago. Afterwards, during an interglacial period, plants and trees grew for many years and developed a thick, brown soil layer.

One of the roadcut's curiosities is the folding that developed in the ancient soil layer and in a new layer of silt the winds of a later time deposited upon it. The folding must have taken place at a time when permafrost anchored the deeper soil but when freezing and thawing of the soil near the surface caused that soil to move downhill. That movement, called solifluction, is a common phenomenon frequently seen on hillside slopes of Alaska and northern Canada. Like folds on an elephant's skin, solifluction lobes skirt many tundra-covered hills. Solifluction can occur on quite gentle slopes because it involves saturation of the near-surface layer with water, and that causes the soil to lose bearing strength. Even so, solifluction typically occurs very slowly, perhaps at a rate of only an inch or two a year. Hence, the fold in the roadcut may have taken the better part of a century to form.

Subsequent to the folding, a new glaciation occurred in the Alaska Range to the south, and again the winds carried in new loess. The light-colored silt layer above was laid down until, about 14,000 years ago, the glaciers receded and no longer supplied new silt for the wind to carry. Mosses and plants grew on the surface and developed the layer of soil found there now.

Deep within the roadcut is a whitish layer of volcanic ash, one of several found in central Alaska and adjacent regions. Several volcanic eruptions during the past hundred thousand years have created widespread ash layers across Alaska and western Canada. These serve nicely as time markers. The ash layer in the campus roadcut is thought to be the Old Crow ash bed probably derived from an eruption, more than 53,000 years ago, of the Wrangell volcanoes or perhaps from another similar volcanic source near the Alaska-Canada border.

Dec 80:452

Pingos

Pingos are surface blisters or ice mounds, 50 to 500 feet across, that thrust up from otherwise flat terrain. In the Arctic, pingos tend to form on the

Roadcuts: *How did it happen? Richard Reger points out the folding of a buried soil layer to a fellow geologist. When the soil layer slid over itself, the top of the permafrost must have been at the level of Dr. Reger's outstretched hand. Repeated freezing and thawing of the soil above caused it to creep downslope and override the frozen material below.*

sites of drained lakes as the thawed silt beneath the former lake, over many hundreds of years, gradually refreezes. Like a closed tin can full of water that bulges or bursts as the last of the liquid freezes, the earth's surface yields from the freezing expansion of watery silt below the lake bed.

In the valleys of the interior, a slightly different process is involved and the pingos are smaller. Here pressure from a "head" or reservoir of water underground in the uplands occasionally will uplift the surface soil and vegetative cover, particularly if the soil is silty and not well-drained. Cracks form, water finds its way near enough to the surface to freeze, forming more cracks, and still more freezing and expansion takes place until a mound is created 5 to 15 feet above local elevation. In the process, the original soil becomes well-drained owing to the pingo's elevation, and sometimes vigorous stands of poplar, birch or aspen will gradually dominate the pingo in stark contrast to the wetland willows, moss and scrub spruce that otherwise typify the silty valley floor.

— *John M. Miller*
Nov 76:33

Rock Glaciers

An active rock glacier is a stream of blocky rock containing ice in the interstitial spaces (the voids between the rocks) that flows downslope by virtue of viscous (molasses-like) flow within the ice component. The top of an active rock glacier flows faster than its base. Consequently, near the toe of a rock glacier, material from the top rolls or slides down the front of the rock glacier to form a slope lying at the angle of repose of the loose rock composing the glacier. By means of this characteristic slope at the toe, one can recognize the rock glacier and that it is active and moving.

Rock glaciers occur by the hundreds in the Alaska Range. They occur in the Wrangells and many other mountain ranges around the world including the San Juan Mountains of Colorado and the Sierra Nevada of California.

For a rock glacier to exist several conditions must be met. There must be a source of blocky rock such as a weathering cliff or mountain slope or perhaps even the terminal moraine of a dying ice glacier. Secondly, the mean annual temperature must be low enough for water percolating down through the

Rock Glaciers: *Two views of a mile-long active rock glacier lying just above the Richardson Highway at Mile 207.7. The rock glacier originates in an empty cirque on Rainbow Mountain. The lower photograph shows particularly well the characteristic steep apron lying at the angle of repose above the toe of the glacier.*

blocky rock to freeze and form an ice matrix in the spaces between the rocks. Third, there must be a slope for the rock glacier to flow along since the force that gives it life is gravity.

The upper surfaces of active rock glaciers in the Alaska Range have been observed to move forward about a meter per year, whereas the motion of the front is about half that amount. The top surface often shows longitudinal ridges and, near the front, transverse ridges that are convex downslope appear.

If the source of rock debris disappears or if the climate warms up, an active rock glacier will become inactive. Consequently, the study of rock glaciers can yield information on past climatic changes.

Sep 78:251

Hoar-Frost Formation

Among winter's beauties are the intricate crystals — called hoar-frost — that form on branches, wires, poles and other objects. Hoar-frost is a sort of wintertime cousin to summer's dew and develops by similar processes.

Dew and hoar-frost accumulate on objects when there is more moisture in the air than the air can carry. Warm air carries in suspension more liquid water than does cold air.

The temperature at which the air is totally saturated is called the dew point. If the temperature of humid air is lowered until the humidity is 100%, then the dew point has been reached. Further cooling requires that the air lose part of its suspended water; the loss can come through rainfall, snowfall or the formation of dew or hoar-frost.

Curiously enough, pure water suspended in clean

WOODEN POLES, HOAR-FROST ON NORTH SIDE ONLY.

METAL POLE, NO FROST.

Hoar-Frost Formation: *By late winter, intricate buildups of hoar-frost crystals have formed on wooden poles and other objects. Warming rays of the sun cause evaporation of whatever frost may have formed on the south side of vertical poles and trees. Conduction within metal poles causes enough heat transfer to remove the hoar-frost crystals entirely from the pole surface.*

air remains in liquid form down to temperatures near -40°C (also -40°F). Below that temperature, the liquid droplets turn to ice — ice fog being a possible result. However, the normal ice fog known and loved in some northern cities comes from man-made injection of water into cold still air.

If, when air is cooled down, it contains enough water to cause the dew point to be above freezing, then dew forms. But if the air is sufficiently dry that the dew point is below 0°C (32°F), then hoar-frost forms.

Hoar-frost consists of crystalline structures that grow from water vapor evaporated from liquid droplets suspended in air. Once hoar-frost crystals form, they can remain as long as conditions for their existence are favorable. But if the crystals or the air around them are warmed up, evaporation from the crystal surfaces leads to their demise. Hence in late winter we see the sun's warming rays removing hoar-frost from the south sides of objects.

It is worth one's while to look at hoar-frost crystals closely. They occur in an intricate variety of forms — needles, cups, plates, fern-like and feather-like — depending upon the temperature at which they developed.

Apr 79:300

Ice Travelers, Beware!

One of nature's nasty tricks for the unwary traveler is the little-known fact that there is a particularly dangerous speed for crossing lake or ocean ice. Moving either more slowly or more rapidly than this dangerous critical speed makes for a safer crossing.

It is not immediately obvious why there is a critical speed at which a moving object — a truck, a snow machine, an ice skater or a taxiing aircraft — is most likely to break through the ice. The reason is that the object moving across the ice at other than very slow speed creates a wave in the ice, i.e., a moving deflection of the ice. Just as a sound wave moves at fixed speed through air, the wave in the ice moves at fixed speed. The speed of the wave in the ice increases with the ice thickness and the depth of the water beneath the ice. A typical speed for the wave in foot-thick (30 cm) sea ice over water 20 feet deep (7 meters) is 20 mph (32 kph).

Now if the object creating the wave moves at the same speed as the wave, the object stays with the wave, just as a successful surfer stays with a water wave riding into the beach. Staying with the wave is great fun for the surfer, but it is disaster in the making for the object riding with the ice wave. The trouble is that the effective weight of the object on the ice builds up and becomes many times the static weight.

Engineers have known about this dangerous phenomenon for many years, but only this year a new method of calculating the stresses on the ice has made it possible to learn how much the effective weight increases when an object moves at the critical speed across the ice. Devised by Professors Howard Bates and Lewis Shapiro of the Geophysical Institute, the new method shows that a 10-ton truck moving at critical speed across ice can create the same breaking stress as a slowly moving truck weighing 100 to 150 tons. Moral: drive slowly on ice to avoid hitting the critical speed.

May 80:398

Thick Ice is Best

A recent article in this column dealt with the danger of traveling across ice at certain critical speeds where stresses build up and drastically increase the likelihood of breaking through. The reason is that an object moving at the critical speed stays abreast of a wave it creates in the ice below, and in so doing causes the stress in the ice to grow to a limit that can exceed the strength of the ice.

I cited an example wherein a 10-ton truck moving at 20 mph across foot-thick ice floating on 20 feet of water could stress the ice as much as a stopped truck weighing 100 to 150 tons. Reader Phil Johnson of Fairbanks, who is knowledgeable about operations on ice and particularly about the take-off and landing of heavy aircraft on ice, points out that the example I quote is not relevant to thick ice over deep water.

Mr. Johnson rightly notes that the stress created by an object moving across ice varies in a complex way that depends upon the salt content of the ice, the ice thickness and the depth of water below. Whereas the critical speed on foot-thick ice over 20 feet of water is about 20 mph, the critical speed on ice 3 feet thick atop 100 feet of water is near 40 mph. More importantly, the stress buildup in thick ice when a vehicle moves at critical speed across it is comparatively much less than over thin ice. The buildup in certain favorable circumstances is less than twice that caused by a stopped vehicle. This is why it is possible to operate heavy aircraft weighing in excess of 100 tons from runways on sea or lake ice only 4 or more feet thick.

Mr. Johnson gives a hint or two on ice safety. He notes that if one can successfully accelerate through the critical speed — as when an aircraft takes off — the stress in the ice rapidly drops off at greater speed. Further he says, "if you can drive onto the ice above the critical speed . . . you are in good shape unless you want to stop."

Jun 80:402

Ice Travel

Each northern fall brings the time of travel on

newly-frozen lakes and rivers, and the question of how thick must the ice be. A general lack of reported measurements on ice thickness for safe travel suggests that successful ice travelers do not measure the ice thickness very often, and unsuccessful ones are too busy to add to the public data pool.

Nevertheless, one can be safe travelling across ice at low speed in a heavy vehicle by following a simple rule given by ice-travel expert Phil Johnson of Fairbanks. Do not venture out unless the thickness of the ice in inches is five times the square root of the vehicle weight in tons. Hence a 2-ton vehicle needs seven inches of ice, and a 4-ton vehicle needs ten inches.

More complex methods are available to compute the load-bearing ability of fresh water ice under various conditions. These methods, and some very useful hints on ice travel, are contained in a new document entitled, *A Guide for Operating Cars and Light Trucks on a Floating Ice Sheet*. It is available from Phil Johnson Engineering, 1045 Lakeview Terrace, Fairbanks, Alaska 99701.

Sep 80:430

Snow in Alaskan Literature

For explorer Vilhjalmur Stefansson snow was something to travel on, build houses out of or eat. In his *Arctic Manual* written for the "Air Corps of the United States Army," the worst thing Stefansson says of snow is, "Toward spring . . . it then becomes granular, mushy, and you and your sledge sink into it as if the drifts were bins of wheat."

Stefansson noted that Eskimos have at least one fundamental discovery to their credit, they being the only peoples of ancient or modern times to build a dome without a scaffold. He claims that it is not the stickiness of snow that allows the Eskimo to avoid temporary supports; rather he implies that it is cleverness in shaping and setting snow blocks of proper consistency.

When it comes to eating snow, Stefansson's only admonition is to be careful where you get it from if there are dogs around.

Jack London dumped snow on the cheechako foolish enough "To Build a Fire" under a spruce tree in the short story of that name, snow that finally caused the cheechako's death. Depending upon when and where he wanted to create a sense of misery or hardship, Jack London put snow into many of his short stories. In several, the word "snow" appears on either the first or the last page.

And as the Northern Lights throb overhead, the driven snow swirls through the passages of Robert Service's poetry, clinging here and there to complete a rhyme or, à la Jack London, to add to the sense of loneliness, horror or, on rare occasion, beauty.

Stefansson's snow is a material to be used to advantage, but the snow of London and Service becomes a living force which, along with the cold and darkness of the northern winter night, fights every traveler — and usually wins.

Apr 78:43

Falling Snowflakes

Snowflakes, cylindrical rocket bodies without tail fins, skydivers and other irregularly shaped bodies tend to fall through the air with their flattest sides downward. This behavior seemingly defies the logic that says an object should orient itself to slip through the air with the least resistance.

The reason for the unexpected orientation of a falling object is the turbulence it creates in the air it falls through. When a snowflake or other body first starts to fall it is moving so slowly that the air passes around it in smooth layers, the so-called laminar flow. As long as the flow is laminar, the air does not act on the snowflake to change its original orientation, even though there is some resistance to the motion because the object pushes some air aside and, because the air is viscous, the object tries to drag the nearest air along with it. The resistance is directly proportional to the fall speed.

Even a snowflake eventually reaches a fall speed that creates turbulence. The air rushing past it (from the snowflake's point of view) curls in behind it in swirling patterns that vastly increase the resistance to the downward motion of the snowflake. The faster the motion and the larger the falling object, the greater becomes the turbulence, and the total resistance now is proportional to the square of the fall speed.

In a real sense, the turbulence increases the area of moving material passing through the air; the area becomes that of the snowflake itself plus the area that the attached turbulent air presents to the surroundings. Even a needle-shaped snow crystal falling pointed end downward, through the action of turbulence, effectively has a resistance many times that which the needle would have if it merely had to push enough air aside to allow its own passage.

The only way the snowflake can minimize the turbulent resistance is to slow down, and the way to slow down if you are a snowflake is to put your biggest face forward so that there is even more air to push against. By putting the biggest area forward, an object minimizes the total resistance to its forward motion through a fluid or a gas, and that is just what our logic says it should do — minimize resistance.

The turbulence not only causes an object to orient until the biggest area is presented to the direction of motion, it also makes the object flutter and move in circular patterns. Falling pieces of cardboard, leaves,

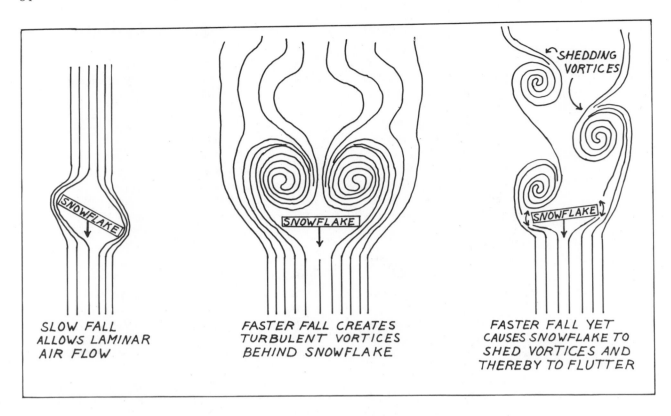

SLOW FALL
ALLOWS LAMINAR
AIR FLOW

FASTER FALL CREATES
TURBULENT VORTICES
BEHIND SNOWFLAKE

FASTER FALL YET
CAUSES SNOWFLAKE TO
SHED VORTICES AND
THEREBY TO FLUTTER

Falling Snowflakes: *Turbulence causes a snowflake to fall flat side downwards.*

snowflakes and even spent rocket motors flutter as they fall. The fluttering results from parcels of the turbulent air breaking away from their attachment to the falling object. Each parcel is in the form of an eddy, a spiralling vortex of motion that seems to take up a life of its own, like a dust devil. When each vortex breaks away, the falling object is given a sideways kick.

Yet another consequence of turbulence is that snowflakes and other bodies tend to catch up with each other. A snowflake caught in the turbulent wake of another tends to move faster and so can collide with the flake ahead and combine with it. This is the same effect that allows a motorcyclist to draft in behind a big truck and get a free, if somewhat dangerous, ride and why geese fly a V-formation; all except the head goose have easier flying. It's also why fish swim in schools; each fish senses the wake of the others ahead and swims accordingly. It's also is the same reason why a group of skydivers are sometimes able to move together to join hands and fall together as a group.

Dec 80:454

How Glaciers Move

Though the terminal end (lower end) of a glacier may be stationary, or even retreating uphill, the ice within the glacier continually moves downhill. The speed of this motion ranges from a few centimeters per day to more than 10 meters per day, but normal flow rates are generally nearer the lower figure.

If the ice at the base of a glacier is much below the temperature of freezing, as happens in winter, or perhaps even in summer at high altitude or in polar regions, the ice bonds tightly to the rock below. Then, the entire motion is within the glacier. The ice itself deforms as individual ice crystals warp and creep past each other.

Most of the deformational creep takes place in the deepest layer of the ice, near to the basal layer. It is here that the greatest stress is placed upon the ice because the stress is proportional to the thickness of ice above. Consequently, little deformation in the near-surface glacier ice occurs; the ice there is mostly carried along by the motions below.

Ice deforms most easily when it is warm. Especially in winter, the ice near the glacier's surface can be comparatively brittle, a fact that helps explain why crevasses form. These tensional cracks or other types of breakage occur where or when changes in stress are too abrupt or rapid for deformational creep to keep up with.

In summer, when the basal layer of the glacier ice warms up to near its melting point, a glacier begins to move by sliding on its bed. Thawing and refreezing take place, and water lubricates the rock surface.

The pace quickens as both sliding and creep act in unison to move ice downhill.

Investigators are finding that the overall rate of glacier flow changes hour by hour and day by day, as well as with the seasons. The reasons for the variation are not understood, though availability of water in the basal layers is suspected to be a main cause. In some instances speedups have been observed after a few days of increased rainfall.

Jul 80:415

Surging Glaciers

Alaska and the Yukon Territory have surging glaciers — ones that advance rapidly at regular intervals. Surging is the sliding forward of the ice at great rates; some glaciers in full surge can advance as much as 100 m (333 ft) per day.

Although surge-type glaciers are fairly common in Alaska and the Yukon — there are several hundred or more — the mechanism of surges is still unknown. Surges are not caused by earthquakes, avalanches, or local increases in snow accumulation, but by some instability which occurs internal to the glacier. No particular size or shape of glacier is required to induce surges. Surging glaciers are not found in one particular climatic zone — some occur in very wet maritime environments and some in drier near-continental environments. Surging glaciers occur in the St. Elias Mountains, eastern Wrangell Mountains, and Alaska Range, but few, if any, are found in the Chugach Mountains.

In 1888, the Tlingit Indians of Yakutat described for a visiting geographer what today would be called a glacial surge that years ago overwhelmed a settlement at the head of Icy Bay in southeastern Alaska.

The Variegated Glacier, just south of the Hubbard Glacier in the St. Elias Mountains, surges at about 20-year intervals. It last surged in 1964-65, when it advanced 6000 m (over 3 miles) in one year's time. Since the early 1970s, scientific field expeditions led by the Geophysical Institute's Dr. Will Harrison have measured and monitored the motion of the Variegated Glacier to learn more about its evolution between surges and the physical changes associated with massive ice advancement. Evidence gathered from this work suggests that the most rapid movement of the Variegated Glacier occurs in summer; the increased sliding of the glacier on its bed probably has something to do with the input of melt water there. This hypothesis is a departure from two more popular ideas for the causes of glacier surging: that an internal temperature change causes the glacier to flow rapidly or that water generated by friction lubricates the glacier bed and causes the rapid flow.

Another better known surging glacier is the Black Rapids Glacier (sometimes called the Galloping Glacier) at Mile 233 Richardson Highway. In the winter of 1936-37 this glacier advanced approximately 4.8 km (3 miles) in 3 months and came within a half mile of the Richardson Highway.

Other surging glaciers in Alaska include the Muldrow, Susitna and Yanert Glaciers — all in the Alaska Range; in the Yukon Territory, the Steele Glacier in the St. Elias Mountains surges. — *Fran Pedersen*
Jul 78:241

Glacial Erosion

Moving glacier ice continuously grinds away at the high mountains of Alaska and the Yukon Territory to create the rugged beauty characteristic of the Alaska Range and the St. Elias and Selwyn Mountains. Glaciologists recognize two processes of erosion — abrasion and plucking.

The glacier ice itself cannot abrade rock. However, given a load of rock debris, the ice layer at the base of a glacier becomes as sandpaper. Much like a slow but steadily-moving belt sander, the sliding base of the glacier can grind away at the valley floor on which the glacier rests.

Measurements of abrasion to a marble block fixed underneath a moving glacier in Iceland showed that 30 feet (10 meters) of ice motion cut away about one-eighth inch (3 mm) of the block. At that rate, the sliding of a debris-laden glacier would probably cut away a yard (1 meter) of rock in about 200 years.

A requirement for continuing abrasion is a steady supply of new abrasive material by downward transport of rock debris to the basal layer of the glacier. Also, the glacier ice must be thick enough to weigh strongly upon the surface being eroded.

The existence of water at the base of the glacier also seems extremely important. If the water is there under too high a pressure, it may lift up against the ice and prevent erosion. A key role of the water is to carry away ground-up rock flour particles. Unless that happens the base of the glacier becomes like a clogged-up file and is unable to continue the erosion.

Plucking out of broken-up rocks from the glacier floor by moving ice that freezes to their surfaces obviously is a more irregular process and, for that reason, one hard to evaluate the speed of. The question of its effectiveness remains as one of the mysteries of the mountains.

Aug 80:416

Slush Flows

The last thing anyone needs is to be caught up in a churning slurry of meltwater, snow and other debris sometimes moving downslope fast enough to carry 75-ton rocks across even gentle slopes. Called slush flows, slush bursts, slushers, slushflow avalanches or water avalanches, these flows tend to occur during

Tors: *Granite tors near Chena Hot Springs. The spires extend up to 100 feet above the near-level cryoplanation terraces. (Photo by A.F. Weber.)*

rapid spring breakup in arctic and subarctic alpine regions.

Slush flows are known to occur in the Brooks Range, in the mountain areas of Alaska's Seward Peninsula and occasionally in the Talkeetna Mountains near Anchorage. During the summer of 1980, a roadgrader on the Alaska pipeline haul road was struck by a slush flow. It caused no damage other than to pack icy slush around the grader's engine, but the driver was lucky that the flow was small.

Much more serious was a slush flow that struck the small coal mining settlement of Longyearbyen, Spitsbergen, on June 11, 1953. Not realizing the danger, people there built several houses and a hospital on a debris fan formed by earlier slush flows. The buildings stood for a decade until the fateful day "a turbulently tumbling wall of slush, rock debris, and ice blocks advanced rapidly down the valley toward the hospital complex. This moving tongue slammed into the upper group of buildings and they disintegrated as if swatted into oblivion by a gigantic hand." This graphic description of the event that killed three and injured twelve persons was given by Fairbanks' geologist Richard D. Reger at a recent Alaska Science Conference.

Slush flows occur during spring breakup in locations where an accumulation of snow becomes saturated with water. Dr. Reger and his co-workers have found that the most dangerous times are when the temperature has risen to about the 40°F (5°C) mark and remained there for 24 or more hours. Afternoon is the worst time for slush flows.

Dry snow avalanches typically release from slopes steeper than 25 degrees, but slush flows can cascade from slopes as gentle as 3 or 4 degrees — practically level ground. Sometimes slush flows churn along slowly, at other times they move faster than 25 mph (40 kmph). A small slush flow may be only a foot or so thick, but those thicker than 50 feet have been observed. Owing to the high density of a slush flow, due largely to its high water content, the flows have high momentum — like a moving locomotive, they are almost unstoppable and, therefore, are highly destructive.

Feb 81:469

Tors

Tors are craggy spires seen on high slopes or hilltops of interior Alaska and elsewhere in the world. They have a special significance, for they are monumental proof that Pleistocene glaciers did not cover the areas where the tors are found. If glaciers had covered the areas, the tors would have been scraped away by the ice. Thus, the tors demonstrate that central Alaska was open to the migration of plants and animals even during the height of the last glaciation.

The most accessible tors in Alaska are those seen on the right-hand side of the road as one nears Chena Hot Springs, northeast of Fairbanks. These granite spires rise up as high as 30 meters (100 feet) above the slopes and table-like terraces upon which they sit. Tors occur on Wickersham Dome where they can be seen from Livengood Road, in inaccessible parts of the Yukon-Tanana Upland, and on a plateau near the Gerstle River crossing of the Alaska Highway southeast of Big Delta.

Tors are created by chemical weathering of rocks, by exfoliation (the flaking off of rock pieces by rapid changes in temperature), and by frost wedging. In Alaska, frost wedging is the main cause. Water enters fractures in the rocks and freezes. Repeated freezing and thawing wedges the rock apart. The debris created by the breaking up of the rocks is transported away downslope by processes involving frost action (solifluction). The result is a tor towering over a nearly flat terrace called a cryoplanation terrace. The tor and the terrace together appear in sharp contrast to each other — and create an unearthly scene.

Jul 78:242

Frozen Pipes

Spring is the time to watch for freezing of buried water and sewer pipes. There is a lag between the months of coldest air temperature (December and January) and the time when the ground freezes deepest. The soil temperature at depth 18 feet reaches a minimum in May; below 20 feet the temperature is a nearly constant 26°F year around in Fairbanks.

As soil freezes it extracts energy from the warmer soil below, causing its temperature to lower. By this process the freezing level moves slowly downward. In water-saturated gravel under a bare ground surface or one covered only by hard-packed snow, the freezing level can move downward as fast as three feet per month. But under a deep layer of loose snow, soil will freeze at a much slower rate. Therefore, to protect buried sewer and water pipes, do not walk or drive over them; better yet, pile loose snow on them.

— Charles Deehr and Neil Davis
Mar 76:31

Freezing of Hot and Cold Water Pipes

Why do hot water pipes sometimes freeze up and burst when adjacent cold water pipes do not? That is an intriguing question recently asked by Anna Kvistad of Clear, Alaska and Tom Busch of Nome.

My first thought on the matter was that the statement of the question itself was in error because I could not understand how it could be possible for a hot pipe to freeze and burst without a cold pipe doing the same, and probably quicker. But then I asked around and found that several people had observed the same seemingly illogical phenomenon described by Ms. Kvistad and Mr. Busch. In fact, hot water pipes exposed to freezing temperatures can freeze and burst while identical cold water pipes beside them remain intact.

The reason for this curious difference is thought to be related to the existence of foreign solid particles in well or stream water, that is, in any except distilled water. Compared to the size of water molecules, the foreign particles are quite large, though perhaps still small enough to pass through even a highly-effective filter. However, prolonged heating breaks up the foreign particles so that they become smaller, and they remain small even after the water is cooled down. Consequently, normal tap water that has been heated for a few hours is different from cold water. This difference affects the temperature at which the first ice crystals appear in water.

To see what happens consider two identical pipes, one with hot water inside and one with cold, and both exposed to outside temperatures far below freezing. Now it so happens that the larger foreign particles within the cold water pipe actually do cause the water in that pipe to begin freezing before the water in the hot water pipe, even if both pipes are brought down to the temperature at which ice made from distilled water melts, 32°F or 0°C. Note that this temperature is the temperature at which ice melts but is not necessarily the one at which the first ice crystals appear as the water freezes, even though we commonly refer to 0°C or 32°F as the freezing point.

According to the leading idea on the subject of bursting pipes, ice starts to form inside the cold water pipe soon after the temperature there drops slightly below 0°C. Heat energy given off as the ice forms increases the temperature of the ice-water mixture to 0°C. As time goes on, more ice freezes in the pipe, but the growth is slow. The slowness of the growth allows water to flow down the center and be forced out the ends of the freezing section of the pipe. The result is that the cold water pipe eventually freezes solid but does not burst.

The situation in the hot water pipe is quite different. Here, previous heating of the water broke up the foreign particles to a much smaller size that does not promote freezing of the water, as in the other pipe. Instead the water in this pipe cools well below 0°C without turning to ice. Such water is called supercooled because it is still liquid well below 0°C. Supercooling always occurs even if the water is vigorously stirred, but still water with very small or no foreign particles contained in it typically will cool several degrees below 0°C before freezing. But when the freezing does take place in the hot water pipe, it occurs very rapidly throughout the entire pipe. The temperature of the ice and water mixture rises to 0°C as in the other pipe, but in this case a far more extensive network of ice forms in the pipe.

So even though the water in the hot water pipe freezes later than in the other pipe, it freezes so rapidly that the pressure created by the volume increase cannot be released by flow of water out the ends of the pipe. Result: the pipe bursts.

Thus we see that cold water pipes really do freeze before hot water pipes, but the freezing process is different enough to sometimes burst the hot water pipe without harming the cold water pipe.

Nov 80:440

Where Pipes Freeze

One of the quirks of fate is that frozen water pipes typically burst at locations where freezing last occurs. Thus an insulated portion of an otherwise poorly insulated pipe is likely to be the place where the pipe breaks.

As everyone knows, the freezing of water causes the material to expand. Ice occupies a greater volume than does the water it formed from. While the expansion of water as it freezes is the underlying cause of bursting pipes and bent buckets, the actual deformation or breakage of the water container results from a secondary consequence of the expansion, namely hydraulic pressure in that part of the water last to freeze.

A series of experiments described by John Houk in the Summer 1974 issue of *The Northern Engineer* illustrates the role of hydraulic pressure rather well. A water-filled metal bucket set on a block of styrofoam ends up with a bulged bottom created by the hydraulic pressure in the last water to freeze, in this case, at the bottom of the bucket. Yet if the styrofoam is placed on the top of the bucket, no bulging occurs because the last water to freeze is near the top surface where there is no metal to be bent.

In other experiments, Mr. Houk wrapped insulation around short sections of otherwise exposed pipe filled with water. The pipe always burst under the insulation, and water leaked into the insulation, proving that liquid water was still present at the time of the breakage.

As the last of the water freezes in a confined space, the increasing hydraulic pressure causes the melting point of the confining ice to decrease. By the time the pressure rises to 8000 pounds per square inch, the melting point lowers to near -5°C (23°F). If that's not enough pressure to break the pipe, the pressure can build to 28,000 pounds per square inch at -21°C (-6°F). That ought to be enough pressure to break just about anything.

Dec 80:443

Freezing of Open Containers of Water

Why is it that a pail of hot water set outside in cold weather sometimes freezes faster than a similar pail of cold water?

More than one scientist has given the flippant answer "Impossible!" to this question and then been suitably embarrassed after learning that it is possible for hot water in an open container to freeze faster than an identical container of cold water. A more cautious person, Dr. D.G. Osborne of University College at Dar es Salaam, Tanzania, commented on this problem by stating, "No questions should be ridiculed . . . for everyday events are seldom as simple as they seem and it is dangerous to pass a superficial judgment on what can and cannot happen."

Actually, the question about whether hot water can freeze faster than cold water is an old one. In 1620, the English philosopher Francis Bacon noted, "water slightly warm is more easily frozen than quite cold." Only in recent years has enough been learned about the physics of freezing water to explain this seemingly unlikely phenomenon.

The best explanation I have found is given by Canadian scientist G.S. Kell, writing in the *American Journal of Physics* in 1969. Dr. Kell presents calculations and experiments which show that an open container of almost-boiling water cooled only by evaporation from the top surface can lose, through evaporation, up to 26% of the original mass of water by the time the remaining 74% turns to ice. That evaporation takes place relatively quickly from the surface of hot water and very slowly from the surface of cold water.

Hence, if one places a wooden or other insulating bucket filled with hot water out in the cold, and places beside it a similar bucket equally filled with cold water, the two will evaporate unequally. By the time both come down to the same temperature, a temperature still above freezing, the bucket originally containing hot water will contain less water than the one originally filled with cold. If the walls of the buckets are vertical, both liquids contained therein still have the same surface area exposed to air; so the rate of evaporation from this time on is essentially the same in both. Since cooling is presumed to continue to be only by evaporation, the bucket with the least water must reach freezing temperature the soonest.

Dr. Kell notes that, if cooling is by evaporation alone, a volume of water starting at near 100°C (the boiling point) will totally freeze in 90% of the time taken by an equal volume at about room temperature.

My experience is that it is pretty hard to make hot water freeze faster than cold. Several tests with metal containers — which, of course, are highly conducting — results in the cold water freezing first. In one instance I was able to freeze the hot water first. To do it, I set two styrofoam cups in holes carved in a block of styrofoam to minimize conduction of heat through the cups. Even then, the cold water usually froze first. But when I put water at 19°C (66°F) in one cup and near-boiling water in the other and placed them in a freezer at -15°C (5°F), the initially-hot water froze first.

This is the type of experiment anyone in the north can do easily, especially in winter, so there is no reason to take anyone else's word about what happens. If you do attempt the experiment, it is important that equal volumes of hot and cold water be placed in identical containers and that the containers be placed in uniform freezing conditions.

Nov 80:441

Lake George Breakout

Whatever happened to the Lake George Breakout? The resulting flooding of the Knik River near Palmer, Alaska, used to be a fairly regular, if not welcome, event. But, fourteen years now have passed since the last breakout in June 1966.

This famous phenomenon results from glacier and snow meltwater being trapped in the valley of Lake George by the Knik Glacier pressing its face against Mount Palmer. After the glacier closes off the valley, spring waters can enlarge Lake George until it covers as much as 25 square miles (65 sq. km) and is up to 160 feet (50 meters) deeper than minimum level.

The rising lake water eats away at the face of the glacier where it touches Mount Palmer until a channel is cut through. Once it starts to flow, the water cuts the channel into a gorge 5 miles long, 100 to 400 feet wide and 300 feet deep. Through the gorge the water flow can be as great as 150 million gallons per minute. That is comparable to the flow in the Columbia River at flood stage.

Flooding from the Lake George Breakout is not known to have occurred until it wiped out three Indian villages on the Knik River just before 1900, although people living in the region said it emptied itself every 15 to 20 years before that. Irregular flooding from the Breakout occurred until 1914. Thereafter until 1966, during almost every June or

July, Lake George floodwaters threatened structures on the Knik River flood plain.

Since 1966, the gorge has remained open and therefore Lake George has not formed. There seems to be no question about whether or not the Lake George Breakout will again occur; it is just a question of when.

Jul 80:414

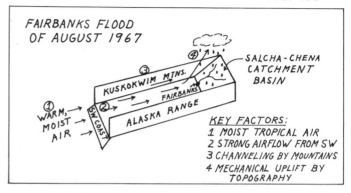

Cause of the 1967 Fairbanks Flood: *A nasty trick of geography.*

Cause of the 1967 Fairbanks Flood

Normal June rainfall in Fairbanks is 1.39 inches; June 1967 was slightly drier, 1.10 inches, in consequence of relatively dry air moving northward over the Chugach and Alaska Ranges into interior Alaska.

However, in July 1967 there developed a low north of Alaska and a high in the North Pacific. These combined to create increasing flow of moist ocean air from the southwest so that Fairbanks received 3.34 inches of rain instead of the normal 1.84 inches.

In early August 1967 large-scale pressure patterns developed to enhance the flow of air from the southwest and an inflow of arctic air from the northwest into northern Alaska. A few days before the flood there occurred a strong movement of warm, moist air into the northwest Pacific from a decaying tropical circulation pattern. This air mass evidently was the real source of the water that created the flood. By August 12, 1967, pressure patterns over Alaska were forcing this wet air toward the northeast through the channel formed between the Alaska Range and the paralleling Kuskokwim Mountains. An increasing depth of saturated air built up over the Alaska Range-Kuskokwim channel as the winds from the southwest persisted. Partially blocking the channel at its northeast end is the Yukon-Tanana upland and the White Mountains — the catchment basin of the Chena, Little Chena and Salcha Rivers.

Continuing pressure on the saturated air mass forced it to rise up over the catchment basin. The associated cooling from the uplift was the final physical process required to produce the heavy rainfall of August 11, 12 and 13. In the 24 hours prior to noon August 12, 3.42 inches of rain fell at Fairbanks, by far the highest ever recorded here. Whereas 2.20 inches of rainfall is normal for the month of August, 6.20 inches fell in August 1967. *(This article based on work of N. A. Streten.)*

Aug 77:177

Arctic Storm Effects

We have been taught that dramatic changes to the earth's surface can be created by almost imperceptible processes acting for very long times; e.g., a tiny stream flowing for millions of years can carve out a large valley. This concept is so embodied in our thinking that it is easy to forget that many geologic processes act in an altogether observable, though intermittent, fashion.

Mount St. Helens is a particularly good example. The mountain is a thousand-year accumulation of ash falls, lava flows and pyroclastic (hot avalanche) flows. Each fall or flow is a perceptible event if someone is there watching, but each forms only a tiny, perhaps almost insignificant part of the whole mountain. And of course, much of the top of the mountain slid or blew away in just a few minutes on May 18, 1980.

Less dramatic but similarly intermittent are the geologic processes that utilize wind and water to erode away or build up coastlines. These days, because of petroleum development, much attention is being paid to the coastline along the Beaufort Sea where it fronts against northern Alaska and Yukon Territory. Scientists are finding that the barrier islands lying along this coastline undergo substantial changes in size and shape in just a matter of a few decades. However, the changes are essentially all due to storms rather than being the result of steady processes.

The most severe storms in the area generally occur in September or October. They involve strong westerly winds blowing over a fetch of open water since, during these months, the pack ice usually is many miles offshore. These strong westerly winds drive seawater onshore to cause flooding of the coastal lowlands and erosion of bluffs facing the sea. The erosion is partly due to the battering of storm waves against the bluffs and partly due to melting of ice layers contained in the bluffs. Undercut by the wave action, the bluff fronts topple down on the beach to be ground up and carried away by the water.

The waves whipped up by the strong storm winds also are particularly effective in cutting up beach materials already deposited and in carrying off the material eroded. Huge amounts of soil material are held in suspension by the violent churning motions in the nearshore waters during storms. Storm waves breaking over vessels anchored in shallow waters have been known to coat the vessels with layers of mud.

When a storm subsides, the water grows quieter and begins to lose its sediment load. Low-lying barrier islands, perhaps awash and partly eaten away by the violence, then reappear with changed shape and location.

One would think that the islands would tend to be moved eastward since the storm winds blow from the west and it is on the western side of shore features that the greatest erosion occurs. However, the islands usually migrate westward. Evidently the reason for the westward migration is that, except during the peak violence of the storm, the normal current in the nearshore region is to the west. Thus the barrier islands slowly step their way westward along the coast, each step taking place during a fall storm and in the days that follow. Some years the steps are only a few feet or are nonexistent; in others, the steps are giant strides, as much as a hundred feet.

Aug 80:421

Storm Surges

Since the gold rush days of 1898, at least 90 storm surges have battered Alaskan coastal villages and towns to cause damage running into the hundreds of millions of dollars, at today's costs.

Storm surges are temporary abnormal changes in sea level that accompany storms in shallow coastal waters. Storm surges can be either positive or negative, that is, a positive surge is one where the height of sea level increases, and a negative surge is one where the level decreases from normal. Strong onshore winds or winds parallel to the shore, where the shore is to the right of the wind flow, cause positive storm surges. Offshore winds or winds parallel to the shore, where the shore is to the left of the flow, cause negative storm surges.

When the wind blows parallel to the shore, the reason why the shore being to right or left of the wind flow is important is the Coriolis effect. Wind blowing across water drags on the water and forces it to move in the direction the wind is blowing. But because of the earth's rotation on its axis, a moving fluid at the earth's surface experiences another force directed at right angles to the motion. This Coriolis force is to the right in the Northern Hemisphere, and to the left in the Southern Hemisphere. The Coriolis force increases in importance away from the equator and toward the poles.

Storm surges occur when a strong wind blows over a long fetch of water, perhaps several hundred miles, in a generally constant direction, and where there is gently sloping, shallow offshore water. Rugged coastlines with deep offshore waters do not suffer from storm surge effects.

A just-completed study of Alaskan storm surges, conducted by James L. Wise, Albert L. Comiskey and Richard Becker, Jr. of the University of Alaska's Arctic Environmental Information and Data Center, shows that positive storm surges up to 13 feet in height have occurred during the past four decades. This study, funded by the Alaska Council on Science and Technology, has resulted in a predictive scheme that can be used to reduce losses caused by future storm surges. Loss can be minimized by knowing which coastal regions are most susceptible to storm surge flooding, and by being able to use weather observations to give a few hour's warning of impending surges.

Typical losses are those involving destruction of boats in harbors, damaged dock and warehouse facilities, destruction of homes and other structures, and washing out of roads and runways. Even wildlife suffers: storm surge floodings during early summer in the Yukon-Kuskokwim delta region have, at times, destroyed 80 to 90% of the production of nesting ducks. If a storm surge occurs at the time of high tide the damage, of course, tends to be the greatest.

The areas of Alaska having the combination of wind and topography that are conducive to strong storm surges include lower Cook Inlet, the north shore of the Alaska Peninsula, Bristol Bay, the Yukon-Kuskokwim delta region, Norton Sound, the Seward Peninsula and, going northward, much of the Chukchi Sea and Beaufort Sea coastlines. Thus, a great part of the Alaskan coastline is susceptible to storm surges. Since ice cover dampens the development of storm surges, the most severe surges generally occur only in summer in the most northern areas.

Among the more well known storm surges are those that have struck the Nome area in the years 1913, 1945, 1946, 1960, 1967, 1974 and 1978. But over the years, towns such as Kodiak, Dillingham, Port Heiden, Shishmaref, Barrow, Barter, Gambell, Seldovia, Homer and Unalakleet have had their share of storm surge problems too.

Sep 81:502

How to Win the Ice Pool

One sure way to win the Nenana Ice Classic is to invest $100,800 to buy 50,400 tickets, one on each minute from about April 18 to May 22. Someone else probably will win too so we probably will lose money. But we can say we won.

If you believe in statistics at all (and who does?) you can use the diagram below to estimate the probability of having a winning ticket. This probability map is compiled on the basis of the actual breakup times from 1917 to 1975; the hour and day of each is shown on the map. From these times a bell-shaped curve was calculated to show the probability of breakup on any specific date. Calculation of the probability of breakups during a particular hour was accomplished by manually smoothing the data, since it appeared that the actual breakups did not, in the parlance of statisticians, follow a normal distribution. Finally, the various results were assembled into the map.

Although a breakup has never occurred during the noon hour of May 6, the probability map says this is the best guess. In principle, such a ticket has 9.6 chances in 100,000 of winning. A ticket falling on the contour line labeled "1" has one chance in 100,000 of winning; one on the "0.1" line has only a chance in a million.

If you choose to ignore the probability contours, which is not a bad idea, you can still glean information from the numbers showing times of actual breakups. Only four breakups have occurred before 9:00 a.m., in 1921, 1923, 1927 and 1941. Except for the breakups of 1940 and 1964, all have occurred between April 26 and May 16.

One technique for picking a winning ticket combines both mathematics and skill. Hang the probability map on the wall, then throw a dart at it aiming for the top of the "probability hill". If you miss altogether, try another method.

— John Miller and Neil Davis
May 76:60

(See drawing next page.)

Harding Lake Levels

What's happening to the water level of Harding Lake, near Fairbanks?

The current low water level of Harding Lake appears to be part of a natural cycle of rising and falling which is tied to climatic cycles and is seen in many lakes around the world. The changes are especially dramatic at Harding Lake because it has a very small contributory watershed; much of its water is provided by seepage. The lake has no visible outlet. While Harding is the deepest unglaciated lake in interior Alaska, it also has extensive shallows which cause the shoreline near some homes to move out dramatically with only a small drop in actual water level.

The University's Institute of Water Resources at Fairbanks has received many reports that the lake was much lower during the 1930s than it is now and the current low began to occur in the early 1970s. Therefore, the cycle may be as long as forty years between natural lows and natural highs. The lake was first settled in the 1920s so it is impossible for us to gauge the exact length of the cycle from residents' reports.

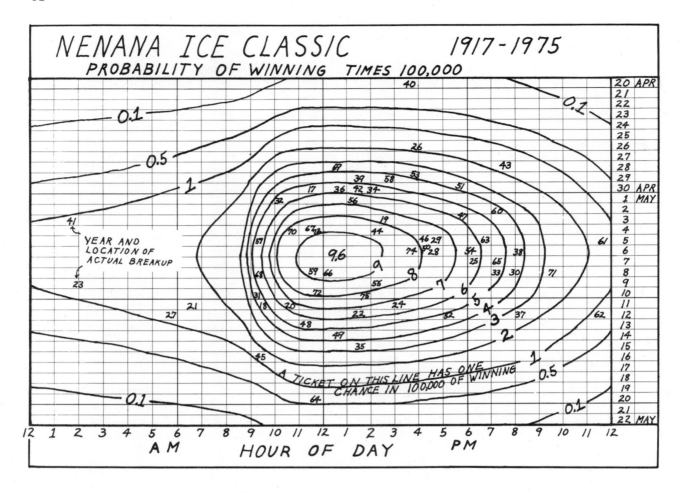

How to Win the Ice Pool: *A gamble at best.*

However, hydrologists from the Institute of Water Resources have been studying the phenomenon, and further work on the hydrology of this lake is being conducted this summer during preliminary studies before extraction of a core of sediments. This core will be extracted by a team of Japanese and Alaskan scientists who will attempt to use the material in the core to determine the past cycles of the climate back through geologic time.

Schemes for diverting additional water into the lake have been proposed and include cutting a trench from the Salcha River to Harding Lake. This scheme would be costly and would add water of much different quality than that Harding Lake normally receives. Investigations would first have to be conducted to determine the effects river water would have on fish and other life in the lake.

Further study is also needed to determine the hydrologic results of any proposed action. The increased lake level that would occur during spring runoffs and the varying summer rains needs to be predicted. Some important social questions are: Who will determine the optimum lake level? Who

will control and maintain the diversion device? And, who will be responsible for property damage due to flooding? Such flooding could occur if optimum lake level was attained early in the summer with the aid of a diversion device and such diversion was then followed by a heavy rainfall. —*Jacqueline D. LaPerriere*
Aug 77:184

Legendary Lake

In the early 1950s, geologic work by Oscar Ferrians in Alaska's Copper River basin showed the existence of the shorelines of a large ancient lake which had filled the whole basin. Old shorelines were found as high as 2650 feet, the height of Mentasta Pass between the basin and the upper Tanana Valley. Carbon dating of material from the area revealed that the highest shoreline existed 9600 years ago.

This lake was apparently formed during the last glacial period by glaciers cutting off the normal flow of the Copper River through its valley below Chitina. At one time, the lake may have actually drained over Mentasta Pass into the Tanana River, but glaciers probably blocked that outlet also and so the lake may have become an inland sea.

Even more interesting is the fact that Mr. Ferrians later read reports of local Indian legends that tell of a large ancient lake in this area. The legends were written down before Mr. Ferrians discovered the lake. This incident demonstrates that historical information can survive for perhaps thousands of years in the form of legends passed verbally from generation to generation.

Oct 76:119

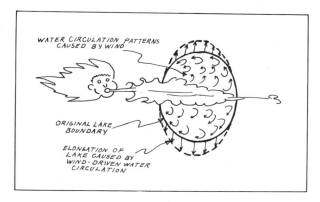

Mystery of Aligned Lakes: *Wind seems to be the cause.*

Mystery of Aligned Lakes

A look at a map of the North Slope from Barrow to Prudhoe Bay reveals the curious fact that nearly all the lakes are elongated with their longer dimensions parallel to one another in a northwest-southeast direction. Not all scientists agree upon the reasons, but a rather compelling hypothesis credits the prevailing winds. Curiously, the prevailing winds are from the *northeast* and blow across the shorter dimension of the elongated lakes. Our common sense suggests that wind and wave action should tend to enlarge a lake in the direction of the wind, but experiments with water tanks and wind devices demonstrate the opposite effect. Wind forces on the surface of a *shallow* lake cause crosswind water circulation

patterns. The resulting wave action could be responsible for thawing and eroding the frozen tundra on the sides of the lake that are at right angles to the wind.

— John Miller
Apr 76:32

Exporting Water

Water supply problems of the western states are increasingly in the news. These problems can only worsen as larger populations demand an increasing supply of water and as deep-well pumping depletes water reserves carried in underground aquifers.

Major rivers such as the Colorado and the Yellowstone figure in the discussions of water supply because of the large volume of water these rivers carry across several states. Together these two rivers carry about 20 million acre-feet of water annually (an acre-foot is one acre covered by one foot of water).

As the western states grow more prune-like, Alaska and British Columbia probably will be increasingly eyed as potential suppliers of fresh water. The day may come when these political entities will have to decide whether or not to export water, and it is possible that they will have no choice in the matter.

What would be involved in exporting 10 million acre-feet of water each year, an amount comparable to the flow of a major western river? Suppose that there were a means to collect a part of the rainfall from a portion of southeast Alaska or British Columbia the size of the Queen Charlotte Islands, about 4000 square miles. Considering the huge rainfall in these areas, it might be feasible to collect four feet of the annual rainfall without it even being missed. Such collection would yield 10 million acre-feet of water.

To carry the 10 million acre-feet of water south at a speed of 5 mph would require a pipe 48 feet in diameter. This is a large but perhaps not impossible object. And while being this fanciful, why not suggest the additional use of it as a flume in which to export another renewable resource, trees?

Feb 79:284

CHAPTER FIVE
THE SEA

Wind-Driven Ocean Currents

Wind-driven ocean currents behave in ways that, at first appearances, do not make sense.

In thinking about the wind blowing over the ocean's surface, one easily recognizes that the moving air exerts a force on the top of the water in the direction the wind blows. Seems obvious that the water should move that direction, too, doesn't it? In fact, the water at the surface will move at an angle to the wind direction.

The reason for the deviation is that the daily rotation of the earth about its axis exerts an additional force on the moving water. That force is at right angles to the direction of the water's motion and is directly proportional to the speed of the water. The combination of this so-called Coriolis force and the force of the wind results in the water surface moving at a 45-degree angle to the wind direction — to the right in the Northern Hemisphere and to the left in the Southern Hemisphere.

To make matters more complicated, the moving surface water tries to force the water below to move also. Going down in depth in the Northern Hemisphere, the water is driven more and more to the right, until at a depth of about 60 meters, the water actually is driven opposite the direction of the wind. Averaged over the top 60 meters, the wind-driven current in the Northern Hemisphere is 90 degrees to the right of the wind direction.

Thus, a west wind blowing against a north-south segment of the Alaskan coast will drive a current along the coast to the south. A wind blowing parallel to the coast or the edge of the arctic ice pack in the Bering Sea will drive water either toward or away from the coastline or the ice pack. If the water is driven away, the result is upwelling to replace the water forced away. Food production rates are highest where upwelling occurs; these are the ocean's richest places.

Feb 79:291

Alaskan Killer Waves

Every once in awhile, the forces of the sea and wind combine to produce the rogue wave. A wall of water a hundred or more feet in height, the rogue wave can easily mash the bow of a large ship or break the ship in two.

Writing in *Smithsonian* magazine, Peter Britton cites a study of giant waves in the Gulf of Alaska. Waves there are found to be no worse than in the northern North Sea, where extreme wave heights are near 100 feet. However, the study indicates that the maximum possible wave height in the Gulf of Alaska is a terrifying 198 feet.

In a sense, rogue waves are statistical accidents. They form when the crests of several different trains of waves, each with its own speed and direction, all come together at the same time. The wave height at that time is the sum of the heights of the individual waves. Since the individual wave trains are moving at different speeds, the rogue wave cannot last long. Either the waves of which it is made separate or the extreme wave may destroy itself by breaking over at the crest.

Storms at sea are the basic causes of large waves that can merge together to create monster waves. Gusting winds start waves growing, and if the wind continues for several tens of hours the waves will steadily grow until a maximum height proportional to the square of the wind speed develops. A 40-knot wind blowing for 45 hours will create 30-foot waves.

Changes in wind direction, reflection of waves off steep shorelines and modification to the wave trains by changes in undersea topography (especially near continental shelf boundaries) can all combine to bring several of the larger storm waves together for a brief minute. If there also happens to be a ship at the point of intersection, that brief minute will be one of terror.

Feb 78:225

Alaska's Freshwater Coastal Jet

High rates of precipitation — up to 340 inches of water per year — along the coast of southeastern Alaska and British Columbia may have important local consequences for fish and marine mammals inhabiting the coastal waters there.

As rains occur and snow melts, there is massive runoff of fresh water into the Gulf of Alaska. No one is certain how much fresh water runs off the mountainous coast since not enough of the stream flows in the area have been gauged. However, Tom Royer of

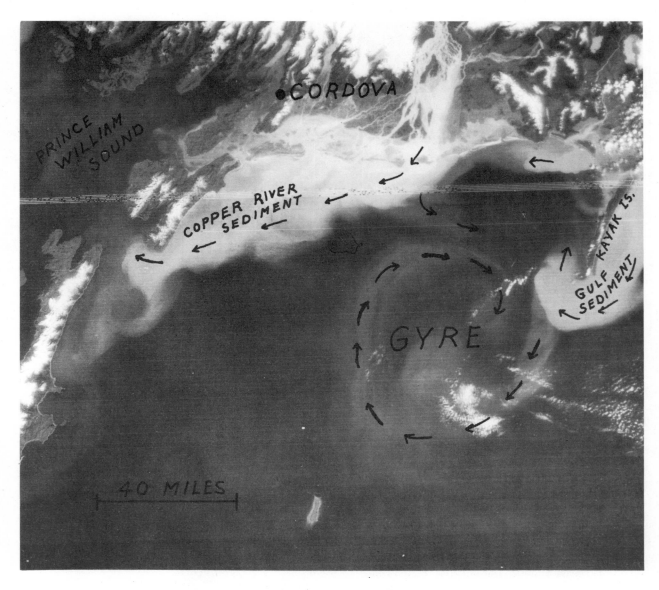

Gyre Versus Oil Development: *The gyre off the mouth of the Copper River.*

the University of Alaska's Institute of Marine Sciences estimates that the runoff easily exceeds by three times the flow down the Yukon River. It is even larger than the flow down the Mississippi River, estimated to average 23,000 cubic meters per second (810,000 cubic feet per second).

A curious thing happens to the fresh water running into the sea. Instead of flowing out southwesterly into the Gulf of Alaska and disappearing into the salt water there, the fresh water forms into a cohesive jet that hugs the coast and flows northerly and westerly along it. There are two reasons for this behavior.

First, the fresh water is lighter than ocean water and, because of the difference in density, the fresh and salt waters tend not to mix easily. Though enough mixing does occur to make the fresh water

too salty to drink, an identifiable stream of fresher water is maintained.

Second, this stream turns to the right as it moves, as do all moving flows of fluid in the Northern Hemisphere. The Coriolis force causing this turning is due to the earth's rotation on its axis. Thus the freshwater stream, roughly 10 miles wide, tends to hang against the coastline as it moves along at a speed of approximately two knots. Boat captains coasting northward can use the stream to speed their passages.

Jun 81:460

Gyre Versus Oil Development

Flowing out of the Copper River into Prince William Sound, suspended sediments show up in Landsat satellite images. Especially in summer these sediments are caught up in a circular current pattern

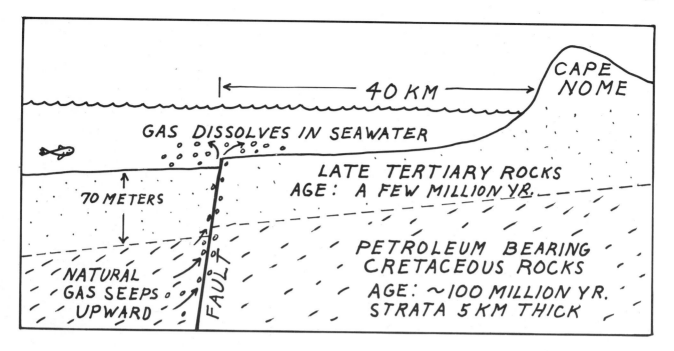

Norton Sound Gas Seepage: *Natural gas seeps up through a fault zone off Cape Nome.*

called a gyre. The persistent summer gyre located southwest of Kayak Island will also trap crude oil, should there be a wellhead accident or tanker spill in the area. Because of the danger, the U.S. Department of Interior recently decided to delete 16 tracts from an oil lease sale in the northeast Gulf of Alaska.

Dec 76:130

Riches of the Bering Sea

Acre for acre, the huge continental shelf area of the Bering Sea may be the most valuable real estate on the earth's surface. This view, expressed by a past director of the University of Alaska's Institute of Marine Science, Dr. Donald Hood, takes into account the Bering Sea's potential for petroleum and mineral development. But most important probably is the renewable food resource.

As our knowledge of the oceans has increased these last few years, we are being forced to abandon the myth that the oceans are an endless and uniform storehouse of food. We are beginning to realize that only certain parts of the ocean are rich and that most of the oceanic volume is a comparative desert.

Primary food production in the ocean is by plant forms that perform photosynthesis, a process that can only take place in the top 200 meters. Required also for maximal photosynthetic production are elemental materials such as phosphorus and nitrogen. These are most abundant in water where photosynthesis is impossible. Thus, where upwelling of deep waters brings nutrients to the surface, photosynthesis proceeds most rapidly.

Rapid mixing of surface water with deep water is the key to high production of food in the oceans. On this score, the Bering Sea has three things going for it. The long reach of shallow bottom extending from Alaska well out toward Kamchatka drags against water currents created by the tides and causes mixing of the deeper and shallower water. Winds blowing across the Bering Sea in winter when it is partially ice-covered causes upwelling at the boundary between the ice pack and the open water. Also, near this boundary and near open leads scattered throughout the ice pack, freezing of surface water causes a circulation to be set up in surrounding water, and this circulation creates vertical mixing.

The region near the ice front seems to be particularly productive because of the mixing. Here marine mammals tend to congregate because of the enhanced food supply.

Feb 79:288

Norton Sound Gas Seepage

Twenty-five miles offshore from Nome's gold beaches, natural gas now bubbles up through the ocean floor.

Found by shipboard water sampling during 1976, the seepage is not the first sign of oil and gas near Nome. Oil films have been reported on the lagoons near Nome and Cape Nome. Sometimes when a southerly (onshore) wind blows, a paraffin-like foam is seen on the beaches.

As early as 1906, there was prospecting for oil on Hastings Creek near Cape Nome. Of two shallow wells drilled, one showed a trace of oil and the other a head of flammable gas under enough pressure to blow the tool stem back up the hole.

Oil seeps have been found in the Sinuk River Valley 30 km northeast of Nome and at the mouth of the Inglutalik River between Nome and Unalakleet.

The light hydrocarbon (hydrogen and carbon) compounds of which natural gas is composed easily dissolve in water. Consequently, a technique of prospecting for marine seeps or monitoring of marine petroleum pollution is to look for the dissolved hydrocarbons in water samples.

Modern methods allow the detection of dissolved hydrocarbon in amounts less than one part in one billion. Concentrations 10 to 20 times normal in sea water were observed in the shallow water off Nome during 1976.

On the basis of a report of the findings of the gas seepage published by Joel D. Cline of NOAA and Mark L. Holmes of USGS, it appears that the gas may be rising up through one or more faults in the ocean bottom rocks. Apparently the gas is formed in Cretaceous age marine sediments laid down about 100 million years ago.

Jan 78:214

Winter in the Arctic Ocean

What goes on under the Arctic Ocean ice cover in the winter? This question lately has occupied the minds and talents of scientists with heightened urgency. The reason for this special curiosity is that arctic oil and gas exploration will necessarily be most intense during the nine-month period of frozen sea ice in the nearshore Beaufort. Mostly used to working on marine problems in open water, scientists and management personnel both have realized that arctic oil and gas leasing offshore in the Beaufort Sea would force industry to operate mainly in winter when the water is ice-covered.

About one year ago, scientists began to wonder about the "big void" they had never looked into: the arctic marine winter. Dogma said that all biological events are at a standstill under arctic winter conditions. Common sense and Eskimo knowledge and certain scientific observations indicated otherwise. Scientists with the University of Alaska and with the National Oceanographic and Atmospheric Administration's Outer Continental Shelf Environmental Assessment Program now realize that some of the most biologically critical events of the annual cycle routinely take place in the dead of winter in North America's arctic waters:

— Arctic Cod spawn between November and February under the arctic ice. These fish are important because they are near the base of the marine food chain leading up to seals, polar bears, and man.

— Mysids also spawn or produce eggs between November and February under the ice every year. They are small shrimp-like animals that are food for many predators in the nearshore Beaufort.

— Ice algae and phytoplankton associated with ice contribute their big pulse of carbon and nutrients long before the winter sea ice breaks up.

— Kelp in the Stefansson Sound Boulder Patch puts on its annual growth spurt in the dead of winter.

All of these biological processes shake the illusions of non-Alaskan scientists that nothing serious can be going on in the "dead of winter." All these processes of reproduction, growth, and survival in winter are requiring special consideration by government and industry now that oil and gas leasing is about to take place in the Arctic.

— Dave Norton
May 79:308

Beaufort Sea Boulder Patches

For the most part, the shallows of the Beaufort Sea have a mud and silt bottom. The one known exception is just east of Prudhoe Bay in the shallows of Stefansson Sound. There, in a 160-square-mile area between the shore and Cross and Narwhal Islands, is a group of boulder patches.

Rocks up to a meter (3 feet) in diameter litter the seafloor. Where they came from and how they got there no one knows. Possibly they were carried out of the mountains to the south by glaciers during a past glaciation. Or perhaps they were rafted into their location on top of ice fragments originating in the Greenland or Ellesmere Island ice sheets, thousands of years ago.

Compared to most of the rest of the floor of the Arctic Ocean, the boulder patches are teeming with life. Like a tropical coral reef, each boulder patch supports a community of kelp and other attached plants and animals, along with various fishes and invertebrates that move around among the boulders.

Originally, the boulder fields and their associated living populations were discovered by scuba-diving scientists from the University of Alaska's Institute of Marine Science back in the 1960s.

Now, there is renewed interest in these anomalous patches because they lie right in the middle of a proposed lease sale area for oil and gas exploration. In fact, they comprise about 20 percent of the area of a joint lease sale proposed by Alaska and the federal government in December 1979. For this reason, the Stefansson Sound boulder patches will be in the news in the months ahead.

— Dave Norton
Apr 79:309

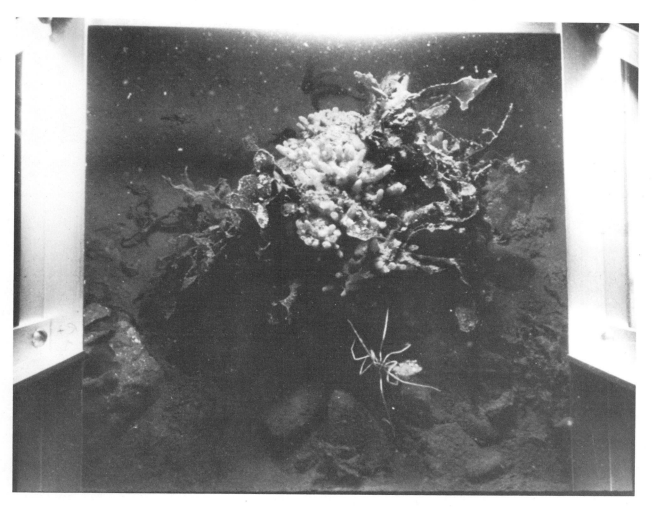

Beaufort Sea Boulder Patches: *View of a small boulder on the bottom of Stefansson Sound, topped by kelp and soft corals. A sea spider can be seen in the lower right.*

CHAPTER SIX
VOLCANOES, EARTHQUAKES, TECTONICS

Go North, Young Continent

It is now being suggested that much of the land in Alaska, like its population, drifted in from elsewhere. The first serious suggestion of this sort was made in 1972 by graduate student Duane Packer and Professor David Stone of the University of Alaska. Based upon the orientation of magnetic particles in rocks formed 160 million years ago, they suggested that southern Alaska had moved from a more southerly latitude to its present location, arriving a few tens of millions of years ago.

Later, in 1974, Packer and Stone reaffirmed their idea and evolved the concept of "Baja Alaska." According to this idea, the Alaska Peninsula used to be aligned parallel to the west coast of North America in a configuration much like that of Baja California today. From such a position the Alaska Peninsula would have rotated and moved north to reach its present location.

More recently, geologists of the U. S. Geological Survey suggested that a large block of land named Wrangellia formed near the equator and sailed northward to form Alaska's Wrangell Mountains as well as parts of the Canadian Queen Charlotte Islands and perhaps even parts of Oregon, Washington and Idaho. They suggest that Wrangellia's trip north started 200 million years ago and was completed in 100 million years.

The very latest bit of evidence comes from fossil palm fronds found near the Malaspina Glacier in southern Alaska. According to U. S. Geological Survey paleobotanist Jack A. Wolfe, the fossil palm and other similar large-leafed tropical plants can grow only in a tropical climate where it is not only warm, but where the daily allocation of sunlight does not change much through the year.

Since Dr. Wolfe's palm fronds were formed about 50 million years ago, southern Alaska's northern journey must have taken place since then. This recent timing of the trip is in agreement with the Baja Alaska concept of Packer and Stone, but does not seem to fit well with the postulated earlier trek of ancient Wrangellia. Time will tell which if either idea is correct.

Jun 78:216

Tropical Fossils in Alaska

The adaptations that plants make to allow their growth in Earth's different climatic regions can be used to learn about the past. Palm leaves found fossilized in the rocks bordering the Malaspina Glacier near Yakutat have a story to tell since palms could not possibly grow there today. Either the climate of Earth was different when the palms grew 45 million years ago or else the rocks in which the fossils occur moved in from someplace else. Most students of the past subscribe to the latter view.

In the tundra of arctic and alpine climates there are relatively few species of plants. Plants there undergo great mechanical stress through rupture of the roots as the soil freezes and thaws and as the

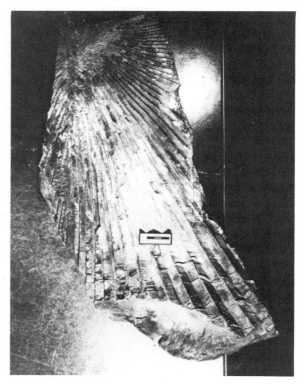

Tropical Fossils in Alaska: *A 20-inch fossil palm leaf that once waved over a tropical forest in Alaska 45-60 million years ago. The fossil was found in rocks near the Malaspina Glacier. (Photo from U.S. Geological Survey, Dept. of the Interior.)*

Alaskan Super Mollusk: *A giant Alaskan ammonite.*

wind abrades any part of the plant sticking up above the rocks or snow. Consequently, tiny plants such as lichens dominate the tundra landscape. A general rule seems to be that the worse the climate, the fewer the species of plants.

In contrast, the equatorial and tropical rain forests may contain as many as 3000 different species in an area no larger than one square mile. Trees of the rain forest tend to have smooth bark, broad evergreen leaves and heavily buttressed roots — all suitable characteristics for a climate where water and sunshine are plentiful all year round.

Plants with gnarled bark, thick waxy leaves (such as spruce needles or cacti) and sometimes a spongy internal structure suitable for holding water are characteristics of climates where water is scarce part or most of the year. In regions where there are large temperature extremes, including below-freezing weather, deciduous plants drop their leaves as part of the effort to become dormant during the bad part of the year.

Paleobotanist Jack A. Wolfe of the United States Geological Survey at Menlo Park, California, has found a number of tropical rain forest fossils along the eastern Gulf of Alaska. These include several kinds of palms, Burmese lacquer trees, mangroves and trees of the type that now produce nutmeg and Macassar oil.

— *Paula Krebs*
Jun 78:188

Alaskan Super Mollusk

Alaskans, being modest by nature, are not inclined to brag about Alaska's being more than twice as big as Texas, its giant mosquitos, strawberries and cabbages or all the other reasons why Alaska is better than other places. Because of this modesty, it hurts to claim that even Alaska's snails are bigger than those of other places.

As proof, I offer the accompanying photograph of a giant ammonite found at Cape Douglas on Kamishak Bay. More than 16 inches in diameter, this fine specimen is in storage at the University of Alaska Museum.

The person versed in such matters will recognize that one reason it hurts to claim this photo as proof of Alaska's giant snail population is that an ammonite is not really a snail. Though both are of the same Mollusca phylum, snails are gastropods (stomach-footed) and ammonites are cephalopods (head-footed). Another reason is that all ammonites died out about 70 million years ago. And, as huge as this Alaskan ammonite is, even larger ones — more than six feet across — have been found in Germany.

Ammonites and many other forms of life such as the dinosaurs died out at the end of the Cretaceous period, for reasons that seem mysterious. This was the time when the highlands of Alaska were starting to rise from the sea, an era that one scientist called "The time of the great dying".

One suggestion for the death of the ammonites is that they lost their sense of symmetry and developed into bizarre, useless shapes. Evidence of this view is found in the curious crenate (leaf-like) shapes seen on the fossil remains. These are the remnants of what were once plate-like septa dividing up the ammonites' shell into cavities (like its only living relative, the pearly nautilus, the animal lived in the outermost cavity of the spiralled-up shell). It is thought that some strange twist of evolutionary fate caused the septa to change from simple flat walls to the grotesque shapes seen in the photograph.

Nov 77:199

Continental Divide

The Continental Divide trends roughly north-south through the United States along the backbone of the Rocky Mountains. It divides the country into watersheds emptying westward into the Pacific Ocean or eastward into the Atlantic Ocean or the Gulf of Mexico.

One would think that extension of the Continental Divide into Alaska would bring it along the lofty Alaska Range and across Mt. McKinley. Instead, as the map shows, the Continental Divide through Alaska runs along the Brooks Range and into Seward Peninsula where it terminates at Cape Prince of Wales. Thus it separates the watersheds draining north and west into the Arctic Ocean from those draining west and south into Bering Sea.

The curious track of the Continental Divide from the Rockies into the Brooks Range led geologists until recently to assume erroneously that the Brooks Range was a structural extension of the Rocky Mountains. But just within recent years geologists have determined that the Brooks Range was uplifted about 100-200 million years ago, sometime earlier than the uplift of the Rockies, 65 million years ago.

So now, most geologists think that the Brooks Range is not structurally related to the Rocky Mountains. Nor is the Alaska Range. It has been formed very recently, within the last five million years, and is still rising.

Mar 78:23

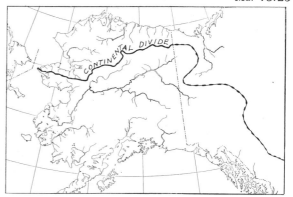

Continental Divide: *It takes a westerly path across the Brooks Range in northern Alaska.*

Tectonics and the Yukon River

Not far from Skagway, just over the border in Canada, precipitation that falls does not run off the few tens of miles directly to the sea. Instead, the mighty mountain barrier which rings Alaska's southern coastline causes the water to flow downhill to the north into the Yukon River watershed. This water must flow north and finally west a distance greater than 1500 miles before reaching the Bering Sea.

Why such a circuitous route? The answer lies in the high degree of tectonic activity of southern Alaska. The mountains there are rising up faster than they are being eroded away by weathering processes.

That the uplifting is very rapid is demonstrated by the troubles a surveying crew had some years ago. One summer they ran level lines from the southern coast to Big Delta. The next year they ran the level lines from Big Delta back to the coast only to find that their survey failed to close. As they discovered during a rapidly repeated survey in the following year, the failure of the first survey to close was due to uplift of the Alaska Range during the two years of the initial survey.

Apr 77:74

The Hills of Home

Jutting curiously out of the level floor of the Tanana Valley, near Fairbanks, are several small hills. Four of these, including Lakloey, Brown's, Sage and Birch Hills consist partly of basaltic rocks. These rocks were erupted through volcanic vents which cut through older rocks (Birch Creek schist) over 90 million years ago. Some of the basalt contains football-like structures called "pillows" which tell us that these lavas were erupted on the floors of prehistoric lakes or seas. These isolated hills are remnants left from erosion that has carried away surrounding rocks over the years.

Most of the hills composing the uplands between the Chatanika, Chena and Salcha rivers are composed of Birch Creek schist and younger granitic rocks (60-120 million years old). Clear Creek Butte, Blair Lake Buttes, Moose Creek Bluffs and Birch Hill are mainly composed of Birch Creek schist. Rocks composing the Birch Creek schist formation are chiefly recrystallized sedimentary rocks which were first deposited as long ago as Precambrian time (greater than 570 million years).

The Wood River Buttes, which emerge from the Tanana Valley flood plain, are composed of iron-magnesium rich (ultramafic) rocks. These rocks are of igneous parentage, as they have crystallized from a parent melt. Being fairly resistant to weathering, they too have better withstood the ravages of time and now stand as low sentinels on the broad valley floor.

Jun 76:39

Alaska's Sand Dunes

Ten thousand years ago, when the last major glaciation occurred (the Wisconsin glaciation), the Tanana Valley was glacier free. Still, it probably looked quite different than it does today. There were fewer trees and probably a lot more sand dunes.

As they ground the Alaska Range to the south into flour-sized particles, glaciers carried the debris northward and delivered it to the winds sweeping up the Tanana Valley. The winds, in turn, deposited the silt onto the hills fronting the valley — 33-Mile Bluff, Moose Creek Bluff, Birch Hill, College Hill, Chena Ridge and the Nenana Bluffs.

Most of the time the silt deposited so fast that extensive humus layers did not build up. In places though, one can dig down to find thin dark layers, an inch or so thick, representing times of low wind deposition rates.

Active sand dunes probably moved across the lowland areas, just as they still do today west of Huslia in the Koyukuk Valley and along the Kobuk River. Low, hill-like remnants, now arrested by growths of small trees and shrubs, can be seen along the Parks Highway, just south of Nenana. There several persons have built their houses on the dunes as a means of getting up above the nearby surroundings.

Even today one sees the telltale signs of blowing soil, blowouts and elongated windrows of silt on top of the snow and moss. Perhaps we are very close to the condition when the plant growth can no longer arrest the dunes. Even a rather slight change — more

wind or less rain — might cause the dunes to move again.

Agricultural development, too, could trigger the change. Replacement of the natural perennial growth by annual crops that do not hold the soil so well could have the potential for long-term disaster.

May 78:90

Dust in Them Thar Hills

Windblown loess (pronounced "luss") forms the surface layer on many of the hills surrounding Fairbanks. The layers of silt-sized dirt particles feather out near the tops of the fills but may be more than a hundred feet thick near the bases. The layers of loess often are frozen. These contain lenses of pure ice and the remains of many mammals: bison, horse, camel, mastodon, mammoth, sabertoothed tiger and even the Fairbanks Lion.

Tall exposures of the loess remain beside the tailing piles on the roads to Ester and Fox. In earlier years the loess was washed away by hydraulic giants so that gold dredges could mine the gravels below.

Little studied, the loess is thought to have been laid down by winds during the last glacial age ending about 6000 years ago. The loess had its source in the broad outwash plain north of the Alaska Range. Though glaciers never covered Fairbanks, they probably extended well north of the Range and carried eroded material far out from the mountains. So the next time you curse the fine dust tracked into the house, remember that it may have had a lofty origin atop Mt. Hayes or one of the other spectacular peaks out across the valley.

May 76:64

Volcano Spacing

Men tend to plant trees evenly spaced in rows, but nature uses a seemingly more random pattern. Therefore, most fixed objects we see in nature are irregularly distributed, and when a regular pattern emerges, it tends to catch our eye.

One such pattern — and a mysterious one — is the rather even spacing of volcanoes on the Alaska Peninsula and elsewhere out along the Aleutians. The Aleutian Islands themselves are just the upper parts of volcanoes perched on the sea floor.

On the west side of Cook Inlet, Spurr, Redoubt, Iliamna and Augustine stand like a row of well-drilled soldiers spaced roughly 70 km (42 miles) apart. Down the Alaska Peninsula to the southwest, the volcanoes are closer ranked but still relatively evenly spaced about 50 km (30 miles) apart.

A possible cause of this remarkable evenness of spacing has been offered by geoscientist Bruce D. Marsh of Johns Hopkins University in an article appearing in the March-April issue of *American*

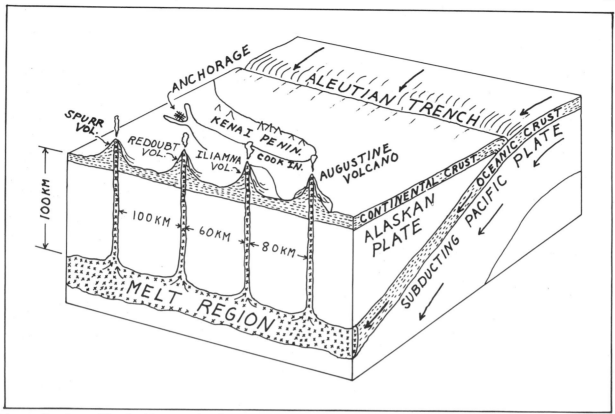

Volcano Spacing: *The Pacific oceanic plate moves northwest to subduct under southern Alaska at the Aleutian Trench. Melting of the subducted material at depths near 100 km creates an elongated pool of magma that floats up through the overlying rocks. The rocks also act somewhat like liquids on the long time scales involved (millions of years).*

Scientist. The idea is easiest to describe, and perhaps to understand, by resorting to examples. One of the best is the behavior of paint if too thick a brushful is applied to a vertical wall. The paint runs down the wall, not evenly, but in fingers spaced some distance apart. The spacing depends upon the thickness of the paint, how viscous it is and perhaps also upon the roughness of the wall to which the paint is applied.

If one liquid is moved through another having different characteristics, this same development of fingering occurs. The same is true of two gases moving against each other, as seen in the pattern of smoke curling up from a cigarette.

This curious tendency for moving liquids and gases to develop filamentary structure is known as the Rayleigh-Taylor instability. It can be described by mathematical formulas which clearly indicate that the fundamental underlying cause is the difference in viscosity of the materials involved. Viscosity tells how well a material clings to itself. The greater the difference in viscosity between two gases or liquids thrust together, the greater is the spacing between the filaments that appear. And even rocks, which we normally consider to be solids, can flow like liquids over a long period of time.

Consequently, volcanoes can be caused by liquid magma floating up through thick layers of highly viscous quasi-liquid-like rocks. The source region quite clearly is an elongated liquid body at about 100 km (60 miles) depth created by the melting of subducted rock. Thought of this way, it seems quite natural that the volcanic magmas would undergo the Rayleigh-Taylor instability and so create an evenly spaced row of volcanoes.

Jun 79:310

Volcano Versus Snow Machine - Volcano Wins

During the eruption of Redoubt volcano in January, 1969, Ray Collins of McGrath was running his snow machine near Nikolai. He and a friend saw a brownish cloud moving down the valley. It precipitated out on the snow leaving a layer ¼ to ½ inch deep. Mr. Collins noticed the volcanic ash sprayed into the air as his Arctic Cat machine ploughed along, but he hardly gave it a second thought. After running some miles, the Kohler engine began to lose power and overheat. Mr. Collins opened the cowling to find ash packed around the air intake and on the cooling fins. After cleaning, the engine was still without much power, but it was able to take the snow machine over the packed outward trail back to

Nikolai. Disassembly of the engine showed it to be destroyed internally by the corrosive, talc-like ash particles.

Jet aircraft flying through ash clouds from volcanoes have had similar problems. Jets that inadvertently flew through the eruptive cloud from Augustine volcano in early 1976 required replacement of both windows and engines.

Oct 76:120

Augustine Volcano

Spewing forth an 8000-foot plume of gas clouds and hot ash, Mt. Augustine awoke from a ten-year sleep in January 1976 to remind Alaskans that we are very much part of a growing land. And while the major activity seems to have abated a bit, intermittent activity has continued and is expected to continue for several months.

Some relics brought back from the Geophysical Institute's scientific hut on the island are grim evidence of one form of death-dealing destruction that sometimes accompanies volcanic eruptions. Sometime on January 23 or 24, 1976, one or more hot gas clouds rushed down the slopes of Mt. Augustine and engulfed the hut. Called "nuées ardentes", the French name for glowing avalanches or clouds, such downward flows travel as fast as 100 miles or more per hour.

From them there is no escape; the metal hut on

Augustine Volcano: *Geologist Robert Forbes holds a partially melted measuring cup distorted by the hot gases of a nuée ardente on Augustine volcano.*

Augustine withstood a blast no living thing inside or in that area could have survived. Temperatures rose, perhaps only for a second or two, to higher than 500°F. Wood objects outside the hut were seared black on the side toward the volcano, yet were virtually untouched on the lee side of the blast. The upper and lower mattresses of a triple bunk inside the hut were essentially untouched. Between them the middle mattress, located beside a glass window, was completely incinerated, the window having been popped out by the gas cloud. Across the room, a plastic towel holder and a plastic measuring cup were partially melted (see photo). Fortunately, no one was in the hut or on the island when the "nuée ardente" rushed down the volcano's slopes.

At other times and places, people were not so lucky. In 1902, the 30,000 residents of the town of St. Pierre, Martinique, were all killed in a few seconds by a "nuée ardente" sweeping down the slopes of volcanic Mt. Pelee.

And, of course, the burned kitchen relics from Augustine remind us of Pompeii. A beautiful city, rich in Roman art and architecture, Pompeii was built up over a period of 500 years upon a lava flow from nearby Mt. Vesuvius. Wracked by a disastrous earthquake in the year 62 A.D., Pompeii was still being rebuilt 17 years later when hot gas and ash flow engulfed the city. Though many of the 20,000 residents died, the event was a boon to the historians of a later age. For 1500 years, Pompeii lay entombed in ash which preserved paintings, statues, buildings and other precious objects. In a sense even the people were preserved; by 1860, casts of their bodies were being obtained by pouring plaster of Paris into the hollows they left in the ash. Nevertheless, it may be hard to convince the former residents of Pompeii or St. Pierre that every cloud has a silver lining.

Almost assuredly, the current saga of Augustine Volcano is unfinished.

Mar 76:1

Alaska Dirt Moves South for Winter

The Mt. Augustine eruption of last January sent huge clouds of dust high into the atmosphere. Winds in the jet stream near altitude 20,000 feet carried the dust great distances horizontally. As the winds aloft were toward the southwest at the time, the Augustine dust traveled down the Alaska Panhandle to Seattle and finally to Arizona before the winds changed, causing the dust to veer up over the central United States. The actual paths, deduced mainly from meteorological observations, of two known eruption clouds are shown on the map. At the time the dust cloud was predicted to pass over Arizona, Prof. Aden Meinel, the founder of the Kitt Peak Astronomical

Observatory, and his wife Marjorie, saw at Tucson a strange-colored, billowy cloud passing over the sky. They took several photographs of the cloud, one of which is reproduced here. Later, they saw a colorful red, glowing sunset that indicated the cloud was a high-altitude one. They suspected then, but did not know, that a volcano had erupted somewhere. Other observers also saw the dust, but the dust clouds thinned and were practically gone by the time they passed out over the Atlantic. Though looked for in

Alaska Dirt Moves South: *Trajectory of the two ash clouds from the St. Augustine eruption deduced from the 300-millibar level meterological data. (Reproduced from* Science *magazine.)*

North America after round the world transit, the clouds were not observed again. One reason for interest in such events is the possibility of global climatic changes brought on by extensive dust layers from volcanism.
— *Glenn Shaw*
Sep 76:111

Augustine Volcano's History

Augustine Volcano's known eruptive history dates back to 1812 but little is known about the activity during that year. Captain James Cook named and charted the volcano in 1778. He described it then as having a conical shape. In 1880 the mountain was described as a "low rounded dome without a peak".

A violent eruption occurred on July 6, 1883 during which the summit was destroyed. Afterwards there was a crater at the top of the mountain, and the new summit was quite jagged. During that

Alaska Dirt Moves South: *The St. Augustine ash cloud passing southwest of Tucson, Arizona. Motion of the cloud is parallel to the streamers and toward the left. The sun is obscured by the lower trunk of the saguaro cactus in the foreground. (Photo from* Science *magazine.)*

The summit of the volcano has been destroyed by an eruption, the previous lava dome having disintegrated and been ejected by the force of the explosion. A small plug of cooled, hardened lava has formed in the vent.

The original lava plug grows, and takes on the form of a dome inside the crater. Pressure from the still plastic magma below forces the plug upward as continued cooling enlarges the mass of hardened material.

The growing dome has completely filled the crater and returned the volcano to its original, conical configuration. This process has taken approximately 90 years at Augustine volcano.

Augustine Volcano's History: *One cycle in the life of an active volcano.*

eruption large seawaves were created. These carried away boats and deluged houses at Port Graham, 50 miles away.

Lava and ash flows accompanied an eruption in 1935. During this eruption a new dome began to grow in the floor of the crater created in 1883. Growth of the dome renewed during explosive eruptions in 1963 and 1969. Since 1958, the dome has grown about 245 feet.

Because of its continuing activity, Augustine is probably the most dangerous of the Cook Inlet volcanoes.

Mar 76:8

The Eruption of Katmai

The recent eruption of Mt. Augustine recalls that of Mt. Katmai in 1912. Katmai's explosion was one of the most powerful to occur in recorded history. Fortunately, its remote location on the Alaska Peninsula, far from major population centers, prevented loss of human life. An eruption of such great force would have buried a nearby city and destroyed its inhabitants.

Residents of Kodiak, 100 miles from Katmai, were among the first Alaskans to observe the eruption phenomenon. A heavy fall of volcanic ash blanketed the town and created considerable apprehension. Initially, no one knew what caused the ash to fall. It was June 6, yet by 6:30 p.m., the town was obscured in total darkness. At the time of the eruption lightning struck the Kodiak radio station. The station burned down and a'l communications with the outside world were severed.

On the morning of the third day after the eruption, the people of Kodiak still groped around in darkness. Ash continued to fall during the day and frequent seismic disturbances were felt. By afternoon, Captain K. W. Perry of the U.S. Revenue Cutter *Manning* decided to evacuate the townspeople. Perry feared that the darkness would hinder his passage through the narrow ship passage leading out of the harbor, but the risk of grounding seemed preferable to remaining to face possible destruction at the hands of nature. Several hundred people crowded aboard the *Manning*. Conditions were uncomfortable, yet the passengers felt more secure in abandoning the town. Everyone remembered the disaster of ancient Pompeii which was buried by the eruption of a nearby volcano.

Kodiak was spared further calamity, and life in the attractive fishing port soon regained its normal momentum. The cataclysmic event caused little serious property damage, but in the awesomeness of its force it ranks with the 1964 Alaska earthquake among the region's great physical disruptions.

Visitors to the Katmai area today see lasting reminders of the eruption in the steaming Valley of Ten Thousand Smokes — a national monument created by presidential order in the aftermath of the blow-up.

— *William R. Hunt*
Jun 76:77

Bogoslof Volcanoes

What do you do when you are President of the United States and you suddenly find you have a brand-new island poking up out of the sea, 20 miles off your shoreline? You claim it and make a bird sanctuary out of it, at least that is what Theodore Roosevelt did in 1909.

The beginnings of the island, Bogoslof volcano, actually existed in 1768 in the form of a rock, called Ship Rock, rising sharply out of the sea. Captain Cook saw it when he sailed by in 1788. Recognition that a new volcanic island was being born came during May 1796. That month an observer standing on Umnak Island, half-way out along the Aleutian chain, saw a new black object appear in the sea, 20 miles off to the north.

As the new island poked up, there were brilliant flames that turned night to day, and many earthquakes and loud thundering noises. Pumice and even stones fell on Umnak. Three days later the flames and the earthquakes subsided to leave a cone-shaped island centered to the south of Ship Rock and connected to it.

The new island underwent some changes during the next hundred years. Then, in 1883 a new companion volcano birthed, about one mile north of Bogoslof. Known as New Bogoslof, and also Grewingk, after an early Alaskan geologist, the newer island now has the name Fire Island.

Over the next six years people observed Fire Island from time to time and watched it grow. A photograph taken in 1883 shows Fire Island to be a curious fantasy of uptilted and jagged spires. This appearance evidently caused the spectators to believe that crustal uplift created the island. Instead, the structure is a lava dome such as often wells up in volcanic vents. Confounded by the lack of a cone appearance, one scientist suggested that subsiding mountains on the Alaskan mainland, 400 miles off to the east, must have somehow pushed up the fantastic tip of Fire Island.

Several years later, in 1906, a new jagged pile of lava thrust up above the sea surface to form yet another island midway between Bogoslof and Fire Island. At that time Fire Island had stopped smoking, as apparently had Bogoslof.

One scientist, presumably the same one who thought subsiding mountains on the Alaskan mainland caused Aleutian volcanoes to grow, predicted that all three islands would wash away within a

George Wharton
1965

Carl Benson
1976

Mt. Wrangell Heats Up: *Two photographs of the North Crater. (Also, see photos on the next page.)*

hundred years. No sooner was this said when new activity commenced in April 1909, giving rise to fiery lights capable of being seen 50 miles away. The very next month, President Roosevelt turned the whole area into a bird refuge. All those hot rocks engulfed in sulfur fumes in their legally assigned new habitat must have impressed the birds no end.

Actually, Teddy Roosevelt acted with foresight because by 1922 a visitor reported the area to have a tomb-like silence interrupted only by the raucous squawking of sea gulls and the terrifying roar of sea lions. He also said the three islands had a look of permanence. Still, all was not done, for in 1927 a new dome thrust up in defiance of the ocean waves which over the years have steadily eroded the Bogoslof Islands. Though changing rapidly, the islands exist today. The ocean may win and totally destroy the islands, but chances are that future eruptions will restore them in some form and that birds will continue to roost there in the intervals between eruptions.

Oct 81:510

Nuées Ardentes

One of the more frightening of volcanic eruption phenomena is the nuée ardente, or glowing cloud. It happens quickly and is hard to escape from; that is one of the reasons why it is wise to evacuate people from volcanoes that erupt explosively.

Nuées ardentes are billowing masses composed of incandescent dust and ash bouyed up by hot gases. A nuée starts with an explosive volcanic eruption that spews the hot material upward or obliquely outward from a vent. After expanding upward hundreds or thousands of feet, the boiling, angry-looking cloud spreads out and falls downslope with ever-increasing

speed and, "at the same time," one viewer said, "developing upward in cauliflower convolutions of dust and ash. These convolutions grow . . . with an indescribably curious rolling and puffing movement which at the immediate front takes the form of forward-springing jets, suggesting charging lions."

With searing temperatures that may exceed 500°F the nuée races downhill at speeds in excess of a hundred miles per hour, typically killing all animal life in its path.

The most famous of all nuées is one that swept several miles down the slopes of Mt. Pelee in 1902 to kill all except two of 30,000 persons in the town of St. Pierre, Martinique. One survivor was in a house on the fringe of the hot cloud, though several others in the same room were killed. The other known survivor was a convicted criminal locked into a subterranean cell. Even there he suffered severe burns and shock. Later he was pardoned and became a celebrity because he had survived. This proves, it has been said, that crime pays.

Apr 80:390

Mt. Wrangell Volcano Heats Up

As the two photographs show, increased heat flow at the top of 14,163-foot Mt. Wrangell during the past few years has radically altered the appearance of the summit.

Our long-time research in the summit area indicates that about 40 million cubic meters of snow and ice have melted from one of the three craters on the rim of the caldera in recent years. The most dramatic changes have occurred in the north crater where the glacier surface has dropped by more than 170 meters (500 feet). This crater, shown in the photographs, is about a kilometer across.

NORTH CRATER, MOUNT WRANGELL, ALASKA

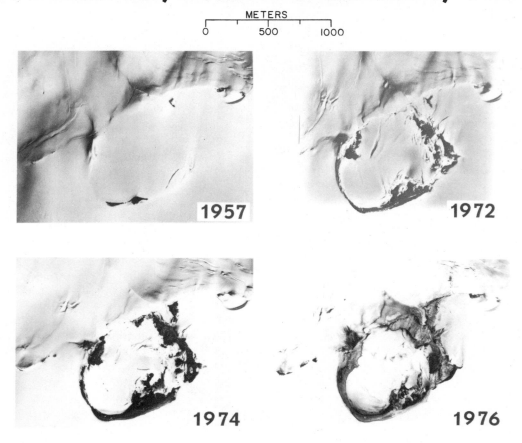

Warming Up of Mt. Wrangell: *Vertical photographs. (Compare with those on the previous page.)*

The volcano bears watching because the increased heat flow can lead to greater water runoff and perhaps flooding, and there is always the possibility of new eruptive activity.
— *Carl Benson*
Dec 76:133

Warming Up of Mt. Wrangell

Of more than a normal interest is the heating up of the summit region of Alaska's Mt. Wrangell the past 20 years. The increase in upward heat flow in a small crater on the rim of the volcano's summit caldera at altitude 4000 m (14,000 ft) does not necessarily mean that an eruption is imminent. But an eruption is an obvious possibility. Mt. Wrangell has been far from inactive in historic times. During the major Yakutat earthquakes in September, 1899, Wrangell increased its output of smoke and ash. The summit caldera, which has a diameter of 6 km, may have been formed as recently as 2000 years ago.

In addition to the usual hazards associated with volcanic eruptions, ice-clad volcanoes like Mt. Wrangell present other hazards to the surrounding areas. Catastrophic flooding by waters from rapid melting of ice and snow on a volcano's flanks have occurred in Alaska as well as in Iceland and the volcanic Cascades of Washington and Oregon.

Mudflows pose another serious problem that can directly devastate property or contribute to outburst flooding by temporarily damming of rivers.

The most recent warming up of Mt. Wrangell began shortly after the 1964 Good Friday Earthquake. Dr. Carl Benson, who has studied the volcano for more than two decades, suspects that the earthquake may have started the warm-up by jiggling something loose in the volcanic plumbing within the mountain.

The warming up of Mt. Wrangell is clearly shown by the melting of glacier ice in the volcano's North Crater. Almost unnoticeable twenty years ago, the North Crater on the caldera rim is now a nearly ice-free pit 200 meters (600 ft) deep. Active steam vents on the crater floor discharge heat energy at a rate of about 100 megawatts. That is enough energy to provide electrical power for a city of perhaps 10,000 people.

Mar 79:288

Maar Formation

During March 1977, a volcano-like eruption was sighted near Becharof Lake 70 miles south of King Salmon. Geologists visiting the area found two holes, the largest about 1000 feet across, on the near-level plain beside the lake. From these holes clouds of steam and ash billowed forth, and lava and rock fragments could be seen spurting upward occasionally.

At first it was not obvious whether the new activity was the beginning of a volcano or a transient breaching of the surface that would eventually lead to the formation of water-filled pits called maars. Maars are found elsewhere in the world, including the north side of the Seward Peninsula, near Cape Espenberg. The accompanying drawing shows how maars are thought to form. It is based upon sketches made

by Dr. Juergen Kienle who, with several others, visited the new eruption.

Jan 77:163

Tolsona Mud Volcanoes

The Tolsona Number One mud volcano lies just a tenth of a mile north, and within easy walking distance, of Mile 173.2 of the Glenn Highway. This is roughly ten miles west of Glennallen, on top of the bluff just east of the Tolsona Creek crossing.

The mud volcano is about 8 meters high (25 feet), 180 meters wide and 270 meters long. Except for a bare region at the crest, the volcano is covered by brush and trees. At the crest, 30 to 40 vents bubble out methane gas and water laced with sodium chloride and calcium chloride salts. The turbulent bubbling of the gas causes mud to be carried up with the water for deposition around the edges of each vent. An increase in the overall activity sometime in recent years has spilled a new layer of mud and salt down from the top of the volcano where it has killed brush and trees growing near the crest.

The seething cauldrons atop the Tolsona mud volcanoes (there are four of them in the area) hide a

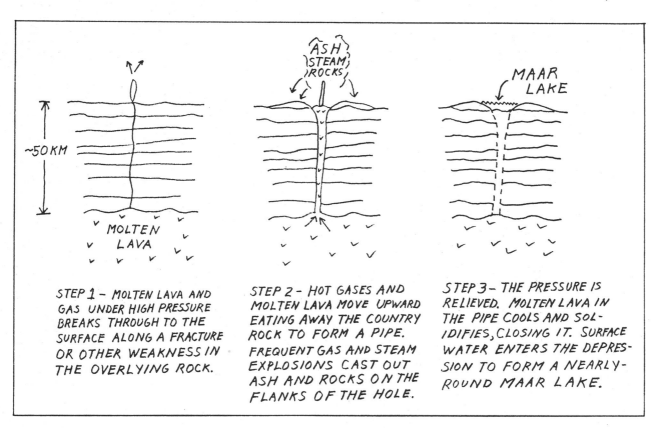

Maar Formation: *The best guess of what happens.*

Tolsona Mud Volcanoes: *Budding scientist, Tommy Pollard, tests the water bubbling up through a vent atop Tolsona Mud Volcano Number One.*

mystery, since no one really knows where the erupting methane gas comes from.

Methane is the simplest of the hydrocarbon compounds, being composed of one carbon atom and four atoms of hydrogen. It is colorless and odorless, but it burns right smartly. Mixed with air in proper proportions, it burns explosively. Consequently, it

has caused many deaths among coal miners, who call the substance marsh gas or fire damp.

One source of methane is decomposition of organic material under anaerobic (lacking in air) conditions. Thus it is possible that the methane bubbling up through the Tolsona mud volcanoes derives from coal beds or other hydrocarbon sources in the rocks not far below. Certainly methane is the chief constituent of natural gas; more than 80% of the gas that will be transported in the proposed gasline to be built in Alaska and Canada is methane.

Another possibility is that the methane bubbling up through the Tolsona mud volcanoes comes from deep within the earth where it was trapped or evolved during the formation of the solid earth itself.

Aug 78:249

Why Hot Springs?

Only a few years ago geologists thought that the water ejected by hot springs was primary water released from molten magmas far below the surface. Now new lines of evidence, including measurements of oxygen and hydrogen isotopes, show that nearly all of the water is recirculated groundwater. The accompanying diagram shows this concept and how a geothermal well might be obtained. Located north of Fairbanks in the Yukon-Tanana Uplands are a number of hot spring localities. These extend from the Salcha River watershed westward to the Seward Peninsula. The better known hot springs in this region are Chena Hot Springs, Circle Hot Springs and Manley Hot Springs, all accessible by road.

Jul 76:87

Alaska's Hot Springs: *More than a hundred hot springs dot the Alaska landscape. They are generated by the return to the surface of water that first fell as rain or snow upon land at higher elevation and then was heated at depth.*

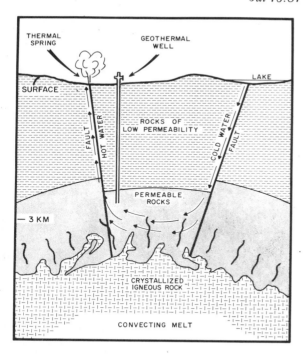

Why Hot Springs? *The hot water fell as rain or snow. (Drawing by R. Forbes and N. Biggar,* The Northern Engineer *5(1), 1973.)*

Alaska's Hot Springs

For a land that has a reputation for being all ice and snow, Alaska has a goodly share of hot springs and flows of warm water. More than a hundred hot springs dot the Alaska mainland and another 24 reportedly gush forth from the Aleutian Islands.

A new publication *Geothermal Energy Resources of Alaska* contains a map and information on Alaskan hot springs and other geothermal resources. Prepared by Dr. Donald Turner and co-workers at the Geophysical Institute, this publication is the first to combine in one place the available information on Alaskan hot springs.

Two features of the Alaskan hot springs map stand out. One is that the springs are scattered all over the state. The other is that the springs group together in more-or-less linear arrays, the reason being that the springs are associated with linear geologic structures such as linear fracture zones or volcanic belts.

Virtually all of the hot water emerging in hot springs starts out as precipitation. From the ground surface it penetrates through faults or water-permeable layers deep enough in the ground to become heated before returning to the surface under hydrostatic pressure. In other words, the water must emerge from the ground at a lower place than it went into the ground.

In the Aleutian Islands and near the volcanic Wrangell Mountains, water can be heated at quite shallow depths by magma (molten rock) not far below the ground surface. The water that emerges from the band of hot springs stretching east-west across northcentral Alaska probably seeps more deeply into the earth where it is heated by still-warm rock solidified long ago.

Oct 80:438

Pilgrim Hot Springs

The year 1979 may have put new life into a mineral hot spring 50 miles north of Nome that for many years has bubbled up 175°F water through the permafrost at a rate of 60 gallons per minute.

In gold rush days, the site was named Kruzgamepa Hot Springs, after the nearby river that heads in Salmon Lake and flows westerly into the Imuruk Basin. Up until the saloon and roadhouse burned down in 1908, the Springs was the resort spa where residents of the southern Seward Peninsula went for hot baths and other recreational delights. A severe influenza epidemic in the years 1916-1918 killed twelve hundred people living between St. Michael and Cape Prince of Wales. The flu left many children homeless so the Catholic Church built a home for them at what is now called Pilgrim Springs (the Kruzgamepa has also become the Pilgrim River). This mission survived until 1942, by which time the children had grown up. A church and a few other old buildings mark the site.

The solitude of Pilgrim Springs was interrupted this past summer by the frenzied thumping of a helicopter working to support geologists and geophysicists. A combined crew from the Alaska Division of Geological and Geophysical Surveys and the Geophysical Institute had converged on the area seeking to get themselves into hot water. The crew dug dirt, pounded rocks, drove pipes in the ground, strung wires around and appeared to walk aimlessly over the area carrying curious-looking electronic gadgets.

When it was all over, the scientific prospecting effort pointed toward a hot area 1500 feet away from the Pilgrim Spring itself. To test the results, a drilling rig was brought in. Concern over the danger of drilling into too hot a spot led to the first hole being drilled off to the edge of the indicated hot area.

A six-inch hole was put down to a depth of 150 feet (50 meters) where it struck an artesian flow of 200 gallons per minute at a temperature of 195°F (90°C). A second well placed midway between the first well and the prime spot dictated by the geophysical work produced similar water at twice the flow rate. Next year, a well will be drilled on the prime spot.

When wells are put down to extract the hot water, one worries that the flow generated in one well might decrease the flow from another or from the natural spring area. But the preliminary geophysical work at Pilgrim Springs suggests that many wells could be drilled without harm. It appears that the Pilgrim (Kruzgamepa) River now carries away much of the heat energy brought to the surface, and that additional wells would merely intercept that energy.

Initial measurements indicate that the river is carrying away energy equivalent to that heat energy contained in a flow of nearly 5000 barrels of oil a day. This rate of oil flow is about the same as that of petroleum products from the North Pole Refinery near Fairbanks.

Jan 80:365

Manley Hot Springs

Of the hot springs strung across northcentral Alaska, Manley Hot Springs has one of the more colorful histories.

The spring is not large; it produces about 200 gallons per minute of water near temperature 58°C (136°F). From that flow one could use current technology to extract about the same amount of heat that would be produced by burning a barrel of fuel oil each hour. This is enough to heat a fairly large building in the Alaskan environment.

In 1901 a prospector named Karshner found the springs at Manley and homesteaded the surrounding land. Gold was struck soon afterward at nearby Tofty and Eureka, bringing thousands of hopeful miners to the region. One of them, a man who called himself Frank Manley, arrived from the Cleary Creek diggings near Fairbanks with several hundred thousand dollars in hand. Manley's money and Karshner's homestead soon combined to create Alaska's first large-scale geothermal project.

Irrelevant, but interesting, was the later finding that Frank Manley's true name was Willard Beaumont. He left Texas "hastily" and was returned there and tried for horse thievery, a charge of which he was acquitted.

Karshner and Manley cleared many acres of land, built a geothermally-heated, 60-room hotel of logs and various other buildings including poultry, hog and dairy barns. Their grain garden and potato crops thrived; in 1910 they shipped 150 tons of potatoes down the Tanana and Yukon Rivers to the Iditarod mining district.

By 1913 the area's placer mining began to decline and so did the Manley agricultural and resort enterprise. Loss of the three-story log hotel to fire was a major blow.

Asparagus and strawberries grown wild and a few remnants of underground aquaducts are among the few remaining relics of that exciting early era. What are the chances of a major rebirth? Perhaps not too bad, considering the rising cost of energy, the ever improving geothermal technology and increasing demand for the high-quality agricultural products that can be produced there.

Jan 79:280

Manley Hot Springs: *The geothermally heated three-story log hotel at Manley Hot Springs. This 60-room structure burned in 1913. (Photo from the University of Alaska Archives, Charles Bunnell Collection.)*

Historic Alaskan Earthquakes

Major earthquakes have been a part of Alaskan life throughout historic time. The first one for which we have specific information occurred on July 27, 1788, somewhere near the south side of the Alaska Peninsula. "Tidal wave; lives lost" is the cryptic entry in a catalogue of Alaskan earthquakes. Ninety years later, on August 29, 1878, the town of Makushin, on Unalaska Island, was destroyed by an earthquake and an accompanying tidal wave.

Perhaps still within memory of some Yakutat residents were the terrible earthquakes of 1899. The town had just spent a week recovering from a Richter magnitude 8.3 earthquake on September 3, when the area was rocked by an even larger 8.6 shock, the biggest ever recorded in North America. Southeastern Alaska experienced several severe earthquakes in subsequent years. Then the magnitude 8.0 earthquake of July 10, 1958, struck, causing five deaths at Lituya Bay and Yakutat.

For death and destruction, no Alaskan earthquakes compare with the Good Friday earthquake of March 27, 1964, in Prince William Sound. One hundred thirty-one people died, and the damage

reached a half-billion dollars in this magnitude 8.3 to 8.6 earthquake.

Despite Alaska's low population and the recentness of its development, Alaskan earthquakes are second only to California's in total damages and deaths caused. In California, 1029 people have been killed by earthquake effects; 700 of these died in the 1906 San Francisco quake. Hawaii lost 173 people in a tidal wave caused by an Alaskan earthquake in 1947. If we add these to Alaska's list, it makes a total of 309 plus the unknown number lost in the 1788 earthquake off the Alaska Peninsula and perhaps others of which we have no record.

Mar 78:26

Measuring Earthquakes

We have been asked the meaning of the Richter magnitude scale now commonly used to report earthquakes.

Some years ago, before seismographs were widely deployed, the Modified Mercalli intensity scale was used. It measured not how strong an earthquake was, but rather how strongly it was felt or how much damage it caused. The Mercalli scale ran from I to

116

XII, I being an earthquake felt only by a few persons under favorable circumstances and XII meaning total destruction.

The Richter scale uses seismographs to measure actual ground motion at a specific distance (100 km) from the earthquake epicenter (origin). Earthquakes smaller than Richter scale 3 are not usually felt even by persons near the epicenter. The Richter scale is logarithmic, which means that a Richter scale 4 earthquake has ten times more motion than a scale 3 earthquake, Richter scale 5 means ten times as much motion as scale 4, and so on.

The largest earthquakes have Richter magnitudes 8.0 to 8.6, but great damage has been done by earthquakes of only magnitude 5 or 6.

Alaska has had more than its share of truly large earthquakes — Richter magnitude 8.6 near Yakutat on September 10, 1899; the Lituya Bay earthquake of July 10, 1958 was magnitude 8 and the March 27, 1964 Good Friday earthquake near Anchorage was magnitude 8.5.

Apr 76:14

When the Shaking Begins

Any person living for a period of a few years or more in the Aleutians or in southern or central Alaska is likely to experience a strong, possibly damaging, earthquake. One's chances of getting hurt in a strong earthquake really are fairly small, but the chances can be made even smaller by taking the right actions.

Above all, stay calm. If inside, stay inside, or if outside, stay outside; entering or leaving a building can be dangerous, especially one of masonry with attached exterior objects that might fall during the shaking.

The safest places to stand indoors usually are near interior walls or within interior doorways. Office desks or other heavy pieces of furniture give good protection if one can get under them. Stay away from windows and outside doors.

If outdoors, avoid overhead electrical wires or objects that might fall. If driving a car, stop the car and remain inside until the shaking ceases.

Collapsing dams, sloshing of water in lakes and tsunamis can be deadly. It can pay to be alert to these possibilities if one is near the water when an earthquake occurs. In many instances, there will be time enough to reach a safer location.

Oct 80:264

Foreshocks and Aftershocks

It is quite obvious that earthquakes are not always random events. In other words, the occurrence of one earthquake often is related to another earthquake. There are patterns of earthquake occurrence that, if understood, can tell us something about the nature of earthquakes and the rocks wherein they occur.

Following almost any sizable earthquake, there is a train of many lesser earthquakes. Simply for the reasons that they occur after the big shock and appear to be related to it, these earthquakes are called aftershocks. Usually, the bigger the main earthquake, the more numerous and bigger are the aftershocks. Following a magnitude 7-plus, tsunami-generating earthquake in the Aleutian Islands in 1965, there were more than 750 substantial aftershocks within the first 24 hours. Sometimes these aftershock trains continue on for months. As time goes by, the frequency and the size of the aftershocks tend to decrease.

The characteristics of aftershocks indicate that they are a continuation of the strain release processes that the main shock participated in, rather than being caused by elastic rebound. Hence, if the main earthquake is caused by a big sudden breakage of the rocks in a particular direction, the aftershocks are caused by lesser breakages in the same direction.

Some major earthquakes are preceded by earthquakes obviously related to the occurrence of the main shock, the so-called foreshocks. Laboratory experiments show that as the elastic limits of rocks are exceeded by a stress, the rocks tend to develop minor cracks before undergoing catastrophic failure. This incipient cracking may be the cause of foreshocks.

So far, seismologists are mostly unable to identify a particular earthquake as being a foreshock, a mainshock or an aftershock until the sequence is over and hindsight is applied. But some regions do display repeating sequences; there, it may be possible to use foreshock activity as a prediction tool.

Apr 79:297

Earthquake Prevention Techniques

Following a major earthquake in southern California some years ago, one of the seismological laboratories there decided to investigate the expected aftershock sequence. They got permission to establish an array of seismometers on a large ranch near where the earthquake had occurred. The seismologists set up the array which fed signals by wires into a large, wrist-sized cable that led into a portable recording van.

They soon got everything working, and signals were humming into the van to show the occurrence of many small aftershocks and some large enough to be felt. Then, suddenly, all the signals ceased. Seeking the cause of the termination, the seismologists went outside the van to find a woman standing with axe in hand beside the seismograph cable which she had just chopped neatly in twain. Defiantly, she explained "we've had enough earthquakes around here lately without you guys making any more."

A similar approach to the problem has been reported by California seismologist Bruce Bolt. In his book *Earthquakes, A Primer*, he tells of a handyman at the seismographic station in the Bahamas. During a strong earthquake in 1965, the man drew out his pistol and shot the jittering seismograph in an attempt to quell the violent ground motion.

Mar 79:296

Ten-Year Earthquake Cycle

February 1977 seems to be adding one more positive data point to the apparent ten-year cycle of earthquake activity in the Fairbanks area.

The *News-Miner* headline on July 22, 1937, read "Fairbanks hit by its worst quake." At the bottom of the same page and extending clear across the page was an ad, "Earthquake Insurance — Alaska Insurance Agency — call John Butrovich, Jr." This magnitude 7.5 quake blocked the Richardson Highway at 33 Mile Bluff and ruined many bottles of liquor in Fairbanks.

The magnitude 7 earthquake of October 16, 1947, was less severe and fewer bottles were broken in Fairbanks stores. From the previous earthquake, area merchants had learned the value of containment wires across open shelves. One wonders if they also followed up on John Butrovich's ad. Earthquakes of May 1958 were strongly felt in Fairbanks but they actually were located nearer Manley Hot Springs.

A magnitude 7.1 earthquake on June 21, 1967, caused minor damage and the temporary evacuation of Bassett Army Hospital.

So far the 1977 earthquake swarms have contained no shocks of comparable size to those of 10, 20, 30 and 40 years ago. The largest so far, magnitude 4.2 on February 27, is many times smaller than the previous main shocks. What the rest of 1977 will bring is hard to say. The worst may be past, but simple precautions such as wires across bottle-carrying shelves will do no harm.

Mar 77:150

Earthquake Lights

When scientists are sceptical about the existence of reported phenomena, they often try to cover up under a layer of humor. Such an attempt by one seismologist led him to remark that "the chapter on earthquake lights is the darkest in seismology."

No longer does this subject lurk in the shadows of scientific scepticism. Among the more illuminating observations that have brought this topic out into the scientific light of day are those acquired by a Jap-anese dentist. He managed to photograph earthquake lights occurring during a ten-year earthquake swarm starting in 1965.

While seismologists are not yet certain of the cause of earthquake lights, they now are highly interested. Not only is it certain that earthquakes can cause lights in the sky; it seems possible that the lights sometimes occur before earthquakes and so serve as warning precursors.

One of the more logical explanations of the cause of earthquake lights is the piezoelectric effect. Certain materials, including quartz, respond to changes in pressure by changes in electrical voltage across their surfaces. The idea is that, as quartz-bearing rocks are stressed, they might produce such high voltages that lightning-like discharges could occur in the air above.

Earthquake lights have been described as looking like auroral streamers diverging from a point on the horizon. Beams like those from a searchlight have been reported. Other reports describe sheets or circular glowing regions, either touching the ground or in detached clouds above ground.

The lights seem to show up best during the time of the main shock of an earthquake and also before and after. From a practical viewpoint, the lights before an earthquake seem most interesting since they shed light on the occurrence of the next large earthquake.

So far, no earthquake lights have been reported in Alaska.

Apr 78:83

Seaquakes

What is an earthquake like at sea? Almost universally, reports by people on ships tell of having thought that the ship had run aground. Rumbling, grating sensations and horrifying rattling of ship superstructures are reported. The noises often appear to come mainly from the bottom of the ship, and there is fear that the ship is breaking up.

Evidently, strong earthquake waves traveling below the ocean floor start compressional wave trains (like sound waves in air) that travel upward through the water at a steep angle. Striking the ship bottom, these waves apparently cause no real damage to the ship.

Much more to be feared by seamen traveling near a shore are the giant tsunami waves generated by nearby or distant earthquakes. In 1868, while traveling near Peru, the unfortunate captain of the U.S. gunboat *Wateree* was forced to abandon ship after a tsunami deposited his vessel on its flat bottom, two miles inland.

May 77:164

Tsunamis

Tsunamis, commonly called tidal waves, are really seismic sea waves generated by earthquakes. In the open sea they travel very fast, perhaps 600 miles per hour, but have almost no effect there because of the low height and great length of the waves.

But as the waves approach land, it is a different story. The waves pile up as the ocean depth lessens; destructive surges as much as 100 feet high can result. Sometimes sea level drops in the minutes before a tsunami strikes, but since it doesn't always, this is not a satisfactory warning of an approaching tsunami.

The Pacific Ocean has had many tsunamis; in the Atlantic only one has been reported. It accompanied the great Lisbon earthquake of 1755. Its devastation to a portion of this best of all possible worlds formed an episode in Voltaire's *Candide*.

One of the worst tsunamis of recent years was generated by an Aleutian earthquake in 1946. The tsunami killed 159 people in Hawaii and destroyed nearly 500 homes. Another similar incident occurred in 1957. This time the establishment of a tsunami warning system prevented loss of life in Hawaii, but there was three million dollars in property damage there.

May 77:165

God Spared the Russians

The first documented Alaskan earthquake occurred during July 1788, perhaps on the 27th day of the month or possibly as early as the 11th. Reports that have survived in the records of the Russian-American Company state that the earthquake lasted 17 days, so there is uncertainty on the dates of large shocks in the series that shook the region of the Alaska Peninsula.

Russian bishop I. Veniaminov cited a report stating "on 11 July 1788 . . . on Unga there was such a strong earthquake that it was difficult to stand up, many landslides fell, and after a time a terrible flood occurred."

Another report said "The earthquake on Kodiak Island was frightful. After the first shocks, the sea suddenly withdrew from the shore. Then the Koniags (Kodiak people) and the Russians fled into the mountains. After a few minutes, water with great speed and appearing like a mountain surged against the shore."

Repeated tsunamis were characteristic of the 1788 earthquakes, indicating an offshore location for these shocks. That people had enough sense to run inland when the sea withdrew from the shore shows that they were experienced in the ways of tsunamis.

Even so, not everyone survived. Writing in 1840, Veniaminov cited stories about how the flood at Sanak Island "preceded as strong and infrequent walls. In addition to this, I saw a remark in a church book, written in old-fashioned handwriting, which stated that on 27 July 1788 there was such a terrible flood on Unga Island that many Aleuts were killed though God spared the Russians."

Mar 80:379

Lituya Bay

T-shaped Lituya Bay is an accident of nature that perhaps shouldn't have happened. But it is the only haven for seafarers facing the open sweep of the Pacific on the passage north from Cross Sound to Yakutat. Many are the sailors who have avoided hours of difficult sea or being storm-battered against the rocky coast by entering the entrance to Lituya Bay at slack flood tide, the only time for safe passage.

Gouged out of steep mountains abutting the sea, Lituya Bay is a place of unusual beauty. The French explorer La Pérouse hoped to make it France's base in Alaska and named it Port of France. He described it as "perhaps the most extraordinary place in the world."

The crossbar part of Lituya Bay is the glacier-filled trench of the Fairweather fault, an active break slicing through the mountains roughly parallel to the coast. At some time in the recent past, a weakness in the rock strata allowed a breach to develop connecting the Fairweather trench to the ocean, and so Lituya Bay was formed. Of Lituya Bay's weird grandeur La Pérouse said, "I never saw a breath of air ruffle the surface of this water; it is never troubled but by the fall of immense blocks of ice, which continually detach themselves from fine glaciers, and which in falling make a noise that resounds far through the mountains. The air is so calm that the voice may be heard half a league (2-3 miles) away."

Something had to be wrong with this northern Shangri-La, and La Pérouse soon learned that there was. On July 13, 1786, La Pérouse's "calm waters" suddenly swallowed up 21 of his finest officers and men as they tried to sound the waters at the narrow entrance to Lituya Bay where currents as fast as 14 mph flow. None of the bodies were recovered, but La Pérouse built a monument to the lost persons on Lituya Bay's central island. He aptly named the place Cenotaph (meaning empty tomb) Island.

Nor was this the only example of Lituya's potential for terror. The seismic forces that built the bay have repeatedly displayed their power. Earthquakes on the active Fairweather fault probably caused the giant water waves which swept down the bay in 1853 or 1854, about 1874, and in 1936. The latest earthquake-caused wave on July 10, 1958, reached a height greater than 100 feet. Speeding along at about 100 miles per hour, it swept right over the top of Ceno-

Lituya Bay: *The central portion of T-shaped Lituya Bay with Cenotaph Island in its center. Towering peaks surround the bay, with Mt. Crillion the tallest at 12,726 feet high. Treeless areas of the shore were wiped clean by the wave which swept down the bay on July 10, 1958. (Photo by Byron Hale.)*

taph Island. It also sank two fishing vessels, and drowned the man-and-wife crew of one.

May 78:91

The Big Splash

Residents of Kodiak and other Alaskan cities with steep-sided mountains nearby have from time to time expressed concern about the potential for damage from landslides. One of the dangers is the creation of splash waves when landslides fall into the sea.

Among other records, Alaska holds the one for the biggest splash wave ever observed. It occurred on July 10, 1958, during a major earthquake in southeast Alaska. Violent ground motion along the Fairweather fault caused a huge landslide in the upper part of Lituya Bay.

Forty million cubic yards of dirt and rocks cascaded down a 3000-foot slope near the head of the bay. The landslide clipped off the front of the Lituya glacier as it fell into the bay. A hugh splash wave surged up the opposite slope to the unbelievable height of 1740 feet (535 meters).

The surging water denuded the slope of trees and soils. Even above the 1700-foot level trees were uprooted and thrown uphill by the force of the water.

This is by far the biggest splash wave recorded anywhere in the world. In 1936 a landslide into Leon Lake, Norway, created a splash wave 230 feet high,

and at Cape Lopatka on the Kamchatka Peninsula, a tsunami wave 210 feet high broke on the coast in 1737.

May 78:109

The Big Splash: *Headland beside the Lituya Glacier that was swept clean of soil and trees to a height of 1740 ft by the giant splash wave. The icebergs seen in the water of Lituya Bay, foreground, were knocked off the glacier by the landslide falling into the bay from a slope to the right of the photograph. (Photo by Byron Hale.)*

Khantaak Island: *The beach remaining near where the tip of Khantaak Island slid into the sea also fell a few feet and was left heavily fissured.*

Khantaak Island

When great destructive earthquakes strike heavily populated areas it comes as no surprise that hundreds or thousands of people are injured or killed. But when great earthquakes happen in unpeopled areas the few deaths that sometimes occur can seem like strange twists of fate.

So it was with three Yakutat, Alaska residents standing on Khantaak Island, just two miles across the sheltered Monti Bay from the town. Mrs. Jeanne Walton and Mr. and Mrs. Robert Tibbles had landed on the tip of the island to pick wild berries. Accompanying them in another small boat were the Yakutat postmaster and his wife, Mr. and Mrs. John Williams. The date was July 10, 1958.

About 9:30 p.m. the Williamses decided to leave for home; Mr. and Mrs. Tibbles and Mrs. Walton decided to stay a while longer. They waved good-by and the Williams' boat left to run back to Yakutat. A few minutes later Mrs. Williams saw trees on the

island whipping back and forth. She looked back toward the beach they had just left only to find that it was hidden behind a wall of water rushing away from the beach toward the Williams' boat. Mr. Williams gave the boat full throttle and outran the wave until its height was no longer dangerous. But when the wave subsided, the beach was gone.

As far as is known, the three people were standing on the gently sloping shore near their beached boat when the first seismic waves arrived from an earthquake centered 100 miles away beyond Lituya Bay, to the southeast. Suddenly the ground beneath their feet fell away and plunged more than 100 feet below the sea.

Though no survivor actually saw the collapse, several persons around Monti Bay viewed the spot within the next few minutes. Where the tip of Khantaak Island had been they saw "heavy black, boiling water". It "looked alive, boiling". Later the heavily damaged hull of the Tibbles boat was found floating submerged near where it was last seen by the escaping Williams couple. The three on the beach were never found.

Why did a half million or more cubic yards of earth sink below the sea? The immediate cause of this peculiar event was the shaking of the unconsolidated sands and gravels that form portions of the bottom and shores of Yakutat Bay. Below sea level these water-saturated materials quickly lose their load-bearing strength when vibrated by seismic waves.

The shallow floor of Monti Bay, near the tip of Khantaak Island where Mrs. Walton and Mr. and Mrs. Tibble stood, simply slid away toward the deeper water. Unsupported, a strip of land 50 by 150 yards fell into the bay creating the wave that chased the Williamses to shore. It is likely that a sizable submarine slide occurred since the tip of the island fell vertically about 120 feet (40 meters).

This is not the only known instance of substantial

bottom changes in Yakutat Bay during an earthquake. Following the February 28, 1979 earthquake just north of the bay, decreases in charted depth by as much as 20 feet were reported, presumably the result of underwater slides such as the one earlier in Monti Bay. A special notice to mariners was put out warning extreme caution when navigating Yakutat Bay since the full extent of bottom changes were not fully known.

Jul 79:327

Sandblows

It was a pleasant summer evening on the Yakutat Foreland until the few people there felt the first earthquake motions. Most ran outside and then were thrown to the ground by earth motions of increasing severity. Unable to rise for several minutes, people heard rumbling and grinding noises in the mountains behind the Foreland and saw the earth ripple into

Khantaak Island: *Following the earthquake, only a cliff remained where, before, there had been a beach gently sloping off into the water. When this picture was taken, the water only a few yards offshore was 100 feet deep.*

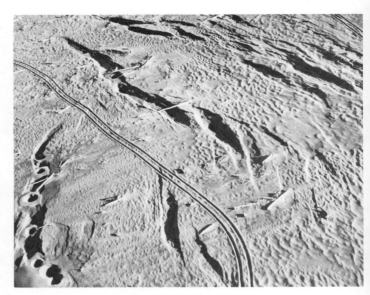

Sandblows: *Bush pilot Donald E. Vent inspects a crater left by a sandblow near Yakutat. Flooding of the area during the eruption of the sandblows has coated the area with a layer of silt and sand, including the fissure just beyond the sandblow.*

Sandblows: *New truck tracks cut across an area of the beach badly fissured during the Lituya Bay earthquake. Older tracks made before the earthquake show faintly. Several sandblows in the fissure at left have partially filled it with sand.*

waves that raced across the nearby ground. In the soft, wet soils of the Foreland the waves opened fissures in the ground and cast up volcano-like eruptions of water and sand.

These so-called sandblows were one of the more spectacular consequences of the great Lituya Bay earthquake of July 10, 1958, though few people saw them, and time soon obliterated evidence of their existence. Tens of thousands of sandblows occurred during the earthquake in the flat coastal region (the Foreland) between Lituya Bay and Yakutat. Some erupted from obvious fissures in the ground. Others were aligned in rows marking out unseen cracks, and many seemed to occur with random placement.

Sandblows form where strong, continued earthquake shaking causes wet, loose soil to consolidate. As sand-sized particles within about 100 feet (30 meters) of the surface are shaken, they reorient so as to fit more closely together. Pressure from the weight of the soil above squeezes water out from the diminishing pore spaces between the sand particles and forces it upwards.

If the water table is not too far below the ground surface, flooding of the surface can result. More usually, water jets up at points determined by zones of weakness or in cracks opened up by the earthquake's shaking. Sand-laden water spouts several feet high are seen, usually a minute or two after the strong shaking begins. The jetting action in a sandblow is easily simulated by holding one's partly opened

fist, thumb upward, about half submerged in water. If one orients the hand properly, a quick closure of the fist leads to a faceful of water.

Jul 79:323

The Mogi Doughnut

Named after Japanese seismologist K. Mogi who suggested the idea in 1969, the Mogi Doughnut is a catchy name for an earthquake prediction scheme. Speaking punningly, the whole idea is based upon the current understanding of why earthquakes occur where they do.

Earthquakes are thought to occur where there are the greatest concentrations of strain in the earth's rocks. Strain is the elastic deformation of material that occurs when stress (pressure) is applied to it. If the strain is too great, the material must break or else flow inelastically, that is, without rebounding to its original form when the stress is relieved.

The rock breakage that creates an earthquake relieves the strain where the fracturing occurs. However, the movement of the rocks near a breaking fault may place increased stress on rocks out away from the fault. In a sense, it is like tearing a piece of cloth. By pulling the cloth at an edge, one can apply enough stress there to break a single thread. But then the stress is shifted to the next thread and it breaks. One after the other, the threads break as the region of highest concentration of tensional stress moves across the cloth.

In Japan, Professor Mogi noticed that large earthquakes tended to occur in the center of a peculiar doughnut-shaped pattern that developed in the ten or so years preceding the earthquake. The pattern involved an abnormal seismic calm in the hole of the doughnut and more than usual activity in the outer ring. Professor Mogi suggested that this pattern meant that the central region would undergo high stress and therefore be likely to have a large earthquake.

A recent prediction of increased likelihood of a large earthquake in the Cape Yakataga region of southern Alaska is based partly upon Mogi's doughnut idea. A roughly circular region north of Cape Yakataga has experienced fewer earthquakes than the surrounding zone. But since the history of seismic recording in most of Alaska is so short, it is not known if the zone of quiet near Cape Yakataga is recently developed and therefore a Mogi Doughnut. Still, other reasons exist for predicting an earthquake in the area near Cape Yakataga. Only time will tell if the Mogi idea is useful for earthquake prediction in Alaska.

Jul 79:315

Rock Dilatancy

Many of the phenomena which precede an earthquake and are now of aid in earthquake prediction are thought to be caused by another phenomenon called dilatancy. Unlikely as it sounds, the idea is that rocks expand when squeezed. To see how this is possible, consider a well-shaken box of marbles. The marbles settle in a configuration leaving minimum spacing, as shown in A. But then if two opposite sides of the box are pushed together, as in B, the marbles move such that larger air spaces exist between them. Hence the total volume increases.

In the theory of dilatancy, rocks are considered to be composed of tiny grains. If the ground surface starts to rise or if water rises in wells, it means that the rocks are being deformed and the rock grains are being dislocated from their minimum volume configuration. The deformation seems to be greatest just before the rocks break — that is, in the hours just before the earthquake.

Aug 76:101

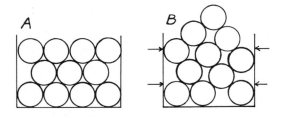

Rock Dilatancy: *Squeezing increases volume.*

Earthquakes and Animals: *Patricia Davis illustrates an unusual animal behavior not yet reported.*

Earthquakes and Animals

Chinese seismologists have underway a major program of evaluating animal behavior as a means of earthquake prediction. They got serious about the matter in 1966 when it was discovered that all the resident dogs left their kennels at a village in Hopei Province just before a large earthquake originated in the rocks below the town.

The Chinese scientists soon collected more than 2000 eyewitness accounts of unusual pre-earthquake behavior, mostly involving domestic animals. The strange behavior was reported to peak in the 24-hour interval just prior to the earthquake; sometimes strange behavior in animals was observed several days before an earthquake. The bigger the earthquake, the more reports there were of unusual behavior.

Several centers now have been established in China to make earthquake predictions by various methods including observation of animals. These centers have set up operational networks to report and evaluate the observations of animal behavior.

An article by a Chinese scientist in the *U.S. Geological Survey Earthquake Information Bulletin* implies that the Chinese think that the strange pre-quake behavior of animals arises from their sensitivity to small foreshocks occurring before the main event. This idea comes partly from experiments on animals having had their sensory capabilities altered by surgery.

A series of observations near Yakutat just before the Lituya Bay earthquake on July 10, 1958, backs up the Chinese conjecture. One person picking berries saw leaves move when they shouldn't have, while nearby others saw birds become disturbed and fly over the trees in unusual numbers. Simultaneously yet another nearby group suddenly started getting bites from fish with every cast into the river. Several minutes later the magnitude 8 earthquake struck. In this instance it seems likely that the birds and fish were responding to vibrations evidenced by the moving leaves but which were not noticed by the people present. Also, it has been suggested that animals may be responding to the release of gases such as methane just before the earthquake.

Mar 71:295

Mammoths and Earthquakes

During the nineteenth century, mammoth finds were frequent enough in Siberia that some persons became professional mammoth ivory hunters. The tusks were in demand for the manufacture of piano keys, billiard balls and other objects. Since the tusks, and even nearly-complete mammoth carcasses, were found in the ground, it was thought by many that the animals themselves lived underground. In parts of China people conjectured that the burrowing of these large beasts beneath the surface was the cause of earthquakes. (If 1976 continues to be a bad year for earthquakes, maybe we better think about setting some mammoth traps.)

Sep 76:113

The Unstable Earth

The question of who owns the land uncovered by a retreating glacier near Juneau came into the news recently. Since we tend to think of geological changes as being slow, questions such as this might seem, at first glance, to be relatively unimportant. Yet, Alaska's high level of tectonic activity, coupled with the effects of climatic change, can alter the geography rather rapidly. New land created by some but not all of these changes belongs to the public rather than to those who own adjacent property.

Earthquakes and volcanic eruptions, of course, can create big changes in a short time. The violent earthquakes of September 3 and 10, 1899, created major changes in the shorelines around Yakutat Bay. In some places the beaches subsided, in others they raised; the earthquake created the world record for uplift — 47 feet, 4 inches — at a location on the west shore of Disenchantment Bay, which lies at the head of Yakutat Bay.

During the 1964 Good Friday earthquake, much of Cook Inlet and the Kenai Peninsula subsided by distances ranging from near zero on the west side of the inlet to six feet on the east side of the peninsula. Off to the southeast, parts of Montague Island rose

30 feet. Horizontal movements as great as 70 feet accompanied the sinking and rising. During the event, the Matanuska Valley grew about five feet wider.

More subtle are the elevation changes that evidently proceed more-or-less continuously. The teacher of a surveying course I once took told about the troubles had by a crew running a level-line from the Gulf of Alaska to Big Delta, some years ago. One summer they ran the line to Big Delta. The next year, they ran back the other way, only to find that their survey failed to close by about four feet. A more speedy repeat of the work demonstrated that the land in the Interior was rising relative to the coast. Hence the moving land, not faulty work, was responsible for the failure to close the survey.

Oct 80:434

Alaskan Clay

Clay suitable for use in pottery occurs in many places in Alaska, but clay from only a very few localities has actually been used in modern Alaskan pottery. Important sources are the extensive clay layers intermingled with the coal beds near Healy. A mixture of Healy clay and clay from near the Chulitna River crossing of the Parks Highway has been found by Fairbanks area potters to be suitable for making thrown clay objects.

In throwing clay, one forms the material on a rotating wheel. Slippage along the flat platelets of the clay particles allows the clay to be formed into bowls and more complex circular shapes. The Chulitna and most of the Healy clay is grayish, but when fired it turns white. Some of the Healy clay that is yellow when found turns brick red when fired.

For sale in many Alaskan shops are brown and cream ceramic pieces made by the slip casting process. In slip casting, a very fluid blend of several clays is poured into a plaster mold. The mold absorbs water from the outer portion of the clay, causing it to become viscous. Then the mold is tipped to pour out the still-fluid center, leaving a rind still within the mold. After further drying, the object is removed from the mold and fired.

The marbleized effect in some clay products sold in Alaska is achieved by simultaneously pouring two different slips into the mold. In these products the cream color derives from a commerical clay obtained outside Alaska, and the brown color comes from a famous Alaskan clay, the Bootlegger Cove Clay.

The Bootlegger Cove Clay receives its fame not from its use by potters, but because its existence beneath parts of the city of Anchorage caused great damage during the 1964 earthquake. Persistent ground shaking caused the clay to liquefy and thereby lose its strength. Subsequently, parts of Turnagain

Heights, L Street, Fourth Avenue and Government Hill slid downward on a potter's "slip" of Bootlegger Cove Clay.

Mar 78:11

Seismic Gaps

When the irresistible force of the North Pacific tectonic plate meets the immovable object of Alaska, the result is an interlinked assemblage of volcanoes and earthquakes. Moving steadily to the northwest at about 6 centimeters (2.4 inches) per year, the North Pacific plate rubs against British Columbia and southeast Alaska and then slides down under the western Gulf of Alaska and the Aleutian Islands.

Rocks at the boundaries between the moving plate and the fixed continent try to absorb the differential motion by bending. The rocks in the Gulf of Alaska region seem to have enough strength to accept 3 to 5 meters (10 to 16 feet) of bending before they break to initiate the event we call an earthquake. The seismic waves created in the impulsive snapping of the rocks are stronger the greater the slippage is along the fault. In a large earthquake the slippage might be roughly 5 m along a fault that may extend horizontally 100 kilometers to perhaps more than 1000 km.

The time taken to build up enough strain (bending) in the rocks to create a 5-m break is 5 m divided by the rate of slippage, 6 cm per year, i.e., about 80 years. On this basis, seismologists think that the entire boundary between the North Pacific plate and the continent should undergo breakage every 60 to 100 years.

Trees as Earthquake Fault Indicators: *Alfred George stands beside a tree split by a small ground breakage through its middle, caused by an earthquake at Huslia, Alaska, in 1958.*

Three regions of the North Pacific boundary have not experienced large earthquakes in 80 or more years. These seismic gaps are in the vicinity of Yakataga, near the Shumagin Islands in the Aleutians and near the Commander Islands west of Attu. According to the seismic gap hypothesis, these three regions are more likely to experience large earthquakes than are the regions along the plate boundary to either side.

Feb 80:372

The Denali Fault

One of the ties between Canada and Alaska is the great Denali fault system that cuts across the whole of southern Alaska, extends on eastward into Canada and then dips back into Alaska near Haines. Its path through Canada and on into Haines is pretty much followed by the Alaska Highway from Koidern, Y.T. (just south of Boundary) to Haines Junction and then by the road on into Haines.

Not obvious to the casual observer, the trench of the Denali fault through the heart of the Alaska Range is easily picked out on topographic maps and is more than obvious in photographs taken from high-altitude aircraft or satellites.

It is now known that there has been major westward displacement of the land on the south side of the fault relative to that on the north. The highest estimates of the displacement give a figure of 400 kilometers (250 miles) during the past 60 million years. Over this time span, this averages out to a motion of about two feet a century or six-tenths of a centimeter per year. Thus, instead of being where it is now, Mt. McKinley — if it existed about 60 million years ago — would have been in eastern Alaska, not far from Tok, since Mt. McKinley sits just on the south side of the Denali fault.

One place to see the Denali fault is where the Richardson Highway crosses it near the terminus of the Cantwell glacier; the glacier itself lies in the rift trench, as does the upper stretch of Black Rapids glacier, off to the west out of sight from this location.

Another spot is on the Parks Highway a few miles north of Cantwell. The bridge across the Nenana River at Windy lies in the fault trench.

Mar 81:463

Trees as Earthquake Fault Indicators

Seismologists are eager to grasp at any straw that might help identify active faults and the dates when motion has occurred along them. At least minor successes have been accomplished by examining the shape and condition of trees and the annual growth ring asymmetries in trees along known faults.

When a fault splits a tree in half, the effect is obvious. Where the ground motion is particularly violent, within a few feet of the surface trace of the breaking fault, limbs are broken from trees and the trunks of tall trees break off, typically some intermediate distance above ground. A swath of dead, tilted and broken trees now makes obvious the trace of the Fairweather fault that broke in July 1958 to devastate Lituya Bay and nearby parts of southeastern Alaska.

Sagging or tilting of the ground along a fault trace causes trees there to tilt or even fall. If these trees continue to grow, their new annual rings show an extreme asymmetry — the rings on the down-tilted side of the tree are much wider than on the up side. This difference leaves a record that can be read by making multiple core drillings around the tree. Then using tree ring dating methods, it may be possible to date earthquakes occurring before historical records were kept. The ability to identify and date very large earthquakes occurring within the past thousand years is important in establishing earthquake risk and for predicting future earthquakes.

Another dating method is referencing ring patterns in earthquake-killed trees to those of trees that have lived through the event and which can be accurately dated. Trees along faults often are killed by drowning because the faults tend to collect normal drainage water. In some instances, there are widespread tree kills caused by general subsidence. Killed by sinking caused in the great 1964 Alaskan earthquake, grimly stark forests of dead trees stand guard around the shore of upper Turnagain Arm, near Portage, Alaska.

May 80:395

CHAPTER SEVEN
NORTHERN PLANTS

Plant Photosynthesis

Plant photosynthesis requires light, normally light from the sun. When the sun is high in the sky more of its light penetrates through the atmosphere to the earth's surface. Knowing this, I have never understood why it is claimed that plant growth during the summer in the far north is faster than at lower latitude. It would seem that the long summer days would not compensate for the low sun angle.

The error in my thinking was corrected by Dr. Don Dinkel of the University's Institute of Agricultural Sciences at Fairbanks during one of his recent lectures. He showed that the rate of plant photosynthesis is not proportional to the intensity of the sun's rays reaching the plant. Instead, photosynthesis begins as soon as the sun comes up and continues until sunset. The rate of photosynthesis does not necessarily increase as the sun gets higher in the sky. Quite the contrary: If the plant leaves get too hot, the rate of photosynthesis actually decreases. Thus it really is true that some plants grow more rapidly and produce more useful food in Alaska than in other states. Further emphasizing the point is Dr. Dinkel's statement that, figured over the summer growing months, the area around Circle in northcentral Alaska has the highest potential for photosynthesis of any region in the world.

Apr 77:154

Fast-Growing Trees

One has the impression that trees in Alaska grow very slowly and cling to life by a thread because of the long, cold winters and six or so months when snow covers the ground. Certainly trees do not grow as rapidly in interior Alaska as they do in Washington and Oregon. Nevertheless, the rate of tree growth in Alaska often surprises the newcomer. The reason for this is that trees in Alaska appear to be adapted to grow more rapidly when the conditions for growth are favorable during the short but relatively warm summer.

Recently two scientists combined their efforts to investigate growth rates of white spruce in Alaska and Massachusetts. Bob Gregory in Alaska and Brayton Wilson in Massachusetts carefully measured the rate at which new tracheids were formed by the cambium. Tracheids are the cells that make up the wood in the formative cambium layer. Gregory and Wilson found that trees in both areas formed the same number of tracheids but that the white spruce in Alaska produced most of these cells in about half as much time as it took the trees in Massachusetts. In other words, the cambium in Alaskan trees was producing tracheids at a rate twice that of the Massachusetts trees. Thus, it appears that white spruce, and other trees which grow in the far north, are genetically adapted to the unique growth conditions which occur here. These observations are borne out by others who have tried to grow Alaskan trees in the "lower 48". All studies show that these trees grow very slowly at lower latitudes. In order to make them grow as fast as they do here, the length of the day has to be increased to match our Alaskan summer day.

— John Zasada
Aug 76:97

Birch Seeds

Even including its wings that allow it to glide through the air, a birch seed measures only three mm across, a distance a bit smaller than the width of a book match. Seen through the University of Alaska's new scanning electron microscope, the birch seed grows into a complicated body with an intricate surface structure.

The scanning electron microscope permits the photography of details of very small specimens. Rather than normal light, the microscope uses a tiny beam of electrons. The beam is scanned across the object and partly reflected from it. The reflected electrons and additional electrons ejected by the impact of the beam on the specimen are collected and used to build up a picture display on the face of a TV tube. Normal photographs of the TV display faithfully record the details of the scanned specimen.

The ability to sharply focus electron beams in the scanning microscope allows the taking of photographs having clarity and depth of field. The resulting micrographs, as they are called since they are not truly photographs, have an almost three-dimensional appearance.

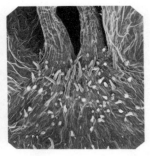

BIRCH SEED

SCANNING ELECTRON
MICROGRAPHS BY
MARY ANN BORCHERT

TOP LEFT - 20X
TOP RIGHT - 200X
BOTTOM - 400X

Birch Seeds: *Electron microscope photographs show intricate details of birch tree seeds.*

But back to the birch seed . . . The 20-times enlargement shows two horn-like projections from the seed body. These are remnants of structures surrounding the female egg when it was fertilized by pollination early in the life of the seed. From the area near the base of these horns, best seen in the 200-times enlargement, the root will emerge when the seed germinates.

As the seed matures, its outer coat shrivels up like the skin of a raisin. The 400-times photograph shows the shrunken walls of individual cells. Hair-like projections stand above the cell walls, for reasons not understood. One possible explanation is given by Dr. Paula Krebs, the Geophysical Institute's resident tree expert. She notes that the hair-like extensions are concentrated near where the root emerges and conjectures that they might help this part of the seed collect the water it will need to germinate.

Mar 78:226

Growing Willows From Seed

Like an unwelcome summer snow, fluffy cotton from willows, aspen and balsam poplar floats through the air and coats the ground in mid- and late summer. These puffs contain tiny green willow seeds, white balsam poplar seeds and tan to pink aspen seeds. Several million to the pound, the separated seeds remind one of salt and pepper grains.

These seeds usually die within a few days, but if they land on a suitable soil environment they may germinate within 24 hours. Several species of Alaskan

willow disperse their seed in September or October. Unlike the seeds of mid-summer, these spend the winter under the snow and germinate in early spring. Seeds of all species can be stored if collected at the time they are dispersed and frozen within several days. Keep them frozen until planting time and then spread them on wet soil or paper towels. Within one or two days, you will have many little trees and shrubs which can be used for a variety of landscaping purposes.

— John Zasada
Jul 76:96

Alaska's Gift — The Pine

Pines no longer grow over most of Alaska, but there is evidence that the area of Alaska and the Bering Sea was the center of development of pines about 260 million years ago. From this point pines spread all over the Northern Hemisphere and even crossed the equator.

Throughout the long history of pines, land masses submerged, rose again, and united to form bridges. Climates changed and deserts or ice fields were formed where pines had lived before. During the Jurassic and Cretaceous periods (181-72 million years ago) pines were migrating from the North American-northern Asia area and southward on both sides of the Pacific, westward in Siberia, and eastward in North America, eventually to Greenland and western Europe. The recent Quaternary glaciation destroyed all pine species in the northern part of the hemisphere. Lodgepole pine survived in places not covered with ice, and after the ice retreated the pine became a pioneer in reestablishing the forests in northwestern Canada and southeastern Alaska.

There are over one hundred species of pines in the world. Pines are conifers, closely related to spruce and are characterized by the needles occurring in clusters of two or more where the needles of spruce occur singly. Pines are conspicuous trees forming extensive forests or occurring mixed with broadleaf trees. Pines are useful; man has known them from time immemorial. He cut them for fuel, and he extracted resin from them. He burned them to clear the land for agriculture, and he planted them for shelter belts. Pines are beautiful; their decorative value is seen in old Chinese paintings, and their branches were used in festivals of ancient peoples. Pine incense was used in religious ceremonies by the Aztecs, the Mayas, and the Romans. Pines were mentioned in Greek mythology. Greek scholars knew a great deal about pines, for these trees occupied a prominent place in the landscape. The oldest known living organism is a bristlecone pine found in California — it is over 5000 years old. This Alaskan export has done well in the world.

— Paula Krebs
Apr 77:161

Right- and Left-Handed Cracks

A scientist co-worker and occasional contributer to the *Forum*, Hans Nielsen, recently noticed that dead spruce trees near his house on Yankovich Road show cracks that spiral in only one direction — clockwise looking down towards the base of the tree. This observation led to a minor after-supper investigation of the subject to see if all cracks are as Nielsen reported.

One finding is that it does not matter which end of the tree one looks at. If the cracks spiral in one sense as seen from the top of the tree, the sense is preserved when viewing from the bottom. They are the same as threads on a bolt or rod, either right-hand or left-hand. To screw a nut on a right-hand thread, one turns the nut clockwise regardless of which end of the rod is attempted.

Secondly, not all cracks in local spruce trees spiral in the same sense. Of more than a hundred examined from several localities, 68% showed cracks spiraling in the same fashion as right-hand screw threads, only 12% showed left-handed spiraling and 20% showed straight cracks. Clearly, there is a strong tendency towards crack spiraling in the right-hand sense.

So far none of us has come up with a plausible-sounding explanation for the preponderance of right-hand spiral cracks. Can any readers do better?

Sep 76:115

Diamond Willow

Red, diamond-shaped depressions in the otherwise creamy white willow wood create the curious, sometimes exotic, patterns exhibited by canes and furniture made from Alaskan diamond willow. Questions sent in by reader J. Norenberg of Fairbanks on the cause of the diamonds, where diamond willow grows and how to work it have led us to pursue knowledge on the subject.

First, there are 33 varieties of willow in Alaska. It is sometimes difficult to tell one kind from another because, when it comes to reproduction, many of the willow varieties are not very discriminating and therefore form hybrids. Nevertheless, it is known that at least five varieties develop diamonds and consequently can be called diamond willow.

The writings of the willow experts contain enough weasel words to demonstrate their lack of confidence that they are certain of the cause of the diamonds. At the center of each diamond is usually found the dead stub of a branch. It is thought that fungi, and in fact a particular one called *Valsa sordida* Nitschke, attack and kill some branches. Then it is thought that this causes the white sapwood surrounding the dead branch to die also. The sapwood, averaging one-quarter inch thick, represents about ten years' growth. Beneath it is the red heartwood forming the base of the diamonds. Diamonds may enlarge enough to touch other diamonds; hence intricate configurations can result.

Though the Copper River is the most famous locale of diamond willow, one variety or another can be found over all the forested areas of Alaska from the Kenai Peninsula northward. Attractive diamond willow is found in the valleys of many rivers including the Yukon, Matanuska, Tanana, Susitna and the Koyukuk.

Nor is diamond willow restricted to Alaska. Large willows with diamonds were being used for fence posts in the upper Missouri River valley during the last century, and canes were being made there of smaller diamond willows. Diamond willow was found to be nearly as rot-resistent as red cedar and therefore durable for underground purposes. Because of its slow growth rate, it is a hardwood; some Alaskan diamond willows are 150 years old, and one only two inches in diameter is likely to be 50 years old. If you cut diamond willow remember that it will not grow back quickly.

It appears that the best places to find willows with good diamonds are locations where growth is slow and stands dense. Thus, valley bottoms rather than hillsides probably will yield the best diamonds. The willow can be cut any time of year, but if cut in winter and dried slowly the wood will probably check and crack less.

In principle, all one needs to do is peel and finish the diamond willow to obtain attractive pieces. This can be more work than one would at first think. Many useful hints are contained in a three-page publication called "Working With Diamond Willow" available from the University of Alaska's Cooperative Extension Service. One wishing to learn more about willows can obtain *Alaska Trees and Shrubs*, authored by Leslie A. Viereck and Elbert L. Little, Jr., and published as Agriculture Handbook No. 410 by the Forest Service, United States Department of Agriculture.

Oct 77:189

Fire and Ice

Were it not for forest fires, it is likely that there would be more permafrost in the valleys of interior Alaska and corresponding regions of northern Canada. It is not that forest fires melt frozen ground, rather that the fires create a long-lasting condition that prevents permafrost from forming.

In regions where the mean annual temperature hovers near the freezing point, permafrost is intermittent. It forms only where the ground surface is insulated or otherwise protected from summer sun's warmth. For instance, it is reported that permafrost is now forming in soil on the north sides of buildings

130

placed on previously frost-free sites in the Fairbanks area. A heavy layer of moss on the forest floor can also lower the year-around ground temperature enough to produce perennially frozen soil.

When new soil is laid down by river flooding or meandering, a succession of northern forest growth starts. Two to five years afterwards the soil supports an open growth of willow and alder shrubs. The shrubs build a closed cover during the next five years, but then balsam poplar trees grow and become tall enough to begin destructive shading of the shrubs below. By the end of the first century following soil deposition, a forest of mature balsam poplar has developed, beneath which some alder still exists and young white spruce trees are growing. The next two centuries see the development of a mature white spruce forest floor with a deep moss layer.

Measurements reported by Keith Van Cleve, Ted Dyrness and Les Viereck, associated with the University of Alaska and the Institute of Northern Forestry at Fairbanks, show that soil temperature decreases as the moss layer in the white spruce forest thickens through the years. Consequent development of permafrost and cold water-logged soil eventually can cause the white spruce to be replaced by the less-stately black spruce which can tolerate these soil conditions.

But that usually does not happen. Natural forest fires occur frequently enough to prevent completion of the full cycle. Almost every non-coastal forest area is burned over at least once each 200 years or so. Each time, the fiery death of the insulating moss layer opens the soil to the sun's rays once again, and a new cycle of life commences.

Aug 80:420

Black Spruce

Somehow black spruce trees seem like the jackasses of the northern forests — sort of ungainly looking, ugly little beasts that can survive under conditions prohibitive to the taller and more elegant birches and white spruce. But, like donkeys, black spruce have their likeable and interesting qualities.

Black spruce are the climax trees on cold, poorly drained soils in Alaska and the Yukon. They rarely exceed 45 feet (15 meters) in height or 9 inches (23 centimeters) in diameter. In a typical stand, the diameter of most trees is less than 5 inches, and growth is very slow. Half the trees in a 30-year-old stand may be less that 2 inches in diameter.

Since black spruce do better than other trees on cold, wet soils, it follows that there tends to be an association between black spruce forests and perma-frost. While this association is true, it is also true that the fortunes of black spruce forests are closely linked to the occurrence of forest fires.

When a fire strikes a black spruce forest, it usually is hot enough to kill most of the trees but not all of the seeds. Black spruce, unlike some other trees, tend to produce seed annually or nearly annually. They start bearing cones at about age 15. Once black spruce seed cones mature, they may remain on the tree for several years. So regardless of when a fire strikes, mature seeds are available, and many are tough enough to survive the fire.

If there are repeated, but not too frequent, fires on dry upland areas where white rather than black spruce tend to be the climax trees, the black spruce will encroach upon those areas. This takeover occurs because black spruce reseed more quickly than do the white spruce.

If there are too many fires, neither the black nor the white spruce will survive. Nearly permanent grasslands develop on drier ground while bogs and shrub thickets take over in wetter areas.

Jun 79:306

Fire of Life

Though well-meaning and worthwhile, propaganda efforts to reduce the careless setting of forest fires have had another effect that is perhaps not as commendable. We have come to fear forest fires and to think of them as devastators of all life in their paths. The opposite may be true for much of interior Alaska, for without fire the forests evolve to plant communities that are relatively unproductive.

A burned area rapidly grows many new plants, and animals soon move in to feed on them. As soon as the fire cools, new shoots of trees, shrubs and herbaceous plants spring forth. Within four to five years, a lush growth forms, perhaps some vegetation being already 10 or 20 feet tall.

Why the rapid recovery? In interior Alaska only black and white spruce must depend upon seeds for new growth after burning. Other plants immediately grow from vegetative parts of plants not destroyed in the fire, unburned stumps and the roots and root-like stems (rhizomes) that have been protected by the moss and soil layers. These parts usually contain buds that remain dormant due to lack of light, low temperature or to growth-inhibiting substances produced by the parent plant. Once the parent plant is killed by fire and conditions are right, the dormant buds burst forth in vigorous new life. *— John Zasada*
Jul 76:95

Fire and Soil

The soils of Alaska and the Yukon typically differ from those of more southern climes where chemical weathering proceeds more rapidly. Due to cooler temperatures in the north, chemical weathering is slower, the result being shallow soil layers with low clay content.

Instead of being mixed into the soil, organic matter of forest land tends to lie in a mantle atop the soil. Farther south, earthworms and other creepy-crawlies foster the mixing of humus into the soil, but in boreal soils these animals are largely lacking. The unincorporated humus mantle is usually several inches thick under birch, aspen and white spruce forests and as much as a foot thick under black spruce forests. Usually it is moderately acidic.

A forest fire usually destroys the humus mantle and in so doing creates several secondary effects that, at least temporarily, help speed up plant growth. One significant effect is the removal of insulation provided by the humus mantle. The soil below then can be warmed more in summer so that a greater depth of annual thaw results. Not only is the soil made warmer in summer, nutrients locked up in near-surface permafrost are temporarily made available to new plant growth.

Destruction of the humus layer by fire makes the remaining soil layer less acidic, and it releases nutrients from the humus to the soil. The amount of usable nitrogen, calcium, potassium and phosphorus seems to increase immediately following a fire because the heat breaks up proteins and other large molecules into simpler compounds or into elemental forms that plants can assimilate.

The combined effects of fire on the soil clearly play a big role in determining the succession of plants that will follow the fire. Just the change in soil temperature and chemistry alone could lead to a temporary plant succession quite different from the forest cover before the fire.

Jun 79:318

Historic Forest Fires

Many references to extensive forest fires in Siberia, Alaska and northern Canada are found in the writings of eighteenth and nineteenth century explorers. Some recognized that lightning was the cause of forest fires, but the explorers frequently attributed the fires to native peoples. Authorities on forest fires, including H. J. Lutz of the U.S. Department of Agriculture, have concluded that early native peoples were, in fact, responsible for many fires.

Some fires were intentionally set to get rid of mosquitos or possibly to increase moose browse. Others were accidental from signal fires or camp fires going out of control.

Indians were not the only starters of fires. In 1915 the "Kennicott fire" was intentionally set by a woodcutter to create fuelwood for use at the Kennicott mine. Sixty-four thousand acres (100 square

miles) was burned. In the same year, sparks from a train set a fire that burned 384,000 acres near Chitina.

Prior to 1940, there were a number of large fires in Alaska and the Yukon that each burned more than 100,000 acres. Among the biggest were the 1,900,000-acre fire at Lake Iliamna in 1935, the Sheenjek River burn of 312,000 acres in 1937 and the Mosquito Fork Flat fire along the old Valdez-Eagle trail that burned over 900,000 acres in 1922.

In Alaska alone it is estimated that there are about 200 million acres of "burnable" land, of which about half is actually forested. Only about 7% of the burnable land can be considered commercial forest capable of producing 20 cubic feet per acre (1.4 cubic meters per hectare) or more of wood annually.

Virtually all the northern forest has been burned over during the last 200 years. It is estimated that a million acres each year is burned, on the average.

The worst year of all seems to have been 1940. That year, fires in the Yukon, Tanana and Porcupine watersheds and on the Seward Peninsula burned 4.5 million acres.

Less serious was a 38,000-acre fire near Fairbanks in 1926 created when a group of children set a tree afire to drive out a squirrel. The next year another Fairbanks district resident started a 5000-acre fire in an attempt to scare away bears that were muddying the water hole used by his horses.

Jun 79:317

Leaves

A leaf is a leaf . . . but not all leaves are created equally. An individual tree or shrub, regardless of its species, will exhibit variation in its leaves. The small-scale characteristics of leaf structure may differ leaf to leaf, and even the leaf size and shape may vary widely. The most apparent variations are those that occur from bottom to top of one year's new growth. Botanists even attach a word to this annual variation — one you are bound to remember: heterophylly.

Poplar leaves provide spectacular examples of heterophylly. In young poplar trees the leaves at the bottom of the shoot may be round and six to seven inches in diameter while those at the top are usually oblong and only one or two inches wide. Highbush cranberry leaves show a similar but lesser variation.

The primary reasons for heterophylly are weather conditions at the time of leaf development and the type of shoot growth. In one type, called indeterminate shoot growth, the winter bud contains only some of the leaves that will grow on that shoot during the next year. The rest of the summer's leaves on that shoot form as the shoot develops.

In contrast, some trees have all the summer's leaves formed in miniature inside the winter bud.

Heterophylly

Balsam Poplar   **Highbush Cranberry**

Leaves: *Variations in leaf size occur in one year's new growth on balsam poplar and highbush cranberry. Both have indeterminate shoot growth.*

These trees are said to have determinate growth; examples are white and black spruce.

Alaskan trees with determinate growth display a burst of activity in June and complete their shoot growth by early July, although their leaves may continue to grow larger as the month progresses. Trees with indeterminate growth continue to grow until late July or early August. In this late part of summer the leaves not found in the indeterminate shoot bud finally form.

Obviously there is a greater chance of wide variation in the leaves growing from those trees and shrubs such as poplar and highbush cranberry that have indeterminate shoot growth. Also, if one wishes to identify the variety of a tree by its leaves, one should be sure to gather leaves from the old growth. Otherwise the effects of heterophylly may make the identification difficult.   — *John Zasada*
Sep 78:252

Cottonwood and Balsam Poplar

It is common for people in interior Alaska and corresponding areas of northwestern Canada to use the name cottonwood when referring to one widespread variety of deciduous tree. But since cottonwoods do not grow in Alaska except on the southern and southeastern coast, the terminology obviously is wrong.

The error is a small one in one sense because the tree referred to, balsam poplar, is practically indistinguishable from its close relative, the black cottonwood. Balsam poplar is the most widespread broadleaf tree in Alaska; it ranges even farther north and west than another close relative, the quaking aspen.

Close up, it is easy to distinguish between balsam poplar and quaking aspen from the leaves and, to a lesser extent, by the branching structure. Where they

appear in mixed stands, the poplar sometimes has small, leafed branches lower down on the trunk. Aspen leaves are nearly round, one to two inches across, shiny green above and pale beneath. Poplar leaves are larger, 2½ to 4½ inches long, and broadly lance-shaped, shiny dark green above and pale green to brownish below. The cottonwood leaf is very similar to the poplar.

If you see a cottonwood tree in interior Alaska, you can be sure it's a balsam poplar, but in southern Alaska it could be either. In areas such as the lower Susitna Valley, near Anchorage, the trees themselves apparently do not know the difference, because they interbreed to produce hybrids. Once in a great while, a poplar goes out on a limb and even hybridizes with an aspen. Only the experts can identify the end product.

Both poplar and cottonwood grow well in river bottoms and sandbars. While poplar may grow to 100 feet high and two feet across, cottonwood can reach to 125 feet and be much larger in diameter. Cottonwoods three feet in diameter at breast height are common. To avoid both bending over and the flare near the tree stumps, foresters measure the tree diameters at breast height, hence the term breast height diameter.

One giant cottonwood near Klukwan, not far from Skagway and Haines, has breast height diameter just over ten feet. The Klukwan giant holds the national record for black cottonwood diameter. Its nearest rival, a tree near Salem, Oregon, does hold the national height record. The Klukwan giant belies the belief that trees tend to get smaller the farther north one goes.

Both balsam poplar and cottonwood have value for fuelwood, pulp and lumber. The large cottonwood stands in the lower Susitna Valley are considered to have the highest potential for economic development of any stands in the valley, though the volume of both white spruce and birch there is somewhat larger. The best cottonwood stands in the Susitna Valley contain as much as 34,000 board feet of lumber per acre. Whereas balsam poplar has somewhat limited utility for lumber, black cottonwood has higher strength and is, therefore, superior.

Persons wishing to learn more about Alaska's trees will be interested in a low-cost but comprehensive book by Leslie A. Viereck and Elbert L. Little, Jr. entitled, *Alaska Trees and Shrubs*. It is published by the U.S. Department of Agriculture.

Jul 81:493

Birch Sap Sugaring Off

The springtime sugaring off party is a New England tradition. People gather to make pure, chewable candy by pouring thick ropes of boiled-down sugar maple sap onto the snow.

Though sugar maples do not grow in Alaska and the Yukon, sugaring off parties are still possible in late April or early May. Then, the sap of birch trees flows upward and makes a reasonable northern substitute for sugar maple sap. The sap from any birch will do.

One of the more common trees in interior Alaska is the paper birch, *Betula papyrifera*. Easily recognized by its white papery bark, this is but one of three varieties of birch trees in Alaska. These hybridize wherever they meet, so the three birches are considered to be three geographical varieties of a single transcontinental species. Two species of dwarf birch also grow here in the north.

Birch sap contains the sugars glucose and fructose, whereas maple sap contains mostly sucrose. Another difference is that birch sap is more dilute than maple. The birch sap has 0.5 to 2.0% sugar, by weight. To make a thick syrup, the birch sap must be boiled down to decrease its volume by 30 or 40 times, but maple sap needs only 25 times concentration.

The end product is a syrup tasting somewhat like molasses. Birch sap tapped directly from the tree is almost imperceptibly sweet. In Siberia it is bottled with the addition of citric acid and sugar and sold as a good spring tonic.

The easiest way to obtain the sap from a birch tree is to use equipment designed for maple trees. This consists of a spout which is a hollow tube inserted into the tree in a hole drilled about 80 centimeters (30 inches) from the ground and 1 cm (1/2 in) in diameter. One centimeter in from the surface of the tree the spout has a 2-3 millimeter (1/8 in) opening on the bottom side for the sap to flow into the tube from the tree; it then runs out the tube and drips from the spout to collect the sap; commercially the sap is piped in plastic tubing under a small amount of suction. It is wise to boil all the equipment to protect the tree from the introduction of fungus and other diseases.

The sap flows for a few days in the spring, when the days are warm and the nights still below freezing. Usually the last two weeks in April is birch sap time around Fairbanks. Some years the sap flow lasts as long as ten days or more, while other years there may be almost no flow at all. At the end of the sap flow, the birch sap turns milky white and becomes bitter to the taste. At this time there are yeasts which appear in the sap which may account for the cloudiness and bitterness. Then the season is ended for another year.

— *Teri Viereck*
Apr 79:313

Sap's Arising

Northerners always await the first signs of spring — the ducks and geese returning, pasqueflowers on a south slope, the warmth of the sun. These all tell that life is returning after the snowy, sparkling winter. One sign of spring that passes unheralded to all but the most die-hard natural history buffs and tree lovers is the almost magical flow of sap in our white-barked birch trees.

Sap flow is the result of so-called root pressure. That is, water is actively absorbed by the root system, but pressure builds because little water is lost from the tree as a whole. Later, the trees leaf out and water-using photosynthesis begins so that the pressure in the roots is relieved.

Birch sap usually begins to flow in late April in interior Alaska and lasts for 10 to 15 days. During the first 5-10 days, the sap is a relatively clear liquid, but as buds begin to break and sap flow decreases the liquid becomes milky in color. This clouding accompanies large increases in the yeast content of the sap.

Sap production varies from tree to tree, and from year to year. Some trees in a stand may produce no sap while others produce 25 gallons or more. Sap collections taken in interior Alaska during 1976 and 1977 showed that some trees were good or poor producers during both years while others were relatively good producers one year and relatively poor the next. Tests have indicated that trees on low-elevation south slopes produce best.

The sugar content of the birch sap (about 1%) is low compared to that of maple sap (2.5%) from which syrup is made. Furthermore, sucrose (ordinary sugar) makes up only 18% of birch sap whereas 99% of the sugar in maple sap is sucrose. Fructose and glucose (honey sugar) are the main sugars in birch sap.

Some people have a special motive for watching for the first sap of spring. They use it to make beer, wine or syrup. In the Ukraine region of Russia sap from several species of birch is collected on a large scale (2000 metric tons in 1970) and used to make wine, soft drinks and health aids.

Birch sap can be used as it comes from the tree or it can be boiled to concentrate it. Probably the most sophisticated sap processing setup in the Fairbanks area is that of Mr. Carroll Phillips who has been collecting and processing sap since about 1968. Mr. Phillips currently taps about 400 trees to obtain 2000-3000 gallons of raw sap. He boils the sap using steam produced in a wood-fired boiler which was brought into Fairbanks in the early 1900s. The process has two steps: during the first, a batch of 70 gallons of sap is reduced to about 3 gallons in 1½ to 2 hours. Secondly, the concentrated sap is placed in a steam kettle and further reduced to 1 gallon of syrup.

Obviously few people have this system available to them. The most common procedure is to boil the sap on the kitchen stove or a wood stove in the back yard. Using this method, it's not possible to concentrate to the degree attainable with the steam kettle without burning the remaining material. After boiling, corn syrup is sometimes added to improve the consistency of the end product.

If you are interested in celebrating the rites of spring by collecting sap for your own use, the following steps will prove successful: 1) Drill a 4-6 cm deep hole in a birch with a hand auger. 2) Fashion a spout from aluminum and insert in the hole. 3) Hang a bucket below the spout to catch the sap as it drips from the tree. Only the clear sap that is produced early in the period is generally used for making syrup, wine or beer.

— *John Zasada*
Mar 81:467

Witches' Broom

In interior Alaska and some parts of Canada, witches' broom (an abnormal outgrowth of branches of the tree resembling the sweeping end of a broom), is commonly seen on black and white spruce trees. From late fall through the winter, the brooms are dark brown or "dead"-looking and are often mistaken for birds' and squirrels' nests. However, in the summertime, these branches are a bright orange or rust color which makes them most conspicuous and distinctive.

Witches' broom on spruce trees is caused by a rust disease (a kind of fungus disease). The rust lives on the spruce tree throughout the year. Each spring, small yellow pustules appear on the new needles of the broom. A strong sweet odor, which is easily recognizable, usually accompanies the maturation of these pustules. Later, much larger and bright orange-colored pustules also develop on the needles from which thousands upon thousands of rust-colored spores (small reproductive cells) are produced. By late August, needles begin to drop off, and the witches' broom turns dark brown.

Witches' broom rust does not infect other spruce trees directly. It usually will infect a bearberry plant first (an alternate host). The spores produced by the infested bearberry will then infect spruce trees to produce new witches' broom.

Although witches' broom does not kill trees by itself, it does deplete the tree of its nutrients and slows down its growth. A heavily infested tree becomes weakened and consequently vulnerable to the attack of other diseases (or the effects of weather) which can lead to the death of the tree.

— *Jenifer Huang McBeath*
Oct 81:255

Burls: *A boy on a burl. The tree is a birch and the boy is Tom Pollard.*

Burls

Burls, spherical woody growths on the trunks of spruce, birch and other trees, are commonly found throughout wooded parts of Alaska. Many are removed from trees and used for furniture making and for decorative roof or mailbox supports or just to set out in the yard as curiosities.

A burl begins life as a gall — a tumor on plant tissue caused by stimulation by fungi, insects, or bacteria. Evidently, only slight irritation to the bark causes a gall. The gall grows to become a burl — a massive, hemispherical or subglobose structure, sometimes very large in size. Once started, the burl grows with the tree, each year building a new growth ring that can be traced along to an unaffected part of the tree where it there appears as a normal growth ring. The growth rings inside the burl are spaced farther apart than the same rings elsewhere on the tree, showing that growth has proceeded most rapidly within the burl. Since the hardness of the wood is related to the rate of growth, the wood inside a rapidly growing burl is softer than the wood elsewhere in the tree. Nevertheless, it is hard enough to be sanded and finished into an attractive surface.

An affected tree may grow a single burl or many; trees with multiple burls on both trunk and limbs have been found. Trees with burls seem to be found in a cluster; if one tree in an area has burls, it is likely that other trees around it have them too. This clumping is suggestive of leafhoppers or aphids transmitting the disease, but no conclusive evidence of this is known yet. Burls weaken trees but do not kill them. The weakening effect, however, makes the trees vulnerable to other diseases which can kill them.

Relatively little is known about burls, for several reasons: It takes a long time for a burl to grow — nearly as long as the tree on which it is found — so research is stretched out over a long period of time. Furthermore there is as yet no major economic reason to learn about burls. Burls do not kill trees nor do they affect a great number of trees, so there is no real need to control their spreading. If burls were eliminated it would mean the end of the small industry that uses them for arts and crafts purposes.

— Fran Pedersen
Oct 78:254

Burls and Human Cancer

There is enough similarity between the growth of burls on Alaskan spruce trees and the occurrence of some cancer in humans that the two could be different manifestations of the same phenomenon.

Every spruce burl that I have seen cut into shows highly ordered structure in the region of abnormal growth. These are not really cells gone wild; instead, they are just growing at a very fast rate under the same rules that govern the structuring in the normally growing tissue. This type of growth also is typical of some animal cancers.

When several burls grow on a single spruce tree, it is likely that they all began growing at once. Evidence for this simultaneity is seen when annual rings in the tree and its burls are counted to determine which year each burl began. So it would seem that whatever

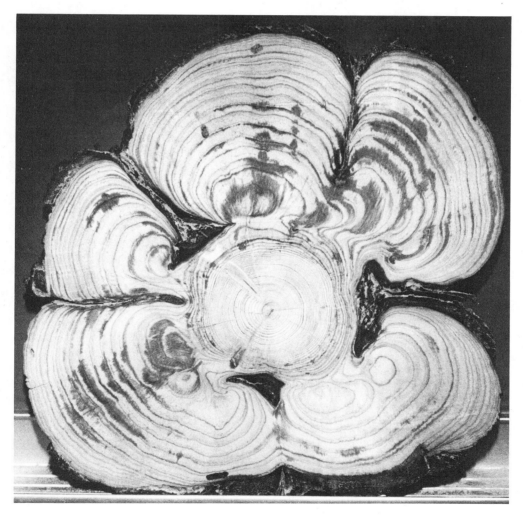

Burls and Human Cancer: *Photograph of a section cut from a spruce tree with five burls that simultaneously grew at the same level on the tree. Annual growth rings can be followed around the tree trunk at center and into each of the burls. The rings show that the growth of burls began when the tree was about 40 years old. This tree was cut on a north slope near timberline by Jim Moore of Fairbanks.*

agent controls the abnormal growth is spread throughout the tree in a single year. And there has to be some mechanism which determines where on the tree burls will grow.

Dr. Les Viereck of the Institute of Northern Forestry at Fairbanks points out that the trees which develop burls often tend to be undergoing environmental stress. Trees near timberline or on north slopes where living is tougher are prone to burl growth. The analogy of smoking's relation to cancer hardly needs mention.

If this suggestion is correct, that there is similarity between the occurrence of burls and cancer, then research into what causes burls in northern spruce trees might advance human cancer research. The simpler structure of trees compared to animals might more quickly yield information on deviant growth processes that could then be applied to the understanding and control of human cancer.

Aug 79:329

Growth of Cancer

Earlier in this column I suggested that studies of the cancer-like burls found fairly commonly in northern spruce forests might contribute to the prevention of human cancers. In response, Dr. Hugh F. McCorkle, a pathologist from Cleveland Heights, Ohio, has written to point out that similar studies have been performed, with somewhat encouraging results.

Medical researchers have learned from studies of abnormal growths in plants and small mammals that abnormal tissue growth, at least in some cases, is a two-part process. First, something has to trigger the process that may eventually lead to a killing cancer. But the cells triggered may not produce malignant tissues unless the tendency toward malignancy is supported by the presence of substances that promote abnormal growth.

An example is provided by experiments wherein a cancer-generating chemical insult was injected into the bladders of rats. The injection did not result in cancer unless the rats were fed a promoting agent — in this case saccharin — for about a year.

This example also illustrates why we are warned against continued ingestion of certain carcinogens such as saccharin. Substances such as saccharin may not in themselves cause cancer. Yet if the body has received another substance or virus that might initiate cancer, continued consumption of the carcinogens may encourage the development of malignant cancer.

The encouraging thing about some of the experimental work with plants and mammals is the finding that sometimes cells can be made to revert from an abnormality that leads along the path to cancer back

to normality. Such a reversion obviously is a means of curing cancer.

Oct 79:338

Evergreen Trees and Marine Bacteria

Alaska's coastal waters contain unexpectedly large populations of hydrocarbon-eating bacteria. This fact comes to light through studies of how petroleum is biologically removed from sea water.

Higher life forms cannot metabolize carbon-hydrogen compounds. But many species of microorganisms — certain bacteria, yeasts and fungi — can gain energy by eating simple hydrogen-carbon compounds, such as those of which petroleum crude is composed.

However if hydrocarbons are introduced to marine bacteria not accustomed to metabolizing the hydrocarbons, it takes time for the bacteria to adapt to the new foodstuffs. So it came as a surprise to discover that marine bacteria in southern Alaska's waters would immediately attack and begin digesting introduced petroleum.

We have found equally abundant populations of hydrocarbon-eating bacteria in Port Valdez, where small amounts of oil are regularly discharged, and in Resurrection Bay near Seward where such discharges are not made. Seeking an answer to this puzzle we searched inland to the forests, where we suspected that rainwater might be washing hydrocarbons from trees and that these compounds were being regularly delivered to the coastal waters by runoff.

Rainwater falling on trees either runs down the stem of the tree or flows outward over the limbs and foliage. Because of their downward sloping branches, evergreen trees are mostly washed by this so-called crown flow. As the water runs down over the bark and needles it dissolves hydrocarbons produced by the tree; among them are the volatile compounds called terpenes. Our laboratory tests have shown substantial quantities of terpenes in the wash water from spruce, an abundant coastal tree.

Apparently the terpene-rich water runs off into the sea where it whets the appetite of the marine bacteria and keeps them in the mood to consume hydrocarbons from any source, including oil spills. Here is yet another example of the interplay between marine and land ecosystems and a warning that what happens to change one may affect the other.

— Don Button
Dec 79:355

Oil-Eating Bugs

Petroleum is a mixture of hundreds of hydrocarbons — chemicals containing the elements carbon and hydrogen. These range from propane (heating gas) through gasoline and lube oil to napthalene (moth balls) and asphaltenes (highway blacktop). As a result of petroleum transportation and natural processes (green plants make hydrocarbons), millions of tons of these compounds enter the oceans every year. About six million (0.3%) of the two billion tons of petroleum produced each year are spilled into the oceans.

Particularly in coastal areas this oil would persist were it not for the bacteria that eat it. Other microorganisms metabolize oil too, as do higher organisms. Whereas humans do not gain energy from ingested hydrocarbons, many species of microorganisms — bacteria, yeasts and fungi — obtain both energy and tissue-building material from petroleum. These microorganisms require both the existence of oxygen and certain minerals to metabolize oil. They are able to attack the oil best when it is mixed with water. Even highway blacktop gets eaten in time, but its dryness, the lack of minerals such as nitrogen and the large size of the asphaltene molecules in blacktop make it tough chewing for the bugs.

Many hydrocarbons dissolve only slowly in water. Others such as the aromatic compounds like benzene are more soluble, and these are toxic to living cells. The aromatic hydrocarbons can attack the fat-like membranes surrounding cells and adversely affect their normal functioning. But, fortunately, bacteria and other microorganisms composing the marine flora are able to feed upon the wide variety of compounds found in petroleum. The ocean water itself aids the process by helping to transport oxygen and minerals to the microorganisms.

By genetic engineering scientists have the means to enhance the capabilities of bacteria to metabolize petroleum, and there have been attempts to develop an oil-eating "super bug." However, even without such assistance, the oceans have a high capacity to biodegrade petroleum. Recently under the T-3 Ice Island in the Arctic Ocean we found active hydrocarbon degradation underway even during the cold and darkness of January. Thus it seems the principal cure for oil pollution is almost everywhere in the oceans, and it has been with us for quite some time.

—Don Button
Mar 77:148

Beefsteak from Wood

Our food, ranging from breakfast cereal to McDonald's hamburgers, comes to us packaged in paper — a product of the forest. Is it possible that the wood from which paper is made has a more important role to play in feeding Alaskans and others? Research conducted mainly in Canada in the past ten years and a growing understanding of Russian technology shows that various parts of the

tree have significant potential as vitamin supplements and major energy sources in livestock feed.

In Russia, a livestock feed supplement called "muka" is made from needles, leaves, twigs and branches less than one-fourth inch in diameter. This material when dried and finely ground has been included in the feed of chickens, dairy and beef cattle and pigs in quantities of five to ten percent of the ration. Livestock productivity is reported to be improved when feed includes these materials.

Even more promising are reports by Canadian wood products scientists that aspen chips cooked at 160 to 170°C and pressures of 100 to 115 pounds per square inch for one to two hours become a source of energy for livestock. This energy comes from cellulose which makes up to 80% of the wood and is similar to starch which is an important component of our diet. Cellulose is generally not available to livestock because it forms a chemical and physical complex with lignin which is not digestible.

After cooking, this material has been combined with barley or corn and fed to sheep and beef cattle. The results of these trials indicate that animals perform as well on these feeds as they do on more traditional rations. It is believed that at least 30 to 50% of the feed can be aspen chips.

These findings suggest that as Alaska develops its agricultural potential, it is not far-fetched to think of Alaska's future farms as growing both barley and aspen or other woody plants for cattle feed.

—John Zasada
Apr 77:159

Energy from Wood

The energy source that powered the Klondike and later gold rushes was wood. It has been said that without the forests of Alaska and western Canada the gold rushes could not have taken place.

Though many of the gold rushers arrived on coal-fired steamers, they had enough else to carry over Chilkoot and other passes into the gold fields that they could hardly carry fuel too. Early-day photographs of the diggings show areas denuded of forest; the miners cut essentially all the trees around to build their cabins and mine shafts, and for fuel to cook and heat with and also to thaw frozen ground.

The miner's use of wood as almost their only fuel source illustrates some of the characteristics of wood as an energy source. Though wood is difficult to transport, it grows almost everywhere so, within limits, is readily available. Also it takes little technology to utilize this energy resource. Anyone with a match or two sticks of wood to rub together (and skill or lots of patience) can make use of it, though the efficiency of a modern air-tight stove beats heck out of an open campfire. With even more technology, the wood can be converted to liquid or gas fuel to burn in engines.

Suppose that today we were to get all our necessary energy from wood, just as the old-timers did, how would we fare using Alaska's forest resource? In answering this question, we have to remember that the forests grow slowly. To avoid running out of energy someday, there is a limited cut we can allow ourselves to take each year. Otherwise the forests cannot remain as a truly renewable resource. We would also have to assume that we really could convert the wood to liquid fuel to power our cars, airplanes and other motored devices.

Alaska has about 120 million areas of forest land of which about 28 million acres are productive enough to be considered commercial forest. That designation is given to land capable of producing at least one-quarter cord of wood per acre each year. The coastal forests of southern and southeastern Alaska can produce more, somewhat over one cord per acre per year. All told, Alaska's commercial forests, if managed only to produce wood for fuel, could yield about 40 million cords of wood each year, on a sustained basis.

The burning of 40 million cords of wood each year would produce a lot of heat (and smoke); it would release about as much energy as is contained in the oil flowing down the Trans-Alaska pipeline in 113 days, 600 trillion BTU. This is far more energy than the 400,000 Alaskans now use. The pipeline can produce all the energy currently needed in about 16 days each year.

Of course this discussion is somewhat nonsensical because we would never allow our forests to be used only for producing fuel, nor would we likely want to use wood as our only fuel source. Nevertheless, it is obvious that Alaska has enough forest to make far more use of wood for fuel than it does now.

But even with the vast forests we have, local shortages of fuelwood are showing up. The problem is that the trees don't always grow in easily reached places, and transportation of wood for long distances usually is prohibitively expensive.

Apr 81:479

Self-Defense for Plants

Pity the poor plant! While the plant-eating animals (herbivores) can move at will from plant to plant, taking bites where they choose, the plants must stand and endure the indignities. Recent research, however, shows the plants are not quite as defenseless against herbivores as their immobility might suggest.

Biologists at the University of Alaska's Institute of Arctic Biology are studying the interactions between snowshoe hares and the plants upon which they feed. The abundance of snowshoe hares changes in a cyclic

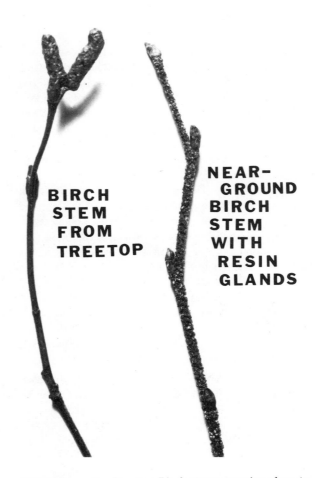

BIRCH STEM FROM TREETOP

NEAR-GROUND BIRCH STEM WITH RESIN GLANDS

Self-Defense for Plants: *Birch stems growing close to the ground are heavily protected by resin glands containing chemicals that discourage snowshoe hares and other herbivores from eating them.*

pattern, with peak densities reached every ten years or so. Populations in various areas of interior Alaska are now nearing their ten-year peak. At such times, the effect of hares on their food plants is near catastrophic. There is strong selection in favor of any plant that has developed a means of escaping the herbivores. Thorns are one obvious means of discouraging herbivores. Many other plants have evolved various forms of chemical defense. Some simply taste awful to discourage the herbivores. Others inhibit digestion by the herbivores, making it unprofitable for the herbivore to eat them. Yet others are outright toxic, and cause illness or death to the herbivore that overindulges. Many of the plant-derived chemicals that we use, for example quinine and aspirin (which was originally derived from willows), apparently originate as chemical defenses in plants.

All plants are not equally defended. Those that grow, use and drop their leaves in a single season (deciduous plants) seem to invest less in defense than those that retain their leaves over a number of growing seasons (evergreen plants). There are even differences within a single plant. Young shoots and branches growing close to the ground, within easy access of the hares, tend to be heavily defended. Older shoots and branches growing out of reach of hares are protected by position and are much less protected chemically. When a birch tree is felled, making the upper branches available to hares, they are quickly attacked with gusto. Penned hares fed branches cut from the tops of trees thrive; the same hares fed only root suckers growing near the ground die of starvation.

The deterrent chemical in birch is a resin that is contained in resin glands along the stem. Stems from the top of a tree have few resin glands, but the well-defined lower branches appear grainy because of them. The resin may make up 44% of the total weight of root suckers, but only 3% of the weight of top branches. This large difference points out the lengths to which plants will go to avoid being eaten.
— *Stephen MacLean*
Jun 80:401

Thoughts on Digging a Hole for the Outhouse

With winter behind, northern residents turn to their spring chores, which sometimes include digging a new hole for the outhouse, or clearing and tilling land for a garden. These tasks usually will bring the poor soul with the shovel into painful contact with a basic observation of plant life in the north: there's a heck of a lot of roots down there!

Why should northern plants invest more heavily in roots than their more southerly counterparts? They certainly are not needed for water intake; in fact, plants in wet sites seem to have the most roots. The roots are not needed to support the modest plant that grows above ground and rarely encounters more than a gentle breeze. The remaining major function of roots, uptake of mineral nutrients, seems the most likely cause for the extensive root systems of many northern plants.

As with other organisms, prudent behavior by plants leads to success in natural selection. In this case, prudent behavior implies investment of resources where they will contribute the most to growth.

Long summer days and summer's warmth permit northern plants to capture solar energy and convert it to sugar efficiently. For the plant to grow, this sugar must be combined with nutrients taken from the soil to produce the molecules that make up the plant.

Northern soils are slow to warm, with frozen ground persisting through much or even all of the summer. Partly for this reason the dead remains of earlier generations of plants are slow to decompose and release the nutrients back into the soil. Consequently, northern soils are characterized by a large accumulation of dead organic matter, and a shortage of available nutrients. Plants respond to this shortage by investing their resources in extensive root systems

to maximize their access to the low concentration of nutrients. Most of the roots are found near the surface in the organic layer of the soil, where temperatures are warmest and nutrients are released by decay.

So there is a reason for the large number of roots that obstruct the shovel. But that doesn't make the hole any easier to dig.
— *Stephen MacLean*
May 80:397

Fairy Rings. *(Drawing by Pat Davis.)*

Fairy Rings

Perfect dark-green circles in the grass — can they be caused by watering or fertilizing patterns? No human could so err; perhaps a rotary sprinkler, or a spreader did the deed. That explanation won't work either, for fairy rings were observed long before the machine age. From the distant past of folklore comes the story that the narrow dark-green rings are created by fairies dancing on the dew-laden grass in the moonlight.

No less fascinating is the explanation that mushroom mycelium creates fairy rings on our lawns. Mycelium is the term for the underground mass of interwoven threadlike filaments that are a part of mushrooms and other fungi. The mycelium spreads through the soil, decomposing dead grass roots and other organic material as it extends outward in circular fashion. Like fire in dry leaves, mycelium consumes what it can use in the center, and it must grow rapidly to acquire new fuel. Mushrooms, the fruiting bodies of mycelia, are formed at the outside edge of the actively spreading mycelium. The intense green color of the fairy ring is created by fresh fertilizer produced as humus is broken down into nutrients usable by the grass.

Air photos show fairy rings as large as 200 meters in diameter. Such large rings are thought to be more than 600 years old. Several large rings, up to three

Fairy Rings: *Three fairies from the staff of the Geophysical Institute in a fairy ring on the University campus. Fairies, left to right, are Karen Brown Flesher, Trudy Cain and Judy Holland.*

meters in diameter, can be seen on the University campus; some of these yield copious quantities of edible mushrooms. — *Eugene M. Wescott*
Jul 76:85

Tundra Fungi

Every acre of arctic tundra contains more than two tons of live fungi; a birch forest in interior Alaska contains well over a ton. Thus, fungi constitute a substantial component of plant life in the north, as elsewhere. Completely lacking in chlorophyll, fungi survive by feeding on other organic materials. By decomposing dead trees and plants, fungi play a crucial role in maintaining soil fertility.

Hundreds of thousands of different fungi exist. We are familiar with those that form blue and green molds on oranges, cheeses and lemons and the white, grey or black furry outgrowths on bread, meat or jam left in damp places. The mushrooms of the meadows

and forests and the beautiful displays of *Amanita, Boletus* and *Russula* — the so-called toadstools — are fungi. Fungi are the principal agents in the fermentation of wine and beer, ripening of cheeses, the production of antibiotics like penicillin and industrial production of vitamins and citric acid.

Scientists at the University's Institute of Arctic Biology are trying to learn the characteristics of tundra and forest fungi that allow them to live in cold soils and to release nitrogen and phosphorus as they decompose organic remains. Since they are a crucial component of life in the tundra, it is important that the resistance of fungi to oil spills or other environmental perturbations be known. If the stability of the fungi is undermined, an entire forest or tundra grazing land can be destroyed.

The next time you are in the forest or tundra, bend down and look closely. Better yet, put your ear to the ground and listen to the fungi grow. If you

happen upon a person who remains long in this position — posterior up, ear down — you probably have just met a mycologist; mycology is that branch of science dealing with fungi.   — *Patrick Flanagan*
Sep 77:183

Reindeer "Moss"

No science fiction writer or practitioner of the controversial new field of genetic engineering would ever think to invent such an unlikely plant as reindeer "moss".

Reindeer moss is not a moss at all. Rather it is one of the world's 15,000 lichens. Before the discovery of the microscope lichens were thought to be mosses, hence the strange names some go by. More strange yet is that a lichen, unlike any other plant, is not a single organism. Instead, a lichen is a combination of two different plants — algae and fungi — growing together in an inseparable relationship called symbiosis.

By virtue of its ability to perform photosynthesis, the algae supplies the lichen with food. The fungus furnishes mechanical structure and the water needed for photosynthesis. This water comes out of the air, so the lichen has no roots and is able to grow on rocks or other objects such as tree bark. The lichen may extract some minerals from whatever it is attached to; otherwise all its needs come from the air. Because lichens take their livelihood from the air instead of the ground, they are terribly sensitive to air pollution, and simply will not grow near cities where pollution is bad.

Because of the ability to avoid using soil as a source of materials for life and the ability to withstand extreme cold and dryness, lichens such as reindeer moss can live in arctic and antarctic locations where other plants cannot. When there is enough moisture in the air and when it is warmer than -10°C (14°F) such lichens show signs of life and growth; otherwise they lie dormant.

Under the worst conditions, it can take 100 years for lichens to regrow after being eaten by arctic and subarctic reindeer, caribou, moose and musk ox. Nevertheless, the lichens are crucial forage for these animals, especially in winter. The slow growth rate of lichens may be a factor that causes the population cycle of Alaskan caribou and reindeer to range from 50 to 100 years.

Sep 80:428

Albino Plants

Every once in a while the careful observer will run across an albino plant. Albino seedlings of Alaskan white spruce, aspen, birch and balsam poplar have been found, as have albino root suckers from aspen

Albino Plants: *An albino seedling of white spruce pokes up through the soil amongst normal seedlings. Since the albino seedling has no chlorophyll, it cannot manufacture food, and will soon die. (Photo by John Zasada.)*

and fireweed plants. Other species of northern plants perhaps also exhibit occasional albinism.

Albino seedlings probably result from the combination in the seed of genes that were recessive in the parent plants. The albino root suckers are thought to develop from mutation in a single cell or in a group of cells, because the rest of the plant from which the albino stem grows can be normal.

As in animals, albinism in plants is caused by lack of pigment. However, in plants the lack is fatal because the missing pigment is chlorophyll. Without chlorophyll, the albino plant has no way to manufacture the food needed for survival and growth to maturity. Albino seedlings usually live only about a week, but albino root suckers tend toward a bit more longevity because they can draw food from the parent plant.

Even though albino plants do not live long, their occurrence is useful to those who study forest genetics. The genes that create albinism can be used as markers to examine the rates and patterns of seed dispersal from those trees which carry those particular genes.

To find albino plants, look for those with white or pinkish leaves and stems. If the albino plant is

142

growing from the stem of a normal plant, there may be transitional features at the juncture. For example, I recently found a fireweed root from which normal shoots were growing up to one point on the root. At that point grew a stem showing mixed albino and normal characteristics; beyond it twelve totally albino shoots grew.

Not all mutations or unusual gene combinations are harmful. In fact, by watching for favorable abnormalities it has been possible to develop important new varieties of fruit, flowers and ornamental plants. Not all plant abnormalities are due to mutations or unusual gene combinations since external causes can create abnormal appearances. Examples are the cancer-like burls that grow on northern spruce and birch trees and the witches' broom that certain fungi cause in spruce.

— *John Zasada*
Oct 80:433

How Does Your Garden Grow?

One measure of how well garden crops will grow is the range of temperature each day. Many Alaskan crops, such as peas, oats and potatoes, will have growth only if the temperature is above about 40°F (4°C). Others, sweet corn, beans and tomatoes, grow only if the temperature is above about 50°F (10°C).

Up to a limit (in the high 80s), the growth is greater the warmer the day.

A growth index called the "growing-degree unit" has been compiled for several Alaskan locations. To obtain the index value for each day, the Fahrenheit maximum and minimum temperatures are added together and the sum is divided by two. This gives a sort of average temperature for the day. From this average temperature, one subtracts 40°, the temperature at which most Alaskan crops start to grow. Added up over the course of the summer, the total growing-degree units so obtained is a good indicator of agricultural potential.

Some surprises come out of the calculations of growing-degree unit totals. The famed Matanuska area (1763 units) ranks only third behind Big Delta (1791 units) and Fairbanks (1852 units), but it does handily beat out Homer (1274), Kasilof (1433) and Kodiak (1572). Because of its warm summers and long days, the Fort Yukon area has even more growing potential than the Fairbanks area.

These results would seem to prove that the farther north you live, the better will be your garden. Residents of Point Barrow and Barter Island may not believe the proof and might be inclined to point out that having continental climate helps a lot.

Actual tests with crops do support the indications of the growing-degree calculations. Dr. James Drew, head of the University's Institute of Agricultural Sciences, cites sweet corn as an example. He says that, aided by ground-warming mulches, sweet corn will not mature at Homer. With mulch, it will mature about one year in three at Matanuska, and it will every year at Fairbanks. At Fort Yukon, north of the Arctic Circle, sweet corn needs no help at all to mature every year.

Dec 77:204

The Greening of Brown Thumbs

Some people seem to have an inborn ability to grow plants, but I am beginning to suspect their green thumbs come from knowledge rather than luck. Having been born with two brown thumbs, I figure it is time to try to learn some of those secrets the expert gardeners appear to have absorbed automatically.

Among the most important, obviously, is an understanding of what constitutes a good growing medium for plants. A reading of some texts on soil and plant science indicates that the ideal growing soil for most garden plants is one that is roughly 45% mineral soil, 5% organic soil, 20 to 30% water and 20 to 30% air.

One can substitute for the solid soil particles but not for the water or the air. That, in fact, is the idea behind hydroponic gardening. Even there, it is common to let the plant roots be supported by a matrix of gravel or other inert material. At frequent intervals the matrix is flooded with a water bath containing minerals and fertilizer, or else a stream of gas is bubbled through the solution continuously.

A plant begins to wilt as soon as there is insufficient water around the small root hairs that take in the water needed by the plant. Root hairs are numerous and tiny; typically they are less than a half-inch long, and there may be as many as 100,000 of them per square inch of root. If these hairs are exposed to dry air for even a few minutes they usually die.

Nor can most plant roots withstand being totally immersed in water for too many hours since that too will kill the root. The key to root survival and a good rate of plant growth is for the root hairs to be exposed continuously to an environment that contains both liquid water and air that is rich in oxygen and saturated with water vapor.

This environment is provided by the pore spaces between the solid particles in soil. Ideally, the walls of a pore space are coated with a thick layer of liquid water; thick in this case means only a tiny fraction of an inch. At least some of the pore spaces must be large enough to contain an atmosphere of water-saturated air in contact with the root hair as well as the layer of liquid water.

A soil with adequate particle size distribution will take up a goodly supply of liquid water in the layers

The Greening of Brown Thumbs: *Though claiming no gardening expertise, Albert Belon, associate director of the Geophysical Institute, had harvested more than twenty ripe tomatoes from these two Tanana variety plants before the end of June, when the picture was taken. Whenever the soil at the top of the pots feels dry, approximately every other day, he pours a gallon of water into the tray holding the plants. The water travels upward through an inch of gravel into the soil, thoroughly wetting it to the top. Continuous production of juicy red tomatoes proves that this method provides both ample aeration and moisture to the root hairs.*

lining the pore spaces and still allow excess water to drain away. Then during the hours and days ahead, the water layers will keep the air in the pore spaces saturated by giving up water molecules to the air and directly to the root hairs. Eventually the water layers become too thin to easily give up water; that is when it is time to add water again.

Remember when watering a garden that the water needs to get down where the root hairs are, perhaps even a few inches deeper so that there is a better reserve for the plants to draw from using capillary action. Remember also, that the water filters down slowly, often taking several hours to get to a depth of one foot. This is why slow watering of a garden or lawn for several hours at a time is recommended.

Jul 80:410

Gardening With Plastic

Black polyethelene sheeting is used to retain soil moisture and prevent weed growth around high-value crops at moderate and low latitudes. First introduced in the pineapple fields of Hawaii, the black sheeting now is often laid down using specially-built machines at the time plants are set out.

Whereas the black sheeting works well elsewhere, it is not suited to growing crops at high latitude where the soil is cold and summer days are long. Clear polyethelene sheeting placed around crops such as corn and squash that need warm soil will allow the sun's rays to reach the ground and warm it during the hours of sunlight. At night, the clear plastic will allow more soil heat to escape than would black plastic sheeting, so for those few hours the black actually would be more desirable.

However, Dr. Don Dinkel of the University of Alaska Experiment Station at Fairbanks says that the use of clear polyethelene sheeting will raise the average soil temperature by as much as 20°C (38°F). That much increase will cause substantially faster growth of many plants.

While black plastic itself absorbs heat from the sun, Dr. Dinkel indicates that the plastic usually is not in good enough contact with the ground to transfer the absorbed heat to the soil. Consequently,

the black plastic will not create more than minor warming of the soil.

The important thing for many crops the northern gardener wants to cultivate is to make the soil as warm as possible. Warm soil fosters rapid uptake of moisture and nutrients through the plant roots. Therefore, use clear plastic on northern gardens for those crops that prefer warm soil.

Jul 80:412

Triticale

The breeding of a male donkey to a horse mare produces a mule — a big, sterile hybrid superior in some ways and inferior in others. Similarly, crossing wheat and rye yields the sterile hybrid triticale. It, too, has certain advantages and disadvantages.

Plantings of triticale made over a four-year period at the Fairbanks Experiment Station have consistently produced a higher yield than other small grains — 24% higher than barley, 28% higher than wheat and 39% higher than oats.

But, as is the case with the mule, there are problems, according to the University of Alaska's Frank Wooding who conducted the tests with triticale. It takes about 109 days to grow mature triticale, which is just a bit too long for most Alaskan localities. Barley, wheat and oats require only 81, 97 and 99 days, respectively, and therefore can be grown in the interior and southern parts of Alaska and Yukon Territory.

Another problem of triticale is its susceptibility to the fungus disease called ergot. Ergot forms black pods on the grain spikes that are poisonous to livestock and human beings. It causes abortion in pregnant animals and lameness and gangrene.

Fortunately it is possible to chemically treat triticale seedlings so that they will develop into fertile, seed-producing plants. Therefore there is hope that improved strains of triticale can be developed that will be disease-resistant and adapted to growing in the north. Rapid progress can be expected. Triticale was first grown only 30 years ago; already a number of different varieties have been developed.

Aug 78:258

CHAPTER EIGHT
NORTHERN ANIMALS

Ice Worms

" 'A cocktail I can understand — but what's an ice-worm please?' Said Deacon White: 'It is not strange that you should fail to know, since ice-worms are peculiar to the Mountain of Blue Snow.' "

And so Robert Service's barroom heroes led Major Brown down the snowy path to belief that ice worms really do exist. Before his eyes was placed a bottleful "picked and put away to show the scientific guys."

"Their bellies were a bilious blue, their eyes a bulbous red, Their backs were grey, and gross were they, and hideous of head. And when with gusto and a fork the barman speared one out, It must have gone four inches from its tail-tip to its snout."

Robert Service perhaps knew that real ice worms were discovered on the Muir Glacier in 1887. Ann Saling, writing in the March 1978 issue of *Search*, tells much of what is known about ice worms. They live in the coastal glaciers of southeastern Alaska and as far south as Mount Rainier.

Four species are known, ranging in length from 1 to 3 cm (an inch more or less). Nearly as colorful as the ice worm concocted by Service, real ice worms can be white, yellow, brown or black.

Squirming around between crystals of ice and through the many interconnected channels in granular snow, ice worms generally stay near the surface of glaciers. Most species of ice worms rise to the surface at dusk, where as many as a hundred in one square meter can be observed. During the day some species remain in puddles of meltwater where they anchor their front halves in the ice — for reasons not explained.

Ice worms eat airborne pollen grains, fern spores and the red algae that lives in snow and sometimes colors it pink. Unable to exist at temperatures much below freezing, ice worms must remain in temperate glaciers. The only ice worms ranging as far north as Dawson were the four-inch giants that Robert Service's Sheriff Black, Skipper Grey and Deacon White fashioned of spaghetti and ink.

Apr 78:53

Ice Worm Habitats

Recently I was surprised to learn that ice worms are found occasionally in glaciers of the Alaska Range. Ice worms are numerous in the warmer glaciers of southeastern Alaska, British Columbia and Washington state, but they cannot tolerate temperatures much below zero Celsius.

Real ice worms — not the spaghetti and ink concoctions of Klondike poet Robert Service — live in pools of water and crawl around between ice crystals near the glacier surface. When I expressed amazement that ice worms could exist in the comparatively cool glaciers of the Alaska Range, glacier expert Larry Mayo of the United States Geological Survey stated that the glaciers there are not necessarily all that cold.

Even though temperatures in the mountains are sub-freezing many months of the year, glaciologist Mayo points out that the Alaska Range glaciers do contain water in liquid form the year around. From time to time, crevasses become water-filled. Also, channels cut in the glacier ice by running water sometimes get blocked up and then fill with water.

In winter the water near the edges of these bodies freezes into ice rinds that may be several tens of centimeters thick. Even so, if a pool of water is big enough, its center remains unfrozen, proving that the temperature at depth can remain above freezing.

Ice worms have been observed to move around in the ice at depths near two meters (six feet). Even in the Alaska Range, the glacier ice at that depth obviously can remain near freezing and so can provide at least a marginal ice worm habitat. But life there can't be easy. Perhaps it's as Robert Service said:

"And as no nourishment they find,
to keep themselves alive.
They masticate each other's tails,
till just the Tough survive."

Apr 80:391

Alaska's European Rabbits

The European rabbits on Middleton Island in the Gulf of Alaska and on Umnak, Rabbit and Hog Islands in the Aleutians have an involved history which began about two million years ago. Then, they inhabited Africa, Asia and North America, later entering South America during the ice age era a few tens of thousands of years ago.

Phoenician traders found the forefathers of the Middleton and Aleutian rabbits in Spain about three thousand years ago. The rabbits became an item of trade and soon were domesticated all over Europe. There, different breeds were evolved. Released in England by the Normans to grow wild, the domesticated rabbits soon took over and were a dominant pest for a thousand years. Introduced into Australia, the European rabbits soon were devastating pasture land there, too.

Once released, the European rabbit multiplies and does well in places where there is open grassland and not too many controlling predators such as fox, coyote or wolf. Grassy islands seem to be especially suitable. Consequently, European rabbits have done well on the comparatively dry San Juan Islands of the Puget Sound area and on Middleton Island and several other islands in Alaska.

Harvestable populations of European rabbits have evolved from unknown numbers introduced on Umnak Island in 1930 and on Rabbit Island in 1940. Three female and one male rabbit placed on Middleton Island in 1954 multiplied like rabbits until their descendents numbered between 3600 and 7000 in 1961.

There also have been successful transplants of snowshoe hares onto Kodiak Island and several Aleutian islands, but introductions of hares and rabbits to the wet, forested islands of Southeast Alaska have been unsuccessful.

Jan 79:281

Twice Through a Rabbit

It appears that there is more to being a rabbit than one is led to believe, hearing only the stories and jokes about the animal's reproductive capability.

Indeed, one learns much that is surprising by reading an Avon paperback by R.M. Lockley called *The Private Life of the Rabbit.* Among the topics covered there is the curious manner in which a European rabbit processes its food. It is a scheme designed to allow for a relatively short eating period followed by an extended interval for food processing.

Rabbits typically graze during the afternoon and evening hours. As they fill their stomachs, they also void fecal matter in the form of hard pellets — about 360 each day. Simultaneously, the new food taken in passes down through the stomach into the caecum. The caecum, also called the blind gut, is a stomach-sized sack opening onto the digestive system just above the rabbit's intestine. In the blind gut the ingested food is formed into soft pellets surrounded by a glossy membrane made of mucous secretions of the blind gut.

The coated soft pellets travel down the intestine and are passed back to the rabbit's mouth through the anus. The reingestion into the mouth may occur above ground while the rabbit is still grazing, but usually it occurs underground in the rabbit's burrow. Rabbits never pass hard pellets below ground nor do they urinate there; hence their burrows remain clean.

The reingested soft pellets go to the stomach where they remain intact for about six hours in a part of the stomach removed from newly ingested food. During this time bacteria in the pellets cause rapid fermentation of carbohydrate material. Finally the pellets dissolve to yield substances of nutritional value and also the wastes that travel on down the intestine to produce hard pellets.

Feb 79:285

Moose Farming?

Very little seems to be known about the way of life of the Tanana Athabascan Indians who lived around Fairbanks before the foreigner came to the area. Ivar Skarland is one of the few to have studied the early ways of life; studying his writings, one gets the impression that life in this area was fairly primitive.

It now seems apparent, however, that the Interior Indians may have purposely modified the environment to produce more food. Verbal reports indicate the Indians recognized that spruce forests provide no food for moose and that they set fires to produce more moose browse. Only in recent years does there seem to be recognition that the fighting of natural forest fires is often a waste of money and that it adversely affects the balance of life.

Like the boy who passes teenage, approaches 21, and notices that his father is growing more wise, our modern society matures and sees the sophisticated intelligence and foresight in many of the practices of our aboriginal ancestors.

Jun 76:71

(See drawing next page.)

Halibut Fishing

The Tanaina Indians who originally inhabited the area took advantage of Cook Inlet's high tides to fish for halibut without going offshore. According to Cornelius Osgood who studied the early day peoples of this area, halibut remain in deep water in winter, but in summer do come into the shallow waters of Kachemak Bay. Elsewhere in Cook Inlet, he says, halibut were either unavailable or at least were not caught.

The Tanaina men drove a stake into the beach at low tide, leaving about three feet above ground. To the top of this stake, they tied a short stick. On a spruce root line a large hook was suspended from the

Moose Farming. *(Drawing by Pat Davis.)*

end of the stick to a height of one foot above the beach. The spruce root line extended along the stick and down the vertical stake to where it was tied to a very large rock, a rock so heavy that two men could just carry it.

A humpback salmon fourteen to sixteen inches long was split open so that the hook could be inserted with the barb sticking out of the salmon's back a short distance. The bait and hook were intended to be large enough to discourage the smaller halibut but not the big ones. After the tide came in and a big halibut took the hook, the fish usually broke the array of sticks, but hopefully not the spruce root line. Then as the tide went out the big fish would be left stranded on the beach, ready for the women to clean and cut up. Not only were the Tanaina men clever in the wiles of fishing, they had a proper sense of proportion in the division of labor between the sexes.

May 78:220

The Alaskan Mosquito

Spring signals the passage of the snow and the cold. Out come the flowers, the leaves — and hordes of mosquitoes. With the Equal Rights Amendment awaiting final ratification, one almost hates to mention that, of the two sexes, only the female mosquito bites people — extracting their blood and causing them to itch by injecting anti-coagulant into the skin.

The mosquito life cycle consists of eggs, larvae or wrigglers, pupae, and adults. All life stages except adults are aquatic and can occur in a variety of places such as ponds and standing pools of water, in artificial containers, in hollow trees, and in moist areas of

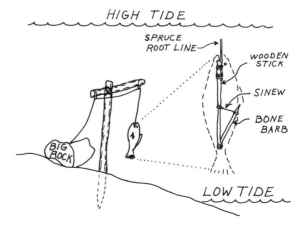

Halibut Fishing.

148

The Alaskan Mosquito: *Only the females bite.*

fields, bogs, and forests. The flat valleys of interior Alaska are ideal breeding sites for mosquitoes because of the constant abundance of slow-moving and standing water.

There are 25 to 40 species of mosquitoes in Alaska, most of which are classified as *Culex*, *Aedes*, *Anopheles* and *Psorophora*. All of them feed on either people, animals, or birds, but no Alaskan mosquitoes carry diseases.

Mosquitoes are present from April through September in many parts of the state. Adults of a particular species may only be present for a few weeks and then another species becomes prevalent, or several species may be present at the same time. This is the reason we encounter various sized adults throughout the summer.

The sexes of mosquitoes can easily be differentiated by the form and shape of the antennae located on the head. Male antennae are very hairy or "feathery" in appearance, while those of the females have only a few short hairs — and don't forget, they bite.

The large adult mosquitoes one sees in early spring spend the winter as adults hibernating in leaf litter, under felled trees, or other protected places. These emerge ready to strike when temperatures begin to warm in late April. Other species overwinter as eggs

or larvae; the adults of the species do not emerge until mid- to late-summer.

Control measures against mosquitoes may be aimed at the larval or adult stages. Areas that harbor larvae can be eliminated by proper drainage or be sprayed with approved insecticides. Measures aimed at adults are the use of protective clothing, screening, repellents, or insecticide sprays. Pyrethrins, malathion, and dichlorvos (DDVP) are the most important insecticides registered for use by EPA for mosquito control.
— *Richard Werner*
May 78:152

Mosquito Repellents

Mosquito repellents do not repel mosquitoes because the repellents smell or taste badly to the mosquitoes. Instead, the repelling action is by a more subtle process that blocks sensory functions.

Female mosquitoes — as usual, it's the females that are the trouble makers — do not much use the sense of sight or touch in seeking out victims or the most stingable parts of victims. A mosquito will become restless and commence to fly around if there is an increase of carbon dioxide in the surrounding air. At first, the direction of the flight path may be random, but if the mosquito finds warm and moist air she tries to stay in it. Since animals give off carbon dioxide as well as heat and moisture, the mosquito can quickly home in on a patch of exposed skin in preparation for a good meal.

Sensory hairs on the mosquito's antennae detect changes in carbon dioxide content, humidity and temperature of the air. If these sensors detect a lowering of carbon dioxide, humidity or temperature, the mosquito turns aside to look elsewhere for signs of life. It is this turning to seek more promising hunting ground that causes mosquito repellent to work.

Tests of mosquito repellency on more than 25,000 organic compounds show that the best repellents are heavy, irregularly-shaped molecules. Size and shape are more important than composition, according to R. H. Wright (July 1975 issue of *Scientific American*). The molecules simply block the pores in the mosquito's sensory hairs and cause her to think that she is flying toward a colder, dryer or more carbon dioxide-free region. So she turns aside and fails to land on target, the result being no mosquito bite.

May 80:399

Musk Ox Versus Man

Stories of bear attacks abound, and there even may be people around who tell of having been kicked by a moose. But there are few neighborhoods, like ours, that can boast of a resident who has been gored by a musk ox.

Musk oxen are not generally known as aggressive animals. In fact, they are famous for the passivity of their defense tactic: they simply form a ring around their young when danger threatens.

So how does one get gored by a musk ox? Ask Dr. David Klein, Professor of Wildlife Management at the University of Alaska, Fairbanks. Professor Klein has learned that female musk oxen are to be managed carefully.

Dr. Klein was helping several others move the

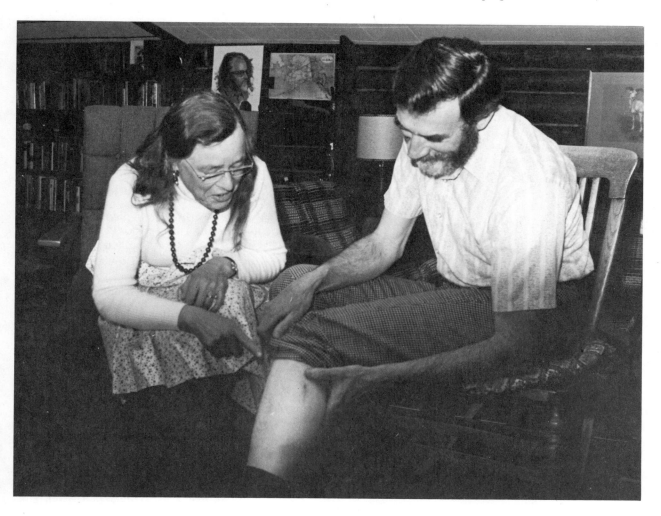

Musk Ox Versus Man: *Physician Betty Elsner points a sympathetic (or scornful?) finger at Professor David Klein's musk ox wound, now healing well.*

musk ox from one holding pen to another after she had undergone a natural abortion. Apparently, the hormone changes in an animal mother when giving birth can tend to make her somewhat irascible as well as more protective of her young. While Dr. Klein was pushing on her trying to get her to move, the cow swung her head quickly enough to dig her sharp horn into his leg.

Another participant in the action, Dr. Robert White, said he didn't think it was all that exciting. He claimed that Dr. Klein and the musk ox were just leaning against each other so hard that the cow's horn sort of poked a hole in Dr. Klein's leg.

Well, they say that there are two sides to every issue. I guess one's view just depends upon whose leg the ox gored.

Anyway, it is known that a single musk ox can be quite dangerous. An isolated musk ox will attack an intruder out in the open. Within recent years, a man in Norway was killed by a musk ox when he approached it closely for photographs.

Jul 79:319

Musk Ox Teeth

Humans are not the only ones to have dental problems. The musk ox, so well adapted in many ways to life in harsh environments, has more than its share of dental anomalies. Here in Alaska a large number of musk oxen have rotated teeth of a kind similar to that occurring in young people and which they correct by wearing braces. Some musk oxen have peg-shaped teeth, and some have teeth that are congenitally missing.

In Greenland, I worked with musk oxen for the Danish government. After examining skulls found in the field and in museums, I became aware of the musk ox's dental irregularities. Since last autumn I have been working on the "Musk Ox Project" at the University of Alaska, Fairbanks, and have been able to examine the teeth of 13 animals here. In one animal the outermost front teeth had never developed, in four animals these teeth were peg-shaped, and in three of the oxen one or more premolars were rotated approximately 90 degrees.

In humans it has been shown that similar dental anomalies are influenced by genetic factors. Based on the similarity of the dental anomalies in human and musk ox, I believe that the anomalies in musk oxen also are genetically influenced. In Greenland the frequency of the dental anomalies is very great in some areas while very low in others. Therefore, it appears that the musk oxen in Greenland occur in several discrete populations.

All the musk oxen currently in Alaska are the descendents of some 30 animals caught in Greenland in 1930. In that part of Greenland where these oxen were captured, missing, peg-shaped and rotated teeth are found in about 30% of the animals. That the same dental anomalies are still found in musk oxen in Alaska today after nearly 50 years of living under conditions quite different from those in Greenland, is strong evidence for genetic rather than environmental control of dental anomalies in musk oxen.

A major reason for examining the teeth of musk oxen is that differences in the incidence of tooth anomalies in various parts of the musk ox range, from Alaska through arctic Canada to Greenland, can show whether musk ox herds exist isolated from one another or whether there is continuous exchange between herds. If animals readily move, then similar tooth anomalies should be found in all parts of the musk ox range.

About 25% of white North Americans have disoriented teeth, and about 5% have missing or peg-shaped teeth (wisdom teeth excluded). Since controlled breeding experiments with humans are not feasible, not enough is known about the genetic and environmental factors that may cause tooth anomalies in humans. Consequently, knowledge gained from controlled breeding experiments with animals sometimes results in better treatment of human disabilities. Further investigation into the causes of dental anomalies found in musk oxen might well yield benefits for mankind. The ten animals now held captive at Fairbanks and the 175 at Unalakleet, Alaska, provide good samples for these studies. — *Poul Henrichsen*
May 80:384

Reindeer and Caribou Populations

Today there are perhaps 270,000 caribou and about 24,000 reindeer in Alaska. In 1935, biologist Olaus Murie estimated the caribou population at between one and two million. Others estimated that about 600,000 Alaskan reindeer existed then. Why has the last 45 years brought such a drastic change?

It makes sense to consider together the populations of reindeer and caribou because they are the same species of animal, *Rangifer tarandus*. Though reindeer and caribou interbreed, there are some differences. Male reindeer tend to be a little smaller than caribou bulls. Reindeer may be a little more white, may have shorter legs and may be slightly more placid than caribou. These differences are so tenuous that it can be hard to tell if one individual is a reindeer or a caribou. However, if you find a caribou with an ear notch or other form of branding, you can be sure it's a reindeer.

Though there had been caribou in western and northwestern Alaska some years before, by 1880 there were few or none. University of Alaska biologist Dr. David Klein suspects that the introduction of firearms during whaling led to the demise of caribou in coastal Alaska.

Whatever the cause, the lack of caribou allowed the successful introduction of reindeer at Teller in 1892. Over the next 45 years the reindeer population soared and spread like wildfire across the Seward Peninsula and north and south along the western coast of Alaska. Also like wildfire, the surge in reindeer numbers probably destroyed the range the animals ate from. So for this reason, and perhaps some others, the population crashed to about 30,000 animals by 1950.

The human management of reindeer and caribou obviously requires a bit more long-range planning than is needed to grow cows in a pasture. If the cows eat all the available grass, there is a chance of a new crop the next year. But lichens, not grass, form a large part of the diet of reindeer and caribou, especially in winter. Once a crop of lichens is eaten down or otherwise destroyed, it can take up to a hundred years to recover. More usually, it takes 15 to 50 years for full recovery. Even so, that is a long time.

On Alaska's Seward Peninsula, 14 managed reindeer herds comprising a total of about 20,000 animals have been maintained at roughly the same total population for over 20 years. That stability of the reindeer population may indicate that the herders have a successful management strategy.

It would be interesting to know what would happen over a period of several hundred years if there were no human management of caribou and reindeer in Alaska and western Canada. The reindeer and caribou herds presumably would merge and all be called caribou. Based upon what has happened in the past, it seems that the descendent populations would wax and wane like that of the snowshoe hare, but with a longer cycle. Instead of the 7- or 8-year cycle of the hare, the caribou is most likely to be in the range 50 to 100 years. The cycle might consist of population booms and crashes or it might be less drastic.

Sep 80:427

Grouse Sounds

For years I thought one of my distant neighbors had a faulty chain saw that would die after firing a few times. John Collette in a letter to the editor of the *Fairbanks Daily News-Miner* described the sound as that of a big diesel generator starting up, then stopping, and also as that of a giant kid dropping two-foot marbles onto a concrete surface. Yet another description is that the sound is similar to a motorcycle engine starting, coming up to speed and then dying.

The male ruffed grouse produces this sound as part of a courtship ritual by beating the air with his wings.

This drumming noise is composed of sound waves of such low frequency — about 40 cycles per second — that many of the grouse's predators are unable to hear it.

The ruffed grouse struts and drums during courtship in the deciduous forests where he lives. According to University of Alaska ornithologist Brina Kessel, the spruce grouse, which lives in coniferous forests, courts by strutting, jumping and clucking. Another relative, the sharp-tailed grouse of the open country, courts by "dancing, clucking and cooing." Seems to me the ruffed grouse puts on the best show, but obviously some female grouse prefer cluckers and dancers to drummers.

May 78:213

Wolf Rabies

Wolf rabies in North America has been known to occur only infrequently, though in the eastern Mediterranean wolves are important carriers of the disease. There had been only six verified cases of rabies in American wolves prior to 1977, when at least six wolves in one Alaskan pack died of rabies within a period of weeks.

While studying a wolf pack of ten animals on the upper Hulahula River of northeast Alaska, Richard C. Chapman noted strange behavior by one member of the group. Between vicious attacks on other members of the pack, this wolf wandered back and forth and pursued other unusual and aimless activities.

Writing in the July 28, 1978, issue of *Science* magazine, Chapman told about the wolf later approaching his tent. After being driven off by shouting and banging of pots, the wolf later returned and was beaten off twice more by raps on the head with an old boot. Chapman finally shot the wolf with a pistol. The dead wolf was found to be rabid; its stomach contained wolf hair, moss, wood chips and sand. Evidently, the wolf transmitted rabies to other members of the pack since two to three weeks later six of the remaining wolves in the pack died.

Transmission of rabies from wolf pack to wolf pack in northern Alaska is thought to be unlikely since the density of wolves is low (one per 180 square kilometers), and each pack tends to keep in its own territory. However, wolves do chase and attempt to kill arctic foxes. Unlike the wolves, the foxes do at times range over great distances, and they are often afflicted by rabies. Since rabies can be contracted by eating a rabid animal or even inhaling contaminated air, the wolves can easily get rabies from foxes.

Aug 78:256

Hibernation

In marked contrast to all large mammals, including man, a number of small northern and alpine mammals are capable of reducing voluntarily, and often conspicuously, their metabolic rates and their body temperatures for extended periods of time. This process, because it occurs in the winter, is known as hibernation and provides a mechanism by which the animal can escape the rigours of a long and often hard winter, when food is limited. Hibernation is largely confined to small herbivores such as marmots, ground squirrels, chipmunks, dormice and northern bats (the black bear is an acknowledged hibernator although it does not conform to the accepted pattern). Entry into the hibernating state is characterized by a large reduction of the metabolic rate (sometimes down to as much as 1/200th of the normal rate) and body temperature (in some cases down to 32°F). Some animals arouse periodically and quite regularly, especially the ground squirrels, and experience wide variations of body temperatures. These are conditions which cannot be tolerated by animals such as man whose mechanism for regulating his metabolism is extremely sensitive to temperature. In fact, it is the latter observation that gives research on this problem some force, as hypothermia (becoming too cold) in man is often injurious, if not fatal. It is therefore interesting to understand how a hibernator can survive hypothermia, thus possibly identifying some mechanisms that can be used as therapeutic measures in treating it in man.

For some years, the Institute of Arctic Biology of the University of Alaska at Fairbanks has had a large program concerned with the metabolic adjustments that the hibernator must make before its entry into, or exit from, the hibernating state. Within this institute I currently perform research on this topic under a grant from the National Institutes of Health. Marmots and arctic ground squirrels are used almost exclusively in this research.

When an animal enters the hibernation chamber it ceases feeding for the entire period, thus facing prolonged starvation and widely varying body temperatures. It is obvious that the animal has some elaborate mechanisms that permit it to regulate its metabolism over a wide temperature range, and to husband efficiently its finite energy reserves for long periods. These mechanisms are manifested at the physiological and at the biochemical levels. It appears that, between regular bouts of arousal from deep hibernation, the animal allows its blood glucose to fall slowly to extremely low levels. Upon arousal, the glucose is restored and the animal once again descends into deep hibernation. The source of almost all of the energy used for this is fat, which in some animals may be well over 50% of the total body weight. That there are fundamental differences between hibernating and non-hibernating ground squirrels was made clear by some interesting experiments conducted by

(among others) Dr. L. Keith Miller of the Institute of Arctic Biology. He demonstrated that the nerves of a hibernating animal continue to conduct impulses down to temperatures far below those at which similar impulses from summer (non-hibernating) animals cease to conduct. This is further supported by the finding that most, if not all, of the animal appears to "restructure" much of its intracellular machinery into a new form that can function and be regulated efficiently over a wide temperature range. These alterations are at the molecular level, and available evidence indicates that they are "turned on" by a hormonal stimulus or "trigger". One of the most provocative results of the current research is that all of the enzymes so far studied undergo this transition three to four weeks before the onset of hibernation. The opposite change also occurs before the end of the hibernation season when the animal finally emerges. The significance of this is that the new characteristics would not do the hibernating animal much good if it did not possess them upon entry into hibernation — there is little value in adapting to something that has already occurred. Further, this means that the ground squirrel anticipates, apparently without any recognizable external signal, a very dramatic change in its metabolic status. It is this last aspect that draws together the separate but converging threads of the annual cycles of the hormonal "trigger" and the resultant biochemical and metabolic changes that turn a summer ground squirrel into a hibernating one.

— *Hans Behrisch*
Dec 76:138

On Hibernation

About 15 years ago several scientists reported to the annual Alaska Science Conference the results of a study on the behavior of hibernating Alaskan bears.

They had located a sleeping bear in a den and proceeded to measure the bear's body temperature. One of them would crawl into the den and insert an electrical rectal thermometer into the bear, then back out of the den quickly.

The scientists were surprised to learn that this hibernating bear moved around a great deal. The movement was interfering with the measurements of temperature because the bear kept ejecting the thermometer. This, of course, necessitated another hazardous entry into the bear's den.

At last the bear settled down, and a good series of temperature measurements was obtained. It showed that the bear's temperature dropped steadily. After some hours, the scientists became quite excited because they were measuring a temperature lower than they thought any animal experienced in hibernation. Even beyond that point the temperature of the bear slowly declined.

Finally the scientists again entered the den to withdraw the thermometer and then discovered the reason for the low temperature readings. The bear had died.

Jan 78:205

Bark Beetles in Spruce Trees: *A section of inner bark showing beetle feeding galleries.*

Bark Beetles in Spruce Trees

Bark beetles attack spruce trees in early summer. These brownish-black beetles are common throughout Alaska and the Yukon Territory where they kill trees by boring through the bark and feeding and breeding in the phloem (inner bark) — the thin layer of soft tissue directly beneath the bark. If the beetles girdle the phloem, the tree will die since the phloem is the vital path that transports food manufactured in the needles down to the roots.

The primary indication that beetles are attacking a tree is reddish-brown dust which accumulates on the bark, in bark crevices, and on the ground beneath the attacked tree. Globules of resin or pitch tubes at the beetles' entrance hole into the bark are another sign of beetle attack. Entrance holes are found from the base of the trunk upward to the top and even in the branches. Different species of bark beetles, of which there are about 20 in Alaska, attack the tree at different heights. To determine if beetles are present, remove the bark around an entrance hole to locate the adult beetle and larval tunnels. Changes in foliage coloration, from one month to one year later, are another indication of attack.

Beetles sometimes attack healthy, vigorous trees and are usually trapped in a mass of resin and "pitched out" of the entrance hole. Trees that have been attacked in this manner will have patches of resin flowing down the trunk.

Various activities which disturb the environment of spruce contribute to bark beetle attack. These activities include timber harvest, land clearing, and severe winds which cause windthrown trees. Bark beetle attacks on trees in urban and suburban areas are encouraged by stress on the trees caused by mechanical damage during building construction, excessive removal or addition of soil from or on the area over the tree roots, soil compaction around the base of trees, and sewage drainage fields adjacent to tree roots.

The best method for preventing the spread of beetles from infested trees to live, healthy trees is to fell, cut up, and burn the entire tree at the first sign of beetle attack. Preventive sprays can be applied to surrounding live trees to protect them from attack in the critical period of beetle flight, May to July.

— Richard Werner
Jul 78:238

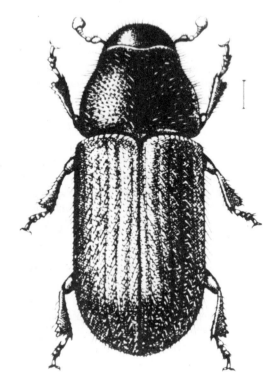

Bark Beetles in Spruce Trees: *An adult bark beetle — top view of the nasty beastie.*

154

Supper On Ice

Protected sites in the mountains of Alaska and Canada support snow beds that may last well into the summer, or even throughout the year. These snow beds may seem inhospitable sites for life, yet birds are often seen foraging on them. The attraction is a surprising abundance of dead or inactive insects that make good eating.

Many insects and other arthropods have a dispersal phase in the life cycle, in which they may travel great distances. Some, like juvenile spiders and mites, are aided by threads of silk that act like balloons in the wind. Others use their wings. In either case, they may be carried long distances by the wind. Insects have been captured in nets hundreds of miles at sea, and thousands of feet above the mountain tops.

Large snow beds cause local downdrafts, and thus act as traps for this "aerial plankton." The insects that end up on the snow may have originated many miles away. Studying snow beds at Eagle Summit, in interior Alaska, Dr. John S. Edwards and his colleagues from the University of Washington found that large carpenter ants formed a major part of the insects on snow beds, even though carpenter ants were not found living in the surrounding tundra. These ants were winged reproductives, unsuccessful participants in the annual nuptial flight from colonies in the spruce forests found at lower elevations. Small flies and aphids also contributed large numbers of insects to the snow surface.

Eight species of birds, ranging in size from small Lapland longspurs and water pipits to common ravens, were observed feeding on the snow bed feast, neatly removing and eating the fat-filled abdomens of carpenter ants while leaving behind the head and thorax, with their unpleasant dose of formic acid.

The arrival and subsequent death and decay of insects originating at lower elevations contributes valuable nutrients to the alpine ecosystem. In any one year, the quantity of nutrients added is small, but, accumulated over many years, this may represent a significant source of critical nutrient elements.

— Stephen MacLean
May 80:396

The Bowhead Whale

Fearing total extinction of the bowhead whale, the International Whaling Commission has now limited Alaskan Eskimos to a total of 12 killed or 18 struck whales per year, much to the consternation of the villagers on Alaska's northwest coast.

Decline of the bowhead whale (the Greenland or arctic right whale) began about 300 years ago. By then, European whalers had essentially wiped out the North Atlantic right whale which they hunted for baleen and whale oil. During the hundred years

ending in 1775 nearly 60,000 right whales were taken. By 1840 commercial hunting of the arctic right whale in the eastern North Atlantic was not feasible for lack of whales.

Yankee whalers breached the last Arctic stronghold of the right whale north of Bering Strait in 1843. Nine years later 278 ships reddened Alaskan waters with their kills of the bowhead, probably taking more than a thousand whales. So efficient were these whalers that they depleted the fishing by 1908. Now the Whaling Commission believes only about 1300 bowheads are left.

The bowhead grows to a length of 60 feet and weighs about a ton per foot. Each side of the huge upper jaw holds 300 or more plates of black baleen up to 10 or 11 feet long. Hairlike extensions of the plates strain out the tiny crustaceans upon which the bowhead survives. A large bowhead may yield as much as 275 barrels of oil, one-tenth of which may come from its tongue.

Though the bowhead is no longer commercially valuable, other whales are being hunted in Antarctic waters. Whale oil is used as a lubricant, for cold-rolling and quenching of steel and for manufacturing soaps, cosmetics and detergents. Whale meat is used as human and animal food. The baleen is still used for corsets and bristles. Whale byproducts are used for fertilizer and for cattle and poultry feed.

But even the Antarctic whales are disappearing. Each year it has been necessary to reduce the legal catch in international waters. In 1971 the U.S. ended licensed commercial hunting of whales.

Dec 77:207

Baleen

The 600 or so plates of baleen carried in the upper jaw of a bowhead whale were so valuable during the heyday of whaling that the take from a single whale could pay the expenses of an entire voyage, leaving all else for profit. The long, tough fibers forming the baleen plates were so strong that they were used for many applications now taken over by fiberglass or plastics. Had radially wound auto tires been invented a hundred years earlier, the best of them would have been called "baleen-belted radials."

Baleen plates ranging in length up to ten feet are attached by one end to the upper jaw so that they hang down on either side of the whale's massive tongue. The plates are set side-by-side crossways in the jaw with the frayed-out hairy bristles toward the inside of the mouth, next to the tongue.

To feed, the baleen whale swims with open mouth through swarms of small creatures known as water fleas or schools of somewhat larger shrimp-like crustacea — the small creatures baleen whale eat are collectively called krill. When the mouth is closed,

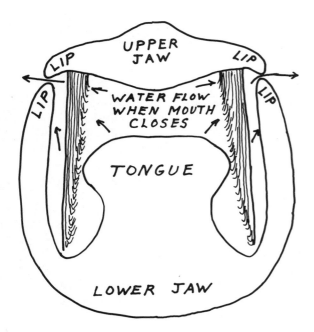

Baleen: *Schematic cross section of a bowhead whale's mouth showing how baleen filters out the krill.*

the tongue moves upward toward the roof of the mouth and forces the collected water sideways out between the baleen plates. The soft hairy fibers on the inner edges of the plates form a heavy, brush-like mat which effectively stops the krill and holds it inside the mouth. The krill is then swallowed into the whale's stomach where several tons can be retained at one time.

Jul 78:235

Recovery of the Gray Whale

Of the baleen whales, least is known about the medium-sized gray whale.

The gray whale was commercially discovered by whaling captain Charles M. Scammon in 1857 as he explored the coast of Baja California, on his way home from a bad season in the North Pacific. (Scammon Bay, Alaska was named after Captain Scammon, though apparently, he never visited this Bering Sea port.)

Captain Scammon and other whalers soon established a fishery to take the 25 barrels of oil to be gotten from each gray whale. Cornered in their shallow Baja California calving grounds, the gray whales were so easily caught that they were nearly totally destroyed within 20 years.

By 1900, gray whales were not seen along the California coast and were thought to be extinct. A few reappeared there in the 1920s but whalers attacked them again. Hunting was banned in 1946 when, according to August Pivorunas, writing in the July-August issue of *American Scientist*, not more than a few hundred gray whales could have been left in the entire Pacific Ocean.

Now, less than 40 years later, 10,000 gray whales roam the American coast. The gray whale winters around the Aleutian Islands from where it migrates each year southward along both the American and Asian coasts.

Why has the gray whale recovered so rapidly, while other baleen whales are not able to rebound quickly from over-harvesting? The answer may be in their feeding habits. Grays are the only whales that feed on the shallow ocean bottom. They eat worms, kelp and other small bottom creatures as well as the small crustaceans called krill that other whales eat near the ocean surface.

Perhaps the gray whales' affinity for shallow water makes them hard to hunt in the open ocean and more prone to stay in national waters where fishing regulations can be strictly enforced.

Sep 78:339

Life Underfoot

Tread lightly when you walk through the north woods; there is life everywhere you step!

Each year the leaves and wood that fall combine with roots and humus matter to make food for an abundant and varied group of animals who live in the forest floor. These are tiny invertebrates, animals without backbones, that make up for their lack of size by sheer numbers.

Locked in frozen soil and dormant throughout the long northern winter, an abundance of life becomes evident in the spring. Studies by University of Alaska biologists show that the life in the floor of black spruce forest becomes more abundant as summer progresses. Soil mites, eight-legged relatives of the spiders, increase in abundance from 150,000 per square meter shortly after snow melt-off to 500,000 in each square meter by August. To convert that to more meaningful units, I drew a line around my size 11 boot and found that each step on the forest floor covers about 44 square inches. Thus, by August, each footstep pads down on more than 10,000 individual mites, the largest of them about the size of a pinhead.

Second in abundance, at least in the (barely) visible range, are the springtails; these are small, primitive relatives of the insects. Like the insects, they have six legs, but throughout their evolutionary history they have lacked wings. Many of them react to danger by catapulting through the air using a springing organ otherwise kept tucked beneath the body, hence the name springtail. These animals reach a mere 2000 or so per footstep.

156

Together, the soil mites and the springtails form a mass of about 34,000 pounds per square mile. That is equal to 320,000 field mice or 43 moose. With this much meat on the hoof, predators are sure to be found. The main predators of invertebrates are spiders and centipedes, multi-legged marauders of the northern forest floor. A view of the ferocious jaws of these animals quickly reveals their purpose in life. In tropical forests centipedes may grow to be 6 inches (15 cm) in length and inflict a dangerous poisoned bite, but evolution has spared us this risk in the north.

So a special posture is recommended for nature lovers in the northern forest: hands and knees on the forest floor, nose near the ground, eyes directed downward. As you search through the litter layer with magnifying glass in hand, you'll find a whole new world of life in miniature.

— Stephen MacLean
Feb 80:374

Earthworms

Earthworms apparently are rare enough in subarctic Alaska and the Yukon that a face-to-face meeting with one is uncommon. Perhaps the earthworms' cousins, the almost-legendary ice worms, are more numerous in the north.

Earthworms live in strange places. They survive in sewage beds, manure piles, beneath the bark of trees, and in tropical ferns growing high above the ground. Able to live submerged in water, earthworms have been found in mud beneath deep lakes, and also in moss on rocks above the treeline in the Himalayas and the Andes.

Despite this versatility, earthworms require acidic to neutral soil (pH between 4.5 and 8.4). This requirement, more than anything else, seems to prevent earthworms from living in northern soils, where the forest soil typically is too acidic.

Many years ago, a student dug up earthworms from soil adjacent to a dormitory on the University of Alaska campus at Fairbanks. During the summer of 1980, U.S. Geological Survey geologist Florence Weber found an earthworm in organic soil 20 inches below the surface in the valley of the upper Salcha River, near Fairbanks.

It may be that earthworms are like pigeons; they exist only at far north locations where people or some other organisms have created a suitable environment. If this be true, the existence of earthworms in soil may be a hint that the site where they are found is a current or previous human habitation.

In an attempt to pin this matter down better, I invite readers who have found earthworms in northern Alaska or the Yukon to write or call me. Putting the information together, we might be able to create an informative map of the locations where earthworms exist in this part of the world.

Sep 80:429

Alaskan Earthworms

Thanks to Fairbanksan Bob Cummings, who has loaned me two books on earthworms, I've learned more about the topic. One book in particular, *The Earthworm Book* by Jerry Minnich, published by Rodale Press in 1977, is a goldmine of factual and interesting information.

Like snakes, earthworms are cold-blooded, so they slow their activity when the temperature moves toward the freezing point. Even those earthworm species that live at latitudes where the soil freezes are easily killed by sudden fall freezes unless there is substantial mulch cover to slow the freezing process. The earthworms evidently prefer some time to burrow deeply enough to stay below the frost line, but can survive the winter in frozen soil. Even so, one can be pretty sure that where there is permafrost there are no earthworms.

Of the 1800 known species of earthworms, Jerry Minnich says that the only recorded natural Alaskan is the species *Bismastos tenuis*, one of the smaller earthworms. He suggests experiments to see if the deep-digging (to 15 feet) nightcrawlers, *Lumbricus terrestris*, and the common field worm, *Allolobophora calignosa*, could be successfully introduced for the purpose of building garden soil. Bob Cummings is experimenting with both and says that earthworms found at Chena Hot Springs near Fairbanks are the common field worm species. Earthworms also occur at Pilgrim Hot Springs, near Nome.

Oct 80:435

Northern Butterflies

Though more southerly states such as Colorado can claim 250 or more resident species of butterflies, at least 78 species flit around the Alaskan countryside.

Summer coolness rather than winter's cold limits the number of butterflies in the Arctic. Not having a source of heat within their bodies as mammals do, and yet needing a certain minimum body temperature in order to fly, butterflies must gain heat from their environment. In winter they are, of course, inactive but those who live over the winter in the adult stage avoid freezing damage to their body tissues by stocking up on self-manufactured antifreeze materials each fall. Some arctic butterflies survive, in larval stage, over two winters.

A few species of butterflies live only in the northern tundra. They can survive there in summer because they have become experts on making use of solar energy. By doing so, butterflies are capable of raising their body temperatures as much as 17°C (30°F) above ambient.

This information comes from Dr. Kenelm Philip who, though an astronomer by training, has pursued a hobby interest in butterflies until it has become his main avocation. In the process, he has become the leading expert on Alaskan butterflies. In his home near the University of Alaska at Fairbanks, he has developed an extensive butterfly collection numbering in the thousands. He also has many fine photographs of butterflies, showing all stages of their development from eggs, through usually five larval stages, into winged adults.

In describing the behavior of those species of butterflies living in the far north, Dr. Philip notes that one of the surprises is that at least one species is found mostly on south-facing rockslides. The reason is, he says, that the butterflies find these slides to be warmer than other areas. The rocks collect the sun's heat, and then the butterflies collect the heat from them, sometimes by laying their wings down against the hot rocks.

So that they can absorb more heat, northern butterflies tend to be darker than their low-latitude relatives. Females tend to be darker than males, probably because their reproductive task is more difficult, and, as Dr. Philip points out, reproduction is the only purpose in life of the adult butterfly.

Northern butterflies also are smaller than others because smallness is an advantage when it comes to absorbing heat from the surroundings. By contrast, mammals, which are heat generators, gain by being large.

Certain butterfly species are particularly clever about gathering up the sun's heat directly. When cold, they stand with wings folded and lean away from the direction of the sun so that they present the biggest area to the sun. When too warm, they lean into the sun to create minimum area. When disturbed, they also lean into the sun to minimize their shadows and thereby make themselves least visible to predators. One kind also soaks up heat by holding its wings at just the right angle to reflect the sun's rays directly onto the butterfly's central body.

Yet another interesting behavioral pattern of butterflies has been observed in the upland areas. Collectors have found that certain species tend to cluster on hilltops, but that the vast majority found there are males. The mystery of why this occurs was solved when the collectors looked at the sex of butterflies flying up- and down-slope below the hilltops. These butterflies were mostly females. Furthermore, it was found that the butterflies headed uphill were all virgins and those going down were impregnated. Thus, it seems that the butterflies are clever enough to use the local topography to increase the chances of getting together for reproduction.

Jun 81:491

Alaska's First 300 Birder: *Dan Gibson, Alaska's first 300 birder. His tally does not include the wooden duck on his lap.*

Alaska's First 300 Birder

How many of Alaska's 381 known species of birds have you seen? If it's as many as 200, you are in select birdwatching company — probably fewer than 30 persons have seen as many.

Being one of those ignoramuses who might not be able to distinguish between a pigeon and a sea gull, I'm the sort of person who appreciates jokes about birdwatching more than the activity itself. Nevertheless, I could not help getting caught up in the excitement of the moment when Dan Gibson, an ornithologist with the University of Alaska Museum, learned that he was Alaska's first 300 birder.

Dan's 299th and 300th sightings occurred recently in Juneau. A friend there tipped him off that two unusual birds were in town. Gibson flew to Juneau specifically to see the reported mountain bluebird and evening grosbeak. At the time, Gibson did not know he had broken the 300 mark. That news came later in a letter from the Smithsonian Institution informing Dan that a bird he had observed in the Aleutians and thought was a gray spotted flycatcher was actually a sooty flycatcher from eastern Siberia. Not only did the news of the sighting boost Dan Gibson to the 300 mark, it raised Alaska's known bird population from 380 to 381.

In the whole United States there are over 800 known species of birds; worldwide there are about 8500. A past president of the American Birding Association evidently is the world's number one birder: he has seen over 5000 species. Dan Gibson, Alaska's number one birder, has seen over 602 birds nationwide. Alaska's number two birder, Terry Hall, has seen over 680 nationwide. This places him in the country's top ten. So far only three people have seen over 700 bird species in the United States and Canada.

Alaskan birding has gained new vigor the past few years. Just as canaries were used in the mines years ago to test for carbon monoxide, wild birds now serve as indicators of environment and its change. The upswing in serious bird observation has increased the number of known species; at least 12 new species were added to Alaska's list in 1977. Between them, Terry Hall and Dan Gibson were responsible for spotting four of the new species.

Jan 78:202

Magnetic Navigation By Birds

Careful tests with homing pigeons and other birds displaying the ability to judge direction show that the birds are affected by changing magnetic fields. Small coils placed near the birds' heads to create unnatural magnetic fields there do disturb the ability of pigeons to find home. Magnetic storms do the same. If birds are released at places where the earth's magnetic field is anomalously strong, their homing ability is entirely disrupted.

A possible reason why birds can sense the earth's magnetic field and perhaps use it for navigation is given by Charles Walcott and co-authors in the September 7, 1979 issue of *Science* magazine. Dissecting a number of pigeons, these scientists found the equivalent of a compass needle in each pigeon's head.

Next to, or essentially in, each pigeon skull, they located a tiny piece of tissue 1 mm by 2 mm (about 1/16 in by 1/8 in) that was somewhat magnetic. Searches inside this tissue with an electron microscope revealed the presence of more than ten million tiny crystals each four times as long as wide. Other tests demonstrated that these crystals were magnetite, the iron-oxygen compound of which compass needles are made.

As yet, it is not proven that the millions of miniscule magnetite "compass needles" in each homing pigeon's head are used for navigation, but it seems likely that they are. These multiple compass needles are so tiny that they could readily oscillate in a rapidly-changing magnetic field such as might accompany electrical storms, earthquakes and also displays of Northern Lights. So here also is a possible explanation of why birds sometimes seem to sense impending geophysical events.

Oct 79:345

Magnetic Bees

Beekeeper Dave Tozier of Fairbanks points out that bees as well as homing pigeons and migratory birds have been discovered to contain magnetite, the material also known as lodestone.

Magnetite, an oxide of iron, is the most common natural magnetic material found. If ground up into small pieces, each, no matter how tiny, has a magnetic north-seeking pole and a south-seeking one; in essence, each tiny piece is a bar magnet. It now appears that many animals have the ability to form within their bodies tiny crystals of magnetite, and thereby to create within themselves a way to sense the earth's magnetic field. The birds do it, the bees do it; so do some fish, and even bacteria.

Within homing pigeons, pods of magnetite have been found near the skull, but in bees the magnetite crystals are located in the frontal portion of the abdomen. The crystals are oriented transversely and horizontally in the bee. That is, in the bee, the magnetite effectively creates a bar magnet oriented crossways as are the wings of an airplane. There is evidence that the bees sense the orientation of the earth's magnetic field and that their lives can be affected by it. If bees navigate using the magnetic field, presumably it is by using the magnetite in the abdomen, but how the sensor there is linked up to the bee's brain function is a mystery. With the magnetite located where it is, the bee surely does not fly by the seat of his pants — maybe it's more of a gut feeling of which way to go.

Anyhow, according to an article in the September 15, 1978 issue of *Science*, bees tend to align their honeycombs magnetically north-south. They also can set their daily cycle of activity by the regular daily variations in the earth's magnetic field, if other normal cues such as the amount of daylight are absent.

Such observations raise several interesting questions about the bees that live at high latitude near the auroral zone. During major magnetic storms, the times when extensive auroral disturbances are seen, the magnetic field fluctuates, and much more so at the auroral zones than at lower latitudes. Northern beekeepers might gain additional pleasure from their endeavor by trying to determine if their bees behave differently during magnetic storms. A daily log of the bees' behavior could later be compared with indices of magnetic activity that are derived from magnetic observations in Alaska, Canada and elsewhere. Several types of indices are available; there is a daily index, a three-hour index, and even one that is prepared to represent magnetic activity at the auroral zone every two and one-half minutes.

Another question involves the fact that any navigator trying to determine the cardinal directions using a compass has increasing difficulty as he goes poleward because the earth's magnetic field trends more vertically and exerts less horizontal force on the compass needle. (At the magnetic equator the earth's magnetic field is exactly horizontal, and at the magnetic pole it is exactly vertical.) If bees do use the magnetic field to navigate by, they probably have the usual navigator's problem with the lack of horizontal force in the earth's high-latitude magnetic field.

Feb 80:370

Gizzard Stones

Just about everywhere one cares to look, nature has placed objects to fascinate the mind. Even in the dirt particles beneath our feet there are many intriguing stories about the present and the past; the trick is to be observant and to question what one sees.

Several years ago, archeologists sieving Fairbanks area dirt in search of small prehistoric bones and human artifacts found in their screens many highly-polished small pebbles of quartz and chert. Puzzling over the origin of these usually rounded but sometimes angular shiny stones, the scientists considered several possibilities.

They decided that wind-blown sand or ice crystals could not be the answer because these agents would carve facets on the polished stones. Nor did polishing from natural tumbling of the soil by frost action seem to explain the combination of rounded and angular shapes found, since tumbling causes all stones to become round.

Then Charles Hoskin and his co-workers realized that these objects might be gizzard stones, called "gastroliths", ejected from grouse and ptarmigan of long ago. Comparison of the stones with those taken from the gizzards of modern grouse and ptarmigan led to the conclusion that the polished stones were, indeed, gastroliths. The polishing given to bird gastroliths comes from chemical action and physical grinding as willow and spruce buds, seeds and other hard-to-assimilate foodstuffs are ground up in the birds' gizzards. Sharp, angular stones are picked up in spring and summer; as the year progresses, the stones become more rounded.

One mystery remains. Some of the gizzard stones found in the soil are larger than present-day birds are known to use, a hint that some grouse or ptarmigan of the past were larger than those that live now.

Nov 80:439

Fossil Food

We're used to the idea of using fossil fuel; indeed we depend upon it heavily. But consider how one's future might look if it was necessary to eat fossil food in order to exist.

That is just the situation faced by certain aquatic larvae and shrimp-like crustaceans living on Alaska's North Slope. Their cousins living in warmer climes subsist year around by eating microscopic photosynthetic plants that grow in the water or on rocks and mud at the bottoms of ponds. However, on the North Slope, the growing season is too short to grow enough food for the little critters to eat all winter. They make up the deficit by eating peat, in a second-hand sort of way.

Peat has been accumulating on the tundra since vegetation was re-established on the North Slope about 12,000 years ago, when ice age glaciers receded. Today, the vegetative residue of 12,000 years is present as a layer of peat 1-2 m (3-6 ft) thick overlying the tundra and topped by the living plants of today. Only the top foot or two thaws each summer; the rest is solidly frozen as part of the permafrost layer. However, at lake shores, riverbanks or at the coastline, the permafrost is exposed to summer warming; then blocks of peat and soil topple into the water to be thawed and dispersed by currents or waves.

Bacterial populations grow on this organic matter and other microscopic animals feed upon them. Insect larvae and the crustacea then feed upon these organisms, and thus the peat carbon is passed up the food chain as a constituent of each link. The food chains are very similar to those utilizing aquatic plants or tundra vegetation growing today, but a delay of several thousand years has occurred between the plant growth and consumption of the vegetation.

It is possible to determine the extent to which any species of fish, bird or invertebrate depends upon the "peat subsidy" by analyzing the radiocarbon content of its tissues using standard radiocarbon dating techniques. Since peat is several thousand years old, any organism feeding upon it acquires an apparent radiocarbon age proportional to its dependency on peat in its food chain.

As might be expected, pronounced seasonal shifts occur as aquatic plants become available in summer. Grayling in the Colville River depend almost entirely on the seasonal plant growth (via flying insects) during summer, but, as winter forces shifts in feeding habits, they acquire about 33% of their food energy from peat.

With other species the peat subsidy is even more pronounced. The least cisco (a species of whitefish) feeds in the nearshore marine environment during summer but then shifts to peat-based food chains for almost 40% of its energy requirements during winter. An oldsquaw duck reared in tundra ponds contained an astonishing 64% peat in its makeup.

The fish, ducks and other birds surely don't think about it, but unless their intake of fossil food is slower than the rate of peat growth, someday they will have to change their winter eating habits. Of course, the long delay between the formation of the peat and the time it is eaten means that any changes that do take place will occur very slowly.

— *Don Schell*
Jan 81:457

Plastic Pollution in North Pacific Seabirds

We normally think of Alaska and northwestern Canada as being fairly pristine and free of many of the environmental pollutants that occur in more populated areas of the world. However, recent work on seabirds in Alaska indicates that this is not always the case. Almost 25% of individual seabirds examined have contained plastic pellets or fragments of plastic which they have picked up from the surface of the ocean. In some species the frequency of contaminated birds is frightening; 83% of the short-tailed shearwaters and 75% of the parakeet auklets examined contained plastic particles.

This plastic is primarily polyethylene, a type used in making plastic bags and squeeze bottles commonly found around the house. The plastic enters the ocean during manufacture or shipment, or from the at-sea dumping of garbage by merchant or fishing boats, and is moved around in the ocean by currents and winds. It appears that most of the plastic in the North Pacific is produced in Japan, and that plastic which enters the ocean there is transported by major oceanic currents to Alaska where it is eaten by seabirds. Birds in the Gulf of Alaska and the Aleutian Islands contain more plastic than do birds in the Bering Sea, primarily because currents that carry the plastic do not transport much water into the Bering Sea.

The plastic remains in the stomach until worn down and appears to be harmful to some of the birds. Birds having large amounts of plastic in their stomachs generally weighed less than birds containing little plastic. Some of the bird's stomachs were found to be entirely filled with plastic and stretched to their maximum capacity; a full stomach decreases the tendency for animals to eat, and this probably decreases the survival ability of the birds. In addition, the ingestion of large amounts of plastic appears to have decreased the ability of parakeet auklets to breed successfully, for breeding adults averaged

half of the plastic that non-breeding adults did. Thus, as in the case of DDT produced in the Northern Hemisphere ending up in the bodies of Antarctic penguins, plastic accidentally introduced into the ocean in the North Pacific may end up in the bodies of seabirds in Alaska, and may have serious implications for the future of these birds in Alaska.

— *Bob Day*
Apr 80:388

Purpose of Porpoises' Porpoising

As porpoises swim near the ocean surface, they are often seen to jump completely out of the water, the behavior called porpoising. This leaping into the air has been suggested to be a playful antic, but it has a benefit that goes beyond merely having fun. For the porpoise it is a matter of conserving energy as it swims.

Porpoises and dolphins — there is no sharp distinction between the two, except that porpoises are smaller and lack the characteristic beak nose of dolphins — are high-speed swimmers able to move at sustained speeds near 20 mph. To achieve such speed, these mammals must swim at least five or ten feet below the ocean surface. If they try to swim nearer the surface, the passage of their bodies creates waves on the surface, a process which consumes considerable energy. Thus, the porpoise or dolphin will tire quickly if it swims very close to the surface for long periods.

Being mammals, porpoises and dolphins must breathe air, hence they must surface at frequent intervals. By experience, they have learned that high-speed swimming and the necessary breathing that accompanies it is best accomplished by swimming well below the surface and then leaping through the highly resistive surface region as quickly as possible. They shoot up out of the water and breathe before falling back through the surface layer to a depth where there is less resistance to their passage. Thus, a porpoise's porpoising has a real purpose.

Porpoises and dolphins also have discovered that they can surf by riding the bow wave of a ship or by riding in storm waves. They cleverly locate their bodies in just the right position in the wave to enable them to move at the speed of the wave with no effort whatsoever.

Apr 81:477

Keeping Salmon Inside the 200-Mile Limit

The April 1977 issue of *Sunset* magazine offers a clue to what might conceivably be a means to develop the offshore salmon fishery in a way that will most benefit American fishermen. The article describes year-around fishing in Puget Sound for resident salmon. These are fish that stay in the sound instead of migrating far offshore in the normal fashion.

Evidently the resident fish grow from hatchery-produced smolt which have been released later than usual. Starting in 1971 marine biologists in the Puget Sound area began a delayed-release program. The result is a soaring population of chinook (king) and coho (silver) salmon.

Suppose a delayed-release program were to be begun in Alaskan waters. Is it possible that the program would lead to a high population of salmon living their entire lives inside our new 200-mile limit where only we could catch them?

Apr 77:157

Salmon Sense of Smell

It now seems to be generally accepted that salmon find their way back to their spawning grounds through their acute sense of smell. Just as each major city of the world has its own set of identifiable odors, each stream apparently has a unique set.

An illustration of just how acute is the salmon's ability to distinguish between different scents is given by C. Herb Williams writing in the November 1978 issue of *Pacific Search*. He cites experiments by Canadian scientists showing that salmon will slow or stop their migrations when certain human smells are present. A solution of one part human skin in 80 billion parts water dumped into a river caused salmon to stop migration for as long as a half hour.

The cause of the offensive smell is an amino acid called serine. It is found in the skin or hoofs of various animals, including dog, deer and sea lion. The amount of serine in human skin depends upon the sex, age and race of the individual. Women and children produce less serine than adult males. Blacks produce less serine than American Indians or Latins, and these groups have far less than the worst serine offender — the white adult male.

Williams' article notes that these differences in serine productivity can explain why some people have better luck at fishing than others, why the kid with a string on a stick may sometimes outfish his well-outfitted father.

Perhaps one solution to the serine problem is the use of commercial scents. Another used by some fishermen is to rub their hands with anise oil; anise is an herb of the carrot family. Whether or not these balms really help may be a secret known only to the salmon.

Jan 79:278

Lunar Effects on Salmon

According to folklore and almanac entries, there are certain activities best undertaken during particular phases of the moon. Even if one does not subscribe to such advice, there is no denying that some animal behavior is related to the 27-1/3-day rotation of the moon about the earth.

Evidence is mounting that salmon and related species of trout born in fresh water migrate back to the sea at times influenced by the phase of the moon. A possible explanation of this phenomenon is given in an article in the February 6, 1981 issue of *Science*, written by E. Gorden Grau of the University of California and several co-authors.

By measuring the amounts of thyroxine in young salmon, these scientists have found that the level of thyroxine dramatically increases near the time of new moon. Thyroxine is the hormone produced by the thyroid gland to control growth. The surge of thyroxine seems to cause salmon to undergo smoltification, a process whereby the fish ready their bodies to enter salt water. Fish released from hatcheries too soon or too late after smoltification occurs have high mortality or fail to grow properly. Hence, there is definite practical value to knowing what triggers the surge of thyroxine in the young fish.

The peaks of the thyroxine hormone appear to occur within a day or two of the time of new moon, the time when the moon is fully dark and is located between the earth and the sun. Tides are greatest at new moon and also at full moon, so if the production of thyroxine in salmon is related to the gravitational forces causing tides, one might expect the thyroxine surges to occur both at new and full moon.

Instead of such gravitational charges triggering the thyroxine surge, the investigators suspect that the trigger has more to do with the amount of moonlight falling on the fishes' habitat. It is known that seaward migration of salmon is restricted to the night-time hours, and the migration appears to occur mostly during the two weeks of the lunar month starting at new moon.

Feb 81:470

Earthquake-Sensing Fish

Do fish have the ability to sense the occurrence of very small earthquakes, earthquakes that might be forewarning of bigger events to come? It seems that they might, according to an article in the August 1980 issue of *Geophysical Research Letters* written by University of Texas researchers, Cliff Frohlich and Ruth Buskirk.

Experiments with codfish, goldfish and other fish have shown that fish are able to sense very small changes in pressure and motion within the water where they live. That is, they are able to hear very weak sounds. As in air, a sound heard in water is the result of compressional waves traveling through the medium, except that sound waves travel about five times faster in water than they do in air.

162

In addition to sound detection in the inner ear, a fish is able to sense sound stimuli with extensive arrays of hair cell receptors along its body and also with sensors that detect changes within the swim bladder. These multiple sensing abilities combine to allow the fish to detect tiny sounds, some of which are far lower in frequency than a human can detect.

People do sometimes hear sound waves in air associated with passing seismic waves in the ground below. Sound waves generated in water by earth-quake waves in the rock below are much stronger than those generated in air. That and the fish's ability to sense weak sound waves combine to permit fish to "hear" earthquakes that are ten to a thousand times smaller than a person can hear.

Researchers Frohlich and Buskirk suggest that fish may detect nearby earthquakes resulting from tiny breakage of rocks along small faults, faults with lengths as short as a meter-stick, perhaps even shorter.

Oct 80:432

CHAPTER NINE
OUR HERITAGE

Roots

If only more Alaskans had roots in the cultural richness of the region. A common framework of reference is desperately needed. In a political year it would be fine if we could say of a candidate: "He's as slippery as . . . was;" or "He lies almost as well as . . . did;" or "We haven't seen such a phoney since . . . beguiled us."

Aside from Soapy Smith of Skagway fame, Alaskans lack regional heroes. And even Smith, a grand rogue, is too far removed from us to serve very well.

Lacking any appreciation of Alaska's past, we are driven to rely on national historic characters when we seek inspiration. Although America's tradition is rich in scoundrels and con men, we miss regional models. At one time Alaskans could identify with clarity the villainy of Seattle fishery interests and the strangling perfidiousness of the Morgan-Guggenheim Syndicate. Here were villains to be hissed and scorned, recognizable objects to blame and defile for all our woes.

Alaskans are divided on many issues. If they could dip into a common, local heritage and fling mud at their foes from a common pot, they would be richer. We need a common heritage as much as a common language. It just doesn't do to relate current problems wholly to facets of the national experience. Great controversies are raging and adversaries, in their ignorance, are unable to score telling points against their enemies by drawing upon the past. A few history buffs know that monumental stereotypes exist for all contemporary antagonists. And it is always relevant to link the evil of the past with the present. But you must know your roots.

— *William R. Hunt*
Apr 78:75

People of the Bering Land Bridge

Uncertainty still exists about the sequences of migration across the Bering Land Bridge that originally peopled North and South America.

It is fairly certain that humans were in the Americas at least 12,000 years ago and perhaps even tens of thousands of years earlier. Evidences of pre-Eskimos and pre-Aleuts in Alaska have been thought to be less old, so it has been conjectured that they were relative late-comers, following after groups of peoples who moved across the Bridge and migrated southward through western North America.

A somewhat different, seemingly quite logical, hypothesis was published in 1967 by W. S. Laughlin of the University of Wisconsin. His idea was that the Bering Land Bridge might have been occupied by forerunners of the Aleuts and Eskimos simultaneously with the presense of those pre-Indians who moved through and came on southward.

Laughlin noted that there was plenty of room on the Bridge for two populations since at maximum exposure the Bridge was a thousand kilometers wide, north to south. At least there would be room if the two populations had different lifestyles analogous to the modern differences between Athabascans, on the one hand, and Aleuts and Eskimos on the other. The Eskimos and Aleuts live primarily from the sea and the Athabascans from the land.

Laughlin argued that it was logical for the Mongoloid peoples of Asia who were used to living along the shore to invade the southern coastal boundary of the Bering Land Bridge when it existed 10,000 to 30,000 years ago. His idea was that they would have an easy time of it because of the richness of that coastline, especially the eastern part of it where strong coastal upwelling would support many fishes, sea mammals and birds.

While these coastal people remained comparatively stationary, as a maritime livelihood dictates, other peoples could pass eastward across the Bridge to the north of them. These people would have to be hunters who followed the game and lived off it. Their lifestyle would demand that they live in small groups able to move on as local scarcities of game might demand. One can imagine that any contacts between the coastal dwellers and the nomads might

164

have been hostile, just as were most contacts between Eskimos and Athabascans in recent times.

Once the Bering Land Bridge began to close, the nomadic hunters would have been cut off on the west by the waters. Then the pre-Aleuts and pre-Eskimos on the eastern end would have extended north along the new shoreline and along the shores of the Arctic Ocean. There is good evidence that the Eskimos, who spread eastward along the shore as far as Greenland, did in fact come from western or southwestern Alaska. Yet another possibility is that the Eskimos who spread into Greenland actually arrived in Alaska by boat from Siberia after the Land Bridge closed.

While Laughlin's joint residency hypothesis seems to make good sense, archeological finds during recent years fail to substantiate it. If his idea is correct, it is expected that archeological finds in the Aleutians and on the nearby Alaska Peninsula should reveal cultural differences between the ancient people who live there and those inland and farther north. Instead, the most recent finds seem to show a high degree of similarity. Of course, much of the evidence that might support Laughlin's hypothesis is now beneath the cold waters of Bering Sea.

Jul 81:494

The Changing Scenery

About 15,000 years ago, toward the end of the last ice age, enough of the world's ocean water was locked up into glacier ice that the Bering Land Bridge still existed.

The actual form of the land surface in Alaska and western Canada has actually changed very little during the past 15,000 years, but its outward appearance has altered radically. The Bering Land Bridge is no longer visible, it having been submerged by water 200 feet deeper than previously. This submersion has now stopped; in fact it stopped about 6000 years ago. Since then, the shorelines have maintained themselves at approximately their present locations.

And of course, the coastal region of southern Alaska and western British Columbia has been largely bared of the extensive glacier ice that covered it during the ice age. Now, deep fiords, broad coastal flats and forested valleys appear where there was only ice before. No people could have lived in this region then.

Even where there was no ice cover in the interior valleys and uplands of Alaska and Yukon Territory, the appearance of the land has changed. Just within the last 15 years, people who study such things have concluded that the vegetation during the ice age was quite different than it is now. Instead of the forests and mossy swamplands we are familiar with, there must have been broad expanses of prairie land largely covered by grasses, sedges and flowers.

Examination of pollens laid down in lakes and other areas at that time show that spruce and alder were lacking, though there were some birch trees. In a recent lecture at the Geophysical Institute, USGS geologist David Hopkins suggested that the ice age summers were comparatively dry. That dryness not only caused a different vegetation cover, it also led to the existence of widespread sand dunes in the valleys of the Yukon River and its tributaries.

Dr. Hopkins noted that this was the time when mammoths, horses, bison and wapiti (American stag or elk) ranged over the countryside. He suggests that these grazing animals might actually have contributed to the maintenance of the open grasslands, for the same reasons that domestic pasture lands are more productive when grazed. By eating grass, animals, like lawnmowers, promote better growth and they also drop fertilizer. Dr. Hopkins noted that the fertilizer left by even one mammoth was not inconsequential, since each ate 200 or more pounds of grass each day.

One interesting point about the ice age climate is that, in some ways, it might have been much like that experienced in interior Alaska the past three years, warm in winter, wet in spring, and dry in summer. Were the weather we have been having these past few years to continue, we could be trending toward more extensive open, dry grassland than now exists. Of course, no one really knows whether the somewhat unusual weather of the past few years is just a fluctuation from normal or if it signals the beginning of climatic change. But whatever happens, we will be able to stroll over the countryside without watching each footstep, since we know that the mammoth won't be back.

May 81:486

Beach Ridge Archeology

We are familiar with the idea that archeologists reach the remains of older cultures by digging deeper into the ground. The famous Arctic archeologist, J. Louis Giddings, used another technique; he simply walked farther back from the ocean beach. He found several localities in western Alaska where there were series of low ridges lying parallel to and behind the existing beach. Giddings reasoned that these ridges, each only a few feet high, were former beach crests. Each should be older than those between it and the sea, and each, Giddings hoped, would yield the remains of the people who lived on the beach crest at the time it represented the shoreline.

In 1958 Giddings and his co-workers began an investigation of the beach ridges at Cape Krusenstern, northwest of Kotzebue. They mapped a total of at least 114 beach ridges extending back two miles from the shore. These beaches were formed over the

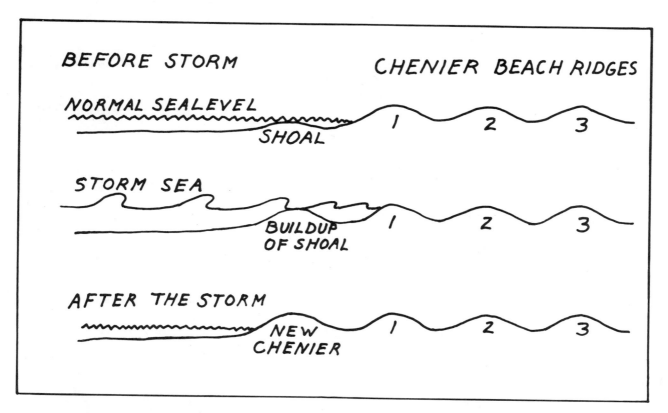

Krusenstern's Chenier Plain: *How repeated storms build a series of even-height beach ridges.*

last 5000 years; on the average a new beach formed about every 40 to 50 years over this time span. The beach ridges revealed a continuous record of human occupation. Giddings was able to identify eight cultural stages, the oldest dating back to about 3000 B.C.

One of the major yields of the Krusenstern beach sequence came from Beach 53 occupied in 1800 B.C. Several house remains found there showed that the occupants had a culture unlike any found elsewhere in western Alaska but somewhat similar to cultural groups living in the Great Lakes region in 3200 B.C. and afterwards.

The full story of Giddings' archeological work in western Alaska is contained in his highly readable book, *Ancient Man of the Arctic,* published in 1967 just after his death. It is available now in Alaskan bookstores.

Mar 77:153

Krusenstern's Chenier Plain

At Cape Krusenstern, northwest of Kotzebue, 114 or more low beach ridges separate a marshy lagoon from the sea. Each ridge is younger than the ones behind it; all were formed during the last 5000 to 6000 years. Since the most seaward ridge was occupied by early man, archeologist J. Louis Giddings

was able to formulate a chronology of occupation by noting which ridge a particular excavation was on.

How did these strange ridges form? They are all about the same height and altitude and so could not be formed by slow changes in sea level. Furthermore, it is known that sea level has not changed during the past 5000 years. Similar beach ridge formations occur on the Louisiana shore and near the mouth of the Amazon River. Based upon studies of these features, called cheniers or ritsens, reported by geological oceanographer W. Armstrong Price, we can see how the chenier beach ridges at Cape Krusenstern formed. In the process we learn something about the frequency of major storms in Kotzebue Sound.

I suspect that the source of the sandy material forming the cheniers is the Noatak River. Its mouth lies just 50 km to the east. Fine-grained clay, silt and sand particles emptied into the sea by the river are probably carried along the shore by westward-moving currents. The nearshore water is fairly quiet so that the suspended particles settle out to form low offshore shoals. Cape Krusenstern is exposed to a long stretch of sea and the violent storm winds that occasionally strike Alaska's northwestern shore. Strong wind from the west can raise the sea level several feet. Heavy storm surf can then build a new beach ridge atop the former offshore shoal. When the storm is over, the sea retreats leaving the new ridge above normal sea level.

Based on the number of ridges and the 5000 year time span, such storms must have occurred roughly every 45 to 50 years. Each time, the local residents must have abandoned their homesites and built new homes on the new ridge. Over the course of the years, the people migrated about two miles, leaving behind the artifacts that describe their existence.

Aug 77:99

Mammoths and Mastodons

Cave drawings of mammoths prove that these extinct mammals coexisted with man, and it is virtually certain that mastodons did also. It seems likely that human beings killed off both species perhaps 8000 to 10,000 years ago, but there may have been other reasons for their extinction. Both mammoths and mastodons existed in Alaska; the remains of mammoths are found frequently — mastodon finds are relatively rare.

The woolly mammoth found in Alaska was up to 9½ feet tall at the shoulder; it had a high humped head and a downward slope to the back, the hind quarters being rather small. The tusks curled upward in a circular fashion and the teeth were fairly flat and formed of alternating vertical platelets of ivory and bone. Mammoths ate grasses and spruce; it is said that one could consume 300 pounds of spruce a day. Though stocky, the mastodon was more elongated in structure. He had a low forehead and tusks that curved mainly forward. The molar teeth were cusped rather than flat.

In 1937, in the mucks at Ester more than 100 young mammoth teeth were found in an area a few yards across, together with burned bones and two man-made artifacts. Also a broken tool point was found frozen against a portion of a mastodon skull. Finds such as these seem to prove that early residents of the Fairbanks area ate mammoth and mastodon flesh. However, archeologists investigating the finds did not make such a strong claim.

Aug 76:108

Mastodon and Man

So far, there seems to be no universally accepted proof that man actually hunted mastodons and mammoths in the Americas, even though cave drawings do prove that man and these elephant-like mammals coexisted. But now from Venezuela comes conclusive evidence of a mastodon kill.

Anthropologists from Venezuela and Canada recently unearthed a young mastodon that had been butchered by man at least 13,000 years ago. The remaining bones showed marks where tendons had been cut away with stone tools. A weapon point and another flaked tool were found with the bones, the point being within a natural cavity in the animal's pelvic bone. Fragments of chewed twigs thought to have been in the slain mastodon's stomach enabled carbon dating of the find.

Near the ancient watering hole beside which the young mastodon lay were found the remains of horse, bear, sloth, and other mastodons. Two bones of an adult mastodon clearly had been used as chopping blocks.

At Ester, Alaska, near Fairbanks, more than 100 teeth of young mammoths were found in 1937 lying in a small area. Very likely this was a man-caused concentration, but it does not constitute proof that man, mastodons and mammoths coexisted in Alaska.

Aug 78:239

Curious Mammoth Find

Bones of mammoths and other prehistoric animals are found rather frequently in the north at locations where the soil has remained frozen. Usually the bones are found relatively deep in frozen ground, well below the near-surface layer which freezes and thaws annually.

Hence it was unusual that a mammoth tusk and two teeth were found within four feet of the ground surface in 1979 by a housing contractor excavating for a basement next to the Fairbanks campus of the University of Alaska. Particularly surprising is that the tusk and teeth were found on an open park-like crest of a hill. No permafrost was found in the excavation nor would one expect any at this well-drained sunshiny location.

However, signs of deterioration were evident. The tusk and the teeth broke into pieces, more or less of their own accord, after being exposed to air, and the skull that had encased them could be seen as only a thin golden-brown layer in the soil.

The mammoth remains were found in a foot-thick layer of humus-rich, wind-blown silt that was the ground surface for many years at the time the mammoth lived. After the animal died, more wind-blown silt deposited on the site and built the surface up to the present-day level.

Probably the mammoth died some thousands of years ago. But still it is not obvious how the mammoth remains could have been preserved for any length of time at such a warm, unrefrigerated site. Perhaps the site has not always been so warm. Not far away, dense spruce trees keep the underlying forest floor cooler in summer, perhaps cool enough for permafrost to exist in some places.

Aug 79:333

Mammoths: *A four- to six-month-old mammoth found in July 1977 during gold mining operations near Susuman, Magadan Oblast, USSR. The animal is 144 cm high at the shoulder and has reddish fur. Estimates of the time of death are between 10,000 to 15,000 years ago. (Photograph presented by Dr. Kontrimavichus, Institute of Biological Problems of the North, Magadan, provided courtesy of the University of Alaska's Institute of Arctic Biology.)*

Mystery of the Mammoth and the Buttercups

In the early part of this century the famous Beresovka mammoth carcass was discovered in Siberia. Nearly intact, the animal was found buried in silty gravel sitting in the upright position. The mammoth had a broken foreleg, evidently caused by a fall from a nearby cliff 10,000 years ago. The remains of its stomach were intact and there were grasses and buttercups lodged between its teeth. The flesh was still edible, but reportedly not tasty.

No one has ever satisfactorily explained how the Beresovka mammoth and other animals found frozen in the subarctic could have been frozen before being consumed by predators of the time. Some have proposed a sudden change in climate, but this hardly seems a likely explanation. The scientist who uncovered the Beresovka mammoth conjectured that the animal fell into a snow-filled ravine that protected the body until it was perhaps covered by gravel during a summer flood.
— *Judy Holland*
Nov 76:122

Caribou Stew at Onion Portage

Onion Portage is one of the most important archeological sites in Alaska. Excavation of the soil there has revealed layers of tools and other artifacts extending back to at least 8000 years.

A seemingly un-Alaskan name, Onion Portage derived its name from the wild onions that grow on this shortcut between two parts of the Kobuk River.

The use of the site by man over such a long time span is evidently related to this being a location where caribou have always crossed the river on their annual migrations between feeding grounds. Before guns were available, man speared the swimming caribou from small canoes and then butchered the carcasses on the beach at the Onion Portage site.

Archeologist Louis Giddings discovered the site in 1940. Since then, excavations revealed layer upon layer of sand and silt containing the refuse and tools of many cultures. Except at the very bottom of the opened pits, where signs of ancient soil slumping were evident, the horizontal soil and refuse layers were undistributed. Thus a detailed chronology based upon carbon age dating could be developed.

The very oldest artifacts taken from Onion Portage were similar to those found in the Aleutians and from northern Japan of the same period, about 6000 B.C. At that time the Bering Land Bridge did exist, so people could easily travel on foot over this broad region. How many exciting archeological sites like that at Onion Portage must now lie beneath the waters of the Chukchi and Bering Seas!

Mar 77:44

College Man

". . . the most important single landmark in the history of interior Alaskan archaeology" stated archeologist Frederick Hadleigh-West when discussing the "Campus site" located on the University of Alaska at Fairbanks. Now marked by a Coastal Indian totem pole — much to the chagrin of most archeologists — the Campus site is one of the few sites known to be occupied by ancient man in central Alaska. Just where he came from or when is uncertain. The similarity of worked tools and points found on the Campus site to Asian artifacts suggests that he came from somewhere west of Irkutsk (Lake Baikal). He probably crossed the Bering Land Bridge just before it last disappeared, perhaps 10,000 or 11,000 years ago. Several other archeological sites have been found in the Interior. They were inhabited by what is referred to as the Denali culture. This seems like a reasonable name, but there is a more fitting one for the scraggly-haired fellow who sat on the brow of College Hill those many years ago. His proper name should be College Man.

Jul 76:45

Seek and You Shall Find

Is that rock you kicked out of the trail the other day just another rock or was it a copper or gold nugget, a meteorite or a skin scraper chipped out by ancient man?

It may be difficult to tell on the spot what a particular object is, but it is certain that one will never know without looking and thinking. Interesting objects are not that difficult to find especially in Alaska, where it is easy to walk ground little trod by modern man or perhaps never walked upon at all.

Almost any man-made or man-worked object found along the trail or on the beach can be an item of interest. The north is kind to objects of bone, wood, metal and stone, much kinder than regions farther south where water and plants and other life forms work more rapidly to cause rust and decay.

Iron objects do deteriorate rapidly near salt water, but perhaps it's not impossible to still find remnants of the old whaling days on Alaska's northern and western shores. The early mining days are now removed far enough in time to make finds of implements interesting, at least to the finder.

Places where the soil is newly disturbed by water, wind or human activity are potential sites for finding artifacts. The fact that these are protected by state and federal law in no way detracts from the thrill of finding them. Suspected finds can be reported to the University of Alaska or to various state and federal agencies.

May 78:212

Local Archeological Find

Excavating for the new Ester firehouse, workers recently unearthed the remains of a bygone culture.

Local Archeological Find: *Two artifacts of Alaska's past.*

Definite evidence of earlier man was found in a midden pile covered by a deep moss layer and upon which a 30-foot high birch tree, three inches in diameter, was growing. Dating procedures place this culture in the early post-Felix Pedro era, i.e. not older than 73 years and not younger than 66 years ago.

Containers found in the midden indicate that the people of this culture existed solely upon whiskey, beer, pop and catsup and that they anointed themselves with large quantities of various liniments for tired and aching muscles. Most consumed goods obviously were imported, but there were exceptions. Two of the excavated containers, presumed to be pop bottles, contain the inscriptions "Distilled Soda Water Co. of Alaska" and "Nome Brewing and Bottling Co.". Each is fitted with a clever stoppered cap actuated by a wire top protruding through the mouth of the bottle. The stopper is a metal and rubber disk that seals from below when pulled upward. Bottle collectors call these "blob top" bottles; the body of the bottle is molded in a machine invented in 1903. The top is formed from an extra blob of glass.

We are seeking correspondence with anyone who has information on the two Alaskan firms that dispensed these bottles.

Sep 76:104

Man — The Deadly Killer

Even without his modern developments — guns, tracked vehicles, airplanes or even riding horses — man is the most formidable big game hunter evolved on this earth. High intellect, a superb body and perserverance combine to make man the deadliest hunter. Not as fast at running short distances as some animals, man nevertheless is capable of running any animal into the ground. He has the mental drive and the physical ability to chase an animal for days until that animal can go no farther.

Indians of interior Alaska used that method for moose hunting long ago. Finding a relatively fresh moose track, the Indian hunter followed it, moving in half circles so as not to follow the trail directly. After a time, perhaps several days, his circular track would close upon itself without crossing the moose's trail. Then the moose was located and was perhaps too tired to escape. The hunter moved in for the kill with spears or birch bows and arrows. Carrying the meat home probably was not a big issue because, in those days, the Indians tended to follow the animals rather than to live in riverside villages as they do now.

Jul 76:86

Bows and Arrows

Forum's first correspondent from Canada, Mrs. Marian Schmidt of Dawson, asks if Indians used the bow and arrow for moose-hunting prior to the time of the Russians and other newcomers of the eighteenth and nineteenth centuries. She reports that natives of her area suggest that the bow and arrow may be a recent introduction.

Perhaps the bow and arrow was reintroduced to this area only recently; however arrowheads and arrow shaft straighteners have been found in strata laid down long ago. Thus it is nearly certain that the bow and arrow has been in use in Canada and Alaska for thousands of years.

Indians along the Alaska-Canada border used, for moose and other big game hunting, a birch long-bow (five to six feet) strung with either three-ply twisted sinew or two-ply twisted babiche (rawhide). Some tribes held the bow vertically, others horizontally. Arrowheads for big game were made of horn and copper, in lengths three to seven inches. Both simple and compound arrows were used for large animals. The simple arrow had an arrowhead tightly bound to the shaft, whereas the compound arrow employed an arrowhead designed to fall off the shaft after penetration of the animal's hide.

Sep 76:112

An Alaskan Mummy

Though she lived 1600 years ago, quite a bit is now known about one Eskimo woman resident of St. Lawrence Island, located midway between Siberia and Alaska in the Bering Sea. The entire story is told by the woman's body, found frozen when beach erosion exhumed her.

Prior to reburial in her homeland, a variety of sophisticated analyses of the woman's naturally mummified body have indicated something about how she lived and how she died after her child-bearing years at age 53, or thereabouts. A fractured skull and moss fibers inside her lungs indicated that the woman had died during the cave-in of her sod house. Asphyxiation (smothering) directly caused her death, rather than the blow to her head.

Had she lived in modern times, researchers might have attributed the carbon deposits in the woman's lungs to her being a habitual smoker of cigarettes. Instead, the cause is more likely 53 years around open cooking and heating fires.

She had other troubles, too. Her teeth were worn down, and she suffered from coronary artery disease, a condition we tend to associate with living in a stressful technological society. She once had pneumonia, and she had a sideways curvature to her spine that probably gave her an abnormal walking gait.

On the brighter side of life are elaborate tattoos revealed by infrared photography of the woman's arms. Most of the markings are in the form of alternating bands and rows of dots extending partially

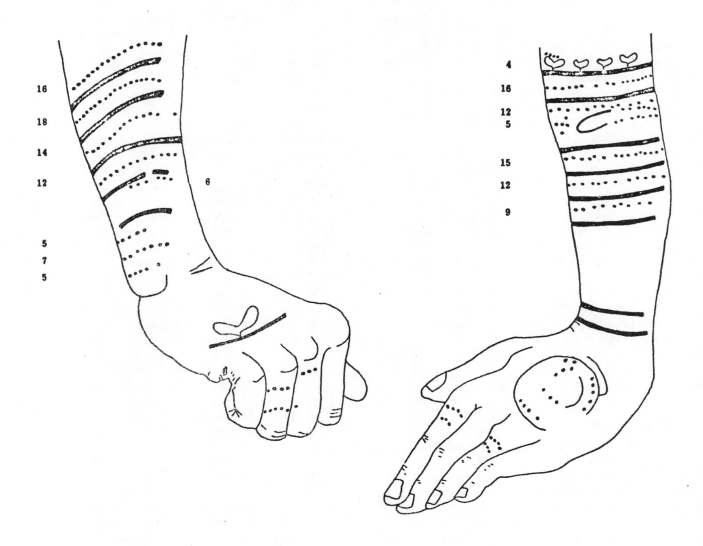

An Alaskan Mummy: *The pattern of tattooing on the forearms of the 1600-year-old frozen body from St. Lawrence Island, Alaska.*

around the lower arms. Variety is provided by a row of roundish designs on one arm similar to one on the back of the opposite hand and by a completely different circular design on the other hand. It would be interesting to know what these patterns represent, just as it would to be able to know more about the Eskimo way of life 1600 years ago.

Jul 80:413

Alaska Native Languages

There exist in North America two major language families comprising a total of 20 separate languages that were born or cradled in Alaska. More people now speak these languages than at any time in history.

Yet, in Alaska, these languages are only holding even or are declining.

One language family, Eskimo-Aleut, is spoken by 95% of the 118,000 Canadian Eskimos and by essentially all 42,000 Greenlander Eskimos. But in Alaska, only about 70% of 34,000 resident Eskimos and Aleuts speak the Eskimo-Aleut languages.

Even more striking is the decline in Alaska of the other language family called Athabascan-Eyak-Tlingit or Na-Dene. Today about 90% of the 23,000 Athabascans living in Canada speak this language family, as do more than 96% of the 170,000 Apaches and Navajos who live in the American Southwest. In

Alaska only 31% of 8000 Athabascan Indians speak the language family.

According to Professor Michael E. Krauss of the University of Alaska's Alaska Native Language Center, the reason for the decline of native languages in Alaska is severe suppression of native languages during the first six or seven decades of this century. Before 1900, outside influences helped the native languages by developing written versions and teaching Natives to read and write them. Russian Orthodox priests developed written Eskimo and Aleut languages and missionaries of the Anglican church operating near the Alaska-Canada border developed written Athabascan languages. Other missionaries, particularly Catholic, Episcopal and Moravian, joined the task in later years.

By 1910, the trend reversed. In all schools administered by the United States Bureau of Education and in many of the mission schools, children were prohibited from speaking their native language. Their parents were urged to speak only English at home in order to prevent the native language from being learned. The suppression worked well.

In 1972, the Alaska Legislature passed a bill giving Alaskan children the right to use and cultivate their native language in school. In a school having eight or more students whose primary language is other than English, Alaska law requires the school to have a teacher fluent in that language. This law does not extend to schools operated by the Bureau of Indian Affairs, which operates the schools where about 75% of children speaking Native languages are enrolled.

Those interested in learning more about Alaskan languages will enjoy reading a new publication by Dr. Krauss entitled, *Alaska Native Languages, Past, Present and Future*, available from the Language Center in Fairbanks. His estimate of the future of many Native languages is grim. Of the 20 languages spoken, Dr. Krauss expects only five to live into the second half of the 21st century.

The first to go will be Eyak, now spoken by only two or three residents of the Cordova region. None are younger than 60. All speakers of Alaskan Tsimshian, Alaskan Haida, Holikachuk, and Tanana are past 40. No one under 20 speaks Tlingit, Ahta, Ingalik, Koyukon or Han.

Each of these languages differs from the other and each has a rich vocabulary, soon without anyone to speak it. However, each language will be preserved in written form as a result of linguistics work already accomplished or still underway at the Alaska Language Center and elsewhere. Anyone wishing to engage in linguistics research in Alaska is invited to contact Irene Reed, director of the center.

Aug 80:419

Alaskan Firsts

Most trends, fads and new developments seem to come to Alaska a year or so after starting someplace else, but it wasn't always so. Sitka's shipyard industry, which produced 25 vessels up to 1860, built the first steam powered ship to be constructed in the Pacific. Aleut craftsmen there cast steam engine parts and also church bells, some of which were exported to California.

A magnetic observatory to record variations in the earth's magnetic field, probably the first on the west coast of the Americas, was established in 1842. The Sitka magnetic observatory remains as one of the world's key stations. In 1861, Sitka had the only pipe organ in northwest America. It had two scientific institutes. One was for zoological research; the other, for the study of terrestrial magnetic phenomena, was supported by both the British and Russian governments.

Jul 76:72

The Alaska-Siberia Telegraph

The Alaska-Siberia Telegraph (also called the Collins Overland Telegraph or the Western Union Russian Extension) was a pioneer attempt to establish a telegraphic communications link between North America and Europe, via the Bering Strait.

The plan for the Alaska-Siberia Telegraph was originated by Perry McDonough Collins, while undertaking a commercial venture in the Amur Valley of Siberia.

Collins envisioned an intercontinental telegraph link from California, north through British Columbia, across Russian-America to Siberia, via the Bering Strait, and across Siberia to Europe. Realizing the critical need for intercontinental communications — and knowing of the repeated failures of Cyrus Field's attempts to lay the Atlantic cable — Collins proposed his idea in 1859 to the U.S. Secretary of State. The commercial potential of the project was obvious to Collins and to the Western Union Telegraph Company, which became very interested in his plan after Congress authorized the construction of the Pacific line to California in 1860. Collins negotiated agreements between various governments and with Western Union; and in 1864 he submitted a petition to Congress asking for aid in a survey of the proposed route, a right-of-way through U.S. territory, and a subsidy in the form of contracts for the dispatch of government messages. Secretary of State Seward (of later folly fame) strongly supported Collins, and President Lincoln signed an act in 1864 permitting construction to begin in the summer of 1865.

Explorations for the line were divided into three parts: one was in British Columbia, where the telegraph line from San Francisco terminated; another embraced the Yukon River and Norton Sound areas with headquarters at Saint Michael; and the third was situated on the Amur River in Siberia. In 1866 a fourth group of about 40 men was sent to Port Clarence to build the line that was to cross the Bering Strait to Siberia.

In Russian America, little progress was made during the summer and winter of 1865. The late arrival of the construction parties, the shortage of supplies and the difficult climate all contributed to lack of progress. Despite the setbacks suffered by the Russian American division during 1866, by autumn of that year the entire route was surveyed and found suitable. Rather than suspend work for the winter season, as had been the practice before, it was decided to begin construction and to continue work through the winter. The Western Union men, most of them unaccustomed to the severe northern winters, found working in these conditions a difficult experience. They had to light fires to thaw out the ground before they could begin to dig in the frozen earth. One of the workers, George Adams, commented, "Building a telegraph line with only dogs and sleds for transportation in the frigid zone is not as much fun as it is cracked up to be."

By the spring of 1867, over 45 miles of line were completed in Russian America, and stations were built and thousands of poles were cut and distributed along the route. But that year's work didn't matter, for in July of 1866 the laying of the Atlantic cable was successfully completed and the first trans-Atlantic message to England was sent. The men in the Russian American division were unaware of the decision to cease work until July of 1867.

Although the Collins Overland Telegraph did not succeed in establishing an intercontinental communications link, it did bring important secondary benefits to Alaska. The telegraph expeditions were responsible for the first systematic examination of the flora, fauna and geology of the area. And in this way members of the telegraph project were able to play a minor but significant role in the purchase of Alaska by providing useful data on the valuable, but relatively unknown, new territory.

— Fran Pedersen
Oct 77:68

The Alaska-Canada Boundary

The Alaska-Canada boundary was originally established in February 1825 by Russia (then owner of Alaska) and Great Britain (then owner of Canada). The demarcation between Alaska and Canada was to begin at 54°40′ N latitude, just north of the mouth of the Portland Canal (near Prince Rupert, B.C.), follow the canal until it met 56° N latitude, then follow the mountain summits situated parallel to the coast as far as 141° W longitude, then follow that meridian northward to the "Frozen Ocean." The boundary line along the mountain summits was never to be farther inland than ten marine leagues (about 50 kilometers) from the ocean.

Following the purchase of Alaska by the U.S., it was found that the wording concerning the boundary line not being farther inland than ten marine leagues from the coast was interpreted differently by the Canadians and Americans. The Canadians argued that the measurements should be made inland from the mouths of the bays, whereas the Americans argued that the measurements should be made from the heads of the bays. The differences in interpretation were critical because it then determined whether or not Canada had access to the sea. The gold strikes in the Klondike and in southeastern Alaska in the late 1800s made valuable the terrain in question.

The southeastern boundary dispute was settled in October 1903, when an international tribunal upheld the American interpretation of the Treaty of 1825. Had it not done so, Haines, Dyea and Skagway would now be Canadian territory as well as the shore approaches to the Chilkat, Chilkoot and White Passes.

With mining activities increasing in interior Canada and Alaska, it became important that the 141st meridian international boundary line be determined and marked to separate the two countries, and in 1906, a convention was signed by Canada and the U.S. requiring this be done.

A first step in the surveying of the boundary line was to find out precisely where the 141st meridian was. Earlier work showed that the most practical starting point was the meridian's intersection with the Yukon River. Astronomical observations made there could be precisely timed by means of telegraphic connections to Vancouver, B.C., and Fort Egbert (Eagle), Alaska. Astronomers, engineers and surveyors of the U.S. Coast and Geodetic Survey and the Canadian Department of the Interior worked together north and south from the Yukon, once they had decided the exact north-south direction, a task they took not at all lightly. Part of their task was to cut a 20-foot swath through all trees encountered. It was all hard work, so it behooved them to make sure, right at the start, that the correct trees were being cut.

Boundary monuments of aluminum bronze were set along the 141st meridian, each, where possible, visible from some other marker, though not necessarily an adjacent marker. Each weighed about 55 pounds and was set in concrete with 200 pounds of cement.

In 1913, after eight summers of work, surveying and marking of the 141st meridian were completed. There were 191 monuments stretching the 350 miles

of the 141st meridian beginning at about 200 feet short of the Arctic Ocean and ending at the south side of Logan Glacier.
— *Fran Pedersen*
Jan 78:193

Kennecott — A Spelling Error

Though perhaps untrue, there is a rumor that the town of Chicken, Alaska, got its name when the city fathers met and decided to call it "Ptarmigan" after the official bird of Alaska, only to discover that no one present knew how to spell the word. Supposedly someone said, "Aw hell, let's just call it Chicken!"

In a somewhat similar manner, the industrial concern named Kennecott Copper Corporation got its name — it was an error in spelling. Kennecott Copper Corporation derives its name from the old Kennecott Copper Company, one of many owned by the Morgan-Guggenheim Syndicate created in 1905. This powerful concern held numerous commercial enterprises in Alaska, under its subsidiary the Alaska Syndicate, including the Seattle-based Alaska Steamship Company.

Kennecott Copper Company owned the copper mines surrounding the town of Kennicott, which was the northern terminus of the Syndicate-owned Copper River and Northwestern Railroad that ran 196 miles to Cordova. In naming the company, someone replaced an "i" by an "e" and the error stuck.

Naptowne: *Modern-day fishermen line the banks of Moose River near Naptowne where Eskimos perhaps once caught salmon.*

The town of Kennicott was, in turn, named for the Kennicott Glacier alongside which it sat. Finally, we come to the original source of the name — the Kennicott Glacier was named after Robert Kennicott in 1899. In 1865-66, he was director of the Western Union Telegraph Expedition which had the goal of establishing an overland telegraph route across Alaska to Siberia. As new history books come out, Robert Kennicott must occasionally turn over in his grave at Nulato, Alaska, since about half of those published in recent years refer to him as Robert Kennecott or Robert Kennecot.

Jun 78:234

Naptowne

During the summer salmon runs, fishermen by the hundreds line the banks near the junction of the Moose and Kenai Rivers. Now called Sterling, this used to be Naptowne. Naptowne nowadays is the name of a small suburb just west of Sterling.

Where did this curious name Naptowne come from? Did someone stop for a short rest once, or did someone named Sam Nap settle here years ago?

Another, more elaborate, possibility is that Naptowne was named after its early inhabitants: Eskimos who occupied the coastal area of southern Alaska as far east as Controller Bay, east of Cordova. Sometime not long before historic times, Alaskan Eskimos expanded inland to occupy fishing sites held by Athabascan Indians and which, again, many years later, were held by Indians.

It seems probable that the Eskimos occupied the Moose-Kenai river junction before the area was reoccupied by the Tanaina Indians during the last two hundred years. Evidently the early Russian contact so decimated the Eskimos that they lost land to the less-affected Indians.

The final bit of conjecture is that Naptowne is derived from the Eskimo word "nap" or "napa" which means "many trees" or "forest." Thus in the Kuskokwim region Napamute meant people of the forest. Variations of the name "Napa" have been attached to various locations of the Kuskokwim, and there is one, Napaimute, located on the south shore of Iliamna Lake, across Cook Inlet not far west of Naptowne.

So perhaps the Eskimos who lived at Sterling were known as peoples of the forest or "napas" and that is how Naptowne got its name.

Geologists have applied the name Naptowne to the last of the five Pleistocene glaciations that affected the Matanuska and Cook Inlet areas. The Naptowne glaciation ended about 5500 years ago; its moraines extend out westward from the Kenai Mountains as far as the present-day location of Naptowne.

Aug 78:243

Naptowne Revisited

Intrigued by the name Naptowne, an early name for present-day Sterling, Alaska, I wrote an earlier article suggesting how the name might have originated. The most elaborate suggestion involved the possibility that Naptowne was a modernization of a variant of the Eskimo term "nap" or "napa" meaning "trees" or "forest". Since Eskimos lived in the Kenai Peninsula area prior to its recent occupation by the Tanaina Indians, it seemed possible that Naptowne could have had this origin.

But this elaborate and fanciful idea is wrong — not just a little bit wrong, it is totally wrong. In this case my embarrassment at being wrong is more than compensated for by the several letters to the editors of newspapers that my article elicited and letters sent directly to me. In particular, I thank Roger V. Burke of Ketchikan, Walt Pedersen of Sterling and Jeffery Paul Petrovich of Anchorage. These knowledgeable persons have provided factual information on the early history of the Sterling area.

Probably the most valuable single source of information is the book *A Small History of the Western Kenai* by Walt and Elsa Pedersen, who live at Sterling. Walt Pedersen played a major role in the modern settlement of the area. That settlement commenced in August 1947 when the area was opened to homesteading, prior to the existence of the Sterling Highway. A letter from Walt Pedersen states that the Indian settlement at Moose River was called "Nilhungua," or "Nilhunga" or "Nilnunga," the last probably being a spelling or typesetter's error.

As the first homesteaders moved in, an attempt was made to give Nilhunga the name "Donjay" in memory of Don J. Saindon, who had drowned at Ketchikan. But this name was not adopted into common usage.

The name Naptowne was introduced by the homesteading families of brothers Alex and George Petrovich from Indiana. The nickname for their hometown of Indianapolis, Naptowne, was first suggested by George Petrovich's wife Elvessie, according to her son Jeffery Paul Petrovich. Alex Petrovich, the first postmaster, chose the name, and the Naptowne Post Office was established at the Naptowne Inn operated by the Petrovich families.

Mail mis-sent to the villages of Napaskiak and Napaimiut in the lower Kuskokwim, endless jokes about napping and numerous misspellings led residents to a request changing the name of Naptowne. According to a letter to the editor of the *Cheechako News* from Laura L. Tyson, second Postmaster of Naptowne, there was much controversy before a petition for a name change was submitted to the Post Office Department. This petition, originated by Walt Pedersen, resulted on October 1, 1954, in the change to the name Sterling in honor of Hawley Sterling of the Alaska Road Commission who had supervised the engineering of the highway which bears his name, but who died before seeing it completed.

Naptowne as a town name is gone, along with the hard pioneering of the era during which the name pertained to the Sterling area. However, the name has achieved a permanency because of its application to the last of the five Pleistocene glaciations that covered much of the Cook Inlet area. In the Sterling area the name remains with the Naptowne Rapids of the Kenai River. Also, the Naptowne Trading Post, a second-hand store, sits alongside the Sterling Highway on the original Petrovich homestead.

Aug 78:263

Up Mt. McKinley with Cook

We never have to worry about being overwhelmed by science. The human capacity to believe or disbelieve is too potent a force to be overcome by knowledge.

I reached this view with mixed gloom and glee after climbing Mt. McKinley with explorer Frederick Cook. Cook claimed he did it in 1906. For the last few months I have followed the literary trail left behind over the 70-odd years since.

The record is amazing. It is little wonder the mountain hides its face in mist and shame. So many lies have littered its slopes.

In 1909 the Explorers Club of New York and the American Alpine Club looked at Cook's claims and dropped him from membership. Yet Cook, a highly respected member of the exploration establishment, had been elected President of the Explorers Club and had helped found the American Alpine Club.

At the time Cook accused his foes of lying, taking bribes, and slander. After the dust settled, sober men studied Cook's mountain narrative, shouldered their packs, and set out to investigate the ground.

Several parties made it to the peak. Over the years Belmore Browne, Herschel Parker and Bradford Washburn photographed the mountain. They discovered the same peaks Cook passed off as the summit in his publications. All were considerably lower and distant from the true one. No one ever found the record he allegedly left carefully just below the top. The hearty Fairbanks men who first reached the top of North Peak in 1910 carried a flagpole along. It was seen clearly by others.

Cook has been dead quite awhile, but his spirit lives on. In recent years there have been three books published in which his claims have been maintained. No new evidence has been offered. No one has been able to climb by Cook's alleged route or even make sense of his description of it.

The only man with him kept quiet for awhile, then confessed in 1908 that they had not come anywhere close to the top. Cook and his fans insisted that his companion had been bribed.

Cook should have been able to demonstrate his climb convincingly when it was challenged. He could not offer scientific, which is to say, plausible, evidence. So he wrote a book as strange as fiction. Others rehashed the evidence and declared him a fraud or a martyr, depending upon their individual assessment.

When is the Truth supposed to appear? Why cannot a Big Lie be nailed down? Cook's most recent biographer even admits that Cook's photography — his evidence — was fraudulent, yet manages to defend the claim nonetheless.

Probably there will always be true believers. Faith cannot only move mountains, it can keep Cook's spirit reaching for angels on the summit.

Maybe we ask too much of reason.

— William R. Hunt
Oct 77:179

CHAPTER TEN
LIVING IN THE NORTH

Alaska's Problems

What do northern scientists think are the most serious problems facing Alaska? More than 500 scientists and technologists have responded to this question posed recently by the Alaska Council on Science and Technology.

Roughly half of the respondents focused on the general problem of how to develop and manage resources without destroying environment and lifestyle. Strong concern was raised for the problem of how to extract nonrenewable resources without devastating Alaska. Some took the skeptical view that there is no way Alaska can avoid the impacts of an expanding population and its associated development — the best that can be done is to seek ways to minimize the impacts.

Though nonrenewable resource development was a major issue, still more scientists were concerned with the issue of how best to develop *renewable* resources, especially fisheries, timber and agriculture. In essence, they seemed to say that nonrenewable resources are only a temporary asset and that it is better in the long run to worry about the resources that can last forever.

Problems specifically involving individual people or their relations with each other came in for comment too. The problem voiced most was how to develop harmonious coexistence of our different cultures and lifestyles. Other needs stated were improved education and health delivery, and how to cope with self-destructive behavior, especially among young people. In this regard, Alaska's main killer, accidents, was cited.

Technical problems also received much attention, the one most addressed was Alaska's need to develop energy self-sufficiency by expanding the use of energy sources other than oil. Many also expressed the need for Alaska to develop technologies particularly appropriate to the north. Among these a favorite expressed was to evolve more on-site processing of resources (e.g., lumber mills and petrochemical plants) to avoid having to transport large amounts of raw material by pipelines, road and rail.

Sep 79:342

The Engelmann Curve

In the first cowboy movies, the color of a man's hat told if he was a good guy or a bad guy. We still often try to simplify a complicated matter by pinning black or white labels on different sides of the issue, and we don't always allow for shades of grey.

An example close to all northerners right now is the complicated question of how much protection for the environment should we demand when we build a pipeline, a dam or some other engineering project.

A refreshing way to view this problem because it helps one to see the shades of grey is the "Engelmann Curve." I put this name on the curve since it was Dr. Rudolf Engelmann of the National Oceanographic and Atmospheric Administration who described the idea of it to a group of scientists recently. The idea may or may not have originated with him.

The idea is this: Suppose an industry builds a project without any consideration for environmental factors or even the minimum engineering standards of construction. Consequently the project fails — the building falls down, the dam collapses or the pipeline breaks. The cost to the industry is high (Point 1 on the graph). If the failure causes additional damage to the environment, there will even be a higher cost to society (Point 2).

Obviously it is wiser for the industry to take some preventive action. From the industry's viewpoint,

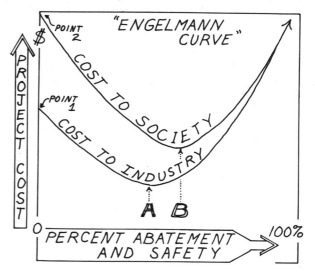

177

there is an ideal percentage of abatement that will place the project at the minimum of the "Cost to Industry" curve (Point A).

But usually, for society as a whole, it is cheaper to increase the investment in abatement over to Point B where a minimum in the Cost to Society curve occurs. Then if a higher percentage of abatement, with its accompanying greater safety, is taken, the total cost to industry and society both climb. If a too-high margin of safety, say near 100%, is demanded, the cost may skyrocket the project out of existence.

Neither industry nor society benefits in the abatement regions far below Point A and far above Point B. So the only real conflict comes in the cost difference represented by the separation between Points A and B. Assuming one can decide where Points A and B should be located, should industry pay the cost difference or should society?

May 79:305

Oral Electricity

For some years, I've accused my wife of deliberately trying to cause me pain by inserting in my salami sandwiches the sheet of aluminum foil that sometimes sticks to the last slice in the package. Each time I am awarded by a disdainful laugh and a comment that biting into a little bit of aluminum couldn't possibly hurt anyone who claimed to be tough enough to live in the frozen north.

Therefore, it was with great glee that I received from University of Alaska geology professor Daniel Hawkins an article he had found explaining why biting aluminum foil hurts so much. The article states that considerable pain or discomfort can result from a tooth filling coming into contact with certain metals.

The standard dental filling is an alloy of silver, tin and mercury. When a piece of aluminum or similar electrically active metal is placed in the mouth a wet-cell battery is formed. The tooth fillings form one electrode, the piece of aluminum the other, and the mouth's saliva becomes the electrolyte. By actual measurement with a voltmeter and an aluminum gum wrapper, my mouth battery creates about one-half volt. If the voltmeter probe is touched to different fillings, slightly different voltages result, indicating different amalgams used by the dentists I have patronized over the years.

The sharp pain comes when the mouth battery is short-circuited by touching the aluminum electrode to the dental amalgam electrode. Then a quick surge of current flows. Though the current is relatively weak, it is strong enough to be painfully sensed by the nerves of the teeth. The current quickly stops, so the pain is brief.

Jun 78:233

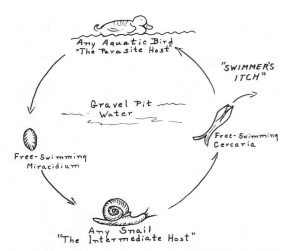

LIFE CYCLE OF AN ALASKAN SCHISTOSOME

"Swimmer's Itch".

"Swimmer's Itch"

If you itch, as I do, and have been swimming recently in water-filled gravel pits in Fairbanks, cheer up, you have probably been parasitized! The itch-producing organism is an Alaskan, nonhuman schistosome, classed as a Trematode and a member of the Platyhelminthes, or Flat Worms, phylum of the Animal Kingdom.

This schistosome, or blood fluke, is normally parasitic in wild ducks, where it is to be found in the blood vessels near the small intestine. Eggs laid by the female schistosome drop out with the bird's excrement. In a watery environment, ciliated embryos, termed *miracidia*, hatch from these eggs and attack and penetrate fresh-water snails. The snails, such as *Lymnaea stagnalis* and *palustris*, serve as intermediate hosts. In the snail, the miracidia undergo morphological and reproductive changes which result in the production of forked-tailed larvae, or *cercariae*. These cercariae leave the snails in July and August and swim as free-living organisms in the water of the gravel pits. They are seeking out another aquatic bird to start the cycle over again.

Schistosome dermatitis, or "swimmer's itch", is caused by the penetration into human skin of the 0.5 mm long cercariae. This penetration produces a prickling sensation, and small red spots of pinpoint to pinhead size may develop. These may disappear in a few hours, but they may persist until replaced by papules, or pimples, in some 10-15 hours. These papules vary in size from 1 to 5 mm in diameter. Intense itching accompanies development of the papules. These may be surrounded by an area of erythema, or reddened skin. The rash may persist for a week. The reaction apparently depends upon individual sensitivity. But, don't worry, once the cercaria finds out that it has not penetrated a bird, it will soon expire.

The major danger of "swimmer's itch" is probably secondary infection caused by breaking through the skin while scratching with fingernails. Go see your friendly doctor for palliative treatment of the itch. If you persist in swimming in the gravel pits, towel-dry vigorously after coming out of the water, especially under your bathing suit; you may be able to reduce the number of forked-tailed "nasties" on your skin that way!

— Fred Milan
Aug 77:178

Cold Water Drowning

Spring starts the season when children fall through the ice; later in the year many adults drown while swimming or boating in Alaskan waters. Drowning is the second-leading cause of accidental death in Alaska.

Cold is usually an enemy to life, but in some instances it is a friend. In recent years scientists have learned that people can be submerged in cold water for long periods without brain damage or other lasting harm.

In March 1975, an 18-year-old man was submerged in a freezing Michigan pond for 38 minutes. Declared dead, he was on the way to the morgue when he gasped and caused a diversion of the transporting vehicle to the nearest hospital. Two weeks later he returned to college and continued to be an A student. But two hours of resuscitation were required to bring him around.

The lesson is very clear. Rescuers should not give up when someone appears to have drowned in cold water. Resuscitation should be continued at least until the person's body comes up to normal temperature — hours may be required.

However, it is absolutely necessary for resuscitation to be started within a very few minutes after the victim is taken from the water. The reason is that a person plunging into cold water undergoes the "diving response." As soon as the cold water strikes the person's face, the diving response is triggered. It reduces the blood supply to the skin and most muscles and saves it for the heart and brain. A person comes out of the diving response when taken from the cold water, so speedy action is needed then.

The younger the person, the better the chances for survival. Newborn mammals are remarkably resistant to drowning, but as they grow older, their effectiveness in using the diving response decreases.

Doctors have found that relatives tend to give up too soon when a family member is thought to have drowned. The doctors explain this giving up as a result of guilt feelings about the apparent drowning.

The moral is — don't give up — especially if the water is cold, as it almost always is in Alaska.

Apr 78:29

Surviving Hypothermia

Immersion in cold water or any situation which causes one's body to shake or shiver hard from cold can soon lead to the condition called hypothermia. Hypothermia kills if the temperature of critical body organs is held too low too long. Death usually comes from failure of the heart owing to disorder in its rhythm. If one could keep his heart beating regularly, he could tolerate long periods of hypothermia.

For fishermen or others in situations where there is a definite chance of sudden immersion in cold water — and northern waters are almost always cold — the best protection against hypothermia is an approved buoyant vest or jacket worn all the time, not just laid in the boat. Warm clothes help a lot, especially waterproof clothes that will help trap body-warmed water around a person's torso.

If one falls in the water without a buoyant vest, one should tread water to keep the head out of the water, since heat loss through the head is rapid. And of course, one is not going to last long with the nose below the water. If one is protected by flotation gear it is best to lie quietly in the water with elbows pressed to the sides, hands on the chest and legs drawn up with crossed ankles. The idea is to keep the body surface area exposed to water as small as possible, especially the torso.

When rescued, let others move you. Your exertion will move cold blood from the arms and legs to the body and possibly cause heart failure. Drink hot liquid but not alcohol. Rescuers should, in an emergency, place a hypothermia victim between two naked heat donors.

Aug 78:246

New-Born Mammal and the Diving Seal

While man is incapable of deep and prolonged dives, many species of marine mammals found in Alaskan waters perform such feats regularly and with no ill effects. Even a pearl diver or other well-trained human can remain submerged for only a few minutes, but the common harbor seal can remain active underwater for as long as 20 minutes. Clearly, the diving marine mammal has some built-in mechanism which allows it to continue to operate when the oxygen supply is cut off. Without such a special ability, a mammal builds up excess carbon dioxide in the blood and may undergo a lapse into suspended animation.

Compared to non-diving mammals, one diver, the seal, has a large supply of blood, a greater concentration of the oxygen-carrying pigment in the blood, and

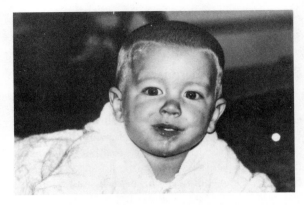

New-Born Mammal and the Diving Seal: *Two look-alikes, with more than looks in common. (Baby photo by K. Behrisch; seal photo by Meredith Tallas.)*

a network of arteries with very elastic walls that permit blood pressure to be maintained more easily. At the onset of a dive, the seal displays a pattern of reflexes known collectively as the diving response. This response entails a profound slowing of the heart-beat frequency and a near-total clamping off of the blood supply to the muscles, kidneys and viscera. The only tissues to which the blood supply is maintained are those of the brain, lungs and the heart itself.

While diving, the animal is in essence divided into two distinct compartments: one receiving blood with a diminishing content of oxygen and the other receiving virtually no blood or oxygen. Those tissues deprived of blood still function to some degree and are not damaged by the asphyxiation of the dive.

The marine divers are not the only mammals in which selective distribution of the arterial blood occurs. Indeed, every mammal at the time of birth becomes asphyxiated, sometimes severely. At birth, the fetus emerges from the bathing fluid of the sac surrounding it, and it loses its mother's circulation via the umbilical cord. The difficulty and the duration of the birth are highly variable. If the young mammal goes without oxygen (remains asphyxic) for too long, the oxygen content of the blood becomes inadequate to satisfy the demands of the brain, and permanent cerebral damage may then occur.

Brain damage occurs all too frequently during human childbirth. Perhaps by learning more of how diving mammals can tolerate repeated long-term asphyxia, we can find ways to lessen the damage of slow births.

We do know that as mammals are born, there is, as in the adult diving seal, a division of the body tissues into those receiving a blood supply and those not. Interestingly, all mammals, even the seal, lose this response to asphyxia during the days or weeks after

birth; but in the seal and other divers, the response develops again later.

For years, we have been trying to understand better how the body chemistry of mammals adapts to the lack of oxygen at birth or during long dives. Our work follows along the lines evolved over four decades by the well-known Alaskan scientist, Laurence Irving. At the Institute of Arctic Biology, we work with harbor seals that exhibit the diving response and certain other mammals that do not. We look mainly at how different tissues operate in the absence of oxygen. One aspect of this work is the measurement of the activities of enzymes that produce energy for tissue function.

In the adult seal, those enzymic sequences that function in the absence of oxygen to produce energy are much more active in the tissues that receive blood during the dive than in those that do not receive blood. Further, the enzymes in the blood-starved seal tissues are far less active than in the corresponding tissues of non-divers. Somehow those tissues that are without circulating blood are able to stretch out the time over which their limited energy stores can be utilized. Tissues in the newborn mammal also seem to have this ability to slow down the rate of using available energy.

Birth is a one-time experience that in the fetus requires the ability to withstand conditions of low oxygen availability. To avoid permanent damage to critical tissues, the fetus sends blood to the most important places: brain, lungs and, of course, heart. But unlike the adult diver, the newborn mammal has not evolved a distribution of enzyme activity that allows it to undergo prolonged asphyxia again and again. So while the fetus is prepared for the oxygen lack during birth, its emergence from the uterus must not be delayed if damage from lack of oxygen is to be avoided. — *Hans Behrisch and Meredith Tallas*
Apr 78:37

Yogis, Bears, Seals and Babies

At first glance it seems a bit curious that an Alaskan physiologist would travel to India to measure the oxygen intake of a meditating yogi. But it turns out that yogis have much in common with many Alaskan mammals and also human babies during the birth process.

Measurements by the University of Alaska's Dr. Robert Elsner, who usually studies diving seals, have shown that the oxygen intake of a yoga practitioner in meditation can go as low as half that required to sustain normal life. This is quite a feat, though the lowering of metabolic rate is an old trick for hibernating mammals such as black bear and squirrels. The smaller hibernating animals can voluntarily reduce their metabolic rate (oxygen intake) to less than 1/100 of the normal rate and, without harm, drop their body temperature to near the freezing point.

Seals and other diving mammals similarly modify their own metabolic rates so that they can stay under water for many minutes. The mechanism employed involves shunting to the brain and critical organs what oxygen-carrying blood is available and temporarily depriving other tissues.

All this has much relevance to the human fetus as well. Like all mammal fetuses, the human baby has a one-time-only ability to minimize the likelihood of brain damage or death from oxygen deprivation at birth. This special ability is then lost, but seals, whales, walruses and apparently yogis learn how to regain it at will.

Dr. Elsner is hopeful of continuing his interesting studies of yogis, perhaps by bringing one or more to this country where particularly complex measurements can be made.

So while the teaming-up of modern medical research practice and ancient yoga lore might seem far out, reducing human birth defects caused by oxygen deprivation is the promise.

Sep 79:337

Seal Finger

Until about 30 years ago, amputation of the offending finger was the accepted cure for a disease called spekk-finger (blubber-finger) by Norwegian sealers. In Alaska and elsewhere, the disease is called sealer's finger or seal finger.

Seal finger occurs only among those who handle seals. According to medical doctors Elizabeth F. Elsner and James R. Crook of the University of Alaska, the exact nature of the infectious agent is unknown. Doctors have conjectured that a bacteria is involved, but the specific organism has not been isolated.

The infection is thought to be transmitted through a small cut in the finger of those who handle seals.

Within a few days an extremely painful swelling of the finger occurs. As the finger swells up it becomes taut and shiny in appearance. The flesh itself becomes soft but there is no pus. Consequently, lancing provides no relief.

Nowadays, there is good news and bad news about the treatment of seal finger. The good news is that the infection responds rapidly to such antibiotics as tetracycline. Recently a Juneau woman who handled young seals in a veterinary hospital contracted the disease, got tetracycline treatment, and was soon rid of the symptoms. (Her adult son also got the disease but did not receive the correct medical treatment. After $3000 in medical bills and much agony, he ended up with a partially disabled thumb.)

The bad news about seal finger is that once a person gets the disease, it may tend to recur every few years. Former Alaskan scientist, Dr. Kaare Rodahl, states that Alaskan Eskimos have long considered the disease malignant and of 15 cases treated on the Seward Peninsula during a two-year period only five were first-time cases, according to medical practitioner Roy Howard. One doctor suggests that antibiotic treatment causes the seal finger organisms to go into a dormant stage only to become active later on.

Until there is enough research on seal finger to learn of a cure, the best advice for those who handle seals anywhere in Alaska and Canada is to wear gloves and to wash the hands frequently. If possible avoid touching seals or seal meat if you have even minor cuts or scratches on your hands. Perhaps because of better habits in cleanliness, Alaskan Eskimos seem to have had less trouble with seal finger than have Norwegian sealers of some years ago.

Aug 79:335

Migratory Birds and Influenza

Some parts of Alaska are said to have lost more than half their population during the great influenza pandemic (worldwide epidemic) of 1918-19. At least 20 million people died as three waves of flu swept around the globe. Twenty-five million people in the United States, a fourth of the population, became clinical flu cases in the fall and winter of 1918. Of these, a half-million died.

Just why there are sudden worldwide outbreaks of influenza is not yet fully understood. But now it is known that similar flu viruses inhabit humans, horses, swine and some birds. Outbreaks of the disease have occurred almost simultaneously in humans and horses. In early 1976 an outbreak of flu at Fort Dix, New Jersey, was traced to viruses in swine.

An article in the December 1977 issue of *Scientific American* by Martin M. Kaplan and Robert G. Webster suggests the possibility that the virus is rapidly carried around the world by birds. Migrating mallard ducks have been found to carry influenza virus along the Mississippi flyway and through central Canada.

Influenza viruses may be carried through the region of the Pacific Ocean by shearwaters (genus *Puffinus*). Viruses deposited in cold waters of the Pacific Ocean off Alaska may survive for several weeks. Animals, ducks, arctic terns or other birds may pick up the flu viruses from the water and carry them along Alaska's coastal waters or inland.

Thus it seems likely that a huge reservoir of various kinds of influenza virus may be harbored in the world's bird and animal population. From time to time these viruses evolve new strains or combine in ways that make them virulent. When this happens, new vaccines to counteract the virulent strains can be quickly developed, and it is unlikely that future epidemics will equal the horrors of 1918-19.

Jan 78:219

The Common Cold

Do Alaskans and northern Canadians have more and worse colds than people living in the more temperate regions to the south? Evidently not, although colds among peoples of the tropics are less common and less severe than those of residents of temperate climate.

The common cold is caused by virus infection and is communicable only among chimpanzees and humans; no other animals are susceptible. Whether there is a single cold virus or many is not known.

But it is known that getting chilled or wet does not contribute to catching cold. One is far more likely to catch cold following an auto accident, according to Dr. John Bligh, director of the University of Alaska's Life Sciences Division at Fairbanks. In fact, he says, severe trauma of any kind is frequently followed by the victim's catching cold.

The natural resistance to infection when exposed to cold virus varies from person to person, and an individual's susceptibility may change over the years. It may be hard to sort out just how much a person's resistance depends upon attitude and emotional well-being as well as upon physical factors. In my case, I have noticed that I usually catch cold at the end of every vacation. Evidently the shock of having to go back to work is too much for my system.

Jan 78:270

Herpes Virus

The waters of southeast Alaska have something to offer to sufferers of herpes virus. Two species of seaweeds of the Rhodophyta (red algae) group that grow along the coast have been found to relieve symptoms of herpes infections.

Herpes viruses cause a variety of diseases that range from cold sores to the more serious genital herpes which can produce painful blisters. It can cause death to infants and perhaps cancer in women. The virus that causes cold sores is named herpes simplex virus Type 1. Herpes simplex virus Type 2 causes genital herpes.

These viruses attack skin or mucous membrane cells where they become parasitic upon the normal processes in the cells. The infestation is difficult to attack with antiviral drugs because the drugs also attack the host cells. Genital herpes is transmitted sexually and is now considered to have reached epidemic status in the United States, 300,000 new cases being reported each year.

Newborn babies can contract the disease by passage through the birth canal of an infected mother. Death can result if the virus reaches a baby's brain. So far, there is no known cure for genital herpes virus. Once a person is infected, the condition is lifelong.

One encouraging development is that two Alaskan researchers, Natasha I. Calvin and Robert J. Ellis, of Juneau, have discovered that two species of seaweed relieve the symptoms of herpes virus. Dried and powdered, these red algae seaweeds reduce blistering when placed on the affected skin. The natural herbs, known as Alaskan Dulse, can be purchased in several Alaskan pharmacies. Some Alaskan physicians and dentists are reported to be recommending the herbs and may be able to suggest sources of supply.

The Alaska Council on Science and Technology now is funding scientists Calvin and Ellis in efforts to define the extent of the habitat of the red algae and to determine how much is available for harvest. The algae are thought to grow only along certain parts of the subtidal coastline of southeastern Alaska. One of the objectives of the research is to see if it might be possible to produce more of the algae through mariculture.

Jul 81:495

DMSO

Not long ago there appeared on the front page of the *Fairbanks Daily News-Miner* a photograph showing an Anchorage man standing on a Fairbanks street beside a large, crudely lettered sign saying "DMSO sold here." The accompanying story indicated the man was doing a brisk business, selling eight-ounce bottles for $24 each — purportedly for use as an industrial solvent.

DMSO is the commonly-used name for dimethyl sulfoxide, a chemical in use as an industrial solvent for over twenty years. In 1964, DMSO was alleged to have therapeutic value for treating arthritis and diseases or conditions affecting muscles and bones and even mental disorders. The Food and Drug Administration authorized clinical tests of DMSO but studies on animals in 1965 indicated the possibility of nasty side effects such as eye damage, headaches, nausea and skin rash.

Controversy has surrounded the use of DMSO as a drug ever since. Finally in 1978, drug-quality DMSO was allowed as a prescription treatment for interstitial cystitis (an inflammation of the bladder), but was recommended only when all else failed. Whether or not DMSO is effective for this or any other drug purposes seems to be uncertain. DMSO is available on a prescription basis in some countries of Europe and South America. Its use has been approved by the states of Florida and Oregon, but even there, only for restricted clinical purposes. Yet, rigorous clinical testing is needed to prove the drug's usefulness, if any, and the full extent to which its side effects might be permanently damaging. Temporary side effects include headache, nausea, diarrhea and disturbance of color vision.

Perhaps the biggest danger with DMSO is that some people who think it is useful for self-treatment of sprains, arthritis and other problems may be willing to apply industrial grade or veterinary grade DMSO to their bodies, drink it or even inject it directly into their bloodstreams. Because DMSO is such a good solvent and is able to carry a wide spectrum of dissolved impurities through cell walls, severe consequences could result if the impure industrial or veterinary grades of DMSO are used on humans.

Dr. James R. Crook, professor of medicine at the University of Alaska and a specialist in human diseases, expresses the fear that users of DMSO may be unaware of how fast the solvent and materials dissolved in it can penetrate the skin and other parts of the body. Because of the fast action, a substance which by itself might have limited or no effect could cause serious damage or death if accidentally or intentionally applied to the body in a DMSO solution.

Evidently, one reason for the prolonged controversy over DMSO is that it is not patentable as a drug. Therefore, there is little motive for any drug manufacturer to undertake the prolonged and expensive clinical testing necessary to clearly demonstrate whatever benefits and hazards DMSO has, and to obtain Food and Drug Administration approval for its use.

Nov 80:442

Violent Death in Alaska

Why is violent death due to accidents, suicides, homicides, and alcohol steadily increasing in the forty-ninth state? What aspects of behavior put an Alaskan in a greater risk category for violent death than a person living in another state?

Under the auspices of the Washington-Alaska-Montana-Idaho (WAMI) Program for medical education at the University of Alaska, Dr. Robert F. Kraus performs research dealing with these and other questions concerning preventable or violent deaths.

By studying the changing patterns of mortality in the various cultures of Alaska for the period 1950-1974 it has been found that in the non-Native population there has been a slight increase in the percent of deaths due to chronic illness and violence. However, for the Native population there has been a striking change in the mortality pattern. Infectious disease, the main killer in the early 1950s (nearly 70% of all deaths), now accounts for only slightly more than 20% of all Native deaths. During the early 1950s, violent deaths among Natives were less than 20% of all deaths. But now, violence is the principal cause of death for Natives and constitutes over 40% of their total mortality.

This startling change in mortality is one indicator of the social and cultural changes wrought on the Native population in the past 25 years. Somehow the knowledge of these changes must be better utilized to increase the effectiveness of our cross-cultural programs in health and education.   — *Julia Froelicher*
Sep 77:181

Northern Suicide

Research on the causes of death among northerners reveals some disturbing trends. Among those who live in the northern half of Alaska the proportion of violent death by suicide is three and one-half times the proportion in the United States as a whole. Furthermore, among Natives in northern Alaska the suicide rate during the years 1970 to 1974 increased to a figure two and one-half times that which had occurred in the years 1960 to 1964. In 1975, the U.S. suicide rate was thirteen per hundred thousand; in all of Alaska the rate was eighteen per hundred thousand.

Among the statistics on suicide provided to me by Mr. Brandt Stickel of Northern Alaska Health Resources, a private corporation, is a curious one on the difference between the sexes. Native and non-Native suicide rates among northern Alaska males in the age group 15 to 24 is roughly twice that of peers in the United States, but among females in the same age group the rate is ten times the U.S. rate in the peer group.

Statistics on the rate of suicide attempts are less certain than those on actual suicides. However, they do indicate that among northern Natives the attempt rate is at least one and one-half times the rate in urban areas, and nearly ten times the rate in Los Angeles.

At the same time that the rate of suicide is increasing in northern Alaska, the rate of identified alcohol abuse is rising; the rate during 1977 was three times the rate in 1971. It seems that the rising alcohol abuse and suicide rates are related.

Dr. Jim Cole, a staff counselor at the University of Alaska, Fairbanks, notes that the suicide rate among college students is 50% higher than the rate among young adults as a whole. One way to help reduce the number of suicides is for people to be alert to patterns of change that are indicative of someone under special duress and, therefore, in the need of help. Things to look for, according to Dr. Cole, are: 1) an abrupt change in personality, 2) signs of prolonged depression, loss of drive and mental or physical sluggishness, 3) loss of interest in activities or friends, 4) loss of weight, 5) disturbed sleep, 6) drop in academic or work performance, 7) accident proneness, 8) giving away of possessions, and 9) direct or indirect comments that indicate a person might be contemplating suicide.

Some of these signs show up among most everyone on occasion, so it is when clusters of the clues are evident that one should be most concerned.

Anthropologists, psychologists and other scientists who deal with human behavior do not yet understand the reasons why special problems with suicide and alcoholism exist in the north. They do suspect that rapid cultural change with its consequent loss of sense of community is the underlying cause.

Jan 81:455

Spring Suicides

Many residents of high latitude say that it isn't winter's cold that depresses them so much as it is the increase in hours of darkness as winter sets in. Since fall seems to be a somewhat depressing time for many, it is surprising that there are reports of more humans in the arctic regions attempting suicide in springtime rather than in fall. One would think that it should be the other way around: that the increasing light and warmth of springtime would give new hope to a person who is depressed, and that there should be fewer suicides than in other seasons.

A hint as to what might be the cause of the spring increase in suicide attempts is given by Thomas A. Wehr and other authors in an article in the November 9, 1979 issue of *Science* magazine. Their studies suggest that severely depressed persons may have their internal clocks out of kilter. Relative to their sleep-wake cycle, their other bodily rhythms are advanced. Tests involving the sudden advancing of a person's sleep-wake cycle to bring it more in line with

the person's other circadian rhythms were found to pull the person out of depression.

Notice that rapid advance in the sleep-wake cycle is the same thing that happens in the jet-lag that a person undergoes when traveling eastward several time zones. If the air traveler is tending toward depression, perhaps the sudden advance may jar him out of the depression. The effect should not be associated with jet lag traveling westward since that retards a person's sleep-wake cycle.

The extreme seasonal change in the number of daylight hours at high latitude has the potential to modify a person's sleep-wake cycle and cause it to get out of phase with the person's other circadian cycles.

One may tend to go to sleep earlier in fall and thereby slowly advance his or her sleep-wake cycle. However in spring, people, at least those that are not required to adhere to fixed working cycles, may tend to go to bed later as the days grow longer. This tendency would allow the other circadian rhythms to be advanced relative to sleep-wake cycle, the situation that is suggested to be associated with depression.

If all this is true, a person tending toward depression might reverse the tendency simply by going to bed earlier.

Apr 80:393

Residential Fire Deaths

Alaska has the distinction of having the highest death rate due to residential fires of any state in the nation. The problem is greatest in rural areas of the state, since the death rate there is five times that of the state as a whole.

Seventy-five percent of residential fires start out by smoldering, as contrasted with those that flash up right at the start. It is recognized that such fires usually proceed in four stages.

During the first, incipient stage, which may last for minutes to days, there is no easily perceptible smoke, heat or flame. Next, there is a smoldering stage during which there still is no noticeable flame or heat, but the combustion increases enough to create visible smoke.

The third stage usually involves less smoke, but flames break out, and much heat is given off. The final, fourth, stage proceeds rapidly with extensive flames and smoke and the emission of many toxic gases.

Because so many fires go through the various stages, early detection of them has the potential to save lives and property. For this reason the use of smoke detectors in residences is coming into more common use.

The person who wishes to purchase smoke detectors should be aware that not all detectors are equal.

Two types, ionization and photoelectric, are commonly available. The photoelectric type may be more expensive, but most tests show that this type is less subject to false alarms than the ionization type detectors.

Jan 81:459

Whale Oil Versus Smoke Detectors

The emergence of Alaska and northwestern Canada as energy resource areas for the rest of North America is bringing increasing awareness that all here is not just ice and snow. Even so, something happens every once in a while that illustrates the misunderstandings people still have about the north.

Such an instance involves an exchange of correspondence between the Alaska Council on Science and Technology and a representative of the well-known Underwriters Laboratory Inc., the organization whose UL symbol we trust on the many gadgets we buy.

In preparation for a research program it administers for the Alaska State Troopers, the Council had asked if Underwriters Laboratories had done any testing of smoke detectors in small houses typically found in rural areas of cold climate regions.

A helpful response came from the laboratory, but it contained an interesting remark, ". . . it is our understanding that most of the residences of the type described use whale oil for cooking . . . " The letter went on to say that UL had not checked out whale oil fumes on smoke detectors but it was suspected that it might cause false alarms and also crud up the detectors, making them useless. So all you folks who cook with whale oil, beware of the possible consequences.

Feb 81:471

A Sixth Sense?

Do humans and animals sometimes display a sixth sense? If so, how does that sixth sense operate?

People and many animals traditionally have been recognized as having been endowed with five senses. These — sight, hearing, touch, taste and smell — provide the stimuli that allow most animals to sense their environments and to operate effectively within it.

One can argue that animal senses tend to come in pairs, according to the mechanisms involved. Taste and smell form one pair in that both operate chemically. Molecules to be tasted or smelled are first dissolved in water within the mouth or nose, and the actual sensing by taste buds or olfactory cells is through chemical action. Of this pair, taste can be considered as a contact sense because an object to be tasted has to go into the mouth. On the other hand, smell works at a distance; we can smell a flower without contacting it.

Another pair of senses, hearing and touch, operate by mechanical forces only. Touch is the contact sense of the pair whereas hearing is the distance sense. Normal hearing is accomplished by responding to air vibrations that can emanate from distant sources. Curiously, both touch and hearing require motion. Unless there is at least a little motion between one's finger tips and a touched table, the brain does not recognize that the table is being touched.

Now we come to the last pair, the pair that uses electromagnetic forces. By comparison with the taste-smell and touch-hearing pairs, one expects the electromagnetic senses to have certain characteristics. For example, one of the pair should be a contact sense, the other be a distance sense. The names of the electromagnetic senses are sight and — whoops, there is no generally recognized sixth sense! But it seems that there should be. Since sight is the distance sense, the sixth sense should be a contact sense. Also by analogy with the other sensory pairs one expects that the sixth sense operates on low-frequency electromagnetic forces, namely relatively slow-varying electric and magnetic fields.

Does the sixth sense really exist? Possible magnetic field sensory organs have been found in homing pigeons and in Monarch butterflies. Both have tiny magnetic field-sensing materials in their bodies that could be used for navigation. Millions of tiny compass-like magnetite crystals occur in a pod next to the pigeon's skull; in the butterfly the magnetite is distributed in the wings. Now that magnetite has been found in these animals, it seems likely that future research will discover its existence in others.

With regard to an animal's ability to sense slow-varying electric fields, the situation may be less certain. However it is known that bones do exhibit electrical characteristics. These characteristics have been found useful for speeding up the healing of broken bones. An electric current passed through the ends of a fractured bone apparently does promote rapid bone growth in the fractured region.

It might turn out that the saying "I feel it in my bones" is not so far off the mark when it comes to sensing electric fields. But the future might cause us to alter another saying: instead of describing an animal that seems to perceive unseen or unknown things as having a "sixth sense", someday we might say that they have a "seventh sense", perhaps even an "eighth sense".

Nov 79:352

Radiowave Effects on Humans

Damaging effect to the human body by radio waves will result if the waves are intense enough to heat up the body. The extreme example is what happens to meat put in a microwave oven.

If a person's body is immersed in a strong radio-wave field the electrons and ions in the body try to oscillate in unison with the radiowaves. By this means, energy is extracted from the radio wave and converted to tiny oscillatory motions of electrically-charged components of the body. The more the motion, the higher the body temperature.

In the Soviet Union, regulations require that workers not be exposed to radiowave radiation in excess of 10 microwatts per square centimeter. One hundred times this radiation level (i.e., one milliwatt per square centimeter) will create slight temperature increase in humans, the rise being about the same as results from normal light physical activity. Prolonged exposure to this intensity of radiowave radiation probably causes permanent damage. Exposure to 10 to 100 milliwatts definitely causes damage to the eyes; it cooks the eye lens enough to cause cataracts.

Scientists and the government agencies charged with protecting human health in Western countries are unwilling, so far, to agree with claims by their eastern European and Soviet counterparts that very low microwave levels (10 microwatt to 1 milliwatt) are dangerous. However, they admit that it is an open question.

One reason the question is unanswered is that the energy absorbed by a human from radio waves depends upon the relationship between the size of the human and the frequency of the radio waves. Just as a TV antenna of the right length and orientation picks up the best signal (the most energy) from a transmitted wave, so it is with a human being. It appears that the cranial cavity of a mammal will resonate at specific radio frequencies determined by the size of the brain cavity. At these resonant frequencies the human head will absorb vastly more radiowave energy than it will at other nearby frequencies.

An adult's head will resonate at a frequency between 350 and 400 MHz (megahertz). Being smaller, a child's head will resonate at a higher frequency, somewhere between 600 and 850 MHz. Since each individual may have his or her own resonant frequency, a particular frequency radiowave might affect one person more than another. Consequently, testing on humans — even if people are willing to let this happen — can be rather complicated.

Aside from the question of permanent damage by absorption of too much radiowave energy, there is the issue of how much radiation it takes to temporarily modify human behavior or mental ability. It is suspected that a microwave signal modulated (i.e., pulsed) at the frequencies where human brainwaves operate (1 to 20 Hz) may affect mental processes, even if the radiation is too weak to create substantial heating of the brain.

Quite obviously it is a complicated issue to determine the effects of radiowaves upon humans and other animals. Just knowing the strength of the radio signal a person is immersed in is not enough. Critically important may be the frequency match between the signal and the person's body and whether the signal is modulated at a frequency that could match up to a person's brainwave pattern.

Complicating matters even further is the finding that mammals can be made to "hear" pulses of radiowave emission. Pulses at frequencies within a mammal's hearing range can cause periodic heatings of the head. These create pressure pulses in the ear that are interpreted as sound. Further, some studies have indicated radiowave effects upon cell processes that could affect the nervous system, the cardiovascular system and immunity to disease. The effects are not necessarily all bad: certain cancers are being successfully treated with radiowaves, and the future of even greater success looks bright.

Mar 80:386

Radiowave Pollution

Each year we install more electrical, electronic and radio devices to make life convenient and more fun. In so doing we surround ourselves with increasing levels of electromagnetic radiation.

Is this a serious problem? The Russians certainly think so, for they have enacted stringent regulations limiting the radiowave energy that workers can legally be exposed to. The limit is ten microwatts per square centimeter (usually simply stated as ten microwatts, leaving out the unit of area).

How about in this country? No regulations exist, although the government recommends a limit of ten thousand microwatts.

Much investigation of the effects of radiowaves on animals and people has been done in the Soviet Union, but little has been pursued in North America. Some of that research in California has used cats to demonstrate significant changes in chemicals that play a role in brain function at levels as low as 100 microwatts. The average leakage from microwave ovens as measured a few inches outside the door is 120 microwatts.

European investigators claim to have found significant impairment to the mental ability of animals exposed for a half hour to levels near 10,000 microwatts. This level is typical of that found within a few inches of a walkie-talkie, and within a few feet of mobile radios such as are carried in taxicabs.

As yet, the radio pollution level in Alaska and northern Canada is comparatively low. Still, many northerners, especially those who work around or use high-power radio transmitters, are probably being subjected to radiation levels considered illegal in the Soviet Union.

Have you been suffering from "insomnia, irritability, headaches, and loss of memory" lately? Maybe it's time to turn off the nearest transmitter. (This article based on one in the premier issue of the new magazine *Science 80*.)

Nov 79:351

Ion Generators

For more than ten years, controversy has swirled around the usefulness of ion generators sold (at roughly $100 each) to improve air quality in homes and offices. Total American sales of ion generators was near the ten million dollar mark in 1980, so obviously many people think or hope the generators are worthwhile.

The stated purpose of a home or office ion generator is to increase in the air the number of molecules or molecular clusters that carry positive or negative charges — such molecules or clusters are called ions, even though the name ion has a broader meaning for most scientists.

Any volume of natural air near the earth's surface contains roughly equal numbers of positive and negative ions, there being about a thousand or so of each in a cubic centimeter of natural air. Since there are more than ten billion billion air molecules per cubic centimeter, the ratio of ions to neutral air molecules is pretty small.

The relatively few ions that do exist in the air are created mostly by decay of radioactive materials in the earth's crust and by cosmic rays striking the air. Because more cosmic rays come into the polar regions than the tropics, there is tendency for higher ion concentrations in the air at high latitude.

Such a trend bodes well for those of us who live in the north, if it is really true, as many claim, that high ion concentrations make for a better living environment. It certainly is true that in urban areas where air pollution is severe the concentration of ions in the air is very low. In an urban office the ions may number as few as 50 per cubic centimeter.

Ions attach to pollution particles and may assist in sweeping the pollution particles out of the air by interacting with electric fields that exist naturally in the air. If that really happens as claimed, then an effective ion generator is useful. It is also argued that the existence of high ion concentrations in air pro-

motes plant growth, inhibits bacterial growth and generally makes people feel better. Clearly this is one of those issues needing further investigation.

Feb 81:465

Negative Ions and Computers

Evidence seems to be mounting that ion concentrations in the air do affect how people feel. Further, there is evidence that the new trend toward using computerized equipment in offices may be creating a special problem.

Outdoor air contains about a thousand positive and negative charges (ions) within each cubic centimeter. Cosmic rays coming into the earth from the sun and elsewhere break apart air molecules and thereby create much of the ionization that exists in the air. Since more cosmic rays come in at the high latitudes, the high-latitude air normally has a higher proportion of ionized air molecules or molecular clusters. However, in cities and in confined spaces such as offices, processes take place to reduce the number of ions. One important process is attachment of charge-carrying molecular clusters to pollution particles in the air. When that happens both the ions and the pollution particles tend to be swept out of the air by the electric field that exists naturally near the earth's surface.

The loss of ion concentration is thought to be harmful because it does seem that high ion concentrations do make people feel better — just why doesn't seem to be clearly understood. High ion concentrations also apparently inhibit bacterial growth and perhaps foster plant growth. The good effects seem to be attributed to high concentrations of negative ions rather than positive ones; generally, the concentration of both types go together, except in small volumes of air perhaps only a few feet across.

Now a new problem arises, according to an article in the August 1981 issue of *Mini-Micro Systems*, a publication for computer buffs. The problem has to do with CRTs, the cathode ray tubes contained in video terminals and the new-fangled typing stations that seem to be sprouting on desktops all over the country. In the Geophysical Institute alone I counted 70 CRTs, not including cathode ray tubes in test equipment.

The electric field caused by the positive static charge that appears on a CRT in normal operation sweeps the nearby air of negative charges, thereby depleting the negative-ion concentration in the immediate vicinity. Apparently when the ion concentration is lowered by this or any other means — air conditioning does it too — workers complain of headaches, lethargy, dizziness and nausea.

One experiment performed in England on 54 individuals at a computer site seems rather convincing.

Negative-ion generators were installed, but, unknown to the persons being tested, the generators were not turned on for four weeks. During that period the negative-ion concentration was about 550 per cubic cm. A secret switching on of the generators during the next eight weeks of the test raised the ion concentration to 3500 per cubic cm, several times that found in normal outside air. After the experimenters turned on the ion generators, they found that the tested persons had fewer headaches and other complaints than before. Only five percent then said they had headaches, whereas 20 percent of the workers complained of headaches before the ion generators were turned on. The number reporting dizziness and nausea dropped by more than half, down to less than one percent.

Other English tests indicate that the more complex the task a person tries, the more the individual is affected by negative-ion levels. Also females are more responsive than males to negative-ion depletion or enrichment.

Fraudulent or questionable claims made some years ago about the benefits of ion generators muddy the issue of how important ion concentrations are in air around workers. Consequently, there now probably will have to be overwhelming evidence that ion levels do affect people before widespread attempts are made to ensure that proper levels are maintained. But if that comes to pass, we may see regulations requiring installation of ion generators in rooms where air conditioning and CRTs are used.

Sep 81:505

Fairbanks Log House. *(Drawing by Pat Davis.)*

Fairbanks Log House

At Alaskaland, at a few locations around town and out in the bush one sees log cabins all of a style — sod roof on a low-pitched gable that extends out over the porch, the overall structure being rather low. Go to Nome or to other coastal towns in western Alaska and you will see a completely different style of architecture involving frame houses with glassed-in porches, usually facing the sea. These houses are reminiscent of the houses found in the old whaling villages of New England.

It seems likely that the Nome-style house had its genesis in the New England houses, but where did the Fairbanks-style log house come from? Travelers to Siberia, particularly in the regions around Irkutsk, will be struck by the similarity of the Fairbanks log house to the log cabins there. In the Siberian cities the log houses frequently have ornate painted window shutters and eaves but the style is unmistakable. To stroll through a country village today in Siberia is to stroll through Fairbanks 30 or 40 years ago; the houses are identical. It is not too farfetched to think that the Fairbanks log house had its origin in Siberia. Irkutsk used to be the effective capital of Alaska before Sitka was. Also the original wave of Russian influence was reinforced by a second wave of emigrants during gold rush days and up until the 1920s. Many Russians settled in interior Alaska and built log houses like those they lived in at home.

May 76:56

House Building Hints

The new buzz word among hopeful home builders seems to be "solar heat." Careful design can help take advantage of what nature provides, even in Alaska. But the home builder should not let himself be detracted from also considering the fundamentals. In this regard teachings contained in the Book of Eb are worthy of study (*Building in the North*, by Eb Rice, available for the paltry sum of four dollars).

Some of the hints (as interpreted by me):

Foundations — Do not build your dream home on permafrost. If you insist, better investigate carefully and be prepared for trouble.

Insulation — To get the most for your money forget the foam insulations, except for special uses. Friction-fit fiber batts (not foil-backed) are the thing to use. Use at least 6 inches in walls, 12 to 15 inches in ceilings and 6 to 10 inches in elevated floors.

Vapor barrier — It is absolutely essential that an impermeable barrier be placed in interior surfaces. Use two layers of polyethylene film and tape the joints with freezer tape. Let the outside surface breathe.

Windows — Use three or four panes spaced as far apart as possible. Seal the inside pane but let the others breathe so as to avoid internal condensation.

Best of all, read Professor Rice's book.

May 77:167

ALASKAN LOCATION	Dec	Jan Nov	Feb Oct	Mar Sep	Apr Jul	May Aug	Jun
			Elevation of the Sun at Noon on the 21st Day of the Month, Degrees Above the South Horizon				
Adak	14	17	27	38	49	58	61
Ketchikan	11	14	23	34	46	54	58
Juneau-Sitka-Kodiak	8	12	21	32	43	52	55
Haines-Cordova-Homer-Kenai	6	10	19	30	41	50	53
Valdez-Anchorage-Bethel	5	9	18	29	40	49	52
Tok-McGrath-Anvik-Yukon Delta	3	7	16	27	38	47	50
Fairbanks-Galena-Nome	2	5	14	25	37	45	49
Fort Yukon-Bettles-Kotzebue	0	3	12	23	34	43	46
Barrow	Sun	Down	8	19	30	39	42

Roof and Window Design.

Basic Facts About Heat Transfer

Every object gives off energy in the form of waves. These waves, called electromagnetic waves, may be infrared, visible, ultraviolet or radio waves. The color (wavelength) of the waves depends upon the temperature of the object. The sun, being very hot, radiates visible electromagnetic waves which we call light waves. People, plants, furniture, and houses or other objects at temperatures found on the earth's surface emit infrared radiation; that radiation has longer wavelengths than visible light.

An object placed in a room will radiate infrared energy to the room and other things in it. The object also receives infrared radiation from all parts of the room and the other things inside. If the object radiates more heat than it receives, it will cool off; if it receives more than it radiates, the object heats up.

Objects touching one another also transfer heat by conduction. Both conduction and radiation are important to think about when building a house or living in one. We use various types of insulation in houses, the object being to reduce the heat transfer through conduction. Heat transfer by radiation is important when it comes to windows.

Apr 76:48

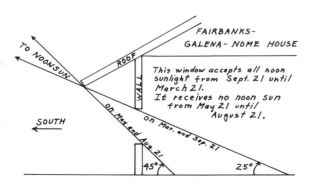

Roof and Window Design.

Roof and Window Design

Alaskans are showing increased awareness that careful housing design can bring economies and pleasant living. Planning for the best relationship between roof overhang and window placement has caused several people to write or call for information on the elevation of the sun through the year. Usually people wish to build an overhang that lets sunlight stream into south-facing windows during the cooler months of the year, but which keeps at least part of the direct sun out during the hottest months.

The accompanying table gives the angle of the sun measured above the horizon at noon through the year. The angles, in degrees, are given for the twenty-first day of each month so as to show the extremes reached on the solstices, June 21 and December 21. The sketch suggests how to design a window and roof overhang relationship that best meets your desires. At the cooler or more northerly locations, one may be interested only in a roof overhang that never blocks out the sun, even on the hottest day.

Mar 78:25

The Greenhouse Effect

Window glass transmits visible light but it does not transmit infrared radiation. Light from the sun readily passes through a window. Objects inside a sunlit room absorb solar radiation. They, in turn, emit radiation, but the radiation emitted is infrared rather than visible light. The infrared radiation cannot penetrate the window. (Visible light can be red, orange, yellow, green, blue or violet; when these colors are mixed together, as in sunlight, we often call it "white light".)

So a window is a one-way street for heat transfer by radiation involving sunlight. A greenhouse, in part, uses this principle to provide a warm environment for plants. The overall process by which radiant heat energy is trapped has thereby come to be

190

called "the greenhouse effect". The trapping occurs because heat radiation is changed from one wavelength to another, from visible light to infrared light.

The greenhouse effect in a house with large windows often makes the house too hot. In winter, it may be possible to use the greenhouse effect to advantage to help home heating.

Apr 76:49

Windows

It seems that house windows in Fairbanks let out too much heat in winter and let in too much heat in summer. Hanging curtains or insulation on the inside does little good because ice forms behind the curtain in winter and, in summer, the curtain heats up and re-radiates the solar heat. The best arrangement, summer or winter, is some type of shutter on the outside to prevent radiation into the house (the greenhouse effect) in summer and outward conduction or convection of heat in winter. These shutters can be made of rigid foam, aluminum foil, wood, or fiberglass with some sort of arrangement for storing them when the windows are to be used as windows.

Wintertime conduction and convection losses through windows are economically reduced by installing windows with three or four panes. Panes less than 3/4" apart permit considerable conduction. To avoid the conduction losses, it is best to install the panes at least 3/4" apart. Icing between multipane windows can be prevented by a water-tight seal around the edges of the inner pane and one hole to the inner space from the outside. The hole should be large enough to let moisture escape but small enough to prevent much air motion, perhaps 1/8 to 1/4 inch.

Conduction: Heat transfer by direct contact.

Convection: Heat transfer by moving air.

Radiation: Heat transfer by electromagnetic waves. Examples are microwave ovens, sunlight, and infrared

light from warm objects. Every object radiates heat in an amount dependent only upon the object's temperature.

Apr 76:50

Cold Trap Entrance

If you are building an "interesting" cabin in the woods and want to keep winter heating costs down you might consider incorporating a cold trap entrance. You must be willing to put up with the inconvenience of climbing down and then up flights of stairs each time you enter or leave the house. However, climbing is good for the legs and the cold trap entrance avoids the drafts and heat loss of a conventional doorway.

The bottom of the barrier wall of the house should extend about 18 inches below floor and ground level (whichever is lowest) to prevent air flow. The cold trap entrance operates on the principal that cold air is heaviest and therefore settles downward. It forms a dense layer that inhibits flow of air through the entryway. The use of a solid door in a cold trap entrance is optional. However, it will impede the flow of cats, dogs, wolves, etc.

Aug 76:67

An Underground House

If you have a building site on a south-facing slope and are interested in lower heating costs in future years, the underground house is worth considering. Whether or not one uses solar collectors or some other exotic form of heat, the house surrounded with dirt on all sides except one offers a real advantage when it comes to outside wall temperature. Instead of fifty below just beyond the insulation, the earth-covered house offers temperatures well above the mean annual temperature (plus twenties or thirties Fahrenheit in Alaska).

Unlike its Eskimo and Athabascan sod-covered forerunners, the underground house need not be

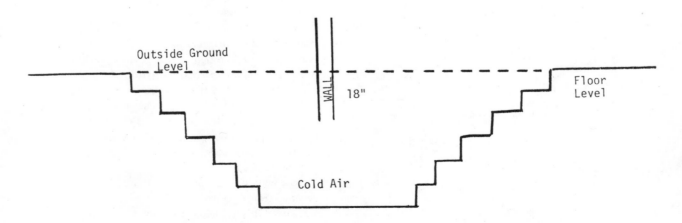

Cold Trap Entrance.

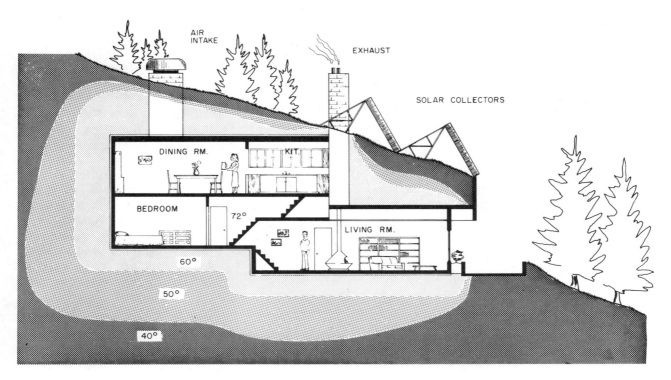

An Underground House Design. *(Drawing by W. Erkelens.)*

dark. Large multi-pane windows placed on the south wall and properly shuttered on cold, dark nights can provide both light and heat when the sun is up, yet prevent excessive heat loss during evening and night-time hours.

The accompanying drawing exhibiting one possible layout of an effective underground house was shown recently by the University of Alaska's John Zarling and Richard Seifert. They are researching the requirements of using solar energy for heating domestic water and housing in Alaska. Their study involves calculations for the communities of Annette, Palmer, Bethel, Fairbanks and Barrow. Their early results show that solar heating is practical for heating of domestic water at some locations, especially those where the cost of imported fuel is high.

Feb 78:217

Shrinkage of Logs

How much do house logs shrink as they dry, and how long does it take? This is another of those reader's questions that should be easy to answer but isn't. It seems that house logs lack the uniformity of other construction materials such as metals, plastics and concrete. Perhaps that is one reason people like log homes.

I found a useful source of information on building with logs and on other types of residential construction to be Axel Carlson of the Cooperative Extension Service of the University of Alaska. Several of

his informative flyers are available free from the Extension Service. Another valuable source for me was an old book published in the 1890s that, from the looks of it, was carried by its original owner, my grandfather, on his trip into the Klondike in 1897. Smaller than a typical paperback, this manual of engineering knowledge has nearly a thousand ultra-thin, gilt-edged pages filled with tiny print. No author's or publisher's name shows in the book, but its cover is adorned with the name Haswell — in gilt print — and a loop by which the book can be attached to a belt for ease of carrying. This book tells how to build and operate windmills, water wheels, steam engines and other devices that energy-conscious Alaskans and Canadians are interested in again, now that petroleum is no longer nearly free.

Meanwhile, back at the cabin, the logs are shrinking. According to Carlson and Haswell, green logs contain water in amounts up to 50%: Birch 30%, spruce 35% and poplar 50%. After two to eight years, depending upon air humidity and how the logs are treated with oil or other finishes, the logs will dry to about 12% water content. While drying, the radial shrinkage will be 1.5% (spruce) to perhaps 5%.

Consequently, one should expect a 96-inch high log wall to shrink at least three inches, and probably more, as it dries. Also expect the wall to seasonally vary in height by an inch or so owing to humidity changes from summer to winter. These changes can be minimized by use of overhangs to keep the rain off and by installing good foundations that keep ground moisture away from the logs.

Mar 80:382

Housing Insulation: *Fairbanks photographer Brian K. Allen snapped this catchy photo showing how bad condensation can be on an air-core door used as an outside door. Melting has caused the ice pattern to sag a bit so that it no longer matches the air core pockets exactly.*

Housing Insulation

Prevention of direct heat flow through a wall or ceiling is not the only reason for installing proper insulation. Three other reasons, according to residential housing expert Axel R. Carlson, are to prevent condensation, to reduce convection drafts within a room, and to avoid cool surfaces for a person's body heat to radiate to.

Whereas some rooms feel warm and comfortable, others definitely feel cold. Chances are the room that feels cold has cold walls and a cold floor. Such a room has convection drafts of cold air down the walls and across the floor. Furthermore, every object in a room radiates energy to every other, and the net amount of energy exchanged depends upon the temperature differences between the objects. Even across the room, a cold wall feels cold to a person's warm face because the face loses energy to the wall by radiation.

A truly serious problem is that cool interior surfaces of buildings cause condensation. If there is not a perfect vapor barrier, the condensation enters the floor, wall or ceiling where it can reduce the insulating value of material in the structure and can form ice. Water stains and other damage can occur when the ice melts.

How critical the vapor barrier is was learned well by some of us several years ago. For free we got a military surplus walk-in freezer which we figured would make a perfect auroral observatory. Nobody thought about the fact that on a freezer the vapor barrier is built onto the exterior of the structure instead of the interior. The first cold snap that winter filled the walls with ice. Since when we walked in we froze, we knew for sure that we had a walk-in freezer and not an auroral observatory.

Sep 80:426

Energy-Efficient Homes

As northerners seal up their homes to save on heating costs, they run the danger of a problem most of us have not thought much about — the quality of air inside the house.

Indoor air pollution is a different beast from the one that sometimes pervades the out-of-doors. In the old days, the energy-efficient Eskimo sod house had a serious problem with smoke from seal-oil lamps and a central open-pit fire. Years of exposure created soot deposits within the inhabitants' lungs equal to that encountered by today's habitual cigarette smokers.

Most modern homes — especially mobile homes — contain materials such as plywood and foam insulation, either as part of the structure or in furniture. Michael Gold, writing in the March/April issue of *Science 80*, notes that these materials release a dangerous pollutant, formaldehyde. The formaldehyde evaporates from processed wood walls and from couches, beds and other furniture. In some newly insulated homes, the concentration of formaldehyde in the air is high enough to cause dizziness, rashes, nosebleeds and vomiting. It also is thought to cause cancer.

A defense mechanism against such problems is to maintain adequate ventilation in a house. That means bringing in new air from outside, the very thing we try to avoid with weather stripping and similar heat conservation methods. One strategy is to use heat exchangers to heat incoming cold air with warm, stale air being ejected from the building.

Oct 80:431

Flashover

Too often one hears about a fire that suddenly sweeps through a trailer house or a building and which kills people before they can get out. Considering how slowly a fire spreads through a pile of logs or even loosely stacked lumber, rapidly spreading fires in structures don't seem to make sense. Obviously, there is something about a fire in a confined space that is different from one out-of-doors.

The key difference is the confinement itself. Once a fire starts, even if initially very small, it releases gases which are hot and perhaps volatile. In a confined space these gases accumulate. As time goes by, the confining space becomes hotter and more gas-filled.

When the temperature rises above 300°F (150°C) many materials start to decompose. Wood, paper, paints, fabrics and plastics then release volatile gases. These gases would drift away from a fire outside, but if the fire is inside, the accumulating gas is a potential horror in the making.

At some point, the gas density and temperature become high enough that flames almost instantaneously spread through the space. This deadly phenomenon is called flashover by fire scientists. Spectacular photographs of a flashover event appear in an article by John F. Kenahan in the January issue of *Science 80*.

Plastic materials are particularly copious suppliers of the toxic and volatile gases that lead to flashover. House trailers and other mass-produced structures such as are found in northern construction camps and similar facilities typically have a goodly share of plastic fittings and furnishings. Even in selecting furniture and fittings for use in a comparatively safe wooden house, one does well to think about which types are least likely to contribute to flashover.

Jan 80:367

Toxicity of Burning Material

The deadly fires that spread through the MGM Grand Hotel and the Las Vegas Hilton during the past year have demonstrated the danger from toxic gases released from combustion of materials commonly found in homes and other buildings. The problem has special relevance for anyone contemplating building a new home or re-insulating an older one since there are substantial differences in the toxicity of insulating materials that one might choose to use.

Researchers at the University of Pittsburgh (March 7, 1981 issue of *Science News*) recently have tested the toxicity of some of these materials by burning them and exposing mice to the smoke produced. Such tests are tough on the unfortunate mice but the results may save human lives.

One of the least toxic materials used in houses is

wood. Fiberglass insulation is almost as good. Smoke from both materials is comparatively slow to kill. In the tests on mice, it took 20 to 30 minutes of exposure to fumes produced from burning measured amounts of wood and fiberglass in a test apparatus to kill half the mice.

By comparison, teflon, used in some cooking utensils, and polyvinylchloride, used to coat electrical wiring and in some wallpaper, are particularly deadly. When burned, small amounts of these materials (less than 5% as much as wood or fiberglass) killed half the mice in less than 10 minutes.

Intermediate in toxicity when burned were the now commonly-used insulating materials such as polyurethane, wool and cellulose. Times taken to cause death in the tested mice ranged from 10 to 30 minutes.

To prevent the rapid release of toxic gases from burning polyurethane and polystyrene (beadboard or Styrofoam) rigid insulation used in homes, building codes now require that they be covered on interior walls by sheetrock or other flame-resistant materials. When so installed, these materials are comparatively safe to use. Still, a person who remains in a burning house too long may never get out because of the released toxic gases.

Apr 81:481

Fiberglass Insulation

The knowledge of the physical characteristics of the various insulations available can be useful to homeowners in deciding which kind to use. Especially in the north, where large temperature differentials exist across outside walls, ceilings and floors, the knowledge can be put to good use. Important characteristics include thermal resistance (R-value or K-factor), water absorbency, strength, change with age, flammability and toxicity under normal temperature and when burned.

Fiberglass, an old insulation standby, had its first beginnings in ancient Egypt when people discovered they could draw hot glass into threads which were placed around vessels for decoration. The modern technique of making fiberglass insulation, developed in 1931, involves jetting of molten glass through tiny heated holes into high-speed air streams wherein the resulting fibers are drawn very thin and to great length. Enough glass to make one large marble forms about a hundred miles of single fiber. Multiple fibers are collected into a mat which is the end product.

Made from sand (SiO_2), limestone ($CaCO_3$) and sodium carbonate (Na_2CO_3), fiberglass is inert, ages well, does not burn and does not emit toxic gases except when in a hot fire. Even then, there is less emission than from wood or any other common insulating material. Fiberglass does not take up water

A Comparison of Insulating Values and Costs
of Available Housing Insulation Materials

Insulation Type	Thermal Resistance (R-value* per inch)	Thermal Conductivity (K-factor)*	Price** in Cents per board foot	Cost** in Cents per square foot per R unit
Fresh Urethane Foam	9.0	0.11		
Aged Urethane Foam (25°F) (foamed in place or in sheets)	5.9	0.17	46	7.8
Fresh Styrofoam	6.2	0.16		
Aged Styrofoam (25°F) (in sheets)	4.5	0.22	49	10.9
Polystyrene Beadboard (in sheets)	3.8	0.26	25	6.6
Blown Cellulose (installed)	3.8	0.26	7	1.8
Fiberglass (rolls or batts)	3.1	0.22	6	1.9
Blown Fiberglass (installed)	3.0	0.33	7	2.3
Celotex (in sheets)	2.9	0.34	46	16
Exterior Fiberboard (in sheets)	2.7	0.37	46	17
Wood (dry spruce)	1.0	1.0	25	25
Cinder Block	0.3-0.5	2-3		
Concrete	0.11-0.17	6-9		

* Approximate values.
** Approximate Fairbanks Area, May 1981.

within the glass fibers, but water passes freely between the fibers. Therefore, fiberglass insulation must be used in conjunction with a vapor barrier placed on the inside, toward the heated room.

Fiberglass in batts has an R-value per inch thickness of about 3.1 and costs (in Fairbanks) about six cents per inch-thick square foot. As blown insulation, it has a slightly lower resistance to heat loss (one-inch R-value about 3.0) but can be purchased installed for about seven cents per inch-thick square foot. Thus, except for blown cellulose insulation which costs about the same, fiberglass in batt or blown form is the cheapest insulation on the market for the insulating value achieved. Of course, for certain applications, other more expensive insulations are more desirable.

May 81:482

Insulation Costs

The accompanying table lists various kinds of insulation available in the north and a comparison of their costs, at least in the Fairbanks area.

A measure of the thermal insulating quality of an insulating material is the K-factor. The K-factor is equal to the number of BTUs transmitted by one square foot of the material of thickness one inch each hour per degree Fahrenheit temperature difference across the material.

More commonly used is the R-value, which is readily calculated from the K-factor. The R-value of a piece of material is simply the thickness of the material in inches divided by the K-factor. Hence, a one-inch thickness of fiberglass batt material has an R-value of 3.1, and a piece 10 inches thick has an R-value of 31.

To compare exact costs of different insulations in your area, a convenient method is to first find out the cost of a piece of insulation one inch thick by one foot square. Then divide the cost by the R-value given in the table for a one-inch thickness of the material.

The R-values given in the table may differ slightly from those quoted by others. The reason is that most R-values quoted are not accurate to better than a few percent.

May 81:483

Rigid Insulation

Rigid insulations increasingly are coming into use in the north. Though a more expensive form of insulation than fiberglass batts or blown fiberglass or cellulose, the rigid insulations have certain advantages that sometimes make them worth the higher cost.

One popular type is urethane that can be purchased in rigid sheets or foamed in place on the job. Also called polyurethane or isocyanate polymer, urethane has the highest R-value (resistance to heat flow) of any material readily available; it is comparatively waterproof and holds up well if protected from sunlight by special surfacings applied within a few days of the time the urethane is laid down.

Urethane owes its thermal insulating and water resistance characteristics to the molecular structure of the material, mainly the large number of tiny closed voids within the urethane material. Urethane is formed spontaneously when certain relatively simple organic molecules are mixed (isocyanate plus polyether). These molecules rearrange themselves and join together into large interlinked chemically-bound arrays called polymers. It is as much art as science to get just the right mix that yields the desired end product since several components are required. Necessary ingredients are isocyanate, a polyether, a catalyst that helps the molecules to rearrange and join, a blowing agent to create closed cells in the structure and also another agent to control the cell size.

The ingredients are partially premixed into two containers for transport. When the contents are finally mixed together under pressure, the rigid urethane foam spontaneously forms. Different characteristics are possible by altering the mix used.

Easily confused with urethane because of the similarity of names is urea-formaldehyde rigid insulation. The confusion is unfortunate because urea-formaldehyde is dangerous and is now outlawed in most states. Urea-formaldehyde evidently is no longer available in Alaska, so one need worry little about it. Urea-formaldehyde and water are produced when urea (CON_2H_4) and formaldehyde (CH_2O) are mixed. The bonding is not strong enough to prevent formaldehyde from being given off, even at room temperature. Formaldehyde does nasty things to people; it gives them nausea, nosebleeds and headaches and makes them vomit.

Two rigid insulation materials now popular in the north are made from the molecule styrene (C_8H_7). One is the blue-colored insulation sold by the Dow Chemical Company under the brand name Styrofoam. Chemically, Styrofoam is identical to the white-colored polystyrene beadboard now readily available. These two insulation materials are made by merely heating collections of styrene molecules. The molecules link together, that is they polymerize, to form a rigid material with many closed airspaces contained.

Though more expensive than urethane, Styrofoam is not quite as good an insulator. However, it has much greater strength. Also, it is somewhat more impervious to water so is particularly suited for use underground and where bearing strength is critical, as under a concrete floor.

Polystyrene beadboard resists water reasonably well, about as well as urethane, but its thermal resistance is poorer than Styrofoam or urethane. Its thermal insulating quality is not much better than ordinary fiberglass, and it is about three times as expensive. However, it can be used underground, as can urethane, if conditions are not too wet and if high bearing strength is not needed.

May 81:484

Special Warning: The final word is not in yet, but there are indications that urethane's thermal resistance is drastically lowered by repeated freezing and thawing. *(Dec 1981)*

Home Heating Costs

There can be no doubt anymore that knowledge applied to house building and home heating leads to money in the pocketbook for years to come. The Geophysical Institute's quarterly journal *The Northern Engineer* is responding to the high level of public interest in energy conservation by frequently carrying articles on this general subject.

One particularly interesting article by Carol Lewis, soon to appear in *The Northern Engineer*, contains information on fuel costs. Her figures are for Fairbanks in early 1979, but one can use the information she gives to calculate fuel costs at any location. So doing, one can make an informed judgment on which is the best fuel to use.

A slightly smaller than average but well-built house will require about 1000 gallons of No. 2 fuel oil for annual heating. According to Ms. Lewis, a gallon of fuel oil contains 135,000 BTUs, but typically it is burned with an efficiency of only 70%. Therefore the 1000 gallons of fuel oil will yield 94.5 million BTUs, enough to heat a house of floor area 600 square feet. In Fairbanks, oil now costs $0.62 gallon, so the annual fuel bill would be $620.

Coal burned at 55% efficiency will yield about 13 million BTUs per ton. To heat the sample 600-square-foot house would require 7 tons at $51.50 per ton or $364 per year.

Propane with 21,550 BTUs per pound burned with 70% efficiency and a cost of $24 per 100 lbs leads to an annual heating bill of $1503 for the sample house.

Electricity gives 3413 BTUs per kilowatt-hour and now costs about 5.7 cents per KWh in Fairbanks. It can be used with 100% efficiency, so the 27,688 KWh required to heat the sample house gives an annual heating cost of $1578.

Black spruce contains about 18.5 million BTUs per cord and probably can be burned with an efficiency near 40%. So burned, 12.8 cords is required to heat the sample house. At $65 per cord, the annual heating cost is $832.

Interestingly enough, the amount of heat available in different kinds of wood depends essentially only on the density of the wood. In millions of BTUs per cord, black spruce has 18.5, paper birch 23.6, cottonwood 14.6, aspen 16.3 and Sitka spruce 17.2 (assuming 80 cubic feet of wood fiber per cord — the total volume of a cord being 128 cubic feet).

From all this it would seem that — at least in Fairbanks — coal is cheapest and electricity most expensive. A word of caution though. Don't forget about the rest of the utility bill, including lights and electrical power for other purposes. When these are added into the total bill, electricity does not fare so badly. The reason is that much of the electrical energy required for these other purposes can be included in — not added to — the requirement for house heating.

Apr 79:304

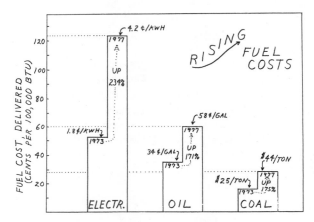

Comparative Heating Costs.

Comparative Heating Costs

Prior to 1962 we heated our Fairbanks house cheaply using coal. It was dirty, the furnace and coal took up lots of space, but mainly we stopped using coal because our stoker quit. She finally refused to get up early, as she had done before, so that the house would be warm upon my own arising.

Investigating the relative costs and merits of electricity and oil, we chose electricity. It was relatively cheap then, clean, used no space and was economical to install. At that time it cost little more for a totally electric house than one heated by coal or oil and using a propane cook stove and electric lights.

By 1973 the situation had probably not changed greatly. In that year Professor Eb Rice published a graph showing the costs of heating with coal, oil and

electricity. The accompanying graph reproduces his data and also gives the costs in Fairbanks for 1977. The graph shows that coal heat is cheapest and electricity most expensive. Coal now costs 175% of the 1973 cost; oil is 171% of the 1973 cost and electricity is 234% of the cost in 1973.

Considering the marked rise in electrical costs, it may no longer be possible to claim that a total electric house has comparable utility cost to one using electric lights, propane cooking and oil or coal for heat. Nor is there a lessening of air pollution by using electricity since, now, much of our electricity is generated here in the Tanana Valley by burning hydrocarbons.

May 77:166

Food Storage and Preservative-Treated Wood

Increasing use of preservative-treated wood for housing foundations in the north leads to a question posed by Doug Yates of Fairbanks: Is it safe to store vegetables in a root cellar constructed of the treated wood?

There are several different types of preservative used to treat wood. Dr. Don Dinkel of the University of Alaska's Agricultural Experiment Station says that it is safe to grow plants treated in the chemical copper-naphthenate sold under the brand name Cuprinol. When first treated, the wood will give off fumes toxic to plants, but the fumes soon go away.

In contrast, the preservative pentachlorophenol, frequently used as to preserve fence posts and which may be sold under the name Woodlife, is definitely poisonous to plants and will kill them.

Thanks to Jack Babcock of Fairbanks Lumber Supply I was able to contact a representative for a firm that pressure-treats wood sold in Alaska. This representative recommends that no foodstuffs be stored in contact with wood treated with his firm's product. It has the brand name Chemonite and the chemical formula ammoniacal-cupric-arsenate. According to him, the only safe wood preservative for food storage containers is one called copper-8-quinolinolate. It is the only wood preservative recommended by the U.S. Department of Agriculture for the storage of food.

The bottom-line answer to Doug Yates' question is a positive yes if the food is to be stored in a root celler having wood treated with copper-8-quinolinolate; the vegetables even can be stored in contact with the wood. It probably is quite safe to store in root cellars where other wood preservatives are used, but the stored food must not come in contact with the treated wood.

Mar 80:380

Northern Self-Sufficiency

Just in the last year or so, we all have become very conscious of the advantage of self-sufficiency in energy and other needs. It is comforting to know that the house will not freeze up if the power goes off because one has a backup wood-burning heating system, or that one has figured out a way to get back and forth to work even if there is no gasoline.

On a larger scale, we are learning how costly it is to import fuel for powering generators or sewage systems in northern villages and towns. Should there be a world-wide catastrophe of some sort we easily see the advantages that northerners hold if they can have their own sources of food, fuel and other similar needs.

Beyond the obvious technical advantages of self-sufficiency there is a more subtle political advantage that self-sufficiency brings, a point which Amory B. Lovins brings out in his book *Soft Energy Paths*. In a sense, it is an obvious thought: the more self-sufficient is a family, a village or a state, the less need there is for help from outside and the less need there is for government assistance and control.

The more interdependent we are as peoples of a nation or of the world, the more government we need to hold ourselves together and to provide our needs. The larger the technical projects we build — power and food distribution systems, water supply and irrigation systems, railroads and highway systems — the more government is required to construct and maintain them.

So, according to this philosophy, if one wishes to minimize government it is best to encourage small technical projects and local self-sufficiency as much as possible. (Thanks to Doug Yates of Fairbanks for suggesting this topic.)

Mar 80:381

The Heat Pump

The heat pump, we are told, is a magical gadget that can be used to heat a house in winter and cool it in summer, depending upon the direction the pump is run. By use of a heat pump, University of Alaska scientist Hans Nielsen is seeking to prove that it is possible to pump enough heat out of the ground to heat a house all winter, even in Alaska.

Each summer, according to Professor Nielsen of the Geophysical Institute, enough heat is absorbed by a quarter-acre of soil to heat a moderate-sized house all winter. The problem is to transfer the energy stored in the ground into the house. Since the temperature of northern soils is normally within a few degrees of the freezing point and the desired temperature of the house is near 68°F (20°C), this transfer sounds impossible. However, it is quite possible if one employs a heat pump, the principle of which has been known for 150 years.

To demonstrate how the heat pump works we need only think about how a refrigerator works, since a refrigerator is a heat pump. When it operates, the food inside the refrigerator gets colder and the room in which the refrigerator sits gets warmer.

In the refrigerator heat pump an electrically driven pump compresses freon vapor to high pressure and to a temperature higher than room temperature. The freon passes to condenser coils exposed to the room where heat is given off to the air outside and a part of the freon condenses to the liquid state (the coils are usually on the back of the refrigerator). The now somewhat-cooler freon gas and liquid mixture passes through a restrictive valve into passageways inside the refrigerator. Extreme cooling accompanies the expansion and evaporation occurring as the freon leaves the valve, so the temperature drops to perhaps -40°F. Since the freon is so cold, it can extract heat energy from the food in the refrigerator. The house is made warmer by an amount determined by how much heat is taken from the food plus the electrical or other energy used to drive the compressor pump.

The heat pump proposed by Professor Nielsen operates exactly the same way. In thinking it through, we only need mentally to replace the food in the refrigerator with the ground outside the house. Furthermore, when the house gets too hot in summer, the heat pump can be reversed to put energy back into the soil to supplement that heat it will receive from the sun.

Jan 80:361

Natural Energy Sources

One can wonder how practical it is to satisfy the human demand for energy with some of the suggested alternatives to fossil fuels. Aside from how practical it may be to use the alternative sources, there is even the more fundamental question of just how much energy is available in each suggested source.

The rate at which the entire human race burns energy in food eaten is about equal to that required to keep a billion 100-watt light bulbs burning. The current worldwide power demand to meet all needs of civilization is about 100 times larger. To avoid hard-to-visualize big numbers, it is useful to talk about the size of potential power sources in terms of the current worldwide demand.

In those terms, some renewable sources of energy clearly are lacking in the ability to solve the world's energy problem, even though they can be important local sources. An example is the power available in tidal flow that could be extracted at places like the Bay of Fundy or Cook Inlet. But the total tidal power available is only about one ten-thousandth of the human energy demand. If all the energy in ocean currents and the waves at coastlines could be tapped, it would supply less than a hundredth of the total human demand.

If one could extract all the energy of motion (kinetic energy) from all water, including falling rain, it would supply only a tenth of the worldwide energy demand, whereas the energy available from the traditional damming of rivers can supply only a hundredth of the demand. Other sources such as wind power, the biological conversion of manure, plant wastes and garbage into gaseous fuels, and geothermal power each fall short, by a factor of ten or more, of being able to supply the current total world demand.

A bigger source of power is the solar-powered temperature difference with depth in the oceans. It is equal in size to the current world demand, as is the photosynthesis that occurs on farmland and in the world's forests. Ten times larger is the energy converted by photosynthesis in the oceans.

The biggest natural source of all is the sun. It provides to the earth 10,000 times civilization's worldwide demand. Even at Point Barrow, the most northerly community on the North American continent, more solar energy falls on the roof of a house over a year than is needed to heat that house for the year.

Apr 80:389

Heating with Wood

How much forest land does it take to keep a northerner's house perpetually in firewood?

To answer this question we begin by defining the size and heating requirement for an "average" interior Alaska house. Axel Carlson of the University of Alaska's Cooperative Extension Service defined an average house as one having about 1200 square feet of floor area and needing 176 million BTUs for heat each year. It would take about 1250 gallons of fuel oil each year to heat such a house.

By photosynthesis, the plants growing on an acre of land can convert and store about 200 million BTUs of solar energy each year. So, in principle, it would seem that an acre could supply a house. In practice, though, we burn only tree trunks and perhaps the largest branches for house heating. This plant material is produced at a far lower rate.

Forests considered to be just marginal for commercial wood production in Alaska and the Yukon will yield about a fifth of a cord of trunkwood per acre each year. Since it takes about 12 cords of wood to supply the 176 million BTUs for our average house's annual heating, as much as 60 acres of marginally commercial forest land are needed to supply the house year after year on a sustained basis.

Of course, the more productive forest lands

bordering the Gulf of Alaska will produce trunkwood at a far higher rate. Balsam poplar and black cottonwood stands of southern Alaska are reported to produce well over a cord of wood per acre annually. So perhaps a 10-acre stand of these hardwoods could supply the heating requirements of a house indefinitely.

May 79:302

Wood Resources

Each passing week's bad news about the rising cost of home heating helps turn a young man's fancy in the direction of firewood.

At the turn of the century, nearly 80 years ago, the average American consumed about 70 cubic feet of wood each year for fuel. For easy thinking purposes, that is an amount roughly equivalent to a 4- by 8-foot sheet of plywood just over two feet thick. It also is about the net volume contained in a purchased cord of firewood when the useless airspaces are accounted for.

Over the years, the per capita annual firewood usage has fallen drastically down to about three cubic feet, roughly the equivalent of an inch-thick sheet of plywood. With widespread new interest in using wood for fuel, we can hope there is no prophecy in the fact that the only time there has been significant increase in the use of firewood this century was during the 1930s depression.

Along with the decrease in use of wood for fuel, there also has been somewhat of a decline in the per-capita use of wood for lumber. Partially counterbalancing these declines have been increases in per capita use of wood for pulp and plywood. Considering all types of use, the American of today utilizes less than half the wood each person used in 1900. Even though the number of people in the United States as a whole has grown much since 1900 the total utilization of wood has dropped from about 12 billion cubic feet in 1900 to 10 billion cubic feet in 1976.

According to an article by Marion Clawson in the June 15, 1979 issue of *Science* magazine, the timber inventory in the United States underwent a drastic decline between 1800 and 1900 when many trees were simply cut and burned in place to make room for agriculture. Since 1900 changes in timber inventory have been comparatively minor. The low point was reached about 1945. The listed inventory has increased slightly during the past 25 years. But, as noted in Clawson's article, it was about 25 years ago that Alaska's timber was starting to be included in the inventory, so one cannot be certain that there has been an actual growth in the volume of useable trees in America's forests.

Jul 79:331

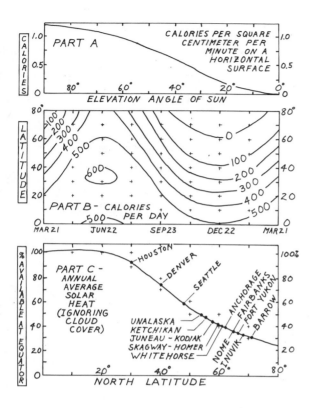

Solar Heating: *This three-part diagram shows in Part A how much solar energy is available when the sun is at different positions in the sky. In Part B it shows how much solar energy is available each day of the year at different latitudes. The curve in Part C allows one to compare the annual energy available at various cities in the Northern Hemisphere.*

Solar Heating

It is easy to see how solar heating can be economical at low latitudes. But will it work in Alaska and the Yukon?

The solar energy available to a collector depends mainly upon the time of day, the time of year, and the latitude of the collector since each of these three geometrical factors determines the angle to the sun. The most possible heat is presented to a horizontal surface when the sun is directly overhead.

As the sun falls lower in the sky, there is less heat energy available for two reasons. First, there is the loss to the shielding atmosphere, and second, the energy that does penetrate through the longer path of air is spread over a larger area, just as is the shadow of any object.

Part A of the diagram shows how the number of calories per square centimeter of surface per minute drops from 1.22 when the sun is overhead (90° elevation) to zero when the sun is on the horizon. This graph does not account for any cloud cover or

excessively water-laden air, both of which will reduce the amount of solar radiation reaching the earth's surface.

Part B of the graph gives contours depicting the number of calories available to a square centimeter of horizontal surface each day at locations between the equator and 80°N. As one expects, the graph shows that at latitudes north of the Arctic Circle (66½°N) solar heating is a complete bust in midwinter — the sun does not even come up. However, in summer, the high-latitude regions do receive solar energy in an amount comparable to that received at the equator.

A comparison of the sunlight available for house heating at the different latitudes is shown in Part C of the graph. Although the annual solar energy available to the latitude region covered by Alaska and the Yukon is only about one-third that available to the equator, the amount is still substantial.

Even considering cloud cover in the interior portions of Alaska and the Yukon, it is evident that more sunshine falls on the roof of a house each year than is needed to heat the house for the year.

The problems then come down to how to collect the solar energy and how to store it. Especially the storage problem is more difficult at high latitude, and neither problem has an easy solution. Nevertheless, solar heating definitely is a practical possibility for heating northerners' homes. It seems most likely that solar heating will serve mostly as a source auxiliary to other methods. But, who knows? Perhaps as our technology improves, solar heating might take over completely.

Apr 79:301

Hai-Toh Lim's Thesis

The other day a big package came in the mail. Inside was Hai-Toh Lim's master's thesis, *Solar energy as a form of supplementary energy for heating Alaskan Inuit houses.*

Two years earlier Ms. Lim's supervisory mentor at Goddard College in Plainfield, Vermont, had called. He had this eager architectural student who wanted to come to Alaska to try to design better houses for northerners, particularly in the windswept coastal regions, and to see to what extent solar energy could be used to heat them. Could Ms. Lim associate with the Geophysical Institute and could the Institute provide enough fiscal support to pay her board and room?

There really was no money, but later when Hai-Toh Lim herself called, her enthusiasm bubbling over the phone sorely threatened fiscal responsibility. Finally a legal and moral way was found to permit Ms. Lim's residency, and some months later Hai-Toh, all five feet of her, arrived behind a big smile.

During her tenure here, Hai-Toh Lim did far more

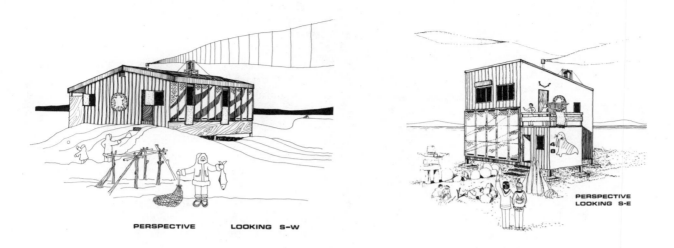

PERSPECTIVE   LOOKING S—W

PERSPECTIVE
LOOKING S-E

Hai-Toh Lim's Thesis: *Single- and double-story housing designs employing the fiberglass and pop can solar collector on the south walls. Essentially, the entire south wall of the one-story structure is covered by the solar collector, and only the lower portion of the two-story building has the collector. (Drawings on this page by Hai-Toh Lim.)*

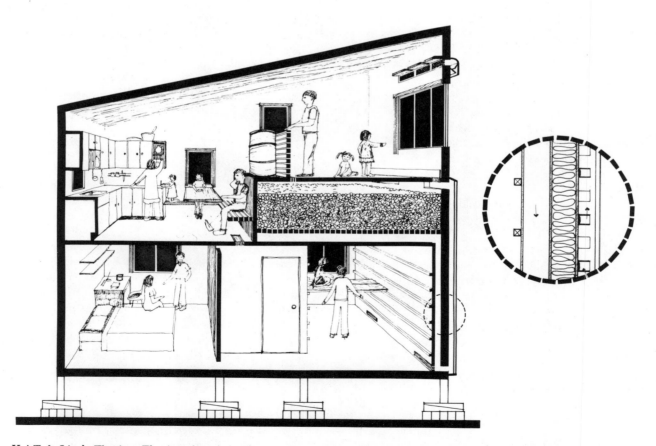

Hai-Toh Lim's Thesis: *The interior view of a two-story design illustrates the pallet-and-rail idea in one sleeping area on the lower floor and a gravel bed for storing heat obtained from the pop can solar collector on the south (right-hand) wall. The inset shows the flow of air in the collector. Quartered pop cans in the upward-flowing air create air movement that increases the efficiency of the collector.*

than sit at the drawing board. With the help of the Institute's shop personnel she built a passive solar energy collector out of pop and beer cans, plywood and fiberglass. She installed it atop the Geophysical Institute and undertook a series of measurements that proved the effectiveness of the device.

Ms. Lim prepared three different house designs incorporating the beer can energy collector and boxes of gravel for storing the heat. She took the designs out into the villages — Anaktuvik Pass, Bethel, Eek and Point Hope — to learn what people there thought of them.

Hai-Toh found that villagers were enthusiastic about certain features of her designs and liked the idea of being able to build the solar collectors themselves out of scrap and other readily available materials. They favored her incorporation of the cold trap entrances concept, the use of solar energy for heating bathwater and her ideas on using movable pallets for sleeping and storage so as to make maximum use of limited space. And, of course, she got critical comments that required her to revise some of her ideas, especially about how she could support a heavy bed of gravel on the second story of a house.

Besides presenting her designs, Hai-Toh Lim's thesis reports on computer calculations and other evaluations that indicate the cost-effectiveness of the solar collector. One surprising result is that, even at farthest north Point Barrow, the designs will pay for themselves in two to four years. A summary of her thesis is given by Ms. Lim in the latest *Northern Engineer*, a publication of the Geophysical Institute. (Those interested in regularly receiving this highly readable quarterly can subscribe at low cost.)

I think Hai-Toh Lim has made a substantial contribution to Alaska. Just how much her contribution cost Alaska is hard to judge exactly. Only a few hundred dollars were paid directly to her, but the indirect supporting services and the time of the many University professionals and faculty who worked with and assisted Ms. Lim — including Axel Carlson, Lee Leonard, Fred Milan, Richard Seifert, Gerd Wendler, Tunis Wentink, and John Zarling — were worth several additional thousands of dollars. Nevertheless, I'm sure Alaska always benefits from the presence of people like Hai-Toh Lim. She has gone to Quebec to look for a job now that she has finished her degree, but she says she would like to come back to Alaska to build one of her houses in a village.

Mar 79:294

Free Heat?

"Scientific new way to get extra heat without using extra fuel!" proclaims a recent advertisement in *The Christian Science Monitor*. For only $4.98 plus 75¢ postage and handling, a concern called American Consumer, Inc., of Philadelphia, Pennsylvania, will send a set of four "sensational" devices. Each device appears to be a flexible aluminum strip called an "Instant Aluminum Radiator." Illustrations show how the strips are to be attached to baseboard heat units, air dust grills or steam pipes.

The implication is that by using these radiating fins to increase the rate of heat exchange within a room, one can increase the amount of heat obtained from a given amount of fuel.

By and large, it's a phony implication.

Such devices placed on a metal stovepipe chimney could increase the heat going to the room and reduce the amount going out the chimney. (This is the idea of the stack robber.) But attached to electric baseboard heating units, to air duct grills and to heat circulating pipes within a house, the added radiators will have no effect of value. Since each "Instant Aluminum Radiator" has 30 square inches of fins, its use is equivalent to putting in the same place a 5-inch by 6-inch sheet of aluminum foil or stiff aluminum sheet.

If you have an application where you obviously benefit by adding four sheets of 5-inch by 6-inch aluminum foil to increase the heat exchange rate, then you might want to order the "Instant Aluminum Radiator." On the other hand, you could just use the aluminum foil.

Nov 77:192

Using Solar Energy Effectively

The 1941 book *Kabloona* by Gontran de Poncins contains a description of an unusual labor-saving application of solar energy by the Eskimos of King William Island in Northwest Territories. The description also illustrates how powerful the sun's rays can be during early spring — April and May — even far above the Arctic Circle.

Long ago, the King William Eskimos noticed that a small piece of fur or a rag would absorb enough solar heat to melt its way into several feet of ice. Normally, if a King William man was in a hurry to create a hole in the ice to fish through, his only recourse was to chop his way through with a cutting tool. But he knew that if he was not in too much of a hurry, he could use solar energy. The accepted method was to lay dog feces on the ice in the right places and then wait for the sun to do all the work.

Mar 80:383

Solid Waste Disposal

It is said that if you get a group of Alaskans or northern Canadians together for an evening's conversation, the talk will, sooner or later, turn to sewage.

Sewage is a topic dear to the northerner's heart; it, like the weather, is something that concerns everyone and gives each at least occasional trouble. Low ground temperatures, water-impervious soils, deep seasonal freezing and permafrost can act individually or collectively to make sewage disposal a messy problem in both rural and urban areas.

One reason sewage gives us so much problem is that we insist upon thinking that sewers and water supplies must always go together. Worse yet, we are inclined to believe that the only way to handle sewage is in a water solution. There are other ways, lecturer Sim Van der Ryne told attendees of the First Alaska Alternative Energy Conference held in Anchorage, November 9-11, 1979. In a conference workshop he held on waste disposal, Van der Ryne described water-free techniques that can be used to safely dispose of solid human waste. The concept is particularly attractive because scarce water and impervious soil are accepted facts of life in many arctic and subarctic localities.

The idea is to retain human fecal matter in vented but otherwise tight containers to which carbon is added regularly. A few handfuls of sawdust, leaves or moss added each day provide the carbon necessary to curtail odor and, later, to promote effective composting.

Holding compartments can be 55-gallon drums or other portable but air-tight containers. Three or four drums provide enough volume to carry a family of four over winter.

When summer comes the next step is to place the capped containers in a greenhouse-like room for a month or so where solar energy can heat the material to temperatures of 180-200°F (68-80°C). Thorough heating to at least 160°F is necessary to kill parasites and disease carriers. It is then possible to safely compost the residue to obtain nutrients for gardens or other plants. However, direct use on leaf crops to be eaten is not recommended.

In addition to being a safe way to handle solid human waste, the waterless method system described by Van der Ryne has the potential for low cost and reliability. Those northern communities that have had experiences with high-cost and failure-prone sewage systems employing water can especially appreciate these qualities.

Nov 79:354

Methyl Alcohol

Not since Prohibition has there been so much interest in the local making of alcohol. This time around, the objective is more noble, the main desire being to produce an economically feasible replacement for petroleum.

The chemically most simple alcohol useful for fuel is methyl alcohol, also called methanol or wood alcohol. Since 1930, most methyl alcohol has been made by chemically combining carbon monoxide and hydrogen. One molecule of CO plus two molecules of H_2 gas yields methanol. Its formula is written CH_3OH.

From the time methyl alcohol was discovered in 1661 until people learned to synthesize it, about 60 years ago, methyl alcohol was obtained by destructively distilling wood, that is, by breaking up the wood fiber with heat and driving off the volatile components. Interest in going back to that method is growing among people who live in the forest regions of western Canada and Alaska because it is recognized that methanol production might be a profitable use of sawdust and other forestry wastes. Wood contains, by weight, roughly 2% methyl alcohol, so a ton of wood will yield about 24 liters (6 gallons) of methyl alcohol.

One source claims a single cord of pitch pine will yield 50 bushels of charcoal, 1000 cubic feet of methane gas, 50 gallons of a burnable mixture of oil and tar, 1.5 barrels of pitch, 20 gallons of turpentine, 1 barrel of tar, and 100 gallons of a gooey mixture of acetic acid and methyl alcohol, in addition to 5 gallons of pure methyl alcohol. So wood can produce a variety of useful substances.

Once the poisonous methyl alcohol and other materials have been distilled off, the remaining cellulose-rich wood fiber can be fed to sheep and beef cattle. Canadian scientists have found that a feed composed of barley or corn mixed with 30 to 50% cooked aspen chips is satisfactory. They did not comment on the taste of the mixture.

Mar 80:385

Gasohol

One of the suggested methods to reduce the need to import petroleum is to produce fuel from agricultural crops. Gasohol, a mixture of 90% unleaded gasoline and 10% ethyl alcohol, can be used in autos without making carburetor adjustments. Whether better or worse mileage results is debatable; most results so far indicate it is worse compared to burning gasoline.

However, the crucial question is if a net energy gain results when gasohol rather than gasoline is used as fuel. Analyses of the energy costs of producing the ethyl alcohol component of gasohol take into account the energy consumed in agricultural production and the subsequent cooking and fermentation processes that yield the alcohol.

Studies reported recently in *Science* indicate that about half of the agricultural energy cost is in the fuel to run the tractors and other machinery. Fertilizers and machinery production make up most of the rest.

Much more energy is required to cook and distill the corn, sugar cane or other crop to be converted to fuel.

If petroleum is used as the energy source for all the processes that lead to the production of gasohol, the whole idea seems to be a loser, and that does not even take into account the energy required for irrigation, drainage or other projects that subsidize agricultural production.

Only if renewable energy sources can be used to produce gasohol can this fuel be considered as a solution to the petroleum problem even at latitudes where high yields of sugar and starch crops can be grown. In the north, agricultural biomass conversions to liquid fuel seem even more likely to be unprofitable.

Feb 80:373

Alaskan Zeolites

Zeolites are a curious group of crystalline compounds that occur naturally and also can be synthesized. An extensive natural deposit occurs in the Talkeetna Mountains north of Anchorage, and there is another near Lake Iliamna on the Alaska Peninsula.

Zeolites have so many uses that University of Alaska geochemist Dan Hawkins likens them to the "schmoos" that some years ago graced the "Lil' Abner" comic strip. Older readers will remember that a schmoo could do many useful tasks and, when eaten, tasted like fried chicken.

In part, zeolites owe their utility to their ability to absorb and give off water. The word zeolite literally means rock that boils; when strongly heated, zeolites froth and give off water. Another curious characteristic is that zeolites, though rigid in structure, are like sponges in that they contain many holes. One of the significances of this open structure is illustrated by new developments of value for energy storage. The amount of natural gas that can be stored in a 19 cubic foot tank at pressure 2300 pounds per square inch can be stored in an eight cubic foot tank of one type of zeolite at only 200 psi. Similarly, it may be feasible to produce hydrogen using wind power, hydro power or solar power during times of peak production and then store the hydrogen in zeolite for later use.

Dr. Hawkins also has suggested that the city of Anchorage, and perhaps other northern cities, might profitably use zeolites to extract methane from sewage for use as fuel.

Apr 80:392

The Eielson Deep Hole

Not far from Eielson Air Force Base is a hole nearly 10,000 feet deep drilled by a federal agency in 1965 for emplacement of a seismic instrument. No longer used for that purpose, the Eielson deep hole is now yielding valuable scientific results and a suggestion for a cheap energy source for Fairbanks.

Based upon age dating of minerals taken from the hole at various depths, Dr. Robert B. Forbes and coworkers have been able to measure, of all things, surface erosion rates over the past 120 million years. By rather esoteric means they find that the average erosion rate over this period is about four or five hundredths of a millimeter each year. That means it would take about 500 years to erode away an inch of rock at the surface.

It is also found that the temperature at the bottom of the hole is very near the boiling point of water. If a cheap way can be found to move all that heat upwards about two miles, every house in Fairbanks will have clean economical heat.

Mar 77:79

Let Them Burn Peat

Alaska's fuel peat resource, like everything else Alaskan, is impressive. In fact, Alaska has slightly over half of the estimated peat resource in the United States. Canada has an even larger peat resource, but then Canada is bigger than Alaska.

According to a recent report available from the Division of Energy and Power Development, 338 Denali Street, Anchorage, 99501, Alaska has an estimated 27 million acres of peat resources. Assuming, as the report does, that the peat in those resource areas averages seven feet thick, that each cubic foot of dry peat weighs 15 pounds and that each cubic foot can provide 6000 BTU, the total reserve amounts to 741 quadrillion BTU.

A big number like that needs to be converted to something one can understand. Knowing that a barrel of oil produces about 5½ million BTU, it is easy to calculate that the Alaskan peat resource is about equal to an oil reserve of 100 billion barrels, five to ten times larger than the known North Slope oil reserve.

Ignoring the environmental consequences and technicalities of how to do it, suppose all that peat could be vacuumed up and fed down a pipeline at the same rate oil energy flows through the Trans-Alaska pipeline. Our imaginary peat-line would flow for about 370 years before the resource finally petered out.

Dec 80:444

Alaskan Energy Use

Alaska pumps into the ground more than twice as much energy as it uses each year.

That, to me, is just one of the surprising facts contained in the new State of Alaska Long Term Energy Plan, now prepared in draft form by the Alaska Department of Commerce and Economic

Development. In 1979, Alaska consumed just over two-tenths of a quad of energy, and it reinjected into the ground just over half a quad of natural gas to keep the pressure high in the Prudhoe and Cook Inlet oil wells.

The term 'quad' is a shorthand name for a unit used to measure energy. It is a term used only in the big leagues; but when it comes to energy production, Alaska definitely has arrived. One quad is the amount of energy contained in a flow of 476,000 barrels of oil each day for one year. By means of the Trans-Alaska pipeline, Alaska exported, in 1979, 2.96 quads of energy. That is about 18 times as much energy as was used that year in the state.

Another surprise is that 25% of the Alaskan end-use demand for energy is due to one refinery on the Kenai Peninsula which makes ammonia and urea from natural gas produced in the Cook Inlet area. Even discounting the energy consumed in that plant, Alaskans have significantly higher per capita energy consumption than do other Americans. Alaskans use almost three times as much energy per capita for transportation and marine use. That such high use exists is reasonable, considering the large distances to travel in the state and the great extent of the Alaskan coastline and the fishing and other activities that transpire along it.

Nevertheless, Alaska's main energy demand is in the Railbelt area, extending from Anchorage to Fairbanks. With 71% of the Alaskan population, this area accounts for 86% of the energy consumed in the state.

Fifty-seven percent of the energy consumed by Alaskans comes in the form of petroleum products. Yet despite being a petroleum exporter, Alaska still imports 43% of the petroleum products it uses. The next most important energy source for Alaskans is natural gas. It satisfies 35% of the energy demand. Solid fuel — coal and wood — supply 2.3% of the energy demand for the state. Electrical demand, amounting to 5.9% of the total energy used in the state, is supplied by a combination of hydro, coal, wood, petroleum and natural gas.

One of the things that is easy to forget is the loss of energy that occurs in the process of delivering energy in useable form to the end user. Losses associated with refining, conversion processes such as electrical generation and with delivery to the user in Alaska burn up another one-tenth of a quad. So for every two BTUs that an Alaskan uses, roughly one additional BTU is lost in conversion and delivery.

One fact that comes clear from the draft of the Alaska Long Term Energy Plan is that Alaskans are nearly totally dependent upon petroleum and natural gas for their energy needs. Coal, wood, hydro and other alternative sources account for only a small

fraction of the total energy consumed. Once the petroleum and gas run out, Alaska will be in serious trouble unless alternatives are developed.

Jun 81:487

The Trans-Polar Air Route

An average day in April 1981 saw more than 28 jets fly across Alaska on the polar air route. Each glided down to Anchorage or Fairbanks to empty the toilets and take on fuel before speeding on. Three-fourths of the planes landed at Anchorage, the other fourth at Fairbanks.

A dozen exotic names adorn the fuselages and tail structures of these airborne behemoths: Japan Airlines, British Airways, Lufthansa, Sabena Belgian World Airlines, Korean Airlines, Scandanavian Airlines, Trans International, Air France, KLM, Trans Mediterranean, World Airways, Pan Am and perhaps others.

Far out of the competition, the United States' former flagship airline, Pan Am, made but one single flight during April. Even Scandanavian Airlines, the organization that pioneered the polar route more than 20 years ago, placed only seventh in the number of polar flights. The big leaders now are, in order, Japan Airlines, Korean Airlines and Air France.

Each of these airliners loads up an average of 17,000 gallons of fuel when it lands. During April, an average month, the 861 planes that touched down in Alaska took on a total of nearly fifteen million gallons of fuel. Actually, Alaska furnishes half the fuel used on the polar route: each round trip involves a fueling in Europe, one in the Orient and two in Alaska.

In a year's time, the polar aircraft load up 176 million gallons of Alaskan fuel. Since each gallon of jet fuel contains 128,000 BTUs, the total energy taken aboard amounts to more than 22 trillion BTUs. This is more than a third of the energy used for transportation in the Alaskan Railbelt region, the region that includes both Anchorage and Fairbanks. It also is just over 10% of the energy consumed in the whole of Alaska for all purposes except that used directly in producing crude petroleum for export.

Jun 81:489

Alaska's Coal

A few years ago, estimates of Alaska's coal resources placed them at approximately 130 billion tons. Now, largely because of better knowledge about the coal beneath the North Slope and the offshore area beyond, the estimates range from 1860 billion to 5000 billion tons.

This, of course, is a huge energy resource if it could all be recovered for use. Full recovery is unlikely because much of the coal is deeply buried, of not the best quality or is at locations where transportation is lacking.

In estimating what portion of an identified coal resource is recoverable, experts considering reserves elsewhere in the United States pick figures ranging from 1% to over 20%. And that percentage generally is applied only to known resources, not those which are hypothesized to exist on the basis of surface outcrops or sparse drilling information. Nor does the percentage apply to resources speculated to exist, such as off Alaska's northern coast, on the basis of even less information. The 1850 billion to 5000 billion ton estimate for Alaska includes these hypothesized or speculated resources.

But suppose Alaska really does have a coal resource amounting to the lower figure, 1850 billion tons, and suppose that 10% of it is recoverable. That means Alaska could recover 185 billion tons. At the rate Alaska used energy in 1979, this is enough coal to last the state more than 15,000 years, leaving nothing for export.

Strangely enough, there is but one operating coal mine in Alaska. The Usibelli Coal Mines at Healy produce about 700,000 tons of coal annually. This coal supplied only 6% of the energy used in the state during 1979.

Alaska's lack of operating coal mines is not because people haven't tried. The Russian-American company opened Alaska's first coal mine in 1855 at Port Graham, a locality on the Kenai Peninsula that had been discovered as early as 1786. The company built a small town on the site and after a year's work exported 88 tons of coal to California. The export venture failed because the coal could not compete with that obtainable from Canada, Australia, England and Chile. Though the mine did supply Russian ships for some years, the company gave it up as a bad show and threw in the towel in 1865.

Since then, dozens of Alaskan coal mines have opened. Most closed shortly thereafter, although some hung on for years. Demon petroleum bedeviled most of the operations. As early as 1902, steamers plying the Yukon River were converting from wood and coal to petroleum. The U.S. Navy, always in the vanguard, followed suit 22 years later. Finally, in 1946, even the Alaska Railroad changed over, despite the abundance of coal practically alongside the track and the fact that the railroad was built where it is in the first place because of the coal.

Another significant factor in the slow development of Alaska's huge coal resources is the quality of the coal itself. Most of the world's really good bituminous and anthracite coals have their origins in terrestrial plants that grew 300 million years ago, during the Carboniferous (Mississippian and Pennsylvanian) period. Burial under overlying sediments brought high temperatures and pressures acting over a long period of time to develop high-quality coals.

Unfortunately, most of Alaska's coals are much younger. They were primarily born in the more recent Cretaceous and Tertiary periods, 30 million to 130 million years ago. Many of these younger Alaskan coals haven't cooked long enough at sufficiently high temperature (100° to $400^{o}C$) to coalify into the high-quality bituminous and anthracite coals most desired. The majority of the Alaskan coal is lignite, sub-bituminous and bituminous.

Jun 81:492

Origin of Alaska's Coal

Unlike petroleum and natural gas which form from plant life in the marine environment, coal derives from plants that grow on land.

Much of the world's coal is thought to have developed from plants growing in swampy areas near ancient shorelines. Some scientists have suggested that there is evidence of occasional intrusion of the seas into areas where coal is starting to form and that part of the coals may actually have derived from plant debris, marine or terrestrial, laid down by these shallow encroaching seas. But it seems clear that some coal beds are strictly terrestrial, that is, formed entirely on land. The coal fields of central Alaska in the Nenana area are examples of strictly terrestrial coals.

The first requirement for forming a coal bed is to accumulate peat-like plant remains in a stratum. Then the peat-like deposit must be covered up by a layer of inorganic material such as clay, silt, sand or gravel which might be laid down by a lake or stream. If the original organic bed is not so covered it merely turns to peat.

However, once the coal-to-be plant remains are covered over, they undergo biochemical changes that cause them to give up oxygen and hydrogen to the overlying sediment beds. Microorganisms play a role in this process by decomposing the cellulose, proteins and lignin materials of which the plants are made. The remains of the biochemical decomposition have high carbon content and these start to transform into identifiable coal particles called macerals.

Now, not everyone is likely to become overly excited about macerals, but coal miners really dig them.

Several types of macerals form. One type is a charcoal-like fibrous maceral made of plant cell walls and which exhibits the structure of the cell walls. Another maceral is vitreous and shiny; it forms from lignin and cellulose remains.

As the biochemical phase of coal development progresses, another geochemical phase begins. It requires the high temperature that comes from deep burial of the coal bed by progressively built-up overburden layers. If a bed is buried to a depth of 10,000 feet, the temperature will rise to the boiling point of water. This is hot enough to create bituminous coal if the temperature persists long enough, perhaps a million years or so. It may even be hot enough to create the higher-grade anthracite coal, but the time taken would be much longer.

Most of Alaska's coals started as plants growing during the Tertiary and Cretaceous ages, 30 to 130 million years ago. Most of America's best coals are much older, having been started during the Mississippian or Pennsylvanian periods, 280 to 350 million years ago. Coals are like people, the older they are the better they usually get. Consequently, much of the coal found in other parts of the country ranks higher than ours. Alaskan coal is largely lignite, subbituminous or bituminous, there apparently being comparatively little anthracite coal in the state.

Aug 81:499

EXAMPLE OF USING THE DATING METHOD:
Dating and microscopic study of ash partings in coal exposed at A and B show it is in the same bed. A second bed lies below the coal exposed at A. Therefore digging at point C should locate coal bed No. 2. Also, digging anyplace between A and B should locate both coal beds.

Coal Dating.

Coal Dating

Two University of Alaska professors have found a new way to help better define Alaska's huge coal reserves. Their idea depends upon the fact that coal is formed on land in extensive sheet deposits. As the years go by, movements of the earth's crust and erosion deform and break up these sheets. Some portions of the coal seams remain buried and others may outcrop here and there. Mapping of those portions not exposed would be helped if it was possible to identify a particular coal seam regardless of where it outcrops.

Professors Don Triplehorn and Don Turner have found that they can use the University's rock dating laboratory to date the coal seams. The coal itself cannot be dated, but volcanic ash deposited in layers within the coal seams can. Called ash partings, these layers contain minerals which can be accurately dated using the potassium-argon and fission-track techniques. It appears that there have been frequent enough ash-depositing volcanic eruptions in Alaska's past to make the dating of ash partings a useful tool.

Dec 77:203

Natural Gas Hydrates

In addition to the petroleum and free natural gas found on Alaska's North Slope, there is the possibility there of another large and, as yet, untapped energy source. This resource is the substance called natural gas hydrates.

Natural gas hydrates are crystalline solids resembling snow that form from mixtures of water and natural gas under certain conditions. Unless natural gas has any associated water removed from it before being fed into a pipeline, gas hydrates may form and plug up the pipeline. The hydrates sometimes have plugged up the fittings placed at the heads of gas wells.

Low pressures and temperatures favor the formation of the natural gas hydrates. Consequently, they are likely to be found beneath the thick layer of permafrost that covers Alaska's North Slope down to depths perhaps near 2000 feet. The hydrates may also occur in the upper reaches of offshore gas fields. In 1970, Soviet scientists announced the discovery of huge deposits of natural gas hydrates beneath permafrost in the Soviet Union. Other deposits have been discovered in the seafloor off the coasts of Africa and Central America.

As yet, it is not known how large the natural gas hydrate resource might be in Alaska and nearby Canada. Nor is enough known about the characteristics of the hydrates to be certain that they can be extracted economically. However, it is likely, according to the University of Alaska's Christine Ehlig-Economides, writing in a recent issue of *The Northern Engineer*, that methods involving reduction of the gas pressure within the deposits or injection of methyl alcohol into the formation will enable profitable extraction.

Aug 81:498

Supersonic Transport Service

May 24, 1976 marked the initiation of Supersonic Transport Service to the United States by the British-French Concorde. This plane, which visited Fairbanks two years ago, seats 128 and flies at a speed of 2.2 times the speed of sound and can cross the Atlantic in 3½ hours. The commercial service which started in May is between Washington's Dulles Airport, London and Paris and will continue for a 16-month trial period. The opposition to the SST flights is based upon the unanswered scientific question: What are the long-term effects upon our atmosphere of the release, at 65,000 feet, of large quantities of water vapor, carbon dioxide, and various oxides of nitrogen and sulfur? The altitude of release of these exhausts is at the base of the stratosphere, a relatively clean and stable layer of the atmosphere, and the location of the world's ozone layer which serves as a protective shield from the sun's ultraviolet rays. The concern, as yet unresolved, is that enough water will be released by successive years of commercial SST flights to react with and deplete the ozone and remove some of this protective layer. Closer to home are the effects of the sonic boom and noise on landing. This question will be judged directly by the people in the communities near the airport. The ozone question will require long-term scientific testing, but the recent flights should get some response from the citizens near Dulles Airport about the noise.

— Henry Cole
Jun 76:82

Alaska's Metric Connection

The United States was officially made a metric country by Thomas Corwin Mendenhall, whose name flows ever onward past Juneau's mountains in the form of glacier ice. In his position as Superintendent of Weights and Measures, he issued the "Mendenhall order" in 1893 which set the United States' standards of length and mass as the meter and the kilogram.

Though the United States has officially been on the metric system for nearly a century, most of us still think in ounces, pounds, quarts, inches, and miles. We are not alone; at least one other country on the planet is still not metric. That country is Sierra Leone, an enclave of about 2.5 million people situated on the west coast of Africa. Several other small African countries may still be on the English system. But even England gave up the English system of units in recent years because of economic necessity.

With its current highly negative balance of payments, the United States may have to go the same route. The country's non-standard automotive and machinery exports are bound to meet increasing customer resistance in an all-metric world.

Had George Washington realized how long it would take for his country to go metric, he would have been horrified. Along with his country, he tried to father adoption of a decimal system of measurement. His first annual message to Congress pleaded for establishment of uniformity in standards, currency, and weight and measures. Successive pleas went to Congress in Washington's second and third annual messages. Thomas Jefferson and John Adams also tried to get Congress to act. Finally the Fifth Congress, in 1799, passed the first act establishing a procedure for standardizing weights and measures.

Nearly 100 years were to pass before the United States legally went metric. In the meantime, France was struggling with the usage of metric and a host of ancient units of wondrous sort. That ended in 1837 when a law was passed forbidding the use of other than metric units.

Meanwhile in the United States, complexity abounded. While Congress wallowed in the problem, the separate States, independently of each other, adopted their own standards. Several fluid measures were in use, including the ale gallon of 282 cubic inches and the Queen Anne, or wine gallon, of 231 cubic inches; England abolished these in 1824 when the imperial gallon was defined to contain 10 pounds of water. The Queen Anne gallon survived in part of North America and is now called the U.S. gallon.

Jan 78:210

High Finance

How much is a billion dollars?

Despite inflation's upward trend which may someday require each of us to carry around sums like this for pocket money, it's hard to envision what a billion means. At the suggestion of one of our local borough assemblymen (the Geophysical Institute's Dr. Bill Stringer), we have amassed some comparative figures to help people understand how much a billion dollars is.

By actual measurement, we have determined that a hundred United States dollars laid side by side will cover an area one meter square (just over a square yard). It takes about 8200 normally worn bills to make a stack one meter high.

So:

— A stack of a billion one dollar bills will reach from the ground 120 kilometers upward so that its top 20 kilometers would be immersed in a normal aurora.

— With a billion one dollar bills, one could lay down a band 70 bills wide along the full length of the Alaska-Canada border from Demarcation Point to Tongass.

— With a lot of paste and a billion dollars, one could paper over the outside of the full length of the Trans-Alaska pipeline twice and still have $140,000 left over for refreshments during coffee breaks.

— There are probably about 50,000 moose in Alaska, so with a billion dollars, one could make a stack of bills beside each moose that would reach at least as high as the moose's head.

— If one sat down to count a billion one dollar bills and could count them at the rate of one per second, every second of every day, it would take more than 30 years to finish the task.

Now you have a clear picture of how much a billion dollars is.

Jan 79:276

Bergy Seltzer

Bergy seltzer is something you have heard but perhaps never heard about. One cynic I know has said that her life could have been fully and happily lived without ever learning about bergy seltzer. For those who do not feel that way, the whole story is laid out here.

Bergy seltzer is a continuous crackling, frying sound that has been heard by submariners and other sailors when close to melting icebergs. Another name for bergy seltzer is ice sizzle, also descriptive of the sound which is attributed to the breaking out of air bubbles from the melting ice.

Among the first to gain insight into bergy seltzer was Per Scholander, a well-known northern scientist. Twenty years ago, he co-authored an article that described the pressures inside air bubbles locked into glacier ice. Measurements showed that the pressure could range from about one atmosphere (14 lbs per square inch) to more than 20 atmospheres.

Glacier ice and some other types of ice can contain huge numbers of air bubbles, which give the ice a cloudy appearance. It seems possible that part of the noise called bergy seltzer can come from the bubbles breaking the ice when melting causes each bubble to come in close contact with the ice surface. However, much of the noise is just the escape of the air under high pressure as the bubble breaks out. Anyhow, placement of hydrophones near melting icebergs enabled U.S. Navy scientists to conclude that bergy seltzer could be detected with sonar perhaps 100 miles away.

Want to hear bergy seltzer but don't have a sonar or an iceberg handy? All that is needed is a glass of water and an ice cube. Drop the ice cube in the water and put your ear down near the top of the glass. The steady fizzle you hear is bergy seltzer.

Sep 80:424

Bubbles in Beer

During the nearly five years that I have been preparing this column, the most difficult question I've tried to answer is one posed by Glenn Estabrook of Fairbanks: "In a carbonated beverage, why do the rising bubbles always seem to stream up from individual spots, as though emanating from distinct localities on the surface of the container?"

For more than two months, I've pondered the question and searched scientific literature for the answer. Finally, I found a partial answer in an enjoyable book *Butter Side Up* written by Dr. Magnus Pyke.

As Dr. Pyke notes, most of us, at one time or another, have watched bubbles rise up in beer or other carbonated beverages such as pop without noticing or thinking about the point Glenn Estabrook has raised. Dr. Pyke goes on to say that it is those who do notice and question why such things happen that are likely to make scientific discoveries.

It is true that bubbles do not appear at random within a glass of carbonated beverage. Instead, they tend to form at particular locations, usually at places on the inside of the glass. Dr. Pyke states that these locations will be found, upon close examination, to be points of irregularity on the bottom or sides of the glass. Also, if a grain of sand or other similar small foreign object is dropped into the glass, bubbles will be seen to form at the sand grain and to rise in a line above it.

So much for what happens; the next question is, why do the bubbles form at places of irregularity? This is a question Dr. Pyke does not answer, but there has to be a reason. The answer to this question has to do with the surface tension within a liquid or gas in contact with another substance, such as the grain of sand or the glass container.

Prior to the formation of carbon dioxide bubbles in a carbonated liquid, the carbon dioxide is contained throughout the liquid. It will collect together to make bubbles in the liquid wherever the pressure within the liquid is lowest. The pressure in the liquid is abnormally low near the boundaries of the liquid because of the surface tension of the liquid. Where the boundary has the most curvature — as on the sand grain or on the irregularity on the glass container — the pressure reaches its lowest. Hence it is precisely here where the bubbles are most likely to form.

Feb 81:468

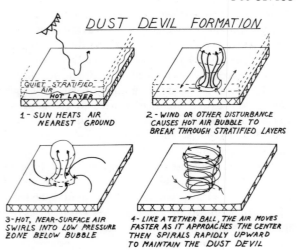

DUST DEVIL FORMATION

1 - SUN HEATS AIR NEAREST GROUND

2 - WIND OR OTHER DISTURBANCE CAUSES HOT AIR BUBBLE TO BREAK THROUGH STRATIFIED LAYERS

3 - HOT, NEAR-SURFACE AIR SWIRLS INTO LOW PRESSURE ZONE BELOW BUBBLE

4 - LIKE A TETHER BALL, THE AIR MOVES FASTER AS IT APPROACHES THE CENTER THEN SPIRALS RAPIDLY UPWARD TO MAINTAIN THE DUST DEVIL

Dust Devils

Dust devils form most frequently in desert areas where the sun beats down on the poorly conducting sand surface. As Meg Hayes of Fairbanks has noted, they also occur in non-vegetated areas such as parking lots, especially if there are nearby large buildings to help cause irregular air currents. The hot desert or parking lot surface heats a thin layer of air just above — setting the stage for the dance of the sun devils.

Even though the hot near-surface air wants to rise

up through the cooler, and therefore heavier, air above, quiet air tends to retain a degree of stability — a resistance to new air motion. One can visualize that resistance as something like the surface tension on water — it is strong but it does have a breaking point.

As the stability limit is approached, almost any sort of irregularity can cause the limit to be exceeded so that a bubble of hot surface air bursts upward. A place on the ground that is hotter than elsewhere will cause the limit to be surpassed there first. Or an irregularity caused by a minor gust of wind, the nearby motion of a car, and even the passage of a rabbit can initiate a dust devil.

The sudden uprush of hot air causes air to speed horizontally inward to the bottom of the newly-forming funnel. One of the rules of the physics of moving air is that its vorticity is preserved. The requirement that vorticity be preserved leads to a large speed-up in the circular motion of air spiraling inward to the bottom of the new funnel.

And so a dust devil is formed; it is an almost self-sustaining whirlwind that maintains a funnel-like chimney through which hot air moves both upward and circularly.

A dust devil may last from less than a minute up to several hours. Air speeds up to 70 mph have been measured in vigorous dust devils. This enables them to pick up dust, leaves or, sometimes, rather large objects. Dust devils tend to form in groups; a large dust devil is sometimes seen to have little, shorter-lived devils traveling along behind it.

Jun 78:227

Washboard Roads

Washboard roads are a familiar part of the northern scene, just as they are in all parts of the world where people travel over unsurfaced roadways. Actually, corrugations develop on surfaced roads, too, as well as on steel or other hard surfaces upon which wheels roll, though the corrugations there are not so noticeable.

For many years people have speculated, usually wrongly, about the exact cause of road corrugations. The real answer comes from a series of experiments and observations conducted in Australia nearly 20 years ago by Dr. Keith B. Mather, now vice chancellor for research and advanced study at the University of Alaska. The lurid details are given in an article by him that appeared in *Scientific American*, Volume 208, published in 1963.

Corrugations develop most easily on dry, dusty roads. The corrugations start to develop at a point where a rolling wheel strikes an irregularity on the road surface. The irregularity might be a dip, a bump or even a small rock.

This irregularity causes the wheel to fly upward above the roadway. A short distance beyond the irregularity the wheel impacts the ground again. Where the wheel lands, it tends to dig in to create another irregularity. The wheel climbs out of this irregularity and, thereby, again flies into the air. Thus, a single irregularity leads to the formation of others evenly spaced down the roadway at locations dependent upon the weight and springing of the vehicle and its speed. Other wheels on other cars coming along behind repeat the process, causing the unevenness of the road surface to increase and spread across the full width of the roadway. On a particular stretch of roadway, vehicles tend to travel at about the same speed and, despite their differences, they bounce about the same, so their collective action is to increase rather than smooth out the bumpiness.

Interestingly enough, it doesn't matter whether a wheel is driven by a powered axle or spins freely on an axle, its tendency to create corrugations is the same. About the only way to prevent the buildup of washboard surfaces is to drive slowly, very slowly, perhaps less than 5 or 10 mph.

Mar 81:472

Springtime Road Restrictions

Several Canadian provinces and most northern states, including Alaska, place special springtime restrictions on the weight of trucks allowed on surfaced roadways. Since, in some instances, the restriction permits only 50% of normally allowed gross vehicle weight, it seriously curtails economic trucking during the breakup period.

The reason for limiting truck loads, and for further restricting them during breakup, is that heavy axle loadings can cause road pavement to flex to the point where the pavement cracks. At first, the cracks may not be visible because they mostly start at the bottom of the pavement and break upwards toward the top. Once the cracks start, they can propagate quickly and lead to breaking up of the entire road surface.

Road builders and maintenance personnel have devised ways to measure pavement deflection under the load of a rolling wheel. One method, the Benkelman Beam test, involves direct measurement of the deflection when a wheeled axle of specified weight is moved along beside a straightedge placed on the road under test. Measured deflections in the road surface amount to a few hundredths of an inch when a standard test weight, 18,000 pounds, is placed on the axle. (Except when special permits are issued, the maximum legal load on a single axle in Alaska is 20,000 pound; on a tandem, it's 34,000 pounds.)

Like a piece of wire, road pavement can be flexed very slightly a great number of times before it breaks.

But also like the wire, the pavement will break rather quickly if the bending is sharp and large.

The flexure a road surface undergoes directly depends upon the load applied. The lifetime of the road surface depends upon the degree of flexing and how many times it is flexed. Consequently, a road surface that would last 20 or 30 years if traveled only by many thousand passenger cars each day might fail in only a few years if subjected to the passage of a far smaller number of extremely heavy trucks.

Enough is known about road surface failure when different loadings are applied that engineers can calculate loading effects and the maintenance costs created by these effects. For example, it has been determined that the road maintenance cost of one 18,000-pound axle rolling along a surfaced Alaskan road for one mile is about six cents. A legally loaded 18-wheeler truck-trailer grossing 88,000 pounds that rolls one mile costs the state about 18 cents. For that same cost to the state, approximately 16,000 small cars weighing 4000 pounds each can travel the same distance (one mile). This is an extreme example, but it illustrates the remarkable dependence a road surface's lifetime has upon the weight of the vehicles that travel it.

At the time of spring breakup, heavy loads cause more road flexing than normal because high moisture content in the roadbed during thaw lowers the strength of the subsurface. Tests in the Fairbanks area show that the flexing is greatest when the spring thaw reaches to depths of two to four feet. The increased flexing then will lead to premature road failure unless special load restrictions are put in effect.

Avoiding unnecessary application of load restrictions while still making sure that they are in effect when needed is a tricky problem. The issue is nicely described by engineer Billy Connor in a document *Rational Seasonal Load Restrictions and Overload Permits* available from the Research Section, Alaska Department of Transportation and Public Facilities, 2301 Peger Road, Fairbanks, Alaska, 99701.

May 81:485

Carbon Monoxide From Melting Snow

A warning all hunters and campers should heed is to be extra careful when melting snow over an open-flame cookstove. Such a seemingly innocent act may have been the cause of the death of arctic explorers S.A. Andrée and Knut Fraenkel. They died in 1897 on White Island, northeast of Spitsbergen. Thirty-three years later their bodies were found where the men apparently died while sitting comfortably in a warm tent. Aside from this conjecture about Andrée and Fraenkel, there are known

instances of serious carbon monoxide poisoning from open-flame campstoves in tents.

Tests have shown that the danger of poisoning is especially great when snow is being melted in pans placed on open-flame stoves such as the Primus-type and Coleman-type cookstoves. These tests were conducted in 1942 by a group that included two scientists well known in the north, Drs. Laurence Irving and Per "Pete" Scholander. Somehow in the years that have lapsed since 1942 the consequences of the tests seem to have been forgotten. Recently, the University of Alaska's Dr. Robert Elsner, who had participated in the tests as an experimental subject, brought them again to light.

The essential problem involves the manner in which a stove operates. An efficient open-flame campstove burns with a blue flame that is very hot, far above $1000^{\circ}C$ ($1800^{\circ}F$). In such a flame the combustion is complete so that the fuel is converted to safe carbon dioxide (CO_2). However if a cold object is placed in the flame, the flame is cooled to a yellow color and combustion is incomplete. The result is the production of carbon monoxide (CO), the deadly killer.

The tests of Irving, Scholander and others proved that the melting of ice or snow on open-flame stoves is especially dangerous. The reason, of course, is that the snow or ice keeps the pan cold until it is finally melted so that incomplete combustion is likely.

Tests made with rats in porous tents where cooking or snow melting was underway showed little or no carbon monoxide poisoning. But if the melting was done in an impervious tent or one iced over, serious poisoning resulted within a few minutes. Even in impervious tents that were somewhat ventilated, dangerous concentrations of carbon monoxide sometimes occurred.

The moral is obvious: be extra cautious when cooking in tents, snow igloos, or other tight shelters especially if melting snow or ice on an open-flame stove. If a tent is made of porous material, make sure it has not become snow covered or been sealed by freezing rain. Extreme caution is called for if the tent is known to be impervious — occasional opening up of such a tent is not enough. Finally do not cook on a stove with a faulty flame, one that is irregular and partly yellow.

Aug 79:336

Lead in Drinking Water

Recent tests on water delivered by some Alaskan community water systems have revealed unsafe levels of lead in the water. Lead concentrations in excess of five parts per billion are considered unsafe, especially for children. Lead poisoning causes weakness, anemia, constipation and paralysis. That sounds depressing enough, but it's not even the whole story; lead poisoning itself causes depression.

Alaska's Department of Environmental Conservation has found excessive lead concentrations in community water systems at the western Alaska villages of St. Michael, Gambell and Shishmaref, and also at the interior village of Birch Creek. The culprit, reports DEC engineer Stan Justice in a recent issue of *The Northern Engineer*, is lead-containing solder used to join copper pipes in the water distribution systems.

Corrosive chemical action similar to that in a car battery occurs to release lead into the water. The copper pipe acts as a cathode, and droppings of excess lead solder inside the pipe act as sacrificial anodes, thereby becoming released in ionic form into the water.

The problem occurs elsewhere but is more common at high latitude for three reasons. In the North, surface water often is used for water supplies. Being soft, this water promotes corrosion more than hard water does. Secondly, water use in the north is often at a low rate, so contaminants such as lead tend to build up. Thirdly, the water in northern distribution systems often is heated to prevent freezing, and this heating promotes corrosion.

Fortunately, as the distribution systems grow older, the excess lead gets eaten away from the pipes. Hence, after a few years, the problem diminishes. Also, users can avoid the highest lead concentrations by running a tap for a few minutes before taking drinking water from it.

Jun 81:488

Arsenic in Well Water

A number of wells in the Fairbanks area contain greater than acceptable concentrations of arsenic. These wells occur within a mineralized belt extending from Pedro Dome — Cleary Summit southwest to Ester Dome. The arsenic derives from arsenopyrite and other arsenic compounds found in association with gold veins of the Fairbanks Mining District. Arsenic is contained both in stream water and well water; in the Ester Dome area between 1/3 and 1/2 the approximately 100 wells recently sampled contain arsenic in excess of the recommended maximum.

Some people of Austria and other regions intentionally eat arsenic compounds believing that they exert a tonic effect. Some arsenic compounds have been used as medical treatment for various disorders and diseases. There are known instances of persons ingesting rather substantial amounts of arsenic without showing evident harmful effect.

On the other hand, arsenic is a known poison which degenerates the lining of the digestive tract and other organs; also it appears to attack the nervous

system to cause numbness and tingling, especially in the legs and feet, and it may be a cancer-causing agent. A recent report by the Institute of Water Resources of the University of Alaska states that a dose of 70 milligrams is known to be toxic to humans (70 milligrams is roughly the weight of a one-inch square of typing paper). A letter recently received from the Alaska Department of Health and Social Services states that a single dose of arsenic may require as much as ten days for disappearance, and a medical doctor told me that it can take years to rid the body of all signs of arsenic once ingestion has stopped.

Giving one pause are reports of an area in Chile where there was high incidence of cancer, stroke and heart failure among children drinking water containing arsenic at the same concentrations being found in some Fairbanks area wells. The unusual incidence of these disorders disappeared within five years of the time the children received only arsenic-free water. Similar findings were made in an area of Nova Scotia.

Quite obviously one is unwise to regularly drink or use for cooking water from an arsenic-rich well. Anyone uncertain about the existence of arsenic or other impurities in his well should contact the local office of the Alaska Department of Environmental Conservation.

Jan 77:30

Arsenate and Phosphate—Chemical Look-Alikes

The finding of high arsenic content in some wells located near gold-bearing deposits of the Fairbanks Mining District has created special concern because of possible health problems. Arsenic can cause skin and mucous membrane cancer and can damage small blood vessels, thereby leading to heart disease, kidney failure, brain damage and decreased tolerance to cold. Young people seem to be affected more than the elderly.

Arsenate and Phosphate — Chemical Look-Alikes.

An arsenic atom will readily combine with four oxygen atoms to form the arsenate molecule. The arsenate molecule is a chemical look-alike to the phosphate molecule, similarly formed from phosphorous and oxygen. Phosphorous is an important element for living organisms. It forms nerve tissue,

212

bones and teeth. Also, it makes up a part of the membrane tissue that surrounds living cells and transports the energy that fuels muscle contraction.

The cells recognize the shape of the phosphate molecule and readily absorb it. Unfortunately, as the diagram shows, the shape of arsenate is so nearly identical that cells do not distinguish between arsenate and phosphate. Thus, if substantial concentrations of arsenate are provided to the body, the damaging arsenate is taken into cells instead of the phosphate which the cells need. This substitution of the bad for the good perhaps explains why arsenic poisoning can retain its latency over the years, especially in children since their bodies are rapidly growing.
— *Don Button and Neil Davis*
May 77:168

Gold Nuggets

A gold nugget surely is one of nature's more improbable products. How can a solid lump of nearly pure gold ever form? Evidently, almost any rock, carefully enough analyzed, will be found to contain a little gold and nearly every other element that naturally occurs on the earth. By what process is gold concentrated into nugget form?

Several theories of mineral deposition exist, each perhaps correct in explaining one or more concentrated deposits of valuable metals. Marine deposition is one idea; it is known that the deeper waters of the Red Sea are abnormally warm and that metal sulfides are now being deposited there. But gold, such as found in the Fairbanks mining district, normally occurs in veins probably formed along fractures or sheared zones near ancient underground molten magmas. The gold and related metals may have been carried upward in a water solution or by similar chemical means. In any case, the nuggets seem not to have been formed directly from molten gold. Individual atoms of gold have been transported from the original magmas and either deposited in openings or have chemically replaced other atoms previously there to form the nuggets. Were the nuggets not proof that such things can happen, one might be inclined to disbelieve the whole idea.
May 76:63

Alaska's Gold

If all the gold that has been mined in Alaska were put in one place, the pile would weigh somewhat more than 1200 tons and a cube formed of it would be 13 feet (about 4 meters) on a side.

At $400 per troy ounce the total value of the gold mined so far in Alaska is 12 billion dollars. Even in these days of inflation and high energy costs, 12 billion dollars is not ptarmigan feed.

According to an article by Mark Robinson and Tom Bundtzen in the September 1979 issue of the *Mines and Geology Bulletin*, the Fairbanks mining district holds the record for greatest total production, well over seven million troy ounces. Juneau follows as a close second with nearly seven million ounces. Nome with four million ounces and the Iditarod district with its 1.3 million ounces are the only other gold mining areas in Alaska that have produced more than a million ounces. The total production of gold across the border in the Klondike district is roughly that of the Fairbanks district, probably somewhat smaller.

The number of people employed in Alaskan metals mining over the years is described by C.N. Conwell in the same issue of the Division of Geological and Geophysical Surveys publication.

Over 8000 people were employed in 1915 but the number was down to 3600 just before the 1933 legal increase in gold price. The number of workers jumped to 6400 then fell to 1400 in 1947 because of World War II.

Alaskan metals mining fell to a low of less than 300 employed in 1970, but the current high price of gold has created new interest. In 1979, approximately 1700 people were employed in exploration activities.
Nov 79:350

Uses of Gold

The winter of 1979-80 has been particularly hard on an old prospector friend of mine. It isn't the cold that bothers, it's the news about the price of gold that is tearing him up.

Each new report of higher gold prices is more likely to drive him into a temporary trance. His eyes glaze, his jaw sets, and he hunkers down on his haunches. Simultaneously, his arms bend at the elbows and his hands come up clasping an imaginary gold pan. He swirls it around a few times, then usually wakes up and again becomes more or less rational.

But these days, all he can think and talk about is gold. He points out that if all of the world's mined gold supply were put into a single cube, the cube would only be 40 feet (12 meters) on a side. That supply is being added to each year at the rate of about 50 million troy ounces (equal to a cube about 15 feet on a side).

It makes my prospector friend happy that the limited supply of gold has many other uses than as a medium of exchange and for jewelry. He figures that these other uses will help keep supply short and price up.

The space age has brought new demand for gold to filter out the intense solar radiation that exists outside the earth's atmosphere. Thin layers of gold

A Strange Sluicebox.

on astronaut's visors protect eyes from both ultra-violet and infrared solar radiation. Gold coatings on spacecraft also help keep temperatures low inside the vehicle. Gold's resistance to corrosion in space leads to its use in coating bearings, thereby overcoming serious mechanical problems that plagued some early satellites having exposed moving parts.

The manufacture of high-pressure seals, reflective window glass and electronic components all utilize gold. Gold is reliable because of its corrosion resistance, its strength and its workability. Consequently gold is in high demand, especially in the rapidly expanding electronics industry.

Fifteen percent of all gold consumed in the United States is for teeth fillings and dental bridgework. Finely divided radioactive gold also has medical use in the treatment of arthritis. This use especially pleases my prospector friend when he is feeling the effects of too many hours standing in the creeks.

Jan 80:366

A Strange Sluicebox

In spring a young Alaskan's mind turns to thoughts of gold. But remembering how much work it is to pan for gold, the clever miner designs a sluicebox.

Sluiceboxes come in many forms but the strangest we ever did see is the one in the accompanying photograph from the Selid-Bassoc collection in the archives of the University of Alaska, Fairbanks. Consultations with several experts led to the conclusion that this Y-shaped sluicebox was so built to aid in the tailing removal problem.

One of the bad things about a sluicebox is that just as many rocks come out the bottom as are put in at the top. These rocks pile up very quickly and somehow must be gotten rid of. Evidently the miner in this photograph diverted the flow from one arm of the Y to the other so as to spread out the tailings over a wider area. By this means he had less shoveling to contend with.

Apr 77:88

Dancing Wires

Suspended telephone and power cables and other objects sometimes are seen to vibrate without apparent cause, as several readers including Ginger Gauss of Fairbanks have noted. Especially on windless winter days it seems that one most often notices dancing wires; but perhaps any motion on such days is unusual and therefore easily recognized.

Every solid object and every stretched wire has one or more resonant frequencies at which it will vibrate easily. A person can make the tip of a rather sizable tree oscillate by repeated pushing on the tree trunk at just the right rate.

The telephone wire or power line is the same. It has a resonant fundamental frequency that depends upon the length and weight of the wire and upon how taut it is. If the wire can be repeatedly tickled ever so slightly at the proper frequency, it will build up a major oscillation. To oscillate, the wire must receive energy from one of two places: either from the ends of the wire or from the strumming of the wire itself by air movement or a falling tree branch.

Dancing wires can get their energy from vibrations of the poles or trees to which they are attached. When two or more vibrating objects are coupled, they can transfer the energy of vibration from one to another. One part of such a coupled system may vibrate for a time and then cease vibrating as another part of the system takes up the vibration.

The usual ultimate energy source for the dancing wires is air movement. It also can be occasional plucking of the wire somewhere along its length or by motion of the earth transmitted to the wire by the poles to which it is attached. The fact that the wire may be carrying electricity has nothing to do with its vibration.

Mar 78:224

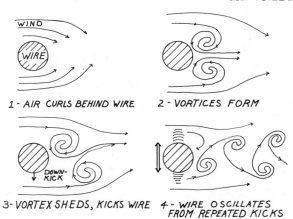

1 - AIR CURLS BEHIND WIRE   2 - VORTICES FORM

3 - VORTEX SHEDS, KICKS WIRE   4 - WIRE OSCILLATES FROM REPEATED KICKS

Dancing Wires.

Dancing Wires: Part Two

In his recent article on dancing wires, Neil Davis noted that one way for wires to receive the energy to cause their dancing is directly from moving air. The mechanism is one involving the formation of vortices behind a wire when the wind blows perpendicular to the wire.

Air moving past the wire is impeded by the wire; the air closest to the wire moves the slowest. The result is a curling up of the air behind the wire to form vortices — rotating spirals within which the air spins faster the closer it is to the center of the vortex.

One by one, the vortices break away from the wire. The breaking away alternates between those formed behind one side of the wire and those formed on the other side. As each vortex leaves, it gives the wire a sideways kick. If the rate of breaking away is somewhere near the natural frequency at which the wire wants to vibrate, large, continuing oscillations will build up — the dancing wires.

Wires on which snow has built up are major obstructions to the wind so that vortex shedding can take place at barely perceptible wind speeds.

Next time you see a wire dancing on a cold winter day, try measuring the direction and speed of the wind by blowing soap bubbles into the air. Aside from proving that the air is moving, it is fun to see how the soap bubbles freeze and roll along the ground.

— Kenelm Philip
May 78:92

Speculations

The last time I extensively speculated on something in this column — a guess about how Naptowne, Alaska, was first named — many of us learned a bit of Alaskan history as various readers corresponded to set the facts straight. Perhaps this experience serves as a warning not to speculate too much here. Still, a request by *News-Miner* editor Kent Sturgis to prepare a special column in honor of this Weekender's emphasis on science tempts me into speculation again.

Why is a science-related column of this type being carried by 13 newspapers in Alaska and Canada? Could it be that the editors of these newspapers know that their readership is made up of people who are more interested in and aware of their surroundings than many who live farther south? Sometimes this awareness exists because many northerners wrest their living from the land, the sea or the air and consequently must astutely observe to succeed and sometimes even to survive.

Not everyone in Alaska or the Yukon earns a living from outdoor activities such as fishing, mining, transportation, timbering or farming. However, many employed in other areas often take vacations that involve pitting themselves against rivers, mountains, mosquitoes or other elements of the north. So it seems that most here have a reason to be interested in the earth and how it functions. Those who are motivated by their own interest to observe their surroundings tend to be good observers.

I first became aware of how expert Alaskans and Yukoners can be as observers of natural events when I investigated major earthquakes that occurred in 1958 near Huslia and Yakutat. A great deal of the information we assembled actually came from bush pilots, villagers, miners, fishermen and trappers who felt the earthquakes or saw their effects. As a supposedly trained scientist, I was, in this era, humbled more than once by having my observational capabilities outclassed by a person without formal education who stood beside me and saw more than I.

But back to the column — many of the articles that appear here are in response to a comment or question resulting from someone else's experience or observation. Many of the 270 articles that have been written since this column's beginning in the *Daily News-Miner* in March 1976 were prepared in consequence of reader interest. The variety of topics covered also has been influenced by the interests of the thirty-plus people who have contributed articles.

Here at the University of Alaska there is a truly remarkable and easily accessible wealth of scientific expertise in almost every subject dealing with northern regions. That asset is used again and again, often without acknowledgment, in preparing these columns.

But the specialists have no corner on science in Alaska. It seems that the majority of northerners are interested in expanding their knowledge obtained by study and practice; according to Webster, that is the definition of science. We often forget in this day of sophistication wherein scientists are usually pictured beside fancy, complicated instruments, that much of science is accomplished by using the eyes, ears and fingers for observational tools and the human brain as an interpreting computer. Everyone has the capability to observe and interpret what goes on around him or her. One gets the impression that northerners are more interested in employing these capabilities than most.

Along this line, one of my favored stories is about the observation and interpretation made in 1969 by an elderly Athabascan woman at Dot Lake. She watched a barium cloud released from a rocket that had been launched from the University's Poker Flat rocket range near Fairbanks. High in the sky over her head, she saw the bright multi-colored barium release cloud suddenly appear, expand circularly and then fade away.

"I know what that was," she said, "It was God opening up a hole from heaven so he could look down from the sky and see the people here on earth. He didn't like what he saw, so he closed the hole back up again." One may quibble with the woman's conclusion, but anyone who has seen a barium release can easily understand why she might interpret it that way.

Interpretations and speculations are often wrong, but if one is to make progress in understanding, it usually is necessary to speculate a bit.

Hopefully, this column provides the reader with the foundation material upon which to form his or her own conclusions and speculations.

Nov 78:274

INDEX

218